KOREA

A Century of Change

ECONOMIC IDEAS LEADING TO THE 21st CENTURY

Series editors: Lawrence R. Klein *(Univ. Pennsylvania)* &
Vincent Su *(Baruch College, CUNY)*

Published

Vol. 1: The Japanese Economy
by Mitsuo Saito

Vol. 2: Asia in the Twenty-First Century: Economic, Socio-Political, Diplomatic Issues
edited by Paula K Chow & Gregory C Chow

Vol. 3: Who Shall Live? — Health, Economics, and Social Choice (Expanded Edition)
by Victor R Fuchs

Vol. 4: India's Economic Prospects — A Macroeconomic and Econometric Analysis
by Thampy Mammen

Vol. 5: Special Economic Zones and the Economic Transition in China
by Wei Ge

Economic Ideas Leading to the 21st Century — Vol. 6

KOREA

A Century of Change

Juergen Kleiner

Department of International Relations
Boston University

World Scientific
New Jersey • London • Singapore • Hong Kong

Published by

World Scientific Publishing Co. Pte. Ltd.

P O Box 128, Farrer Road, Singapore 912805

USA office: Suite 1B, 1060 Main Street, River Edge, NJ 07661

UK office: 57 Shelton Street, Covent Garden, London WC2H 9HE

British Library Cataloguing-in-Publication Data
A catalogue record for this book is available from the British Library.

KOREA: A CENTURY OF CHANGE
Economic Ideas Leading to the 21st Century — Vol. 6

ISBN 981-02-4657-9

Printed in Singapore by Mainland Press

Foreword

Korea is one of the flash points of international politics. Again and again it hits the headlines. The news reports are often surprising, sometimes disturbing. They make us feel that the tensions between the two Koreas, the Republic of Korea in the South and the Democratic People's Republic of Korea in the North, are going to be with us for a while. Only a closer look will reveal the details. Only a study of the thick layers of Korea's recent history will allow us to understand current developments. For those who want to reflect about the trouble spot Korea there is no other way but to become involved.

Modern Korean history is complex. To understand it we have to deal with three sets of problems: We have to describe how two contrasting societies and systems developed on the peninsula which had previously known a uniform rule over many centuries. We have to examine the antagonistic policies pursued by each of the Koreas against the other. And we have to study the involvement of the four big Pacific powers, China, Russia, Japan, and the United States, which have strongly influenced Korea's fate.

We are told that the West entered the Korean War (1950–1953) in order to save the "free world". That may be so, except the Republic of Korea was not a free country at that time. It had an authoritarian ruler, President Syngman Rhee (1948–1960). The signature tunes of his rule were manipulation and corruption. The political situation in Korea got even worse. After a short democratic interlude military dictators followed each other. First South Korea was ruled by General Park Chung Hee (1961–1979), and then by General Chun Doo Hwan (1979–1988), both of whom governed South Korea with an iron fist. A drastic change occurred in mid-1987 when the government suddenly opted for thorough democratic reforms. These reforms did not come out of the blue. The export-oriented industrialization, initiated by Park Chung Hee and continued by Chun Doo Hwan, had been successful in transforming an impoverished country into "a little tiger". The improving economic conditions had created a middle class, yet for many of its members the satisfaction with the economic development no longer outweighed the dissatisfaction with the oppressive political conditions. They wanted to determine their political future themselves. It had become impossible for the government to contain by force the movement for greater participation. Democratic rule followed, during a transitory period under Roh Tae Woo (1988–1993), a former general and close ally of Chun Doo Hwan, and then by Kim Young Sam (1993–1998) and by Kim Dae Jung (since 1998) who had been the most prominent dissidents during the time of suppression.

Today, the Republic of Korea is one of the rare examples of a developing country having made its way to freedom. This is a development that as such is worth a thorough study. The bright picture was somewhat damaged by the economic collapse at the end of 1997 which was caused by a rapid deterioration of export prices and an inability to substitute short-term external debt. International assistance was necessary and instrumental in overcoming the crisis. Since then South Koreans do not enjoy in the same way as before when talking about their country's economic "miracle".

When we take a closer look at North Korea, we are also in for some surprises. Although Kim Il Sung was the towering figure from 1945 until his death in July 1994, his leadership did not go unchallenged in the early years of the DPRK. He had to fight factionalism, and it was only in 1961 that he had overcome this worst of all Korean political diseases. He then occupied the most important positions within the Korean Workers Party as well as within the government structure. The "great leader" became larger than life. In order to legitimize his leadership he developed the *juche* ideology. The North Koreans have had difficulty grasping an ideology characterized by a mixture of crudeness and finesse, self-praise and ritual repetitions. But they have found one aspect of the message attractive; the demand for the independence of the state which has appealed to their national pride.

The North Korean leadership has introduced a system of control and terror in order to secure its rule. The citizens do not enjoy any freedom. Indoctrination starts with the education of children. Criticism is not allowed. Even traveling within the country is only possible with special permission. Contact with foreign countries is extremely restricted. It is not the state's function to serve the citizens, but rather to control the citizens for the empowerment of the government authorities.

When Kim Il Sung died in July 1994 the world could watch the unique spectacle in a communist country of the son inheriting his father's position as supreme leader, a form of succession normally associated with monarchic dynasties. It must be added however, that at that moment Kim Jong Il was already holding the key positions in the DPRK. Therefore, it was of no importance that he was formally elected Secretary-General of the Korean Workers Party only more than three years after his father's death. As Chairman of the National Defense Commission he holds the post which, in September 1998, was proclaimed to be the highest in the state. North Korea's economy has been in deep trouble for many years because the deliberate renunciation of the advantage of the international division of labor has backfired. When the situation further deteriorated due to floods and other natural disasters, Kim Jong Il could not find a way out. He, however, continued to rule unchallenged, demonstrating the resilience of his father. And he still enjoyed his father's support who has been made "the eternal President of the Republic" by an amendment to the constitution in September 1998.

From the very beginning the foreign policy of both Koreas was aimed at unifying the country under its respective flag. These aims excluded each other, as was clearly demonstrated by the Korean War. The driving force behind the war was Kim Il Sung. But he could only go ahead after having received Stalin's consent. It was the United States which saved South Korea, and it was China which saved North Korea in a conflict which restored the *status quo ante bellum.*

In the period following the Korean War, confrontation between the two Koreas prevailed. The list of threats, provocation, clashes and hostile acts has become endless. It reaches into the present day. The occasional dialogue between the two governments was considered to be sensational because it occurred so seldom. It always gave rise to great expectations. In July 1972 both sides in a Joint Communique envisaged efforts to achieve unification. In the mid 1980s North and South discussed economic cooperation and the exchange of organized groups. The international thaw made it possible for the prime ministers of both countries to meet in 1990. In December 1991 an Agreement on Reconciliation, Non-aggression and Exchanges and Cooperation was announced, in which both sides again promised to join hands in order to unify the country. None of these agreements was ever implemented as the policies of both sides continued to differ. North Korea continues to aim at achieving unification on its terms. It will not agree to open its borders under conditions which threaten the present leadership. The South Korean government pursues, under the heading of "sunshine diplomacy", a step by step approach of trying to engage the North in a process of reconciliation and cooperation. This policy is reminiscent of the West German *Ostpolitik* which believed in "change by rapprochement". The South Korean leadership is, however, worried about the possibility that the North Korean state could collapse.

There are no miracles on earth. But the fact that the Korean nation survived in spite of the efforts of the surrounding great powers to subjugate the country comes rather close to a miracle. Until the second half of the 19th century Korea had a tributary relationship with China. Around the turn of the century Russia's influence had become dominant, until Japan annexed Korea in 1910. A harsh rule followed which tried to deprive Koreans of their national identity, a rule which has never been forgotten nor forgiven.

If history knew logic Korea's fate after the end of World War II in the Pacific should have been liberation. But Korea was divided for reasons of military convenience of the two occupying powers, the USA and the Soviet Union. The line which had been drawn in August 1945 to fix military responsibilities hardened and had become insurmountable. The pattern of the Cold War determined the relations of both Koreas. South Korea relied on the support of the United States and Japan, North Korea enjoyed relations with the Soviet Union and China. Since the beginning of the 1990s this situation changed. South Korea established diplomatic relations with Russia and China, North Korea succeeded in holding bilateral talks with the US government using the threat to go nuclear and to develop ballistic missiles. North Korea also negotiated with Japan. In the Four-Party Talks the two Koreas, the US and China attempt to replace the Armistice Agreement of 1953 with a peace mechanism. So, developments on the Korean peninsula continue to be full of suspense.

This book gives a comprehensive account of Korean politics during the last one hundred years. It is intended to enable the reader to study all important aspects of political developments on the peninsula and those surrounding the peninsula. At the beginning of last year's fall semester I asked my students at Boston University why they took a course on Korea. One of them, a first generation American of Korean descent, answered that he wanted to learn something about his ancestors not from his father but from an objective source.

I have lived for more than ten years in Seoul and tried to understand Korea and Koreans. Being a diplomat I remained a foreigner who could afford to study and assess events as objectively as possible. Thus I try to give an even-handed coverage of Korea which hopefully will be useful not only for my students. "The century of smooth talk is over, and the pink treatment damages only the one to whom it is applied" (Theodor Fontane).

I am indebted to General (retd.) Fred F. Woerner, Professor of International Relations at Boston University, for checking the chapters relating to military issues; to Dahlia Boyarsky MA for editing the text; and to my wife Jutta Kleiner for typing the text and tolerating a husband so much occupied with research and writing.

Boston, May 2000 Juergen Kleiner

Contents

PART I

Korea and the Modern Age

Chapter 1

The Hermit Kingdom

A Monument

Someone who tries to reach downtown Seoul coming from the southern parts of the South Korean capital, and who chooses the Yang Hwa Bridge to cross the Han River will observe at the northern bank of the river a modern church. The place where this Catholic Church, called Yang Hwa Jin, was built is a memorable one as Christians, persecuted by the government, had been killed here. A museum attached to the church is dedicated to those Christian martyrs. In front of the museum stands a replica of a stone monument with an inscription. The text of the inscription, which can also be studied on a board inside the museum, reads as follows: "Not to fight a battle against the invasion of the barbarians from the West and agreeing to peace negotiations, means selling-off the country. Posterity is admonished forever. Written and erected in the year of the tiger and the month of the lamb".

The year of the tiger was the year 1866. The Korean government had approximately 100 of these monuments erected in order to stop the people from getting into contact with the Europeans. In the middle of the 19th century Chosun was an extremely isolated country indeed.

Relations with the Middle Kingdom

Chosun in those years was a monarchy ruled by the Yi-dynasty since the 14th century. The Yi dynasty, like its predecessors, found itself in isolation, due to the country's geographic position. In this secluded world of East

Asia there were only limited opportunities for foreign relations. During their long national history, Koreans had to fight against tribes invading from the North as well as the Japanese trying to conquer the country from the South. While the Japanese invasions under Tayotomi Hideyoshi at the end of the 16th century had failed, it had in the process devastated large parts of Korea. Korea had exchanges with neighbors but developed permanent and consistent relations only with its large neighbor in the North, with the Middle Kingdom.

The Chinese made various attempts to conquer Korea but failed. During the rule of the Tang dynasty (618–907) — Korea was unified under the Shilla dynasty (668–935) — the ties between both countries started to assume their characteristic form of tributary relations. This special type of foreign relations had built up into an elaborate system during the Ming and Ch'ing dynasty in China, and the Yi dynasty in Korea. China and Korea regularly exchanged embassies. Korea recognized China as a "great state" calling the relationship *sadae* (serving the great) and expressed this by sending tributes. The Korean kings received a seal from the Chinese emperor which had to be used in their correspondence with the imperial court, the Chinese calendar in order to date official documents as well as their posthumous titles.

The tribute system was of economic importance. It was the only form of external trade authorized by China and resulted in a considerable transshipment of goods across the borders of China. The total value of goods delivered by Korea to China in 1787 is estimated to have matched more than 3 tons of silver.[1] As China was obliged to offer gifts in return, and to accommodate the embassies during their stay in Beijing, the tribute system was not necessarily profitable for the Chinese government.

The cultural aspect of the tribute system was also important. Foreign visitors to Beijing were exposed to the superior Chinese culture. It is difficult to determine whether the cultural impact was based on Chinese intentions or was just a byproduct. It was, however, the vehicle in which China's dominating influence spread to its neighbors.

The main aim of the tribute system, however, was a political one. It was meant to guarantee peace for China along its borders. At the same time it protected the states at China's borders against interference in their domestic

[1] R. Machetzki, "Tributsystem", in *China Handbuch*, edited by Wolfgang Franke and Brunhild Staiger, Düsseldorf 1974, p. 1421.

affairs. These family relations were only offered to those countries which had become Confucian and had accepted the natural rules. The neighboring states were supposed to recognize the tribute system voluntarily. Therefore, military interventions were to be avoided — a principle, however, which was often violated.

The tributary ties with China were a burden for Korea's economy, but a blessing for its cultural development. Politically non-interference by China in Korea's domestic affairs prevailed. As long as Korea recognized China's precedence it remained independent in its internal policies. The investiture of the Korean kings by the Chinese emperors was mainly of a nominal character because regularly the one who already acted as king received the seal from Beijing.

During the centuries of relations between Korea and China friendly feelings towards the great neighbor in the North prevailed in Korea. They found their expression in the term *mohwa*, veneration for China. The aristocracy in both countries had a similar education and shared the same Confucian convictions and conceptions of the world. These views held the Chinese Emperor, the son of heaven, responsible for transmitting the heavenly principles to everybody.

Tung Yueh, who came as Imperial Envoy to Korea in 1488, used the following formula for Sino-Korean relations in his account of his mission: "Because Korea has always shown loyalty and reverence to the Imperial Court, it receives favors such as is given to no other country".[2] His Korean contemporary Choe Pu, who wrote down his account also in 1488, shared this view. He said to a Chinese officer who had shown him hospitality: "Certainly that shows your feelings that though my Korea is beyond the sea, its clothing and culture being the same as China's, it cannot be considered a foreign country... All under Heaven are my brothers; how can we discriminate among people because of distance? That is particularly true of my country, which respectful serves the Celestial Court and pays tribute without fail. The Emperor, for his part, treats us punctiliously and tends us benevolently. The feeling of security he imparts is perfect".[3]

[2]English translation by Richard Rutt, "Chao-hsien fu", *Transactions* of the RAS Vol. XLVIII p. 65.

[3]John Meskill, *Choe Pu's Diary: A Record of Drifting across the Sea*, Tuscon 1965, p. 65.

First Contacts with the West

The Koreans' feeling of security was going to be upset by contact with the Europeans and the Americans. This exactly had been the reason why the Korean government had the stone monuments erected with warnings against contacts with the barbarian.

Beijing was the place where Koreans got in contact with Westerners. Through this contact, the members of the Korean Embassies came to know Europeans and European ideas. Europeans seldom came to Korea and most of them came as sailors of stranded ships. If caught they were jailed and not released. In 1653 Hendrik Harmel and other Dutch sailors who were stranded at the coast of Cheju Island succeeded in freeing themselves after having been imprisoned for 13 years. After reaching Europe via Japan, Harmel's account about his Korean adventure was translated into several European languages and made Korea known in Europe.[4] As he reports, the strange European visitors were treated with a mixture of curiosity, kindness and arrogance.

The contacts with Westerners had one particularly important result. The Catholic faith, which the Koreans had met in Beijing, began to spread in Korea by the middle of the 18th century. It did so even before the first missionaries had set foot on Korean soil. The new faith also met much opposition. Confucian scholars could not find justification for the Christian faith in the part of history with which they were familiar. It was a traditional Confucian approach to check history so as to cope with present events. Some Korean scholars felt the Christian claim that Jesus Christ — whom they considered to be the founder of that faith — was God's son was blasphemous. In addition they realized that this new faith broke away from Korean traditions, particularly ancestor worship. The official version of Christianity found its expression in a textbook on Confucianism edited by the Korean government at the end of the 19th century. The German Consulate took up the matter with the Korean Foreign Ministry in a letter dated 5 October 1896 which complained about the deformation of the Christian religion quoting the following passage from a Korean textbook: "In the opinion of

---

[4]Hendrick Harmel, *Account of a Ship wreck of a Dutch Vessel on the Coast of the Isle of Quelpart, with Description of the Kingdom of Korea*, first publication in 1668, reprinted in Transactions of the RAS Vol. IX 1918, pp. 97 ff.

the new generation the so-called Christian religion of the Europeans is mean, superficial and wrong, and is an example of the viciousness of barbarian customs which is not worthy of being studied seriously. The terms used by Christians for heaven, happiness and misfortune are similar to those used by the Buddhists. They worship the heavenly spirits, but not their ancestors. They insult heaven in many ways and confuse the social system. This is really characteristic of barbarian ruthlessness and not worth to be dealt with in our survey of foreign customs. This is especially true since this religion is in a state of decay at present. Europeans have spread their spawn in all countries in the world except China. Everybody adores this religion. We are surprised to see dthat Chinese scholars and the Chinese people did not avoid the infection".[5]

By the end of the 18th century the Korean government acted against individual Christians. From the beginning of the 19th century Christians were brutally persecuted. The persecutions were mostly triggered by the Christian refusal to worship their ancestors in the traditional way.

Before the turn of the century the first ordained priest, a Chinese, came to Korea; he was followed by French fathers who started arriving in Korea by 1835. Kim Tae Gon (Father Andre Kim) was the first Korean priest to do missionary work in his home country. He became a victim of the persecution shortly after his arrival in Korea in 1845. But the persecutions did not succeed in stopping the spread of the Christian faith. Many Koreans were attracted to this faith because Christianity demanded that all men and women were God's children, and should be be treated equally. There were allegedly 17,000 Catholics in Korea by 1860.

Official church history dates the founding of the Catholic Church in Korea back to 1784.[6] In that year Yi Sung Hun, who had come as a member of an embassy, was baptized in Beijing. When he returned to Korea he baptized Yi Pyok. Together they created a Christian community. In May 1984 Pope Paul John II came to Korea to celebrate the 200th anniversary of the country's Christianization. At that occasion he canonized 103 martyrs.

---

[5] *Ku Hanguk oegyo munso* (*Diplomatic Documents of Old Korea*), *togan* (*German Document*), edited by Koryo taehak kyo Asea munje yonguso (Asian Research Institute of Korea University) Seoul 1966, Vol. 1, pp. 658 and 659 (Translation from German by the author).

[6] E. Plazidus Berger, "Zr Gründung der Kirche in Korea. Ein Forschungsbericht", in *Zeitschrift für Missionswissenschaft und Religionswissenschaft*, Vol. 19 (1985), pp. 98 ff.

The Country's Internal Situation

Korea's desolate situation in the 19th century contributed to attracting many people to this new faith. Many people felt that the traditional concepts were inadequate to cope with modern developments.

Chosun continued to be an authoritarian state ruled only nominally by the kings. Real power was no longer in the hands of the victorious factions of the aristocrats, the *yangban*, but was wielded by the in-laws of the royal family. This development was made easy: since King Chongjo's death in 1800 minor princes ascended the throne for whom regents filled in. It was in particular the Kim clan from Andong which dominated politics at the royal court. Nepotism and corruption were spreading.

The old class system was unsettled. Many *yangban* who were kept excluded from government services became impoverished. Early capitalism was developing, aggravating the contrast between rich and poor. Status was now determined by wealth. Confucianism which had been the official ideology of Chosun for such a long time degenerated into formalism. Interest in science and technology was missing.

The majority of Koreans felt suppressed and exploited. This was particularly true for the farmers who had to carry the heaviest burden. They suffered from an unfair tax system which was often enforced by corrupt government officials. The basis of the tax system was a land tax. The system had many exemptions of which some were based on fiction. This often resulted in the land tax being applied arbitrarily. Those who wanted to be exempted from military conscription had to pay a military exemption charge. Families with many men who were needed for working on the farm had to suffer particularly from this charge. The rice loan system was misused. It had originally been established in order to support farmers. In spring, when rice was in short supply, farmers were to receive rice loans from the government which the farmers had to refund after harvest in the fall. The tax officials had not used the rice loans for its intended purpose, but had started to charge interest. As corruption was widespread among government officials the country's financial system was in disarray.

It was not surprising that injustice and mismanagement caused severe rebellions. Already in 1811 a rebellion broke out in the Northwest of Korea; in 1862 revolts were started in the South and quickly spread over the whole country.

It was the regent Yi Ha Ung (1864–1873) who restored government authority. When King Cholchong died in 1864, a twelve-year-old boy — his posthumous title was: Kojong — ascended the throne and his father was made regent. He was given the title of Taewongun (Prince of the Great Court). This title had been bestowed on other fathers of kings, but Yi Ha Ung was — much to the surprise of the Cho clan which had appointed him — such a strong personality that he became known as the Taewongun. He succeeded quickly in controlling the court, reorganizing government administration and fighting corruption. In order to make the strengthened role of the crown visible he had rebuilt Kyongbok Palace in the heart of Seoul which had been in ruins since the Hideyoshi invasions. It is the Taewongun's reconstruction of the Palace which visitors see today.

Since the Taewongun was afraid that Koreans might be infected by Western ideas, he launched persecutions against Catholics. In the period from 1866 to 1872 several thousand Catholics were killed. It was disastrous for Korea that the Taewongun failed to realize that only a dynamic and future oriented policy could show Korea the path to modern times.

Seclusion

The Taewongun reacted negatively to various Western attempts to take up relations with Korea. Due to this, he increased Korea's isolation even more. The stone monuments, as mentioned above, which warned the Korean population of contacts with Europeans, were erected during his rule. Korea finally became known as the "Hermit Kingdom" in Europe and in the United States in the second half of the 19th century.

Already during the period before the rule of the Taewongun, Koreans were convinced that there was reason to be suspicious of Western intruders. In the view of many Koreans, Europeans and Americans appeared to be propagandists of a religion which, if it succeeded in spreading, would result in a confusion of the social system. The Koreans were also worried about the conflicts between China and Japan on the one side and the West on the other. It could not have left Koreans unimpressed that China had had many conflicts with European colonial powers and since the opium war in 1864 suffered one humiliation after the other resulting in a deep shock for the Middle Kingdom. Seoul had also observed with concern that Japan had been forced by the USA to establish relations.

Time after time European and American ships reached the coast of Korea. Already in the first half of the 19th century British ships had demanded to trade with the Koreans. In 1846 and 1847 French naval ships appeared on Korea's western coast to retaliate for the persecution of Christians. The Korean impression that Christianity accompanies Western interference is, therefore, plausible.

During the rule of the Taewongun, European and American ships approached the Korean coast more frequently. In 1866 the American merchant ship *General Sherman* advanced along the Taedong River. The Koreans sank the ship and killed the crew. In the same year French ships under the command of Admiral Roze showed up at Korea's western coasts in order to retaliate for the Taewongun's persecution of Christians. They were, however, quickly driven off. The same happened to American warships which had come to Korea in order to find out what had happened to the *General Sherman*. In 1871 a small fleet of five US warships came to Korea in order to urge the Koreans to conclude a treaty of friendship. The ships approached Kanghwa, situated at the estuary of the Han River, and engaged in fighting with the Koreans. These intruders were also driven off. The notion that the Taewongun resisted the arrogant style of Western colonial powers is plausible. Unfortunately, he had no idea how to free Korea from its backwardness and how to reform the country.

Oppert's Act of Piracy

Among those foreigners who tried to open Korea to the West, the German Ernst Oppert played a strange role. There are different accounts of the event; even its precise date is not clear. If one pieces together what W. E. Griffis[7] and Oppert[8] reported, events would have unfolded in the following way: Oppert, a German merchant residing in Shanghai, had made several vain attempts to trade with Korea. Together with the French priest Féron and the American Jenkins he devised a plan to open the tomb of the Taewongun's father, Prince Namyon, and take away his mortal remains — which Oppert called relics. Griffis, using official US documents, felt that the adventurers had in mind to extort money from the Taewongun. It seems more plausible that Oppert intended to use the remains of the Taewongun's father as a type of security in order — as he himself put it — "to force the regent and his government to comply with the demand to open the country and sign accordingly treaties

[7]William Elliot Griffis, Corea. *The Hermit Nation*; 4th edition, New York 1884, pp. 396 ff.
[8]Ernst Oppert, *Ein verschlossenes Land, Reisen nach Corea*, Leipzig 1880.

with foreign powers".[9] Oppert dates the expedition "three half years" after Admiral Roze's visit.[10] As the latter one occurred in October 1866, it is likely that Oppert sailed to Korea in the spring of 1868. The adventurers, some Filipinos and a Chinese crew of approximately 100 men left Shanghai with the steamer *China* and the dinghy *Greta* under the flag of the Northgerman Federation, the predecessor of the German Reich. Sailing via Nagasaki they reached the Asan Bay at the west Coast of the Korean peninsula. Using the dinghy they found the tomb of Prince Namyon. The tomb was — and still is today — situated on a hill overlooking a valley surrounded by the Kaya mountains. Four of the men tried digging the tomb with shovels. When they met the stone walls inside the mound they had no tools to open them. They thus had to leave without having achieved opening the tomb. They stayed for some time in the area of Kangwha Island and then returned to Shanghai.

Jenkins was tried by a US consular court, but acquitted for lack of evidence. It is said that Oppert was given a prison sentence in Germany.

Though the event can only be called grotesque it had its influence on the Korean attitude towards Westerners. Desecration of graves met indignation everywhere. For Koreans it was outrageous. For centuries ancestor worship was a central element of Korean religiousness. The ancestors who were contacted via offerings continued to protect the lineage. The attack on Prince Namyon's tomb by Oppert and his cohorts confirmed the impression of the Koreans that the Europeans were barbarians who should not be allowed to enter their country. While Oppert had intended to pull Korea out of seclusion his act of piracy contributed to an even greater seclusion of the country.

References

Clark, Charles Allen, *Religion of Old Korea*, New York 1932.

Dallet, Charles, *Histoire de L'Eglise de Corée*, Tome Premier, Paris 1874, Royal Asiatic Society, Korea Branch (RAS), Reprint Series, Seoul 1975.

Chon, Hae Chung, *hanchung kwankyesa yonku* (*A Study of the History of Sino-Korean Relations*), Seoul 1970.

Koh, Byong Ik, "Concept of Foreign Countries in Traditional Korea", in *Asian Culture Quarterly*, Vol. III No. 4 (Winter 1975), pp. 1 ff.

[9] Oppert p. 272 (Translation from German by the author).

[10] Oppert p. IX.

Chapter 2

Within Reach of the World Powers

The Opening of Chosun

After Japan was forced by the USA to open the country, it undertook energetic efforts to restructure its system of government according to Western patterns. The Meiji reforms of 1868 laid the foundation for the modernization of the country. The Shogunate was abolished, the feudal system phased out, and the Emperor reinstated the central authority. Foreign experts were invited to assist in the establishment of a new educational system, the reform of the military and the industrialization of the country. Unlike Korea Japan had an important military tradition and a well organized division of labor among the trades. The Japanese reformed their country with extreme, unprecedented speed so that it could enter the ranks of the big powers.

Since 1868 Japan tried to rearrange its relations with the Yi dynasty. The Japanese government was no longer willing to accept that contact with its northern neighbor could only be handled by the daiymo of Tsushima. He had been granted the monopoly for trade with Korea after the Hideyoshi invasions; this meant that all trade had to pass through the harbor of Pusan. Korea was becoming attractive as an additional market for Japan's growing industry and was of strategic importance since it was the nearest part of the Asian continent. In 1873 a great debate was held in Japan on whether to send a military expedition to Korea (*seikanron*). In the fall of 1875 the Japanese warship *Unyokan* showed up in Korean coastal waters close to Inchon and Kangwha Island, and got involved in gunfights, thus demonstrating Japanese maritime power. In February of 1876 six Japanese warships turned up at Kangwha Island;

the envoy whom they had brought along, Kuroda Kiyotaka, demanded that the Korean government agree to conclude a normalization treaty with Japan. Japan had quickly learnt the style of European and American imperialism.

The circumstances were favorable for a Japanese success. After the Taewongun had been forced to retire at the end of 1873 King Kojong had assumed full authority. In view of the growing weakness of China and the military defenselessness of Korea he attempted to react flexibly towards Japan. He thought that Korea could win Japan's friendship through correct and polite behavior. Japan thus met with some open-mindedness when it made clear its determination to rearrange its relations with Korea. By deploying warships in the waters before Kangwha Island, Japan exerted pressure on Korea. On 27 February 1876 a treaty was signed, the Kangwha Treaty.

The Kangwha Treaty provided for the exchange of envoys, the opening of two more ports for trade in addition to Pusan, and the exemption of Japanese residing in Korea from Korean jurisdiction.[1] After extended negotiations conducted persistently by Japan the port of Wonsan in northeastern Korea was opened to Japanese ships in 1880 and the port of Inchon in 1883. Japanese goods poured from Japan into Korea. This was facilitated by an agreement which declared a number of imported and exported goods custom free for a number of years. This provision favored only Japan, because Japan and not Korea had an export industry. Many Japanese came to Korea and Japanese influence expanded.

The Kanghwa Treaty was a turning point in Chosun's history. The country made the first step to open up towards foreign countries. It is only fair to stress that this happened not too long ago. As the opening occurred under pressure there was no chance to open the country under self-made conditions, a method favored by reform-minded Koreans. The most important result of the Kangwha Treaty was that it was Japan that showed Korea the way to the modern age.

At the same time the Kangwha Treaty implied a loosening of relations with China. It was nothing unusual that Korea and Japan took up relations with each other, as both countries had enjoyed prior relations already. However, there were provisions in the Kangwha Treaty which gave reason for suspicion. Article I mentioned that Korea as an independent state enjoyed the same sovereign rights as Japan, and that in the future relations between both countries would be entertained on the basis of equality. In other words, the

[1]Treaties pp. 18 ff.

ideas of sovereignty and equality that stem from European international law were applied to both contracting parties. This had not necessarily had an impact on the sort of family relations between the elder brother China and the younger brother Chosun, relations based on a different concept. Japan could, however, make use of these modern terms to question China's supremacy over Korea. And that was exactly the intention of the Japanese government.

The Unequal Treaties

King Kojong and his advisers realized more and more the precarious situation of their country which resulted from Japanese and Russian expansionism. In the fall of 1880 they came to the conclusion that the establishment of diplomatic relations with Western countries could contribute in stabilizing Korea's position. The USA was the first Western country which Korea took up official relations with, since the USA seemed to be best suited to counteract the expansionist tendencies of Chosun's neighbors. The American-Korean Treaty was signed on 22 May 1882 and was quickly followed by treaties with Great Britain (26 November 1883), Germany (26 November 1883), Russia (25 June 1884), Italy (26 June 1884) and France (4 June 1886).[2] These treaties followed the same pattern: They provided for the exchange of diplomatic and consular representatives, they opened cities and ports, they provided concessions for foreign nationals, allowed extraterritorial jurisdiction and established import and export tariffs. These treaties were of the unequal type used by Western powers in relations with Far Eastern countries. They focused on promoting the economic interests of the Western countries. Korea was in no way ready to become active beyond the borders of East Asia. The treaties also violated Korea's sovereignty by granting jurisdiction of Western nationals residing in Korea to the Western powers. The relinquishment of extraterritorial jurisdiction was envisaged in case the Korean legal system would be thoroughly reformed.[3]

China provided help in arranging the treaties with the USA and other countries. It was Li Hung-chang, the leading Chinese statesman of his time, who had intervened. He fostered Korea's opening as he hoped that this would

---

[2]The dates mentioned are those of the signing of the treaties.

[3]For example: Korean-German Protocol signed on 26 November 1883; text in *Akten des Auswärtigen Amts, Handels- und Schiffahrtssachen Asien 27 Band 3.*

be useful to contain Japan's influence on the peninsula. At the same time he tried to maintain China's traditional supremacy over Korea. He did not succeed in getting provisions to that effect inserted into the treaties, but the Korean King sent dispatches to the contracting parties stating that Korea "was a country subordinate to China", but independent in its internal administration and foreign affairs.[4] This reflected the traditional tributary relationship. The dispatches were intended to clarify that Korea did not consider the special relationship with China abolished. From the East Asian perspective this was conceivable, because Korea had relations on an equal basis with other countries but China in the past. Europeans, however, interpreted the statements of the Korean King as an expression of independence and sovereignty, applying Western legal terms to East Asian relations.

The Last Stage of Chinese Supremacy

China did not only use the negotiations with Western powers but every suitable opportunity to establish its traditional claim to supremacy over Korea. The preamble of the Sino-Korean Regulations for Maritime and Overland Trade between Chinese and Korean Subjects, signed on 4 October 1882, mentions Chosun as "a tributary kingdom" which was granted certain advantages.[5] The term of "a tributary kingdom" was also used in Rule I of the Twenty-four Rules for the Traffic on the Frontier between Fengt'ien and Korea concluded in spring 1883. These terms had characterized Sino-Korea relations for centuries. As Japan now questioned the special relationship between the two countries, China had to do more than merely to rely on the niceties of traditional terms. China felt compelled to intervene directly in Korea.

During the last years of Chinese influence in Korea (1882 to 1895) the Korean society showed signs of breaking up. After many years of seclusion the country was suddenly exposed to many contacts with the outside world. There was no agreement among the political leaders on how to use the new experiences in order to modernize the country. A reform of the economic system was urgent. This was true for agriculture where new methods of cultivation had spread. Mining had to be developed. Industrial goods were reaching Chosun.

---

[4]See for example the Dispatch to the US President with translation by Professor H. H. Dubs in Nelson pp. 147 and 148.

[5]Deuchler p. 141.

The use of machines became known, and methods of industrial production were introduced, often with the assistance of foreign experts. Trade had to be reorganized and infrastructure improved. Railway and streetcar systems were established. Postal and telegraph offices had to be organized. Steam ships had to be acquired. As the political elite were occupied with infighting and did not demonstrate leadership, dissatisfaction among the people spread. This development resulted in various revolts, but not in a revolution. The Confucian virtue, which included a sense of duty and the willingness to accept one's position within society, outweighed the reformist forces.

In the summer of 1882 a military unit in Seoul rebelled against irregularities in the grain distribution. This mutiny developed into a rebellion against Queen Min and her clan which had occupied important government positions since the beginning of the eighties, and against the Japanese presence in Korea. Bloody clashes occurred, people were killed, the Japanese top among them. In order to find a solution for the crisis the Taewongun was temporarily re-appointed.

China as well as Japan sent troops to Korea. The Chinese reacted quicker and got the situation under control. They took the Taewongun by force and brought him to China and returned government business to King Kojong. In order to maintain their influence they left troops in Seoul and dispatched Chinese advisers to the Korean government. The interference of the Chinese into Korean politics and administration made them unpopular. Japan succeeded in receiving a commitment of compensations for the damages suffered during the incident.

In December 1884 another coup followed, usually called after the year name, the Kapsin Coup. Its causes differed from those of the 1882 incident. It originated from opposing views on how to proceed with the modernization of Korea. On one side there were the Min who had assumed government control with the support of the Chinese since the 1882 incident and who had sidelined King Kojong. Also the Min and their followers tried to reform the country, but focused only on acquiring Western technology. They wished to maintain and use the existing social structures. Besides Queen Min, whose role has often been overemphasized, Min Tae Ho, president of the newly founded Home Office, and his son Min Yong Ik were the main representatives of the clan which came from Yohung (today's Yoju). On the other side was a small group of reformers lead by Kim Ok Kyun which were later called the Enlightenment Party (*kaehwadang*). Its members were deeply impressed by Japan's reforms and suggested radical changes in the Korean social system. As they did not succeed in realizing their ideas through the government of which they were members, they decided to initiate a coup d'état. When on 4 December 1884 the new post office in Anguk dong, a district in Seoul, was inaugurated in the presence of many government officials they launched their attack. With Japanese assistance they succeeded in ousting the Min and their followers of whom many were killed. But the victory was short-lived, because the Chinese forces under the command of Yüan Shih-kai drove off the rebels and their Japanese supporters. Japan succeeded again in concluding a convention on 9 January 1885 by which Korea was again bound to pay compensations. In the Convention of Tientsin, concluded between China and Japan on 18 April 1885, both countries agreed to withdraw their troops from Korea to give prior written notice to each other before sending troops back into Korea. The withdrawal of troops worked in favor for Japan which had far less forces stationed in Korea than China. China and Japan continued to try to enhance their influence in Korea. The Chinese representative Yüan Shik-kai tried to control the Korean government's business, a clear departure from the traditional Chinese politics of non-interference into Korea's internal affairs.

The most severe of the rebellions which shook Korea at the end of the nineteenth century was the Tonghak revolt. It was a revolt of impoverished farmers who demanded equitable taxation and the halting of rice exports to Japan which had caused rice prices to increase. The revolt was organized by the leaders of the Tonghak movement. Tonghak (Eastern Learning) founded by Choe Che U in the middle of the nineteenth century was a syncretic religion, comprised of elements of Confucianism, Buddhism, Taoism and original Korean religions. The more the economic situation deteriorated, the greater the new religion seemed to be the only way out of misery. And the economic situation deteriorated dramatically because of droughts and of maladministration.

The Tonghak revolt began in the Cholla provinces in the spring of 1894 due to unfair treatment of farmers by a government official. The revolt spread rapidly over the country. When the revolt met success, its leaders demanded far-reaching reforms aimed at abolishing the traditional aristocratic system. As the Korean military was unable to cope with the situation King Kojong asked China for help. This was a disastrous step. Since the Convention of Tientsin had provided a connection between the military activities of China and Japan in Korea, Japan reacted to the Chinese military activities in Korea by also dispatching troops. On 25 July 1894 an undeclared war broke out in the Asan Bay when Japanese warships attacked Chinese ships, which were bringing additional forces to Korea. At the same time Japanese ground forces attacked Chinese troops. The Chinese troops managed to hold out in Pyongyang for a period of time, but in the fall of 1894 they were finally driven out of Korea. The Japanese ended the rule of the Ming clan and forced King Kojong to call back the Taewongun once again. The resurgence of the Tonghak revolt in October 1884 provided the Japanese with the opportunity to persecute the Tonghak leaders and to achieve control over the whole country. The Tonghak revolt which had started as an anti-foreign movement had played into the hands of the Japanese.

The failure of the Chinese military in Korea was not at all surprising. It was not really the whole of China which was fighting in Korea, but only the units under the command of Li Hung-chang. C. v. Hanneken, a German observer, called the Chinese forces "a spotted military".[6] He felt that the armament of the Chinese forces "was better suited for an arms collection than for an army ready for war".[7] The Chinese political and military leadership were irresolute. The agony of imperial China had begun.

Mok In Dok

Among the foreigners hired by the Korean government as advisers upon the recommendation of Li Hung-chang after the 1882 incident was a German, Paul Georg von Moellendorff.[8]

Von Moellendorff, born in 1847, had joined the Chinese Maritime Customs Service as a young man and had later become an interpreter at the German missions in China. During his stay at the German Consulate in Tientsin he had got in contact with Li Hung-chang who remembered the young man when the Korean government had approached him looking for a linguist and expert in international relations. The contract between von Moellendorff and the Korean government concluded in Tientsin on 18 November 1882 provided that

[6] C. v. Hanneken, "Episoden aus dem Chinesischen-Japanischen Kriege", in *Deutsche Rundschau* 1886 p. 391.

[7] Ibidem.

[8] Jürgen Kleiner, "Paul Georg von Möllendorf. Ein Preusse in koreanischen Diensten", in *Zeitschrift der Deutschen Morgenländischen Gesellschaft* Band 133 (1983) pp. 393 ff., Koh Byong Ik, "Mok In-dok ui kobing hwa ku paegyong": *Chindan hakpo* 25–27, 1964, pp. 227 ff.

he had to advise the Korean Foreign Ministry on reforms of all kind. As special fields of work foreign trade and the establishment of a customs office were mentioned. On 13 December 1882 von Moellendorff arrived in Seoul and in January 1883 he was appointed vice-president of the Department of Revenue and Port Administration. The first European government official in Korea now used the Korean robes of office and was called Mok In Dok.

When Li Hung-chang had recommended von Moellendorff to the Korean government he had in mind that the activities of a German adviser might be helpful to contain Japanese expansionist efforts in Korea. Von Moellendorff quickly realized how much Korea was endangered by Japan. He, therefore, focused on the question of how to preserve Koreas independence. He felt that China was not in a position to guarantee Korea's security against Japan and, therefore, sought a partnership with Russia. He saw to it that the friendship treaty with Russia was concluded in the summer of 1884. In the eyes of his sponsors in China he had gone too far. They insisted that he was temporarily released from his functions in the Korean Foreign Office.

Von Moellendorff was not only deeply involved in Korea's diplomatic negotiations, but was active in many other fields. He always worked towards contributing to the country's modernization. As head of the Korean Maritime Customs Service he established customs offices in Inchon, Pusan and Wonsan. He introduced modern technology in the Mint and tried to improve agriculture, particularly sericulture. He promoted mining as well as the porcelain industry and established a machine factory. He was also helpful in establishing a government language school. Many of his initiatives failed. He lacked consistency in his approach, and the Korean government did not sufficiently support the foreign expert whom it had hired.

After the Kapsin Coup von Moellendorff joined the Foreign Office again and became instrumental in concluding the Korean–Japanese Treaty of Seoul on 9 January 1885. In February 1885 he made use of his stay in Tokyo — where he had to deliver the letter of apology provided for in the Treaty of Seoul — to contact the Russian legation and to negotiate the sending of Russian military instructors to Korea. When Russia pursued this idea in the summer of 1885 in Seoul, a storm of indignation broke out and von Moellendorff was relieved from his functions in the Foreign Ministry. This came upon the request of Li Hung-chang on 27 July 1885; later that year he lost all other functions in Korea. He had gone beyond what China considered permissible for a peripheral state.

Von Moellendorff had given selfless advice to the Korean government. He wanted to assist the country to become independent. He had Korean aims in mind. He underestimated, however, China's readiness to defend its traditional position in Korea. And the Korean government did not lend him the necessary support. His activity in Korea was a failure, however, it was a noble one.

The End of a Special Relationship

Ernst von Hesse-Wartegg, who visited Korea in the summer of 1894, described an exchange of embassies between Korea and China in 1890 on the occasion of the death of the widow of a Korean crown prince.[9] Based on Chinese documents he gave the following account: Twenty days after the death of the widow, a Korean embassy traveled by land from Seoul to Beijing and informed the imperial court of the sad event. The embassy requested, at the same time, to take Korea's poverty into consideration and not to send a Chinese embassy to Seoul. This request was rejected, but it was agreed that the Imperial embassy would travel by sea. In November 1890 the Chinese embassy left Tientsin with three warships. In Inchon (Chemulpo) the embassy was welcomed by a large Korean delegation and then guided to Seoul. The delegates were received by the King before the city gate and then led to the royal palace. Here the imperial letter of condolence and the gifts were exhibited and the King had to kowtow. The next day the condolence ceremony was held. After having had a ceremonial banquet, the Chinese delegation left, taking the same way which it had chosen when coming.

Von Hesse-Wartegg tried to prove Korea's "slavish dependence" on China.[10] As can be seen from his account relations between Chi'ng China and the Yi dynasty had become extremely formalistic. The ceremonies were out of proportion with their causes. However, the ceremonies, as described by von Hesse-Wartegg, were an expression of the special relationship between China and Korea. In the Sinic world order it was understood that the Middle Kingdom was superior to its smaller bordering states. Originally, non-interference into Korea's domestic affairs had been predominant. Only since Japan questioned the special relationship between China and Korea the Middle Kingdom

---

[9]Ernst von Hesse-Wartegg, *Korea. Eine Sommerreise nach dem Land Morgenruhe 1894*, Dresden und Leipzig 1895, reprinted by Korea University, Seoul 1973, pp. 86 ff.

[10]Von Hesse-Wartegg p. 86.

had directly intervened in Korea. Direct interventions by China were not typical of the relations between Ch'ing China and Chosun.

It was the last effort of China to maintain the traditional system. The embassies described by von Hesse-Wartegg are among the last which the Middle Kingdom exchanged with Chosun. The Treaty of Shimonoseki of 17 April 1895 which brought the Chinese-Japanese war to a close, abolished the Chinese supremacy towards Korea. In Article I of this Treaty, China recognized the complete independence of Korea. This meant the end of the traditional ties between the elder brother China and the younger brother Korea.

The Treaty of Shimonoseki did not only decide about Chinese-Korean relations. China had to cede Formosa and the Pescadores Islands to Japan. It also had to open cities, ports and rivers and to pay reparations. The cession of the Liaotung peninsula, however, was prevented by protests from Russia, France and Germany. Japan had now become the predominant power in East Asia.

Russian Efforts in Seoul

When Russia expanded to East Asia, it was unavoidable that it got in touch with China and Korea. The interests Russia pursued in Korea were similar to those of Japan. Though tzarist Russia had already requested the establishment of diplomatic relations with Korea in the middle of the nineteenth century, it took until 1884 before a friendship treaty could be concluded. It was the Russian Karl Waeber, who later became Russian minister in Seoul, and von Moellendorff who succeeded in bringing about that treaty. On 8 August 1888 both countries reached an agreement on overland trade at the Tumen River. On the Korean side the American O.N. Denny participated. He was von Moellendorff's successor and also had Korea's independence in mind. By this second Korean-Russian treaty the border town of Kyonghung was opened to Russia. Russia was also allowed to establish a consulate there which had the sole jurisdiction over Russian citizens and Russian property in Korea.

Russian influence at the royal court in Seoul had increased as it was considered to counterbalance Japanese and Chinese efforts. The Min clan hoped that Russian support might be helpful to regain power. The Japanese reacted brutally. On 8 October 1895 Queen Min was murdered in the Kyongbok palace by the Japanese and their Korean followers. The Russians took advantage of the unrest caused by Queen Min's murder and fuelled by the Japanese ban of the topknots, the traditional Korean hairstyle. They brought troops into Seoul and led King Kojong to the Russian legation. Suddenly, the Russian influence was so strong that Japan had to make concessions.

During the years of Russian influence Korean reform efforts could develop, although in a modest way. Behind these efforts was So Chae Pil (Dr. Philip Jaisohn) who had founded the paper "Independent" (*Tongnip Sinmun*) and the Independence Club (*Tongnip Hyophoe*). The gate where Chinese envoys used to be welcomed was replaced by an Independence Arch. The Independence Club requested the democratization of the state and to halt the granting of concessions to foreigners. The Club did not succeed in convincing the conservative government by which it was dissolved.

In 1897 Chosun was renamed the Korean Empire (*taehan cheguk*) and Kojong became Emperor (*hwang che*). The renaming was done to demonstrate that Korea was on an equal footing with the empires of China and Japan. The renaming, however, was contrary to the actual situation. Kojong had stayed for more than a year in the Russian legation and had taken residence in the Toksu Palace only on 20 February 1897. The country had no united leadership and was more and more exposed to the expansionist efforts of the neighbors.

The Russian-Japanese War

The importance of the war between Russia and Japan went far beyond the territorial conflict between the two countries. It had a global impact, but it also had direct consequences for Korea's fate.

Japan had reacted in a flexible way to the Russian efforts to increase its influence in Korea. If necessary it had agreed to a compromise, if possible it had tried to enhance its own influence. In a series of agreements Russia and Japan had attempted to define their interests in Korea. The Lobanov-Yamagata Agreement of 9 June 1896 gave both countries equal influence in Korea. In the Rosen-Nishi Agreement of 25 April 1898 the Russian government conceded not to hinder the development of commercial and industrial relations between Japan and Korea.

An additional bone of contention between both countries occurred over Manchuria. Here Russia took position at the end of the last century, exploiting the weakness of China which became more and more a victim of the colonial powers. Russia's position in Manchuria was strengthened after railways had been built. In 1898 Russia succeeded in leasing from China the southern tip of the Liaotung Peninsula with the two harbors Port Arthur (Lüshun) and Dairen (Talien) for 25 years. Japan observed this development with concern, since Manchuria together with Korea not only protected the Japanese flank, but also was well suited for further Japanese expansionist moves on the continent.

Before Japan dared to clash militarily with Russia, it was looking for diplomatic support for its position. It gained this support by forming an alliance with Britain, the enemy of Russian expansionism. Since April 1885 Britain had maintained a coal station on Komun Island — at that time called Port Hamilton — in order to be prepared for possible conflicts with Russia in Northeast Asia. Apart from this coal station, Britain had not shown much interest in Korean developments. In the treaty of 30 January 1902 Japan and Britain reached agreement about controversial areas in East Asia; Britain was mainly interested in Tibet, Japan in Korea. Both sides assured each other benevolent neutrality in case of an attack by a foreign power and support in case of an attack by more than one foreign country. Though the Anglo-Japanese alliance focused on East Asian areas, it also had an impact on European politics. Britain departed from its policy of isolation, thus initiating a new line-up of world powers.

When Japan suggested to Russia to find an arrangement for their mutual interests, Russia reacted by reinforcing its troops. Japan, at the beginning of 1904 launched an attack on Russia even before it had declared war. On 8 February 1904 Japanese ships attacked the Russian fleet at Port Arthur. Japanese ground forces started to attack Russian forces in Manchuria. The Russians suffered severe defeats. In order to turn around the situation Russia sent down its Baltic fleet. Its long voyage was overshadowed by many difficulties, including mutinies and bunkering problems in particular. The fleet had to take the long way around Africa as Britain blocked the use of the Suez Canal. When the Baltic fleet arrived in the Korea Strait off Tsushima Island at the end of May 1905 it was attacked and defeated by the Japanese navy. Russia was forced to accept the meditation offered by then US President Theodore Roosevelt. The peace treaty was concluded in Portsmouth (New Hampshire) on 5 September 1905.[11]

During the war Japan had landed troops in Korea and had used the country to deploy troops needed to fight against Russia. After Russia was defeated Japan saw to it that its supremacy in Korea was assured. In Article II

[11] Treaties ans Conventions pp. 56 and 57.

paragraph 1 of the Treaty of Portsmouth Russia accepted that Japan would have predominant political, military and economic interest in Korea. Russia also agreed not to interfere in measures of protection and control which the Japanese government might have deemed necessary in Korea.

As can be seen from a memorandum concerning the talks between Prime Minister Katsura and the US Minister of War Taft on 27 July 1905 the Japanese government justified its activities in Korea by arguing that Korea otherwise would lapse back into its old habit of concluding treaties with other countries in a careless way.[12] This argument can only be called malicious for it had been Japan which had made Korea conclude the first of the careless treaties.

The Treaty of Portsmouth brought Japan many other gains. The areas leased to Russia on the Southern tip of the Liaotung Peninsula including Port Arthur and Dairen as well as the railway system in Southern Manchuria were transferred to Japan. Russia also had to cede South Sachalin to Japan. Japan was no longer just the predominant power in East Asia, but had become one of the world powers.

A Japanese Protectorate

Even before the victory over Russia gave Japan freedom of action in Korea, the Japanese government had used every opportunity to enhance its influence in the neighboring country. This occurred particularly during the war between China and Japan in 1894 and 1895, when Japan had pushed a policy of reforms in Korea. The governmental system was reorganized and a state council with eight ministers was established. The examination system was modernized by introducing new, non-Confucian subjects. A new coinage was issued, taxes were to be paid in cash, the expenses of the royal court were separated from the public finances which were put under the control of the ministry of finance. The four classes as well as slavery were abolished. The educational and the legal systems were reformed. At the same time the first Japanese "advisers" appeared. Many of these reforms were necessary, but they were hastily carried out, and with a view to be beneficial for Japan.

---

[12] Andrew S. Nahm, "The Impact of the Taft-Kazura Memorandum on Korea. A Reassessment", in *Korea Journal* Vol. 25 No. 10.

After Russia had accepted not to interfere with Japanese precautionary measures in Korea Japan could further deepen its control over the country. Japan imposed a series of agreements on Korea. Particularly important were the Agreements of 17 November 1905 and 24 July 1907.

The first Agreement contained the following provisions: Future control and supervision of Korea's foreign relations would be the responsibility of the Japanese government; Korea could conclude international treaties only through Japan's mediation; the Japanese government would be represented by a Resident-General and commissioners. Existing treaties between Korea and Japan would remain valid only as far as they were compatible with this agreement and the Japanese government guarantee the safety and dignity of the Korean Emperor. As according to this agreement the fostering of Korea's foreign relation was transferred to the Japanese government, Korea had become a state with limited power to act. Essentially, Korea had become a Japanese protectorate.

Koreans did react against the reduction of their country's sovereignty. Everywhere in Korea people protested against the self-appointed protecting power. Many high government officials were so full of despair that they committed suicide. Soldiers of the dissolved Korean army and other Koreans organized resistance groups (*uibyong*) which fought bravely against the better-equipped and better-commanded Japanese army. Japanese records revealed that there were 2819 clashes between Korean resistance groups and Japanese forces in the period of 1907 to 1910. In 1907 Emperor Kojong who had rejected signing the agreement of 17 November 1905 undertook a last effort to regain sovereignty. He sent representatives to the Second Peace Conference in The Hague. These representatives were met with some sympathy, but no foreign government was willing to raise the Korean question. This was not surprising, because Japan had acted exactly in the same way as other imperial powers. Japan forced Emperor Kojong to abdicate on 19 July 1907 in favor of his son Sunjong. To what extent he was acting under duress can be seen from his declaration to the contrary: "In abdicating my throne I acted in obedience to the dictate of my conviction; my action was not the result of any outside advice or pressure".[13]

On 24 July 1907 the so-called "New Agreement" was concluded. It gave the Japanese government far reaching rights to interfere in Korea's domestic affairs.

[13]Nelson p. 279.

The Korean government could no longer enact laws or ordinances, take any important measures of administration, or appoint high government officials without prior Japanese consent. Japanese recommended by the Resident-General had to be appointed as Korean officials. The Japanese government ensured that these provisions were implemented. Korea's status was now that of a Japanese colony.

At the beginning of the 1990's the question of whether the two agreements of 1905 and 1907 were void from the beginning (*ex nunc*) was discussed with excitement. Korean scholars argued that the treaties were void after they had found out that the original texts of the agreements lacked the Emperor's seal.[14] A report of the German Minister Resident Conrad von Saldern to the German Chancellor dated 20 November 1905, a copy of which was first found in Hungarian Archives and could later be verified in the archives of the German Foreign Office, may give a hint to why the seal was missing: Von Saldern reports that the Emperor, in his discussions with the Japanese representatives Ito Hirobumi, firmly rejected the proposals for the 1905 agreement.[15] Von Saldern continued to say: "This [Foreign] Minister was authorized to negotiate with the Japanese, but not to sign a treaty. The Emperor stick to his 'No' ".[16] What was lacking for the signature of the agreements was the Emperor's consent. Today this would be termed a violation of constitutional provisions. Since Kojong's refusal was well known to the Japanese delegations, as evidenced from the discussion which the delegates have had with him, they could not claim to have signed in good faith.[17] So indeed, the agreement of 1905 was void from the beginning. As for the agreement of the 1907 we do not know similar details. From a historical perspective, the legal question is not crucial, but the incident sheds light on the ruthlessness of the Japanese action.

Resistance against the Japanese rule continued. It was mainly promoted by newspapers, schools and churches. On 26 October 1909 An Chung Gun killed Ito Hirobumi who had been the first Resident-General in Korea at the railway station in Harbin (Manchuria). The resistant movement was quickly crushed,

---

[14]Newsreview, 23 May 1992.

[15]Text of the report and details of its history in *Koreana. Magazin der Deutsch — Koreanischen Gesellschaft e.V.* 3/93 pp. 7 ff.; see also Korea Herald, 14 June 1992, News Review, 20 June 1992.

[16]Koreana loc. cit. p. 11 (Translation from German by the author).

[17]Seidl — Hohenveldern pp. 6 ff.; Malcohm N. Shaw, *International Law*, 4th edition, Cambridge 1997, pp. 661 ff.

however, by the Japanese police. There was also cooperation of Koreans with the Japanese administration. The main support came from a popular pro-Japanese association (*ilchinhoe*). It was dissolved in 1910 after having fulfilled its purpose. By way of a bilateral treaty signed on 22 August 1910 Japan annexed Korea. Korea ceased to exist as an independent state.

Summary

Isolation and xenophobia were quite natural in the secluded world of East Asia. The fears had, however, disastrous consequences for Korea by preventing the country from quickly adopting to modern times. The strong influence of an outdated state philosophy which had always stressed solidarity within the family more than cohesion within the state, the dissolution of the Korean society which resulted in strong tension between government and citizens, and the lack of a united and stable leadership made it impossible for Korea to find new ways by its own efforts. As the country was also caught by the maelstrom of conflicts between the world powers, its independence was endangered.

Korea lost its position as a younger brother of the Middle Kingdom which itself was shattered. The family relations which had allowed Korea to develop independently were substituted by a far stronger dependence on the unloved neighbor Japan which had demonstrated its influence as one of the world powers. Korea was now called an empire. But the term was deceiving since Korea had become the protectorate of another empire. And in addition the Korean Empire was about to completely lose its sovereignty. It was a bad start in the 20th century for Korea.

References

Sources for the treaties concluded by Korea:

Treaties, Regulation, etc, between Corea and Other Powers (1876–1889), published at the Statistical Department of the Inspectorate General of Customs, Shanghai 1891 (quoted as Treaties);

Treaties and Conventions between Corea and Foreign Powers, compiled by H.I.J. M.'s Residency General, 1908 (quoted as Treaties and Conventions).

Deuchler, Martina, *Confucian Gentlemen and Barbarian Envoys; The Opening of Korea, 1875–1885*, Seattle and London 1977.

Kang, Thomas Hosuck, "Confucian Behavior Toward the Modernization of Korea, 1864–1910", in *Korea Journal* Vol. 13 No. 7 (1973) p. 4 ff.

Kim, Kyung Tae, "A Survey of Domestic and International Conditions Relating to the Opening of Ports in 1876", in *Journal of Social Sciences and Humanities* No. 12, Seoul 1975, p. 37 ff.

McKenzie, F. A., *Korea's Fight for Freedom*, New York and Chicago 1920, Reprinted by Yonsei University Press, Seoul 1969.

Swartout, Robert R., *Mandarins, Gunboats, and Power Politics*, Hawaii 1980.

Chapter 3

The Japanese Rule

The Annexation

The Treaty of Annexation signed on 22 August 1910 by the Japanese Resident-General Masatake Terauchi and the Korean Prime Minister Yi Wan Yong provided that "His Majesty the Emperor of Korea makes complete and permanent cession to his Majesty the Emperor of Japan of all rights of sovereignty over the whole of Korea".[1] The treaty further stipulated that the Japanese government assumed control of Korea's administration. This treaty entered into force on 29 August 1910. At the same time, Koreans became subjects of the Japanese Emperor, that is to say they became Japanese citizens. This was publicly announced in a proclamation by the Resident-General on 29 August 1910. A declaration of the Japanese government, addressed to foreign powers, stated that the international treaties concluded by Korea had expired and would be substituted, as far as possible, by the international treaties which Japan had concluded. As the treaty had stated, the annexation resulted in a transfer of Korea's sovereignty to Japan.

Japan quickly made use of its newly acquired sovereignty in Korea. A declaration by the Japanese government on 29 August 1910 determined that the future title of the Korean Emperor would be that of King and that Korea was to be called Chosen. In order to distinguish Korea under Japanese rule from Choson under the Yi-dynasty, the term Chosen will be used for the period between 1910 and 1945.

[1]Text of the treaty in: Annual Report 1930–1932 pp. 180 ff.

Upon insistence of the Japanese government, the Korean Emperor had to publish a "Rescript on Cession" on 29 August 1910, in which he gave reason on why the cession was necessary. He justified it with the inability to overcome "the long-standing weakness and deep rooted evils".[2] "We feel constraint to believe it wise to entrust Our great task to abler hands than Ours, so that efficient measures may be carried out and satisfactory results obtained therefrom". The real intentions of the Japanese government in Korea were revealed in the proclamation of 29 August 1910 by Resident-General Terauchi.[3] The proclamation called it natural and unavoidable that both neighboring countries merge and form an entity. While this did not sound too threatening, it was threatening indeed. As an adaptation of the world power Japan to Korea was out of the question, it meant the Japanisation of Korea. Japan had not only subjugated its smaller neighbor — whom it had earlier promised protection — in a very humiliating way, but now it had also announced a radical program of assimilation. Outside of Korea nobody protested. Those Koreans who intended to object were already informed by Terauchi's proclamation that they should not expect any mercy.

The System of Control

The Japanese government lost no time in making its control felt in Korea. Through an Imperial Rescript on 29 August 1910, the position of the Resident-General was substituted by that of a Governor-General.[4] An Imperial Decree dated 30 October 1910 laid down the details of the administrative organization. The Governor-General will be chosen from the ranks of generals and admirals and appointed by the Emperor to whom he has to report ("to memorialize").[5] Six central offices which functioned like ministries were established: for General, Home, Financial, Agricultural, Commercial and Industrial as well as Judicial Affairs. The governor-general had the sole responsibility for Japanese politics in Korea and was authorized to issue regulations and orders. The Decree made him very powerful. Later his official position underwent changes.

[2] Annual Report 1930–1932 pp. 182 and 183.

[3] Annual Report 1910–1911 pp. 235 ff.

[4] Annual Report 1930–1932 pp. 181 and 182.

[5] Annual Report 1930–1932 p. 33.

He was first put under the control of the home office in Tokyo and later under that of the prime minister. As all governor-generals on duty in Chosen were former high ranking officers, and at the same time, prominent political personalities they ruled Chosen in an independent way which sometimes looked to be even dissociated from politics in Tokyo.

Controlling Chosen was facilitated by an enormous influx of Japanese. It had already begun before the turn of the century, but accelerated after the annexation. In 1910 171,500 Japanese lived in Korea. Their numbers doubled by 1920 to 347,900, and quadrupled by 1939 to 650,100. The Japanese had not only occupied the most important positions in Chosen's administration but had also occupied the top management functions in business.

The main instrument of Japanese control in Korea was the police. In the first decade, the military police came under the jurisdiction of the Governor-General in his capacity as commander-in-chief of the Japanese forces in Korea. The increasing numbers of policemen revealed the seriousness of the efforts of the Japanese administration. In 1910 the police force in Korea was numbered at 7,712. By 1918, it had doubled to 14,358 and reached a strength of 20,647 in 1937. The police acted arbitrarily, thus spreading fear among the Koreans. Reports about torture and other atrocities by the Japanese police were numerous. The police also recklessly made use of flogging, defending its use as the traditional form of punishment in Korea. Considerable numbers of the police force included Koreans. In the Treaty of Annexation, Japan had promised to employ those Koreans in Chosen's public service "who accept the new regime loyally and in good faith".[6] Therefore, it could not totally exclude Koreans from the administration of their own country. For the most part, however, the Japanese made empty gestures. They established, for example, a Central Advisory Council (*chu suin*) composed of 65 Koreans; the council's advice, however, was seldom asked for.

The Vice President of this Council was Yi Wan Yong who, as Prime Minister, had signed the Treaty of Annexation in 1910. Koreans have focussed on denouncing him as traitor. It cannot, however, be overlooked that in the years before Korea's annexations, there were a number of pro Japanese politicians within the Korean elite. Some of them joined Yi Wan Yong in the Central Advisory Council.

---

[6]Annual Report 1930–1932 p. 181.

The Samil Uprising

The tough Japanese rule provoked resistance among Koreans which strict police control could not totally suppress. Leaders of the resistance movement in Korea who were in touch with Koreans abroad decided to hold peaceful demonstrations everywhere in the country for Korea's independence. They were influenced by the idea of the right of self-determination made popular by President Woodrow Wilson. The preparations for the demonstrations were organized by the Protestant churches and by Chondogyo as the Tonghak movement was called since 1905. Both organizations were able to make use of their countrywide networks. Students made important contributions because they could move relatively freely in the country and thus were in a position to establish contacts among the groups. The Buddhists eventually joined while the Catholics stayed away. The "Proclamation of Korean Independence" was signed by 15 leaders of Chondogyo, 16 Protestant leaders and 2 Buddhists.[7] For the first time, representatives of the old upper class, the *yangban*, did not participate in an important national event.

The Proclamation justified the call for independence by referring to many sources, to god, to the equality of all nations, to universal law, and to a balance of powers in East Asia. Japan was only accused in an indirect way, the future of Korea was in focus. However, no organizational pattern on how to achieve independence was given. In a noble way which revealed helplessness at the same time, the Korean people was called upon to pursue the aim of Korea's independence without violence. The Proclamation is not a document for the beginning of a new state, but an outcry of an oppressed people. The document states among other things: "Victims of an older age, when brute force and the spirit of plunder ruled, we have come after these long thousand of years to experience the agony of ten years of foreign oppression, with every loss to the right to live, every restriction of the freedom of thought, every damage done to the dignity of life, every opportunity lost for a share in the intelligent advance of the age in which we live."

The funeral for Emperor Kojong, who had died on 22 January 1919, was considered by the leaders of the independence movement to be a good occasion for the envisaged protests. The funeral was to be held on 3 March 1919, and many Koreans had come to the capital city, now called Keijo by the Japanese,

[7]Text in McKenzie pp. 247–250.

in order to pay their last respect to the former ruler. The people were infuriated by rumors that Kojong had been poisoned or had committed suicide. As the leaders of the movement felt that police control would be particularly strict on the day of the funeral, they scheduled the demonstrations for the 1st of March — in Korean *sam-il*, the first day of the third month. The uprising is therefore called Samil uprising.

29 of the 33 signatories met on 1 March 1919 in a restaurant in downtown Seoul. They displayed numerous copies of the Proclamation, a Buddhist monk delivered a speech and the participants shouted "Long live the independence". When the police arrived, the protestors did not object to being arrested. At the same time, several thousand people gathered in Pagoda Park where a young man read the Proclamation of Independence. Many protests followed in Seoul and throughout other places all over Korea. While many of the demonstrations began peacefully, some turned into violent clashes with the Japanese police which had been caught by surprise. The demonstrations and rebellions continued for weeks, and were then systematically and brutally suppressed by the Japanese police which went so far as to burn down villages.

The number of Koreans who participated in the demonstrations is unclear. The numbers mentioned vary. According to Japanese police reports, 587,641 people participated in the period from 1 March to 30 April 1919.[8] Of those, 26,713 persons were arrested, 553 killed and 1,409 injured. The Samil movement quotes much higher numbers. Whatever the real numbers may have been it is quite clear that it was an important movement which found support throughout Korea.

The Japanese administration could suppress the resistance movement, but the Korean people had succeeded in uniting behind the idea of self-determination and in demonstrating a national consciousness. In Korean history, only the neo-Confucian ideas at the beginning of the Yi dynasty had had a similar effect. The Korean people have good reason to be proud of the Samil-uprising; the 1st of March is celebrated in the Republic of Korea as a public holiday.

The Japanese Reaction

The Japanese government reacted in a flexible and effective way toward the Korean attempt for self-assertion. It reacted flexibly by softening its rule in

[8] Lee Chong Sik (1963) p. 114.

Chosen, and effectively by preventing future protests. It flatly declared that "the change in the times following the World War necessitated a readjustment of the entire administrative system", and that the unrest in the spring of 1919 had made it impossible to proceed with the readjustment.[9] When the so-called reforms were introduced in August 1919, the merger of the two people was no longer mentioned; now it was stressed to place both people "on an equal footing".[10] The new measures were, of course, intended to safeguard the Japanese rule in Chosen.

The system of Japanese administration in Chosen was changed by the reforms of August 1919. In the future, a civilian could also be appointed governor-general. The governor-general was no longer the commander-in-chief of the Japanese forces in Chosen. If necessary, he would have to ask the military commander to bring forces into action. The new regulation was meaningless since all governor-generals appointed after 1919 were former high-ranking officers, who could rely on the loyalty of the military commanders in Chosen. The military police were withdrawn, but the number of the civil police was increased at the same time.

The central administration was reorganized to the effect that it had six bureaus now: for Home, Financial, Industrial, Judicial Affairs, for Education and the Police. It was announced that the access of Koreans to hold government positions was going to be facilitated. This program showed some results. In 1936, there were 87,552 officials on duty in Chosen's public administration, out of when 52,270 were Japanese, and 35,282 were Koreans.[11] Mosft of the high positions were occupied by Japanese. The more World War II was wearing out Japan's human reserves, the more the Koreans could enter the public administration in Chosun.

Local administration was also reorganized after the Samil uprising. The introduction of councils at the levels of the province, city and municipality gave the Koreans a small and modest possibility to influence decisions on the local level. Even the Japanese did not call the system local self-government. The electoral procedures for the councils and their functions varied, and were once again changed in 1931. The councils in the cities and selected municipalities — and later in all municipalities — were elected. Every man who was older than

[9]Annual Report 1930–1932 p. 7.

[10]Annual Report 1930–1932 p. 185.

[11]Henderson p. 106.

25 years, a resident of the municipality for more than 1 year and who had paid more than 5 yen in local taxes was entitled to vote. These provisions favored the Japanese, but gave the Koreans some possibilities for participation.

From the very beginning of their rule, the Japanese had considered education important. The educational system was expanded, particularly by the introduction of elementary education in 1906, and was intended to produce loyal Japanese subjects. Thousands of Japanese teachers who came to the peninsula contributed to reach that aim. The "reforms" of 1919 had announced a cultural policy in order to realize the plan to place both people on the same footing. Governor-General Makoto Saito who had been appointed after the Samil uprising had built schools and founded a teacher seminary. Compulsory school attendance for all children, however, was not introduced. Nevertheless, the number of students increased dramatically. While the number of students amounted to only 111,000 in 1910, they had increased to 1,2 million by 1937. The knowledge of Japanese spread: by 1943 one fifth of Koreans knew Japanese. It must be mentioned, however, that Korean children were discriminated against. While at the end of Japanese rule in 1945, nearly all Japanese children living in Korea had profited from school education, less than half of the Korean children had gone to elementary school. Access to institutions of higher learning was difficult for Korean children. Fortunately a growing number of private schools, among them missionary schools, could fill this void. Access to the only newly founded university in the country, the Imperial University in Seoul — the predecessor of Seoul National University — was limited; only a couple of hundred Koreans could attend it. Regardless, organization and capacity building of the educational system made considerable progress during the Japanese rule.

The Economy

The Japanese administration was determined to develop Chosen's economy for the benefit of Japan. From the beginning, it focused on improving agricultural production, particularly rice production so as to secure the supply for Japan.

Under the heading of Land Survey, a modern system of surveying land and registering ownership was introduced. This was necessary indeed. Land property and property rights had not been precisely fixed or documented. Originally this had been unnecessary. At the beginning of the Yi dynasty, all land had to be returned to the state which had distributed most of it to government officials for the period of their term of office. This system had been undermined by and by. The members of the royal clan kept much of the land for themselves. The expansion of the estates of the *yangban*, the *nonjang*, could not be prevented as the *yangban* were the main supporters of the monarchy. The tax system, based on land ownership, had become totally disorganized. All this was said to have been changed and improved by the Land Survey System. Many farmers, however, did not understand this new approach and failed to register the land they were farming. Consequently, they ended up losing much of the land.[12] The number of farmers who were tenants and not landowners had been considerable in the past. After the Land Survey, their numbers increased. In 1938 more than half of the farmers were tenants. The Japanese administration saw to it that large portions of the land went to the Japanese immigrants or to the Oriental Development Company, a state-controlled organization.

The Japanese administration reached its main goal of increasing rice exports to Japan. Exports increased far more than the rice production. In spite of all the efforts to improve the productivity of rice farming by means of additional irrigation systems, use of fertilizers and modern machinery and use of new varieties of seeds, rice production increased only slowly. The unequal balance between the increase of rice export and the slower increase of rice production resulted in food shortages for Koreans.

During a later stage, the Japanese administration began to industrialize Chosen. The country needed an improved infrastructure. Electric energy was needed for new factories the number of, which grew rapidly. Hydroelectric power plants were set up, particularly in the North. The railway system had been expanded immediately after annexation. Since Manchuria under the name of Manchukuo, a supposedly independent state, belonged to the Japanese empire, the Korean railroads had the function of linking both parts under Japanese rule on the continent. The ports were also developed and became busy with the shipment of goods to and from Japan. Korea was no longer an economically isolated country as Cumings accurately observes.[13]

Since the beginning of the 1930s, the Government-General promoted mining, particularly of gold, coal, iron ore, tungsten and lead. It promoted

[12]Han, Woo Keun pp. 467 ff.

[13]Cumings (1997) p. 166.

as well the development of various industries, mainly the chemical, textile and food industry. Japanese companies, particularly those of the big conglomerates (*zaibatsu*) Mitsubishi, Sumitomo and Mitsui invested heavily in Chosen. By 1940, the chemical industry became the most important, having a share of 39% of the industrial production, followed by the food industry with 18% and the textile industry with 14%.[14] The number of industrial workers was growing tremendously, from 14,500 in 1911 to approximately 100,000 in 1930 and to roughly 550,000 in 1943.[15] This enormous increase also reflects the efforts to boost the Japanese arms industry during World War II.

In order to demonstrate the success of their economic development since the 1960s as a result of industrialization, South Koreans point at the growth rates and the increasing share of manufacturing of the gross national product. It is quite revealing to measure the economic development of Chosen in a similar way.

As there are no statistics available concerning the gross national product of Chosen, a comparison of the gross values of production must be used.[16] If one compares these values (converted into constant prices of 1911) it turns out that real growth rates between 1911 and 1940 amounted to an annual average of 5.4%. While agriculture only grew by 3.4%, mining grew by 10.5% and manufacturing by 13.8%. The percentage of the gross values of production in mining and manufacturing increased at the expense of agriculture. The share of mining went from 1.5% in the years from 1911 to 1915, to 5.6% in the years from 1936 to 1940. In the same period, the share of manufacturing rose from 6% to 35.1%. During the same periods, the share of agriculture decreased from 92.5% to 59.3%. There cannot be any doubt: The Korean economy grew during the Japanese rule and primarily as a result of industrialization.

Why does one seldom hear a positive remark about the economic development of the country during the Japanese time? Various reasons can be listed. The Japanese considered Korea a part of their economic zone to which besides the mother country, Formosa, South Sakhalin and Manchuria belonged. Korea was an integral part of the zone which was economically developed

[14] Chul Won Kang, "An Analysis of Japanese Policy and Economic Change in Korea", in Nahm (1973) p. 82.

[15] Choi Hochin p. 237 table 58.

[16] Chul Won Kang, op. cit. cp. 80 ff. and p. 87; Kwan Suk Kim, "An Analysis fo Economic Change in Korea", in Nahm (1973) p. 105; Young-iob Chung, "Japanese Investment in Korea 1904–1945", in Nahm (1973) pp. 95 and 96.

by Japan. Its development was a function of the economic demands of the motherland. Japan had no intention whatsoever to promote in Korea components of an independent Korean economy. The Japanese government made use of Korea's most important resources, rice and minerals. The speed of the economic development became hectic under the influence of the increasing demands during World War II. The bulk of the Korean population did not profit from this economic expansion. Wages seem not to have increased in real terms. Japanese companies were also not interested in a transfer of technology. Key positions in factories were generally held by the Japanese. The Korean industry was mainly owned by Japanese who, therefore, reaped the profits.

But there were also Korean businessmen who succeeded in founding their own companies — with their own capital and/or loans from the new banking system. One outstanding example was Kim Song Su whose basis of economic power was the Kyongbang Textile Company. He was also the co-founder of the daily Dong A Ilbo and the founder of the Posong College, today's Korea University. Both have developed into patriotic institutions.

In spite of the economic expansion during the Japanese rule, only a crumbling foundation was left for building up an independent Korean economy after liberation in 1945.

Resistance, Adaptation, Collaboration

As the Samil-uprising had shown, Chondogyo, Protestant churches and schools were the mainstay of resistance against the Japanese rule. They could fulfill these functions because they belonged to groups within the Korean society which had remained unaffected by the recent changes. Students were also in the center of an uprising which was ignited by an incident in Kwangju in 1922. Korean and Japanese students had clashed after Korean schoolgirls were insulted by Japanese students. The demonstrations spread all over Korea showing the deep disapproval of the Japanese rule by the Koreans. There were 54,000 students at 194 schools and universities who took part in the uprising.

Behind the scenes, Singanhoe (New Trunk Society) had been helpful. In 1927, the Japanese administration had allowed the nationalists and communists to form a coalition. It was, as Henderson said,[17] "a kind of opposition

---

[17] Henderson p. 84.

party", although it did not have the rights and possibilities of such a party. The members were united by being anti-Japanese, but otherwise they were divided in many ways. The communists tried to use the Singanhoe for their purposes. When they failed, they insisted that the society be dissolved in 1931. The dissolution took place in 1931.

Centers of resistance to the Japanese rule were also the three dailies Dong A Ilbo, Chosun Ilbo and Sidae Ilbo. These papers had been founded in 1920 during the reform period which followed the Samil uprising. Yi Sang Jae, the publisher of the Chosun Ilbo, was the first president of the Singanhoe. Those were difficult times for Korean newspapers, because they were subjected to censorship from their initial founding. Articles, and even whole editions, were suppressed. In 1940 they were finally prohibited. The Dong A Ilbo and Chosun Ilbo were founded again after liberation and continue to exist. In the spring of 1985, 65 years after their original founding, they reproached each other for having been pro-Japanese.[18]

Resistance groups were also organized among the Koreans abroad. Already by the end of the 19th century, many Koreans had emigrated. Their numbers increased after annexation. The emigration did not only happen for political reasons, but very often for economic ones. The desperate situation of Korean farmers made thousands try to find a livelihood outside Korea. Most of the Korean expatriates lived in Japan (by 1934 more than half a million), many in Manchuria (by 1934 more than 700,000) and in Siberia.[19] Additionally, a considerable number of Koreans had emigrated to the United States and Hawaii.

When the various Korean groups in exile gathered after the Samil uprising, they chose cosmopolitan Shanghai as center, even though only a few hundred Koreans had taken permanent residence there. On 13 April 1919 the establishment of a Provisional Government, which was to be headed by Syngman Rhee as Prime Minister, was announced in Shanghai. On this date, only one of the designated cabinet members, Yi Shi Yong, was present in Shanghai. Only after An Chang Ho, who was named Minister of Home Affairs, came to Shanghai did the Provisional Government start working. An Chang Ho had long been linked with the independence movement and had co-founded a branch of the Singanhoe in Pyongan province. In August 1919 the Provisional

[18] See the analysis in The Korea Herald, 21 April 1985.

[19] Choi Hochin p. 375.

Government was reshuffled by a legislative assembly. Syngman Rhee became President, and Yi Tong Hwi Prime Minister. Kim Kyu Shik and An Chang Ho received less important positions. The Provisional Government, which was short on funds, did not succeed in controlling the various resistance groups. There was also no unanimity on how to proceed in order to achieve Korea's independence. Royalists, democrats and communists could not agree. Korean factionalism was at its worst. Personal relations and regional affiliations were often stronger than political ideas and aims. Also Syngman Rhee, who had come to Shanghai at the end of 1920, was not successful in integrating the various factions. On the contrary, the conflicts intensified to such a degree that many members, among them Yi Tong Hwi, An Chang Ho and Kim Kyu Shik resigned. The Provisional Government did not achieve recognition by a single foreign state and had no decisive function in shaping Korea's future. Yi Tong Hwi went on to found the Korea Communist Party in Shanghai in 1920. This party was also troubled by factionalism, but developed into becoming the rival of the nationalist movement even though it pursued aims beyond Korea's independence.

The Korean historiography has a tendency — which is officially supported[20] — to describe the period under Japanese rule as period of resistance. While this may be understandable, it simplifies events. Many Koreans, if not most of them, had come to an arrangement with the Japanese administration. Indeed the majority of Koreans living in Chosen and ruled by the Japanese had no other chance but to live under the conditions set by Japan. For the younger generation, educated during the Japanese rule, it seemed quite natural to occupy positions in the existing institutions. This was the fate of people everywhere in colonies. The Japanese government did not only subject the Koreans using the police, but tried to win them over. Already after annexation, it had offered titles and pensions to influential *yangban* in order to win their co-operation. Many accepted which made it easier for the Japanese to govern the colony.

There was also outright collaboration. This subject was for many years taboo and still remains a delicate topic. But meanwhile some authors have had a critical look at it.[21]

---

[20]Korea Times, 28 March 1987.

[21]Song Gon Ho and others, *haebang chonhu saui inchik* (*Understanding of the History before and after Liberation*), 2nd edition Seoul 1989.

From the perspective of the Koreans, those Koreans who had worked as policemen for the Japanese administration are viewed and hated as traitors. Koreans could, indeed, enter the police forces of the Government-General and even reach high positions. Numerous Koreans made use of this opportunity, as was already mentioned. Because the policemen served as the administration's henchmen, they were particularly disliked and hated by the Korean public. Far less unpopular were those Koreans who served voluntarily in the Japanese army; they served in places far away, and were not seen as the administration's henchmen in Chosen. Koreans could become officials in the Government-General. They occupied mostly lower positions, but sometimes also higher ones: Numerous Koreans were even appointed as governors of provinces.

In order to transform Koreans into Japanese, the administration in Chosen started a large re-education program. It also used Korean employees. The position of head of the Department for Social Education within the Bureau of Education of the Government-General was held by a Korean. This department co-operated with a number of organizations which included the Committee for Radio Propaganda, the Korean Artist Association, the Korean Society for Women's Problems in which many Koreans were active. A number of Korean groups were created which supported the policy of Japanisation; for example, the Korean Association for the Unity of the People Forces and the Association of Authors for the Protection of the Country. One has to agree with Im Chong Guk that the colonial realities were depressing.[22]

The Second World War

Since 1937, Japan was at war with China. In 1940 it expanded its aggression to South East Asia and the Pacific. Japan had started to realize the Greater East Asia Co-Prosperity Sphere. On 7 December 1941 Japan attacked the US navy at Pearl Harbor, Hawaii. Japan had entered World War II. The war had its impact on Chosen which was used as a supply base. From 1939, many Koreans were forced to work wherever the Japanese administration sent them.

More and more Koreans joined the military, some voluntarily, others forcibly. Already since the beginning of the 30s, a smaller number of Koreans

[22]Im Chong Guk, "cheil kongwhagukhwa chimil sae riok (pro-Japanese in the First Republic)", in Vol. II of the publication mentioned in note 21, p. 144.

had the chance to become an officer in the Japanese army. The Korean officer cadets could either attend the military academy in Tokyo or the Manchurian military academy in the allegedly independent state of Manchukuo in Mukden. Quite a number of politicians of South Korea have received their training in Mukden, among others President Park Chung Hee and Chung Il Kwon, a Prime Minister and Speaker. To have received one's training in the military academy in Mukden was something to be proud of in the Republic of Korea. During the war, the pressure to join the military increased tremendously. Finally, in January 1944 conscription was introduced. By 1944, 270,000 Koreans allegedly did military service in the Japanese forces.[23]

During the war, Chosen was ruled in a tougher way than before. Since 1938, instructions in schools had to be in Japanese only. Koreans had to worship at Shinto shrines. And in 1940 they were forced to change their names to Japanese ones. Thus, the assimilation policy of the Japanese government reached its peak.

The Result

The Japanese administration of Chosen reached some of its goals. It succeeded in overcoming the resistance it had to face. It enforced its system and integrated Chosen into the Japanese Empire. Japan made use of the country's resources, mainly of rice and minerals and later also of labor. In spite of proceeding so vigorously and so rigorously, the Government-General failed, however, to reach its main aim, the merger of Chosen with Japan.

The Government-General was very much pre-occupied with the idea of merging both countries. On 1 October 1925 Governor-General Saito called it "natural as well as logical for them to be united into one body politic for their mutual benefit".[24] One of his successors, Governor-General Kazushige Ugaki, went even further when he, in a speech on 11 September 1934, demanded the complete assimilation of Chosen.[25]

For Koreans, the most important task was maintaining their cultural identity. In the editorial of its first edition, the Dong A Ilbo had stressed the

---

[23] Henderson p. 140 note 97.

[24] Annual Report 1930–1932 p. 186.

[25] *Thriving Chosun.* A Survey of Twenty-five Years Administration, compiled by Government-General of Chosun, October 1935 p. 79.

importance of a cultural revival. The editorial mentioned: "It is the greatest desire of our newspaper that the Korean people establish great culture in which everybody remains faithful to the values of life and practises solidarity with others, and that all nations under the sky find their correct place, that they co-operate and assist each other in establishing a great paradise where all ways of life can unfold". And indeed: In spite of the harsh regime of the Japanese, the Korean culture remained unaffected as was shown by the many songs and poems written during the times of trial. The Japanese did not only fail in their policies of assimilation. Under the pressure of the colonial power, the Korean people developed a feeling of national consciousness and identity. This feeling was exemplified in the poem by Yang Chu Dong "I am a Son of this Land".

It is difficult to have a balanced discussion with Koreans about the period of Japanese rule. Koreans are seldom willing to acknowledge that Japan, in a short period of time, contributed considerably to the modernization of Korea. Koreans are used to condemning the Japanese rule which is understandable, particularly in view of the policy of assimilation which brought severe hardships to many Koreans. After 1945, Japan did not undertake any efforts so that Koreans could improve relations with the former colonial power. Japanese government officials made remarks of regret and apologies, but what was missing was a broad-based effort of reconciliation similar to the efforts of the Federal Republic of Germany towards France; but Japan is no Christian country. During the Japanese rule, Koreans, for the first time, got united behind the idea of a nation. At the same time, their national feelings were hurt by the contemptuous attitude of the Japanese towards their history. This is still felt today and expressed by demonstrations of Korean nationalism towards Japan. What Koreans tend to overlook is how much the ideology of their post-liberation leadership on running a state was shaped during the Japanese period. The Japanese model of strict administration, in the absence of politics, was revived later by Park Chung Hee.

References

Sources:

for the Japanes policy in Chosen after 1919: *Annual Report on Administration of Chosen*, Compiled by Government General of Chosen Vol. 1921–1922, Keijo December 1923 and Vol. 1930–1932, Keijo December 1932, for statistics (if no other sources are quoted): Andrew J. Grajdanzew, *Modern Korea*, New York 1944.

Choi, Ho Chin, *The Economic Histotry of Korea. From the Earliest Times to 1945*, Seoul 1971.

Nahm, Andrew C., (editor) *Korea under Japanese Colonial Rule. Studies of the Policy and Techniques of Japanese Colonialism*, Western Michigan University 1973.

Nahm, Andrew C., "Poetry and Songs of the Koreans as an Oppressed People; 1910–1945", in *Korea Journal* Vol. 16 No. 10 October 1976) pp. 4 ff.

Park, Sung Jo, *Die Wirtschaftsbeziehungen zwischen Japan und Korea 1910–1968*, Wiesbaden 1969.

PART II

Divided Korea

Chapter 4

The Origins of the Division of Korea

A Nearly Forgotten Country

The Germans suffered from the division of their country until they regained their unity on 3 October 1990. The division of Germany was — at least to a certain degree — understandable. Germany, which had started World War II, fought against various enemies. At the end of the war, its territory was occupied by the victorious armies of its main enemies and divided into occupation zones. Thus, the foundation was laid for the division of Germany. The former occupation zones of the USA, the United Kingdom and France became the Federal Republic of Germany; the former occupation zone of the Soviet Union became the German Democratic Republic.

But why was Korea divided? Korea, as a part of the Japanese Empire, was only indirectly involved in the Pacific War. It was a country which had been annexed by Japan in 1910. If history knew logic, Korea's fate after the end of the war should have been liberation and not division.

The declaration, published after the meeting of President Roosevelt, Prime Minister Churchill and Generalissimo Chiang Kaishek in Cairo on 1 December 1943, mentioned the independence of Korea. Roosevelt had insisted that Chiang Kai-shek participated in the meeting which had been intended for discussing the future of Asia. Roosevelt was determined to establish China as one of the great powers after the war, the US's efforts resulted, among other things, in the inclusion of China among the five permanent members of the United Nations Security Council. The three statesmen who met in Cairo agreed that Japan had to return all areas of which it had got hold by violence. In reference to Korea, the following formula was used: "The aforesaid three great powers, mindful of the enslavement of the people of Korea, are determined that in due course Korea shall become free and independent".[1]

The Koreans who received the information from Cairo were concerned that Korea's supposed independence would not occur immediately after the end of the war, but "in due course". This was a favorite idea of President Franklin D. Roosevelt. He felt that the smaller Asian countries should first undergo an education before becoming independent. Until the completion of that education, those countries should be subjected to a trusteeship by the big powers. In a talk with Stalin during the conference in Teheran (26 November to 3 December 1943), Roosevelt estimated that Korea's apprenticeship would take approximately 40 years.[2] Stalin agreed. The idea to envisage a transitory period for Korea in which the country would be subjected to a trusteeship had important consequences. It paved the way for two countries, the USA and the Soviet Union, to occupy Korea.

The allies were understandably focussing on the immediate problems of the war and less on their policies after the war. The US government endeavored to win the Soviet Union over so they would enter the war against Japan, and thereby shortening the Pacific War. In so doing, the US government officials grossly overestimated Japan's military strength. The question of Soviet participation in the Pacific War had been mentioned in Teheran and was discussed in detail during the Conference at Yalta in February 1945. The conditions for the Soviet Union's entrance into the Pacific War were fixed in an agreement at Yalta on 11 February 1945. This agreement recognized the Soviet interest in Manchuria. Korea was not mentioned although Roosevelt, in his talks with Stalin, had repeated his idea about a trusteeship for which he now allowed 20 to 30 years. Also, at the Potsdam Conference (17 July to 2 August 1945) Korea's future was mentioned only accidentally. After all, the Potsdam Declaration confirmed the Declaration of Cairo as far as the conditions for the surrender of Japan were concerned. The Soviet Union, which until that date was not at war with Japan, was not a party to that part of the Declaration.

As agreed upon with the allies, the Soviet Union declared war on Japan on 8 August 1945. A few days later, Soviet forces entered Manchuria and the northern part of Korea. It had been the USA which had carried the

---

[1]McCune p. 42.

[2]Henderson p. 41 note 19.

main burden of the Pacific War. Yet, shortly before the war's end, the Soviet Union — invited by the United States — hurried to safeguard its interests in East Asia. These interests had also aimed at Manchuria and Korea in the past.

The surprising announcement of Japan's readiness to surrender on 10 August 1945 made decisions on Korea's future by the US government urgent. The responsible bodies in Washington suggested to the President that the Japanese forces north of the 38th parallel surrender to the Soviet forces and those south of the 38th parallel surrender to the US forces. The two colonels who had prepared the decisions — one of them being the later Secretary of State Dean Rusk — had chosen the 38th parallel because it left the capital Seoul under US control.[3] This line had already been mentioned in internal discussions of the US military at Potsdam when they had envisaged the military occupation of Korea for the first time. The suggestion to choose the 38th parallel as dividing line became part of an instruction, approved by the President, to General MacArthur, Commander-in-Chief of the Allied Forces. This instruction was also communicated to the British and Soviet government. Stalin suggested small changes, but did not comment on the decision to choose the 38th parallel as dividing line for accepting the surrender of the Japanese forces in Korea. After Japan's capitulation, MacArthur's Chief of Staff, Lieutenant General R. K. Sutherland, issued "General Order No. 1" on 2 September 1945 which contained provisions for the surrender of Japanese forces in Asia. This order stated among other things: "The senior Japanese Commanders and all ground, sea, air and auxiliary forces within Manchuria, Korea North of 38 degrees North latitude, Karafuto, and the Kurile Islands, shall surrender to the Commander-in-Chief of the Soviet Forces in the Far East. The Imperial General Headquarters, its Senior Commanders, and all ground, sea, air and auxiliary forces in the main islands of Japan, minor Islands adjacent thereto, Korea South of 38 degree North latitude, Ryukyus, and the Philippines shall surrender to the Commander-in-Chief, US Army Forces, Pacific".[4]

The 38th parallel was considered to be a temporary line to fix military responsibilities. Therefore, it has been called a "military expedient".[5] Yet, once

[3]Dean Rusk, *As I saw It*, New York 1990, p. 124.

[4]Copy of the full text to be found in the library of the 8th US Army in Seoul.

[5]General John H. Hilldring on 10 March 1947, quoted in McCune p. 44 and note 6.

Soviet troops had entered the northern part of Korea, facts were established which could not be removed. It had been unnecessary to invite the Soviet Union to come to Korea; Japan was defeated anyway, and defeated only by the United States. Thus US policy towards Korea after World War II started as a great mistake. The first US forces reached Korea only a month later, on 8 September 1945 to be more precise. The US government had to pay the price for not thinking thoroughly about Korea's future.

The South — A Powder Keg

When the allies had agreed that the Koreans would not govern themselves for a temporary period of time, they had not bothered to imagine how the Koreans and the Japanese in Korea would react at the end of the war. Koreans wished to establish their own independent state immediately. When it became clear that Japan would surrender, the efforts of the Japanese administration in Korea tried to cope with the situation as clever as possible. Governor-General Nobuguki Abe, who was in command in Korea even after the capitulation of Japan, contacted Korean leaders and suggested that they establish a provisional government. He hoped to save the lives and property of the Japanese residing in Korea. He first contacted Song Chin U who belonged to the circle around Kim Song Su and was a respected patriot. Song Chin U declined the offer, probably because he felt that the situation was too unstable. The Japanese then turned to Lyuh Woon Hyung (Yo Un Hyong), a moderate leftist and well-known member of the resistance. Lyuh accepted the offer and started preparations. Already on 6 September 1945, even before the Americans arrived in Korea, the People's Republic of Korea (*Chosun Inmin Konghwaguk*) was founded with people's committees all over the country.[6] Lyuh tried to reach out to both leftists and rightists. In European terms, the movement could be called a national democratic front. It found strong support everywhere in the country. A sort of loose administration had been established by the Koreans. Abe could be pleased.

The US military units, which started arriving in Korea on 8 September 1945, belonged to the 24th Corps which consisted of the 6th, 7th and 40th Infantry Division. During 1945, a total of 80,000 US soldiers came to Korea.

---

[6]Henderson pp. 114 ff.

The 24th Corps had been chosen as the military unit to come to Korea because it had been stationed in Okinawa and therefore was closest to Korea. They were tactical forces which were not prepared to run the administration of a country. Their Commander, Lieutenant General John Reed Hodge, had not received any substantial instructions on how to rule the southern part of Korea. The first precise instructions did not arrive until July 1946.[7] When the Americans arrived at Inchon, they had no knowledge about Korea, not to mention plans and ideas on how to govern the country.

General Hodge, following with his general instructions, set up a military government which was formally organized as US Army Military Government in Korea (USAMGIK). Since the Americans in Korea had no civil affairs units at their disposal, they allowed many Japanese officials to remain in office. Governor-General Abe was released from office in mid-September, and only because of Korean protests. Other Japanese officials, however, worked for the occupation force, at least as advisors. By the end of January 1946, their number had decreased to 60. One does not need much imagination to figure the reactions of the Koreans. Now they were again ruled by a foreign power. This power was well meaning, but unprepared for its Herculean task.

The Military Government rejected all claims by Koreans to rule their own country. From the very start, General Hodge declined to cooperate with the leaders of the People's Republic even though they had formed a *de facto* government. By the end of 1945, he banned the activities of the People's Republic. In the American eyes, the movement had become too leftist.

The Military Government also did not recognize the Provisional Govern ment whose leaders returned one after an other to Korea. Syngman Rhee who already returned on 16 October 1945 received a warm reception by General Hodge who also presented him to the press. Some branches of the American government considered him pro-American enough to be the next Korean leader. Rhee was a respected nationalist, but lacked tolerance and was a man of erratic behavior. He also lacked the ability to establish a consensus among people with differing views. He did not get along with another well-known member of the Provisional Government Kim Ku. Kim Ku returned to Korea from Chungking in November 1905. He had a dubious character and was called "the Assassin".[8]

[7]Henderson p. 125.
[8]Cumings p. 197.

The Military was on friendly terms with a group of conservatives, including Kim Song Su, Song Chin U, Yun Po Sun and others. They were mainly wealthy people who had done well during the Japanese era. Therefore, they had difficulties being accepted in the post-Japanese period.

While the Military Government did not give government functions to any Korean group, it planned that the Koreans should rule themselves at some point in the future. Therefore, it allowed the formation of political parties and social organizations. Due to the absence of forces which would work in the direction of unity, centrifugal forces prevailed. In 1947 the Military Government had registered 354 political parties and social organizations.[9] A number of youth organizations emerged, out of which the Korean National Youth, led by Lee Bum Suk, was the most popular. The youth organizations attracted much attention because of their violent behavior.

Violence and chaos spread. Therefore, the police force had to be reinforced. Their numbers superseded those during Japanese times. The police force also absorbed policemen who had worked for the Japanese. The economic situation of Korea which lost the Japanese experts became more and more precarious. Anti-Americanism emerged. In an open letter addressed to General Hodge, the Chosun Ilbo wrote that the Korean people now suffered more than during the Japanese era on 31 August 1946.

In the fall of 1946, chaos and violence reached their peak with uprisings in the southern parts of the peninsula. The riots started with the strike of railroad workers in the southern port city of Pusan in September 1946. In the strike which spread up to Seoul, 250,000 workers participated. Shortly after the Military Government had dealt with this uprising, another far more dangerous one started in Taegu in October 1946. Workers and farmers fought against policemen, local government officials and landowners — against those whom they considered responsible for suppression. Atrocities were committed by both sides. The unrest spread in waves to other provinces. The rebels demanded better living and working conditions, the abolishment of the rice collection system — reminiscent of the Tonghak rebellion — and the transfer of the government administration to the people's committees. Those parts of the country, where the people's committees had been strong, recorded the most severe riots. This showed that the left was fighting, but the fighting

[9]Cho Soon Sung p. 75 and note 34.

was locally inspired. The Soviet leaders in North Korea supported the rioters through giving them advice and money.[10]

The police, supported by right-wing organizations, needed until the end of 1946 to cope with the situation. In the end, more than 1,000 people, including 200 policemen, had been killed, and more than 30,000 arrested. And there is no doubt: If the US Military Government had not repeatedly used troops to quell the rebellion, Korea would have had its civil war already by that time. The riots were also a clear indication of how much the American rule in Korea had failed.

The Americans tried to organize a provisional Korean government. At the end of 1946 and beginning of 1947, a Korean Interim Legislative Assembly (KILA) with Kim Kyu Shik, a renowned independence fighter, as President and a South Korean Interim Government (SKIG) with An Chae Hong as Chief Civil Administrator were established. The results of the work of these interim organizations were barely effective due to strong Korean discord.

American ignorance and indecision together with Korean impatience and disagreement made for a bad mixture. The possibility that political forces could develop within the country to lead Korea towards independence or even unification was spoiled.

Quick Progress in the North

When the 25th division of the Soviet Army, under the command of Colonel General Chistiakov, crossed the Soviet-Korean border, it had been 40 years earlier that the Russians had lost the Russian-Japanese war and with it their influence on the Korean peninsula. The memories of the defeat were still alive. In Stalin's declaration on the occasion of Japan's capitulation on 2 September 1945, he said: "However, the defeat of the Russian troops in the year 1904 in the Russian-Japanese war had left severe memories in the people's consciousness. This defeat settled on our country like a black patch. Our people believed in and waited for the day when Japan will be defeated and the patch removed. For 40 years we, men of the old generation, have waited

[10] Hyun Su Jeon with Gyoo Kahng, "The Shtykov Diaries: New Evidence on Soviet Policy in Korea", in *Cold War International History Project Bulletin* 6–7 (Winter 1995–96).

for that day. And now the day has come. Today Japan has recognized to be defeated and has signed the unconditional capitulation".[11]

The Soviet Union, which had old interests in this part of the world, was familiar with the situation in Korea. The Soviet Union had at its disposal a large amount of people of Korean origin who or whose parents had migrated to Siberia before or after 1910 and who had become Soviet citizens. Many of these people accompanied the Soviet army when it moved into Korea. They became important intermediaries for the Soviet efforts to control North Korea.

Unlike the Americans in the South, the Soviet Union did not establish a formal military government, but had, from the very beginning, North Korea ruled by Koreans. The Soviet government made use of the various structures of the People's Republic which had also been established in the North since August 1945. It came in handy that the people's committee had a leftist orientation. The Soviet occupation power saw to it that as many communists as possible joined the committees. The North Koreans had the impression that their countrymen, not foreigners, were running the government.

Since February 1946, government authority was vested in an Interim People's Committee for North Korea presided over by Kim Il Sung. The new government started immediately to change the social system. Land reforms as well as the nationalization of Japanese property was introduced. On 3 November 1946, elections were held for the people's committees in which some non-communist groups also participated. The parties of the popular front prevailed. Representatives of the people's committees met in Pyongyang on February 1947, approved the decisions of the Interim People's Committee and established a Legislative Assembly which was presided over by Kim Tu Bong. The People's Committee under the leadership of Kim Il Sung was maintained; it was no longer called an "interim" committee.

The representatives of the Soviet Union stayed in the background. They had quickly succeeded in expanding the Soviet system in North Korea. At this point, the North Korean government was dependent on a close cooperation with the Soviet Union. Kim Il Sung was not just a puppet.[12] As time went by, and he assumed full control of North Korea, it became clear that he was a

---

[11] *Der Sowjetkommunismus, Dokumente*, Band 1: *Die politisch-ideologischen Konzeptionen*, edited by Hans Joachim Lieber and Karl-Heinz Ruffamnn, Koeln and Berlin 1963 p. 406 (Translation from German by the author).

[12] Cumings pp. 224 ff. with details.

Korean nationalist in his own way. He had more in common with his southern opponent, Syngman Rhee, than one might have thought.

The Trusteeship Issue

At the end of 1945, the Foreign Ministers of the Soviet Union, the United States and the United Kingdom met in Moscow to discuss post-war problems. Korea was an item on the agenda. The Moscow Agreement of 26 December 1945 provided for the setting up of a provisional Korean democratic government, the establishment of a Joint Commission of the two occupying powers and the preparation for "a four power trusteeship of Korea for a period of up to five years".[13]

When these decisions became known in Korea, a storm broke out. Representatives of all parties, at first also of the communists, opposed these decisions as they confirmed that according to the will of the big powers, Korea for the time being would not be an independent and free state. Mass demonstrations followed.

As already mentioned, it had been President Roosevelt who had suggested to establish a trusteeship for Korea. Why the US government pursued this idea, even at the end of 1945, is not clear. It is likely that the US thought to prevent the extension of the Soviet rule all over the Korean peninsula. Within the US administration, there was no agreement on the usefulness of a trusteeship. It was the Department of State which promoted the idea, the Department of War and General Hodge had opposed such a solution because they had expected fierce opposition by the Koreans.

US attempts to defend the Moscow Agreement were ruined by a public statement of the Soviet government which explained that the idea of setting up a trusteeship and extending the trusteeship period to ten years was an American idea. The Americans did not have much to reply.

Opposition against any further advances by the communists in Korea became more and more the primary concern of US policy in Korea. The Soviet Union, on the other hand, tried to establish a Moscow-friendly regime and did not try to hide its intentions. The first meeting of the Joint Commission, established by the Moscow Agreement, was held from 20 March to 8 May 1946

[13] McCune pp. 275 and 276.

in Seoul and did not achieve any results. This was not surprising in view of the different opinions on both sides. When General Shtykov justified the breaking-off of the meeting, he told General Hodge that the Soviet Union, being a direct neighbor of Korea, was interested in establishing a provisional democratic government in Korea which would be loyal to the Soviet Union.[14] During the meeting of the Joint Commission, the Soviet representatives had demanded to exclude from the consultations those Koreans who had criticized the trusteeship idea. Since this would have meant the ineligibility of most of the Korean supporters of the Americans, the US representatives objected to it.

Both sides also failed to reach agreement during the second meeting of the Joint Commission which started on 21 May 1947 and dragged on until autumn of the same year. The crucial question was which "Korean democratic parties and social organizations" mentioned in the Moscow Agreement had to be consulted.[15] Mistrust between both sides was intensifying. The Soviet Union as well as the United States were mainly concerned with preserving their influence in their respective occupation zones. The aim of "the re-establishment of Korea as an independent state" as mentioned in the Moscow Agreement was fading away.[16] This was tantamount to the preliminary decision on Korea's division.

The discussions over the participation of Korean parties in the consultations with the Joint Committee had resulted in a fierce conflict between the US military government and the Korean rightists including Syngman Rhee and Kim Ku who protested vigorously against the trusteeship idea. The Americans were unable to gather a moderate, and to some extent, united popular group which would support them. Changing its policy all of a sudden from the end of July 1947, the military government allowed demonstrations against the Moscow Agreement and arrested communists. Lyuh Woon Hyung became the victim of increasing violence; he was murdered on 19 July 1947. Cumings, based on information from Lyuh's daughter, feels: "The police either arranged his assassination or looked the other way so that it could happen."[17] With Lyuh's death, one of the few capable political leaders was missing. The domestic situation in Korea was more confusing than ever since the end of the Pacific War.

---

[14]Cho Soon Sung pp. 122 and 123.

[15]McCune p. 275.

[16]McCune loc. cit.

[17]Cumings (1997) p. 209.

American Disengagement

In 1947, the American hopes to continue cooperation with the Soviet Union came to an end. The US government felt that there was no basis for mutual trust because of the revolutionary aims of the Soviet government. The Soviet Union had demonstrated its aggressive policy when it subjugated the East European countries. From the American perspective, this aggressive attitude was an alarming threat for Europe. The US government concluded that it should be the policy of the United States to prevent a further advance of the Soviet Union. This policy of containment was phrased by President Truman in his message to Congress on 12 March 1947 in the following way: "I believe that it must be the policy of the United States to support free people who are resisting attempted subjugation by armed minorities or by outside pressure. I believe that we must assist free people to work out their own destinies in their own way."[18]

Also in 1947, the negotiations of the four powers on the destiny of Germany came to a standstill. During the meeting in Moscow in the spring of 1947, the foreign ministers of the four powers clashed on the question of a four-power agreement for Germany, of the control over the Ruhr district, of the eastern borders of Germany, and of reparations. When also during the conference of the foreign ministers in London in fall 1947 no agreement could be reached, the Western powers decided to maintain that part of Germany which they had occupied and to strengthen it through a quick reconstruction program. West Germany was included in the Marshall plan program which served as an instrument of the policy of containment.

Nothing of that new policy could be felt in Korea. Here it was not really applied. Statements made by Secretary of State George C. Marshall on 29 September 1947 were revealing. During a meeting of the cabinet, he mentioned that he was dealing with the question on how the Americans could get out of Korea without losing face.[19] Disengagement, and not containment, became the guideline of US policy in Korea.

The Joint Chiefs-of-Staff had already earlier discussed the withdrawal of US forces from Korea. In a memorandum on 25 September 1947, quoted by

---

[18]Truman Vol. 2 p. 106.

[19]*The Forrestal Diaries*, edited by Walter Millis with cooperation of E.S. Duffield, New York 1951, pp. 321 and 322.

Truman in his Memoirs,[20] the Joint Chiefs-of-Staff had argued in the following way: In case of war in the Far East, the US forces in Korea would be a liability. In view of the present shortage of military manpower, the forces stationed in Korea so far could be well used elsewhere. The withdrawal of these troops from Korea would do no harm to the military position of the Far Eastern Command, unless the Soviets as a consequence of this development would establish military strength in South Korea capable of mounting an assault on Japan. The Joint Chiefs-of-Staff concluded that the US, from the point of view of military security, had little strategic interest in maintaining troops and bases in Korea. George F. Kennan, the celebrated author of the containment policy, concurred with the views of the Chiefs. He advocated a strategy of concentrating US commitments on vital interest areas only. In the Far East, he considered Japan to be the power center which deserved US support in order to achieve economic rehabilitation. Korea was, in his view, for the US a peripheral interest area; therefore, he recommended the withdrawal of US forces.[21]

The withdrawal of US forces from Korea, which was now envisaged, was not to be carried out immediately because it could expose South Korea to an invasion from the North. This had also been the suggestion of the Joint Chiefs-of-Staff. Disengagement would only occur after South Korea had been strengthened. The US administration now placed its hopes in Syngman Rhee who was the only prominent leader left with an unambiguous anti-Japanese record left and who had recommended himself as a staunch anticommunist fighter.

Part of the American disengagement policy was to internationalize the question of Korea. The US had Korea placed on the agenda of the United Nations General Assembly in the fall of 1947. The Soviet Foreign Minister Molotov had been informed of that intention by a proposal attached to a letter by Acting Secretary of State Lovett dated 26 August 1947.[22] As the negotiations on the basis of the Moscow Agreement had been unsuccessful, the new proposal suggested early elections in both occupation zones of Korea under UN observation. The Soviet Union objected arguing that the Korean question did not fall within the responsibility of the UN. It countered the American proposal by its

[20] Truman Vol. 2 pp. 325 and 326.

[21] Kim, Seung-Young "American Elites' Strategic Thinking Toward Korea: From Lippmann to Brezczinski", in *Diplomacy and Statecraft*, Spring 2001.

[22] McCune pp. 288 ff.

own suggestion that both the United States and the Soviet Union should withdraw their troops from Korea at the same time. The Soviet government also suggested that Korean representatives from the North and the South should participate in the UN deliberations. These efforts were in vain. The US had the support of a majority in the UN.

On 14 November 1947 the UN General Assembly adopted Resolution A/ Res. 112 (II) which laid down the following[23]:

— elections were to be held for a National Assembly no later than 31 March 1948;
— formation of a National Government by the National Assembly which would take over government functions from military and civilian authorities and arrange with the occupying powers the withdrawal of their forces;
— the establishment of a UN Temporary Commission on Korea (UNTCOK) which would consist of representatives of Australia, Canada, China, El Salvador, France, India, the Philippines, Syria, and Ukraine and which would observe and guide the elections.

It is worth mentioning that the United Nations were involved in the Korean question two and a half years before the Korean War. For the moment, developments seemed to indicate a diplomatic victory for the US. But it was obvious that it would be impossible to conduct elections in the whole of Korea without cooperation from the Soviet Union. The Soviet Union and the other communist countries had not participated in the General Assembly's final vote thus indicating their unwillingness to realize the provisions of the resolution in the North. The resolution resulted in a reinforcement of the division of Korea, since it was speeding up the establishment of two Korean governments.

The decisions of the US government concerning Korea were faulty in many ways. The most serious mistake made was, however, to fail to see the strategic importance of Korea for each future conflict in East Asia.

Two States on the Korean Peninsula

UNTCOK started working in the beginning of 1948 with the Ukraine declining participation. The Commission made a half-hearted attempt to declare itself

[23]McCune pp. 299 ff.

responsible for the whole of Korea. These efforts failed due to Soviet objections; the members of UNTCOK were not allowed to enter North Korea. Thus only elections in the South seemed feasible. Whether to proceed with elections only in the South became controversial because it was obvious that this would be another step to reinforce the division of Korea. Under US influence UNTCOK, however, decided on 26 February 1948 that elections should be held "in such part of Korea as are accessible to the Commission".[24] It was also controversial among Koreans whether it was appropriate to hold elections only in the South. The left was opposed, but also the moderates and some rightists. In April 1948, a reunification conference took place in Pyongyang with the participation of political organizations from the North and the South. This was for many years the last attempt by Koreans to solve the Korean question by themselves. The most prominent participants from the South were Kim Kyu Shik, the leader of the moderates, and Kim Ku. The conference had no concrete results since it was controlled by the communists. Already in the beginning of 1947, Syngman Rhee had declared himself in favor of holding elections only in the South because elections in the North would fail due to Soviet objections.

The National Assembly elections in South Korea were scheduled for 9 May 1948. As the Koreans expected a solar eclipse on this day and as this would have been a bad omen for the new government, the elections were postponed until 10 May. UNTCOK tried to promote a peaceful and liberal atmosphere. As can be seen from the Commission's report (UN Doc. A/575 Add. 3), its efforts had only limited success. The report stated that in the period from 7 February to 9 May 1948, 254 persons and, on election day, another 44 persons were killed. The real figures seem to have been much higher. The circumstances of the first elections in Korea's history which were supposed to be general and free, were more than unpleasant. The Commission had only a small staff available to observe the elections. The UN General Assembly however, concluded that the election results "were a valid expression of the free will of the electorate of that part of Korea" where UNTCOK had observed the elections.[25]

Since the left had boycotted the elections, it was scarcely represented at the National Assembly. The South Korean population, which in the first weeks after liberation, had decided for the left People's Republic, now had a conservative legislature. Of the 200 seats, Syngman Rhee's National Association for

[24] McCune pp. 301 and 302.

[25] McCune p. 306.

the Rapid Realization of Korean Independence won 55 and the Korean Democratic Party of Kim Song Su, the party of the well-to-do, won 29 seats; 85 seats were held by independents. The Korean disease of discord had not been overcome. Political parties had been founded and then dissolved. Personalities had been more important than political programs.

The National Assembly held its first session on 31 May 1948 in the Capitol, the former seat of the Japanese Governor-General, placed by the colonial power directly before the old Kyongbok Palace. The Assembly passed, after hasty deliberations, the constitution on 12 July 1948.[26] The constitution provided for a presidential system; the president, however, was not to be elected directly by the people, but indirectly by the National Assembly. He was vested with far-reaching powers. He appoints and dismisses the prime minister, and needs the assembly's consent only for the appointment. The separation of powers was weak, basic rights were subjected to statutory limitation, and the president had the right to issue emergency orders. Thus, the new constitution could be used as an instrument for autocratic rule.

On 20 July 1948 the National Assembly elected Syngman Rhee as first President of the Republic of Korea. On 15 August 1948, i.e. on the third anniversary of the liberation from Japanese rule, government authority was transferred from the US Military Government to the Government of the Republic of Korea (*Taehan Minguk*). General Hodge, who had been weary with his task in Korea for quite some time, could now quit his job. Major General Coulter became his successor as Commander-in-Chief of US forces in Korea on 23 August 1948.

When Syngman Rhee started to form his cabinet, he immediately got into trouble. His first candidate for Prime Minister, Lee Yoon Yung, was rejected by the National Assembly. Therefore, the President had to agree to a compromise and appoint Lee Bum Suk, the leader of the Korean National Youth Movement, which had developed into a para-military organization. The other cabinet members — such as Chang Taik Sang as Foreign Minister and An Ho Sang who had studied philosophy at Jena (Germany) as Minister of Education — mainly belonged to the political right.

The establishment of a separate state in the North followed quickly. On 9 September 1948, approximately three weeks after the founding of the Republic

---

[26]Text in *Korea 1945 to 1948. A Report on Political Developments and Economic Resources with Selected Documents*, published by the Department of State, pp. 48 ff.

of Korea, the Democratic People's Republic of Korea (*Chosun Minjujui Inmin Konghwaguk*) was established in the North. The way to independent governance had been paved for quite some time. The People's Committee, presided over by Kim Il Sung, had already acted as government. Since the beginning of 1947, a representative body had also existed, but a formal framework was missing. In the spring of 1948, a constitution was completed.[27] The Supreme People's Democratic Assembly was to be the highest body of the country. On the local level the people's committees were to continue their work. The land reforms and the nationalization of the mining and heavy industries, railroads, water and air transport systems as well as of banks were all confirmed.

Elections for the 572 seats of the Supreme Assembly were held on 25 August 1948. The North Korean rulers simply claimed that elections had also been held in the South.[28] On 3 September 1948, the Supreme Assembly ratified the constitution. On 9 September 1948, the Democratic People's Republic of Korea (DPRK) was proclaimed. Kim Il Sung became Prime Minister. In a letter dated 12 October 1948, addressed to Kim Il Sung, Stalin expressed the readiness of the Soviet government "to establish diplomatic relations between the U.S.S.R. and the Korean People's Democratic Republic, and to exchange ambassadors, and along with this to establish corresponding economic relations".[29]

For more than a thousand years, there had been just one Korean state on the peninsula. Now, in 1948, two states existed, each of which claimed responsibility for the whole of Korea. This was expressed in both of their constitutions. Article 103 of the North Korean Constitution established Seoul as the capital. According to Art. 4 of the South Korean Constitution, the territory of Korea shall consist "of the Korean peninsula, and its accessory islands". The South Korean government tried to base its claim of sole representation of Korea also on the resolution of the UN General Assembly of 12 December 1948 (A/Res. 195 (III)). However, operative paragraph 2 of this resolution was vague, stating only "that there has been established a lawful government (the Government of the Republic of Korea), having effective control and jurisdiction over that part of Korea where the Temporary Commission was able to

[27]Text in Jan F. Triska (editor), *Constitution of the Communist Party States*, Stanford 1968, pp. 242 ff.

[28]McCune pp. 246 and 247.

[29]McCune p. 305.

observe and consult and in which the great majority of the people of all Korea reside".[30] That this government was responsible for the whole of Korea the resolution did not mention. Severe antagonism between the two Koreas both claiming responsibility for the whole had to be expected.

The Withdrawal of the Occupying Forces

The resolution of the UN General Assembly dated 12 December 1948 had recommended that the occupying powers withdraw their occupation forces as early as possible. The Soviet Union did not recognize this resolution, but withdrew its troops completely from North Korea by the end of 1948. In a letter dated 19 September 1948 it had already informed the US embassy in Moscow about its plans to withdraw. The US administration could and should have interpreted this move as an indication that Moscow considered North Korea as stable and reliable. The US government drew, however, a different conclusion. Truman wrote in his memoirs: "We, of course, were in favor of troop withdrawals. I have always believed that there is nothing that more easily creates antagonism than the presence of unwanted soldiers, foreign or domestic".[31]

The internal situation of the Republic of Korea was everything but stable. The year 1948 was not only the year of a new start, but the year of dangerous and bloody rebellions. They broke out in the south of the country, on Cheju Island and in Yosu. On Cheju Island, there was a guerilla war of islanders against the suppression by forces from the mainland. The government needed until the spring of 1949 to control that rebellion. The result was disastrous for the islanders. Tens of thousands of them had been killed, more than half of their villages had been destroyed.

Even worse was the rebellion in Yosu, a southern port town in the South Cholla province. It started with a mutiny of soldiers being sent to Cheju Island on 19 October 1948. People joined, the revolt spread, people's committees were restored. The government succeeded in the suppression of this revolt — with American support. Syngman Rhee used this opportunity to take action against communists. Between 4 September 1948 and 30 April 1949, nearly

[30] McCune p. 306.
[31] Truman p. 328.

90,000 persons were arrested. Kim Ku was murdered on 26 July 1949; the murderer Ahn Tu Hi, who was sentenced to lifelong imprisonment, but was released a few days after the beginning of the Korean War, said 38 years later, not to feel any particular guilt.[32]

The turbulent developments in the Republic of Korea did not deter the US administration from its policy of disengagement. The American government just delayed its withdrawal of troops by half a year. Demobilization of US forces worldwide resulted in a concentration of US military power in areas of importance for the US. South Korea did not figure among those important areas even though in China the victory of the communists was imminent.

Since the US administration realized the difficulties of the South Korean government, it promised to make a military advisory group and economic assistance available. The Truman administration, however, faced great difficulties in finding the consent of Congress for the aid program for Korea. The troop withdrawal was implemented; on 29 June 1949 the last US tactical forces left Korea. The US administration had not even given the Korean government a firm assurance that the US would intervene in case of an attack from the North, even though President Syngman Rhee had asked for it. Thus, a policy, shortsighted from the very start, found its appropriate end.

References

Cho, Soon Sung, *Korea in World Politics 1940–1950. An Evaluation of American Responsibility*, Berkeley and Los Angeles 1967.

Chung, Kyung Cho, *Korea Tomorrow*, New York 1956.

Lauterbach, Richard E., *Danger from the East*, New York and London 1947 (with documents).

Lee, Won Sul, *The United States and the Division of Korea*, 1945, Seoul 1982.

McCune, George M., *Korea Today*, Cambridge 1950.

Meade, E. Grant, *American Military Government in Korea*, New York 1951.

[32]Korea Times. 29 March 1987.

Chapter 5

The Korean War Phase One: Towards Reunification

Looking Back

Half a century has passed since the Korean War (1950–1953), yet there will be numerous contemporaries who remember the war.

West Europeans who think back to that period will remember the shock they felt when only five years after the end of the Second World War, another war broke out. The dangers of communist expansion were now taken more seriously. The joint efforts within NATO were strengthened. The decision to rearm the former enemy, Germany, was also the result of the fears triggered by the Korean War in the West.

Americans who think back might probably remember above all the strong tensions aroused by the Korean War within the US political establishment. The war in the Far East was the most severe challenge after the Second World War for the United States as a big power. The US government had to answer the question on whether it was willing to render active military support to a country belonging to its sphere of influence. The Truman administration answered in the affirmative and intervened militarily in Korea. But after many discussions of the pros and cons, the US government finally decided not to wage a crusade to annihilate the enemy and to occupy his territory. However, the notion of a "limited war" is not justified in light of the overall characteristics of the war such as the atrocities committed by North and South Koreans and the down-pouring of napalm and bombs from US air craft onto the civilian population north of the 38th parallel. The decision not to conquer the North was attacked by Republicans. The conflict seemed to reach its peak with President Truman's decision to dismiss the US Commander-in-Chief in the Far East, General Douglas MacArthur, who had suggested extending the war into China. The Truman administration did not succeed in reaching an armistice; this was achieved by the following Eisenhower administration. During the 1952 presidential election — Truman did not run again — the Korean War had been the main issue. Eisenhower, the candidate of the Republicans, had promised to travel to Korea in order to find a way to stop the fighting.

Koreans thinking back to the war will have different memories. They will, above all, remember the many people who were killed, injured, missed in action or taken prisoner. There are no precise figures about the victims of the war. According to Rees, altogether 300,000 South Korean soldiers were killed, wounded or missing; the losses of North Korean soldiers amounted to approximately 520,000.[1] Rees estimates further that the losses among civilians amounted to one million each in the South and the North.[2]

Koreans will further remember the horrible devastation caused by the war. After the beginning of the war, the front moved southwards until only the bridgehead around Taegu and Pusan, the so-called Pusan Perimeter, was left in Southern hands. After the landing of US forces in Inchon and the offensive out of the Pusan perimeter in mid-September 1950, the front moved north. It reached the 38th parallel in the beginning of October 1950. A few weeks later, UN advance guards reached the Yalu River, i.e. the border of China. After the Chinese intervention at the end of November 1950, the front moved south again to approximately 90 kilometers south of the 38th parallel. In the spring of 1951, the UN forces succeeded in repulsing their enemies beyond the 38th parallel. In the following period, the front stabilized close to the 38th parallel. Seoul changed possession four times, Pyongyang only twice, but was subjected to severe air bombardment by the US air force.

I imagine that many Koreans think back to the war with particular fear, since it was fought with a fierceness which only fratricidal wars know of. Both North and South Koreans wished to achieve supremacy in the whole of Korea and fought fanatically and regardless of victims to achieve that aim. Streams of

---

[1]Rees pp. 460 and 461; the *Statistics on Korean War Casualties* (*hanguk chonjeng pihae tonggejip*) published by the Korea Institute of Military History (kukbang kunsa yonguso) in 1996 mentions figures twice as high for the Korean casualties.

[2]Rees pp. 460 and 461.

refugees moved in both directions. The South received approximately 2.5 million refugees during the war from the North.[3]

From a Korean perspective, the demarcation line, which substituted for the 38th parallel, is a truly important legacy of the war. The 38th parallel was considered to be a temporary line in order to fix responsibilities for foreign occupying powers. The demarcation line, however, is a boundary for military forces hitherto involved in an armed conflict. Since no peace treaty followed, the Armistice Agreement of 27 July 1953 has been until now the decisive legal basis for the relationship between North and South on the Korean peninsula. For Koreans, the consequences of the war have a continuing impact. Many talks I have had with Koreans on the division of their country brought us back to the Korean War.

The Outbreak of the War

The war began on a Sunday morning, 25 June 1950, at 4.00 a.m. The fighting between North Korean and South Korean forces started along the 38th parallel. Simultaneously, North Korean assault forces landed at Kangnung and at Samchok on the East Coast of South Korea. The North Korean forces which had begun their actions with heavy artillery fire advanced quickly. Already on 28 June, the fourth day of the war, they took Seoul and continued to move south. Their main strike was along the line Seoul, Taejon, Taegu, i.e. along a track where today a highway is running.

It was obvious that the North Korean forces were superior to their South Korean enemies, in numbers, in experience as well as in equipment. Both the Soviet Union and the USA had envisaged establishing earlier local military forces in the parts they had occupied. In North Korea, this development had been quick. Thousands of Koreans who had fought together with the Chinese communists and had returned home had become the backbone of the Korean People's Army (KPA). Nearly the entire high command of the KPA consisted of veterans of the war in China.[4] When the Soviet Union withdrew its forces from North Korea, it left arms, equipment and military advisors behind and later augmented the KPA's equipment. Therefore, the North Korean

[3]Rees p. 441.

[4]Cumings p. 241.

forces had strong artillery, 150 T34 tanks and 180 aircraft at their disposal. The Americans had originally hesitated to set up a Korean military because it was difficult to justify such an attempt. Therefore, USAMGIK only set up a constabulary force which, however, became the predecessor of the Korean army. When the US forces left South Korea, they also left arms, equipment and military advisors behind. But the South Korean forces had mainly light weapons at their disposal; tanks and aircraft were missing. The KPA had tactical forces of 89,000 men (plus 23,000 in reserve divisions; 5,000 men at headquarters and 18,800 men in border guards), the South Koreans had tactical forces of 55,000 men (plus 33,000 men at headquarters and in supply units).

When the North Korean forces approached Seoul unstoppably, people panicked. Many thousands tried to flee south. In the early hours of 28 June — at 2.15 a.m. — South Korean troops blew up, without advance notice, the road bridge and the three railway bridges which crossed the Han River. Many people who were using the bridges to flee south were killed. Destroying the Han River bridges was also a military blunder because it prevented the South Korean units fighting at the northern outskirts of Seoul to retreat with their equipment southward. Not only the civilians but also the military leaders had panicked. After the first days of fighting, the South Korean army showed signs of breaking up.

The American Reaction

The news of the outbreak of the war reached Washington — the time difference is 14 hours — on Saturday evening. Neither President Harry S. Truman nor Secretary of State Dean Acheson was in Washington. President Truman spent the weekend with his family in Independence (Missouri), Acheson was at his farm in Maryland. On Sunday evening, the most important members of the cabinet got together at Blair House in Washington.

The outbreak of the war in Korea caught the US administration by surprise. For years, it had considered the question on how to react to an attack in the Far East and had come to the conclusion that the US had no strategic interests in Korea. Therefore, the US had implemented a disengagement policy in Korea which became obvious to everybody when the US withdrew its troops from South Korea. In his famous and later often criticized speech before the National Press Club on 12 January 1950, Secretary of State Acheson had drawn the US defensive perimeter in the Far East from the Aleutian Islands via Japan and the RyuKyu Islands to the Philippines.[5] The countries outside this perimeter, he had stated, have to rely, in case of an attack, on themselves and on the commitments of the civilized world under the UN charter. The Chairman of the Foreign Relations Committee of the Senate, Senator Tom Conally, later stated more precisely that the US would probably not intervene in case of a great military conflict in Korea. This policy also had the support of General MacArthur. Nevertheless, in his "Reminiscences" the general wants to make us believe that he, the hard-liner, had already opposed Acheson's policy before the war. But in an interview with the New York Times on 2 March 1949, he had defined the US defensive perimeter in the Far East in the same way Acheson had in January 1950. In view of these preparations and statements of leading politicians and military leaders, one should have thought that the US government would ignore the war in Korea.

But the contrary happened, and it was mainly Acheson who was responsible for the US entering the Korean War step by step:

— A conference at Blair House on 25 June 1950 decided to instruct General MacArthur to use navy and air force units to take supplies to Korea and evacuate Americans.
— The next day General MacArthur received orders to use the navy and the air force to support the South Koreans against targets south of the 38th parallel.
— On 29 June 1950, General MacArthur was also authorized to attack targets in North Korea but at a distance from the borders with China and the Soviet Union; to deploy units of the US army to protect a harbor and an airport in the Pusan area; and to protect Taiwan against a possible attack from China by using the 7th Fleet and air force units.
— On 30 June 1950, President Truman agreed to a proposal by General MacArthur — who had meanwhile visited Korea — to send a US regiment to the front and move two US divisions from Japan to Korea. The US administration also decided to impose a blockade on North Korea. With these decisions the USA had entered a war again.

The quick decisions to enter a war surprised the American public. The administration, however, was prepared to take this step. Indeed Korea had

[5]Text in Kaufman pp. 126 and 127.

been left out of the US defensive perimeter, but the American East Asian policy had meanwhile been overlapped by a new strategy towards the Soviet Union which had become inevitable since the Soviet Union, in the summer of 1949, had exploded a nuclear bomb, and since a little later China had finally been conquered by the communists. Secretary of State Acheson and Secretary of Defense Johnson had prepared a long report, dated 7 April 1950, which President Truman passed onto the National Security Council (NSC). This report (Document NSC 68), which had not yet been made public, brought about important changes to US foreign policy.[6]

The containment policy received an aggressive accent. It was defined as a policy "which seeks by all means, short of war, to (1) block further expansion of Soviet power, (2) expose the falsities of Soviet pretensions, (3) induce a retraction of the Kremlin's control and influence and (4) in general to foster the seeds of destruction within the Soviet system that the Kremlin is brought at least to the point of modifying its behavior to conform to generally accepted international standards". In the report, this policy was called a policy of containment, but it contained elements of rollback, a term also used several times in the report. It assumed that the military facilities of the US and its allies have to be strengthened which so far did not correspond to the dangers of Soviet expansionism. A quick reinforcement of military and economic facilities was, therefore, urgent.

The US defensive perimeter was not defined in Document NSC 68 which mentioned essential territory of the allies, vital positions and possible local conflicts caused by the Soviet Union. South Korea was only mentioned as recipient of US economic aid. However, the message of the report was clear. The USA considered itself the champion of the free world against the totalitarian and aggressive world of the Soviet Union, "a defeat of free institutions anywhere is a defeat everywhere".

In view of this policy, there was no other option for the US but to enter the Korean War and defend its Korean protégé. Although the US had withdrawn its troops from South Korea, the country remained an American creature and remained within the American sphere of influence. The US could not allow this territory to be conquered by an ally of the Soviet Union. The US administration further considered the North Korean advance to the south as an attack on the free world. It was afraid of a chain reaction if it did not intervene in

[6]US Department of State, *Foreign Relations of the US. 1950, Vol. I* pp. 235 ff.

Korea. "I felt certain", President Truman wrote in his memoirs, "that if South Korea was allowed to fall, Communist Leaders would be emboldened to override nations closer to our own shores".[7] It had become obvious that the big power had to defend each and every part of its empire if it wanted to maintain its legitimacy. Korea, for which the disengagement policy had been meant, had become the pilot project of the containment policy. Earlier mistakes were revised under the pressure of war, a revision for which the American people had to pay a high price.

The American intervention in Korea took place formally through participation in collective measures for the restoration of peace by the United Nations. But the US was the driving force behind the UN moves. The basic decisions were taken in Washington, not in New York at UN headquarters. On 25 June 1950, even before the Conference at Blair House, the Security Council upon American request called "for the immediate cessation of hostilities" (S/Res. 82).[8] In its next resolution on 27 June 1950 (S/Res. 83), the Security Council went one step further by recommending that member states support the Republic of Korea in order to repel the armed attack and restore international peace and security in the area. On 7 July 1950, the Security Council recommended (S/Res. 84) to put those forces committed by UN member states in a "unified command" under the United States. Upon request of the Security Council, President Truman appointed the US Commander-in-Chief in the Far East, General Douglas MacArthur, Commander-in-Chief, United Nations Command. By a letter dated 15 July 1950, President Syngman Rhee assigned to General MacArthur "command authority over all land, sea, and air forces of the Republic of Korea during the period of the continuation of the present state of hostilities".[9]

Without any doubt, this was an important step in the history of the United Nations. The Security Council did not impose military sanctions according to Art. 42 of the UN Charter. The Council was not in a position to do so, because none of the member states had provided — as envisaged by Art. 43 of the UN Charter — military forces by special agreements. The Security Council however, did not just determine the breach of peace but recommended based on Art. 39 of the UN Charter to counter the breach of peace militarily. Whether

---

[7]Truman p. 333.

[8]Text of the Resolutions and the other UN decisions in: Kim Se-Jin, Unification, pp. 122 ff.

[9]US Department of State, *United States Policy in The Korean Conflict*, pp. 10 and 11.

these resolutions were really binding was not certain. Article 27 paragraph 3 of the UN Charter stipulates that resolutions of the Security Council in non-procedural matters need the consent of all five permanent members. The Soviet Union did not participate in the vote on the three resolutions because it boycotted, at that time, the sessions of the Security Council in order to protest against the fact that China was represented by Taipei and not by Beijing in the Council. UN practice, however, accepts that not casting a vote because of absence does not prevent the Council's decisions to be valid. In spite of some doubts, it deserves to be noted that the United Nations, by sanctioning military measures against an aggressor, took an extraordinary decision. Yet, it should be mentioned again that the decisions of the UN were just additions to those of the United States.

The most important ally of the United States during the war was the United Kingdom. Fourteen additional states made military contributions, and five other UN member states contributed medical units. Even though these contributions were numerically modest, they were important because only these contributions made the action a collective one. At the beginning of 1953, 400,000 South Koreans and 350,000 Americans were fighting along with only 44,000 soldiers from other UN member states under the UN flag in Korea.[10]

In a North Korean document, which the Americans got hold of, the following is mentioned: "Kim Il Sung has directed that the war be carried out so that final victory can be realized by 15 August, fifth anniversary of the liberation of Korea...".[11] These plans were ruined by the intervention of the US. The Americans came late, but not too late. On 5 July 1950, the first exchange of fire between American and North Korean troops occurred near Osan. The weak US units were unable to halt the North Korean advance, but they did slow it down, thus securing the military reinforcement of the Pusan Perimeter. North Korean troops succeeded occasionally in breaking through the Pusan perimeter which was formed by the Naktong River. The Commanding General, Eighth US Army, Lt. General Walton H. Walker reacted in a flexible way; the US air force supported the ground forces effectively. At the end of August/beginning of September 1950, the Pusan perimeter enclosed just a little more than 10,000 sq km. That was all that was left of the Republic of Korea. North Korea came close to success, but the defenders held the Pusan Perimeter.

---

[10] Rees p. 33.

[11] Appleman p. 345.

Who Started the Korean War?

The best way to start a war is by firing back. Then the other side is the aggressor, and we are reacting, to use the words of Art. 51 of the UN-Charter, "by exercising the inherent right of self-defense". In the Korean War, both sides followed this pattern. South Korea as well as North Korea claimed and continue to claim that the other side was the aggressor.

In its resolution of 25 June 1950 (S/Res. 82) the Security Council noted, with grave concern, the armed attack upon the Republic of Korea by forces from North Korea and determined "that this action constitutes a breach of peace".[12] This has always been the position of the West. North Korea was the aggressor; in South Korea the West was defended.

North Korea, on the other hand, has claimed since the first days of the war that it was defending itself against an aggression from the South. North Korean radio programs, on 25 and 28 June 1950, asserted that South Korea had attacked near Haeju during the morning of 25 June and now had to bear the consequences of the North Korean resistance. North Korea and its friends have always considered the American involvement and the UN actions as illegal. There were also some voices in the West which showed sympathy for the interpretation that South Korea was the aggressor. The war, they claimed, had been caused by a provocation of American rightists in cooperation with President Syngman Rhee.

The UN Commission on Korea (UNCOK), which had succeeded the Temporary Commission (UNTCOK), reflected in its first report to the Secretary General, dated 25 June 1950 (VN Doc. S/1496), the conflicting statements of both sides.[13] The next day the Commission reported "that judging from actual progress of operations, Northern regime is carrying out well-planned, concerted, and full-scale invasion of South Korea" (UN Doc. S/1502).[14] Indeed the quick advance of the KPA to the South during the first weeks of the war underlined this impression. Within six weeks, the KPA had conquered South Korea with the exception of the Pusan perimeter. These successes could only be explained as a result of a blitzkrieg.

---

[12]See note 8.

[13]UNCOK reports in: Department of State, *United States Policy in the Korean Crisis*, pp. 12 ff.

[14]op. cit. p. 12.

From the moment they were founded, both states on the Korean peninsula claimed responsibility for the whole of Korea. The policy of the two Korean states was, therefore, antagonistic. It is not at all surprising that the area along the 38th parallel had already been a zone of high tension before the war. There were hundreds of incidents, and sometimes real battles in the year 1949. Even raids across the 38th parallel occurred. Both sides acted aggressively. Saber–rattling was to be heard from both sides. On 31 October 1949, Syngman Rhee announced that his government would solve the question of unification by war if necessary. Kim Il Sung was aggressive in his new year's message for 1950. He claimed the Syngman Rhee clique and the American imperialists had blocked the efforts of the North towards reunification. Therefore, the North had been compelled to establish strong bases. He called upon his forces to complete their preparations for war and to decide to annihilate the enemy.

The circumstances prevailing in June 1950 suggested that the North should try to use a good opportunity. The US tactical forces had been withdrawn from South Korea, and the country had not even received a guarantee of US support in case of an invasion from the North. South Korea had furthermore been declared to be outside the US defense perimeter. Internally South Korea was plagued by riots, caused by thousands of guerillas whom the government called communists. The fight against the guerillas was intense and cruel; army units had to be deployed to deal with the rebels. Syngman Rhee's position had been weakened by the elections for the 2nd National Assembly on 30 May 1950. His National Association had received just 6.8% of the votes, and he did no longer enjoy a majority in the Assembly. Taken together, this was a great chance for the North to try to unite the country under its flag.

That the plans of Kim Il Sung were pursued is proven by documents which the Americans obtained. Reconnaissance Order No. 1 of the General Command of the KPA to the Commander of the 4th Division dated 18 June 1950 written in Russian, spells out in detail what information on the South Korean defense positions was to be gathered before and after launching the attack and how this information have to be passed on.[15] A Combat order No. 1 of the Chief-of-Staff of the 4th division dated 22 June 1950, written in Korean,[16] outlined the details for the attack via the Uijungbu corridor to Seoul. Preparations, the order

[15]Kim Chum Kon pp. 299 ff., Appleman p. 20.

[16]Kim Chum Kum pp. 303 ff.

made clear, were to be completed by 23 June 1950. These are unambiguous documents.

We have meanwhile additional confirmation by documents released from Soviet archives which make it clear beyond doubt that it was the North Koreans who attacked.[17] In a report dated 26 June 1950, the Soviet Ambassador to the DPRK, T. F. Shtykov, described in detail the preparations and the course of the military operations during the first two days of the war.[18] As he reported, all preparatory measures for the operations were completed by June 24th. The military operations started in the early morning hours of 25 June 1950 by direct fire and artillery barrage. Then the infantry went on the attack. The South Korean forces were completely taken by surprise and put up a strong resistance only in the direction of Ongjin, Kaesong, and Seoul. Shtykov also confirmed that the North Korean Navy undertook two amphibious landings on the first day of the war. He noted with satisfaction that the KPA advanced deep into South Korean territory, but he also noted insufficiencies in their operations.

The Soviet Union was deeply involved with the preparations for the war and the major decisions during the war. It was Stalin himself who was in charge. Originally one had to be content with the explanations Khrushchev gave in his memoirs.[19] He argues that the war was not the idea of Stalin but of Kim Il Sung. The North Korean leader had assured the Soviet leadership that the first nudge would cause an explosion in the South and that the war would be finished soon. As a good communist, Stalin did not try to dissuade Kim Il Sung.

Since many Soviet documents have become available — quite a number of them were handed to President Kim Young Sam when he visited Moscow June 1994 — more details have become known. It was indeed Kim Il Sung who pressed for a war against the South. In view of his economic, technological, and military dependence on the Soviet Union, he needed Stalin's consent. His first proposals were rejected by the Soviet government, because it considered the risk too high that a war initiated by North Korea would drag on and negatively affect Soviet interests. A telegram of the Soviet Embassy in Pyongyang quoted Kim Il Sung as having said the following to diplomats of the Soviet Embassy

[17]See the articles by Weathersby.

[18]Weathersby (1995/1996) Document 14.

[19]*Khrushchev Remembers*, With an Introduction, Commentary and Notes by Edward Crankshaw, translated and edited by Strobe Talbott, 1971 pp. 401 ff.

on 17 Jan 1950: "The people of the southern portion of Korea trust me and rely on our armed might. Partisans will not decide the question. The people of the south know that we have a good army. Lately I do not sleep at night, thinking about how to resolve the question of the unification of the whole country. If the matter of the liberation of the people of the southern portion of Korea and the unification of the country is drawn out then I can lose the trust of the people of Korea."[20] Finally, at the end of January 1950, Stalin indicated his consent by a telegram dated 30 January 1950; he instructed the Soviet Ambassador in Pyongyang to inform Kim Il Sung "that I am ready to help in this matter".[21] Since US forces had been withdrawn from South Korea and the communists had seized power in China, he would have considered the risks of war in Korea as bearable.

Stalin was helpful indeed. He provided arms, ammunition, and sometimes even food and military advisors. He not only supported North Korea, but also China. The Soviet air force provided air cover for Chinese troops crossing into Korea and engaged American planes.[22] Stalin gave advice which often took the form of an order to the North Korean and Chinese leaders. He continued to be informed not only by his representatives in Pyongyang and Beijing, but also by the North Korean and Chinese leadership. He remained very much in command of all decisive steps in the war.[23]

Kim Il Sung had been the driving force to start the war; yet he could only begin it after he had received Stalin's consent. He thus shares the responsibility for the war with the Soviet leader.

The Advance Toward the Yalu River

On 15 September 1950, 70,000 men of the X Corps landed at Inchon, Seoul's harbor at the Yellow Sea. Inchon was not a very suitable place for such an amphibious landing. Access to the harbor from the sea is through a narrow and shallow bay; tides are so huge that larger ships can only enter the harbor on particular days and at particular hours. Therefore, there had been much

[20] Weathersby (1995) p. 8.

[21] Weathersby (1995) p. 9.

[22] Weathersby (1995/96) Document 35. *1949–51,*"

[23] Evgueni Bajanov, "Assessing the Politics of the Korean War", in *Cold War International History Project Bulletin*, 6–7 (Winter 1995/96).

opposition against the plan of landing at Inchon, but General MacArthur, who during the Pacific War had successfully carried out many amphibious operations, had won. He was justified by success. The American troops gained a foothold quickly and advanced towards Seoul. At the same time, the Eighth US Army together with South Korean troops broke out of the Pusan perimeter and pushed the KPA towards the north. The situation became difficult for the units of the KPA because their supply lines were cut by the X Corps. On 27 September 1950, units of the Eighth Army and the X Corps met at Osan. After heavy fighting, Seoul was taken. The KPA had to retreat so quickly to the north that it had to abandon most of its equipment. At the end of September 1950, South Korea was in the hands of UN troops.

When the war broke out, Secretary of State Acheson had stated that the fighting had the sole aim "of restoring the Republic of Korea to its status prior to the invasion from the North".[24] This goal had been achieved; the communist aggression had been repulsed. If the US administration intended to stick to its containment policy, then there was no reason for the UN forces to cross the 38th parallel and marched north. But that was exactly what happened.

The South Korean government had always stood up for reunification, and President Syngman Rhee had made it clear during the war that he would not be satisfied with the restoration of the *status quo ante bellum.* Since now victory was on the Southern side and the KPA seemed to be thoroughly crushed, Rhee argued forcefully to continue the war until unity was achieved. It was not surprising therefore, that the first UN troops crossing the 38th parallel to the North were South Korean units. This happened on the East Coast in the beginning of October 1950.

In the US, the position to continue the war was fostered by political and military considerations. If the aim was, as spelled out in NSC 68, "to induce a retraction of the Kremlin's control and influence", there was now an opportunity. The military also envisaged to annihilate the KPA. In order to do so, operations had to be carried into the North. Instructions from the Joint Chiefs-of-Staff, dated 15 and 27 September 1950, authorized General MacArthur to move north, provided that neither a Chinese nor a Soviet intervention was expected.[25]

---

[24]Spanier pp. 88 and 89.

[25]Text in Kaufman pp. 141–143.

On 7 October 1950, the UN General Assembly passed a resolution (A/Res. 376 (V)) which recommended steps to secure stable conditions "throughout Korea". An instruction by the Joint Chiefs approved by President Truman, dated 9 October 1950, authorized General MacArthur to continue fighting in North Korea even after a Chinese intervention as long as fair prospects of success existed. With this decision the US administration had changed its policy in Korea from containment to rollback. The inconsistencies of US policies towards Korea had reached another peak.

The advance of UN troops to the north occurred on two tracks. In the west the Eighth Army, under the command of Lieutenant General Walker, crossed the 38th parallel at Kaesong on 9 October 1950, conquered Pyongyang on 19 October and crossed the Chongchon River at the end of October. A South Korean patrol reached the Yalu River at Chosan on 25 October 1950. In the east the X Corps, under the command of Major General Edward M. Almond undertook another amphibious landing at Wonsan and Iwon at the end of October/beginning of November. The amphibious operation was unnecessary. When X Corps units landed at Wonsan, the city had already been taken by South Korean forces which had come overland. The X Corps marched north. Units of the 7th Infantry Division reached the Yalu River at Hyesanjin on 21 November 1950. The advance on two tracks was problematic. The X Corps reached positions which were further north than the front line of the Eighth Army in the west. Between both units was also a huge gap.

The Intervention of the People's Republic of China

The war in neighboring Korea could not be a matter of indifference to the Chinese government. Since the end of August 1950 it commented on the developments in Korea in various public statements.[26] The tone of the statements changed from expressing concern to warning against an extension of the theatre of war. In a telegram on 20 August 1950 addressed to the UN Secretary General, Prime Minister Zhou Enlai had stated that the Chinese people cannot but be concerned with regards to the solution of the Korean question. At the same time, he insisted that the People's Republic of China should participate in the discussions of the Security Council. In a speech on 30 September

[26] Whiting pp. 79, 108 and 115, gives details plus sources.

1950, he attacked the US and declared that the Chinese people would not stand by to see its neighbor invaded by the imperialists. On 3 October 1950, Zhou Enlai asked the Indian Ambassador in Beijing, Sardar Panikkar, to come and see him and informed the Ambassador — whom he had asked before to make Chinese views known — that China would send troops across the border to defend North Korea if UN troops crossed the 38th parallel.[27] On 10 October 1950 the Chinese foreign ministry warned again that China could not remain inactive in view of the American invasion into North Korea.[28] Since 19 October 1950, China deployed troops south of the Yalu River. Even though many divisions were sent to North Korea, the move went largely unnoticed; the Chinese units moved only during night-time and were camouflaged during daytime.

The first battle with Chinese troops occurred on 25 October 1950 near Onjong, that is to say at the eastern flank of the western front. The Chinese forces succeeded in pushing the South Korean Sixth Army back behind the Chongchon River. At the same time, the Chinese forces attacked the middle part of the western front near Unsan. The Eighth Army, which had pushed north, had to be withdrawn behind the Chongchon River. In the east, the Chinese attacked north of Hungnam and succeeded in slowing down the advance of the X Corps. After these first successes, the Chinese forces retreated. The UN troops did not want to believe that they were facing Chinese units when they first clashed with them at the end of October 1950. US intelligence officers concluded that the UN forces had clashes with reinforcements of North Korean units by personnel of the Chinese forces. But before long, there was no denying the fact that the new enemy consisted of Chinese divisions, mainly light infantry, poorly mechanized with no heavier weapons than mortars, but well-trained and experienced in flexible warfare. In the beginning of November 1950, China admitted that Chinese "volunteers" had supported the North Koreans.

The warnings reached the main addressee, the US administration, which however did not take the warnings seriously. On 15 October 1950 on Wake Island, General MacArthur assured his Commander-in-Chief, President Truman, whom he met for the first time, that China would not enter into the war in Korea. If the Chinese tried to get to Pyongyang, "there would be the greatest

---

[27] US Department of State, *Foreign Relations of the US, 1950 Vol. VII* p. 839.

[28] Ibidem p. 914.

slaughter".[29] This view was apparently shared by the US leadership which found it sufficient to stress from time to time that the US would not violate the border at the Yalu River. The US government did not review its position even after it became aware that the Chinese continued to dispatch troops across the Yalu River. Since the deployment was done covertly, the precise number of Chinese troops in North Korea was unknown to the US leadership but the figures it knew should have made it reconsider its policy seriously. The US administration's estimate in the beginning of November 1950 was that there were already 80,000 Chinese soldiers in North Korea and that 24,000 additional men could be transported daily across the Yalu River.[30] The conclusion drawn by the US government was amazing: It continued to follow its previous policy.

General MacArthur found backing for his proposal to continue the offensive, to march to the Yalu River in order to conquer the rest of Korea. Because of the risks involved, concerns were raised. MacArthur was instructed by the Joint Chiefs to exercise restraint, but he was not told to halt the offensive. It was apparently most difficult to stop the victor of Inchon since he had achieved another impossible victory. The US administration also shared MacArthur's conviction that China, a weak country, a satellite of Moscow, would not dare to defy the big power, the USA. A decision to halt the offensive or to withdraw the front would not have been easy. Therefore, the US government preferred not to take note of the signs indicating a massive Chinese involvement.

The Chinese intervention in the Korean War had to be coordinated with North Korea and the Soviet Union since the war was fought on Korean soil and with the backing of the Soviet Union. The Chinese leadership was not included in the talks between North Korea and the Soviet Union which in the beginning of 1950, had resulted in to the decision to invade South Korea. Mao Zedong complained years later — on 31 March 1956 — to the Soviet Ambassador P. Yudin that during his stay in Moscow on December 1949 and January 1950, the issue had been the strengthening of North Korea but not the seizure of South Korea.[31] When Kim Il Sung discussed details of the attack with Stalin in Moscow on April 1950, the Soviet leader insisted that Kim ask Mao Zedong for his approval. Kim Il Sung went to Beijing in May 1950 where he obtained

[29]Goulden p. 268.

[30]Poteat p. 196.

[31]Weathersby (1995/1996) Document 115; Chen Jian pp. 87–90, relying on other evidence takes a different view.

Mao's consent.[32] This seems not to have been a difficult exercise since Kim Il Sung had already a year earlier, in May 1949, received a promise by Mao to assist him once the fighting ended in China.[33] Shortly before his meeting with Kim Il Sung, Mao had told the North Korean Ambassador in Beijing that the unification of Korea by peaceful means was not possible. He added his assumption that the Americans would not enter a third world war for such a small territory.[34]

Not everybody in the Chinese leadership shared Mao's optimism. This became evident when the UN forces approached the 38th parallel at the end of September 1950 and the danger that they might invade North Korea became imminent. Kim Il Sung was desperate. In a letter to Stalin on 29 September 1950, he admitted that the KPA alone would not be able to stop the advancing UN forces and asked for "direct military assistance from the Soviet Union".[35] Stalin, who wanted to avoid a direct military confrontation with the US, passed the demand for help to China by a letter to Mao Zedong and Zhou Enlai, dated 1 October 1950.[36] Since there was no unanimity for this move in the Chinese leadership, Mao gave a negative answer to Stalin's demand in a message dated 2 October 1950.[37] On 9 and 10 October 1950, Stalin tried to convince Zhou Enlai and Lin Biao, who were the main opponents of Chinese entry into the war, that it was China's responsibility to preserve the existence of North Korea, but to no avail. Stalin was so frustrated that on 14 October 1950 he advised Kim Il Sung to evacuate North Korea and pull his troops out to the north.[38] A day later, he asked Kim to postpone the pull-out since Mao had prevailed

[32]Weathersby (1995) note 9.

[33]Weathersby (1995) Document 6.

[34]Weathersby (1995/1996) Document 13.

[35]Alexandre Y. Massourov, "Stalin, Mao, Kim, and China's Decision to Enter the Korean War Sept. 16–Oct. 15, 1950: New Evidence from the Russian Archives", in *Cold War International History Project Bulletin* No. 6–7 (Winter 1995/1996), pp. 94 ff., Document 6.

[36]Massourov, Document 10.

[37]Massourov, Document 11. This text differes sharply from the version published by the Chinese in which Mao informed Stalin about the decision to send troops to Korea; this message seems to have been a draft which was not dispatched. See Sehn Zhihua, "The Discrepancy between the Russian and Chinese of Mao's 2 October Message to Stalin on China's Entry into the Korean *War*", in *Cold War International History Project Bulletin* No. 8–9.

[38]Massourov, Document 18, 20 and 21 which refers to that advise of which no text is available.

and the Chinese leader had decided to intervene militarily in Korea by sending a first echelon of nine divisions.[39]

What were the motives of the Chinese leadership for entering the war? As their hesitation to give into Soviet pressure illustrated, the decision was made on the basis of Chinese interests. In his telegram on 20 August 1950 to the UN, mentioned earlier, Prime Minister Zhou Enlai had said: "Korea is China's neighbor. The Chinese people cannot help but be concerned with regards to the solution of the Korean question". This could have been a statement of an emperor of the Ming or Ch'ing dynasty. China had always considered Korea as a border state the peaceful development and peaceful intentions of which were of utmost importance. For centuries, the relations between both countries had had the form of tributary relations which had the political aim to guarantee the Middle Kingdom peace on its borders. The Treaty of Shimonoseki at the end of the 19th century, which had followed the Sino-Japanese war, had cut the old ties between China and Korea. Since then, China, threatened by adversaries from inside and outside, had been too weak to assert its interests with regards to Korea. But China was now free from foreign rule and united by the communists. Therefore, it was in a position to turn its attention again to the Korean peninsula. Since the end of June 1950, there was a war being fought in neighboring Korea and in the fall of 1950 the UN forces started to move north. That meant that the War Theater was approaching the Chinese border. The fall of North Korea seemed possible. The possibility of a Korea under the flag of the South was looming. Such a neighbor, an ally of the USA, which had supported the Chinese nationalists until the last moment, was not welcome in Beijing. China felt that its security was directly in danger.

Mao Zedong originally insisted that there was no reason to be afraid of the Americans. But contrary to what he believed, the Americans had intervened militarily and continued to support South Korea. Meanwhile, Chinese airspace at the Yalu River had been violated, and American politicians had made militant statements. Secretary of the Navy Matthews had played with the idea of a preventive war in a public speech on 25 August 1950. The Chinese leadership, without experience in foreign relations, might have misinterpreted such statements. Diplomatic relations between Washington and Beijing would have been useful in conveying the views of both sides, but they did not exist. "There is only one explanation", the newspaper Jen-min jih-pao wrote

[39]Massourov, Document 19.

on 22 September 1950,[40] "the American imperialists are deciding to extend their armed aggression against China". Since the end of 1949, the Chinese leadership had considered a confrontation over Taiwan, Vietnam and Korea as unavoidable. Zhou Enlai had talked of "the concept of confronting the United States in three fronts".[41] And now, as the US intervened in the Korean War, the Chinese felt that the moment of the first showdown with the Americans had come. In order to be prepared, the Chinese leadership already decided in the beginning of July 1950 to establish the Northeast Border Defense Army in Southern Manchuria.[42]

For China, it was ideologically easy to enter the war as it meant support for a communist brother state. "North Korea's friends are our friends. North Korea's enemy is our enemy. North Korea's defense is our defense. North Korea's victory is our victory", a Chinese newspaper article said on 25 August 1950.[43] To prevent the collapse of socialism in Korea, which Stalin had evoked in his talks with Zhou Enlai and Lin Biao, will have been another aim of the Chinese leaders when they decided to send their divisions to Korea. The intervention seemed further well-suited to have a negative impact on Japan's reawakening strength and on Japan's relations with the US. That the Chinese communists were much concerned about Japan is demonstrated by the Sino-Soviet Friendship Treaty on 14 February 1950 which was directed against the "revival of Japanese imperialism".[44]

Peculiarities of Sino-North Korean relations also had their impact. The Chinese leadership was well aware of the fact that the Koreans had made many sacrifices when they were fighting on the side of the Chinese communities during the civil war.[45] Since 1946, North Korea had served as a strategic rear area for the Chinese communist forces in the northeast and North Korea had generously assisted the Chinese forces.[46] China was ready to compensate the North Koreans for these efforts. Kim Il Sung was reluctant, however, to ask the Chinese for help in the civil war against the South because he was afraid

---

[40]Whiting pp. 105 and 106.

[41]Chen Jian p. 94.

[42]Shu Guang Zhang pp. 58 ff.: Chen Jian pp. 135–137.

[43]Whiting p. 85.

[44]Text in J.A.S. Grenville, *The Major International Treaties 1940–1973. A History and Guide with Texts*, (New York 1974), pp. 370 ff.

[45]Cumings (1997) p. 284.

[46]Chen Jian pp. 107–109.

that the Yenan faction in the KWP would be strengthened. Only after the UN forces had crossed the 38th parallel did he ask the Chinese for help. On 1 October 1950, he sent a letter to Mao Zedong asking him to send troops to Korea.[47] With this, the Chinese leadership was formally in a position to intervene in the neighboring country.

In the eyes of the Chinese, the war of the North Koreans was a just war because it was waged against the imperialists. The Chinese leadership as well as the Chinese commanders were convinced that they, with their experience gained in the civil war, could beat the American troops in spite of the superiority of the enemy's fire power, equipment, mobility and its absolute mastery of the skies and the sea. The Chinese thought that by their tactics — attacking weak enemy positions, penetration, circling and disintegration close combat, night strikes, and quick battles — they could wear the UN forces down.[48] Mao and his followers believed that in war, men were more important then weapons. The war gave China the chance to appear as the champion of communism in Asia and thus had an expansionist touch. Whether it was intended or not, the fact was that by entering the Korean War, China under its new leadership returned to the world stage. This sort of return implied a lasting disturbance of Sino-American relations. After the direct military clash with China — the Chinese People's Volunteers in Korea were units of the People's Liberation Army — it became impossible for the Democratic administration to implement its rather liberal policy towards China which had already been under fire from the Republicans. President Truman had originally intended, as he had stated on 5 January 1950, to drop Formosa and the nationalists of Chiang Kaishek. This policy was driven by the hope that a conflict would arise between Moscow and Beijing of which the US might profit. The Chinese policy of the Truman administration fell by the wayside. This result, which prevented a rapprochement between the US and China for years to come, will have been welcomed by the Soviet Union. That the Soviet Union had that result in mind and, therefore, had encouraged the Chinese to enter the war, waged by North Korea, is unlikely and, in any case, cannot be verified.[49]

[47] Chen Jian, p. 172.

[48] Shu Guang Zhang, pp. 76 and 77.

[49] According the Newsweek, 14 July 1997 the Chinese Communist Party Magazine *Hundred Year Tide* in a revision of official Chinese history portrays Stalin as the ultimate mastermind of the Korean War.

On 24 November 1950, General MacArthur came to Korea to witness the offensive on the western front, but he had no chance to see his troops winning. Even before the offensive had begun, the front at the Chongchon River, held by the Eighth Army, collapsed under the attack of Chinese forces. The Chinese first overran the South Korean troops deployed on the right flank and then surrounded parts of the front. The retreat of the UN forces changed into fleeing. On 5 December 1950, Pyongyang was lost. On the eastern front the situation was very much the same. The X Corps had no chance to continue on its offensive. The marines were pushed back in a bloody battle at the Chosin reservoir. Troops and equipment of the X Corps had to be evacuated by sea. At the end of December 1950, North Korea was back in communist hands.

The North Koreans and Chinese did not stop there. On New Year's Eve, apparently inspired by their success, they started an offensive to conquer South Korea. On 4 January 1951, Seoul was taken once again. The new Commander of the Eighth Army, Lieutenant General Matthew B. Ridgway, who had succeeded General Walker, who had been killed in an accident, managed to stabilize the front of UN forces along the line Pyontaek–Samchok, running approximately 90 km south of the 38th parallel. Ridgway boosted the morale of his troops and started a war of attrition. The UN troops did not give the Chinese forces a chance for flexible warfare and for encircling operations. The UN forces made use of their superior and well-coordinated firepower. The Chinese forces which made use of human wave attacks could not match these tactics. From the end of January 1951, the UN troops moved slowly north. On 14 March 1951, Seoul was taken back for the second time. In April 1951, the UN troops had reached a line somewhat north of the 38th parallel.

References

Sources: US Department of State, Publication 3922, *United States Policy in the Korean Crisis*, Washington July 1950; US Department of State, Publication 4263, *United States Policy in the Korean Conflict*, Washington September 1951; US Department of State, *Foreign Relations of the US, 1950, Vol. I and VII, 1952–1954 Vol. XV*, Washington 1976 bis 1984; Kim Se-Jin (editor), *Korean Unification. Source Materials with an Introduction*, Korea 1976 (quoted as Kim Se Jin, Unification).

Appleman, Roy E., *United States Army in the Korean War, South to the Naktong, North to the Yalu (June-November 1950)*, Office of the Chief Military History, Department of the Army, Washington 1961.

Chen, Jian, *China's Road to the Korean War. The Making of the Sino-American Confrontation*, New York 1994.

Clark, Mark, *From the Danube to the Yalu*, New York 1954.

Fleming, D.F., *The Cold War and its Origin, 1917–1960, Volume II 1950–1960, Chapter XXI: The Crucification of Korea* (S. 589 ff.), Garden City 1961.

Goulden, Joseph C., *Korea. The Untold Story of the War*, New York 1982.

Kaufman, Burton I., *The Korean Conflict*, Westport 1999.

Kim, Hak Joon, "International Trends in Korean War Studies", *in Korea and World Affairs*, Vol. XIV No. 2 (Summer 1990).

Kim, Young Ho, "The Origins of the Korean War: Civil War or Stalin's Rollback"? *in Diplomacy and Statecraft* Vol. 10, March 1999, No. 1 pp. 186 ff.

Knorr, Klas and Morgan, Patrick, *Strategic Military Surprise*, New Brunswick 1983. Poteat, George Howard, *Strategic Intelligence and National Security: A Case Study of the Korean* Crisis, University Microfilms.

Ridgway, Mathhew B., *The Korean War*, Garden City, New York 1967.

Shu Guong Zhang, *Mao's Military Romanticism. China and the Korean War, 1950–1953*, Lawrence 1995.

Spanier, John W., *The Truman-MacArthur Controversy and the Korean War*, Cambridge 1959.

Weathersby, Kathryn, "To Attack, or Not to Attack? Stalin, Kim Il-Sung and the Prelude to War", in *Cold War International History Project Bulletin* Issue 5, Spring 1995, pp. 1 ff (with documents translated from Russian).

Weathersby, Kathryn, "New Russian Documents on the Korean War. Introduction and Translations", in *Cold War International History Project Bulletin* Winter 1995/96 (available online http://cwihp.si.edu/cwihplib.nsf/).

Whiting, Allen S., *China Crosses the Yalu. The Decision To Enter The Korean War*, New York 1960.

Chapter 6

The Korean War
Phase Two: The Division Hardens

The Dismissal of General MacArthur

The UN troops had suffered a horrible defeat at the Chongchon River. Within five weeks, they were driven out of North Korea. Since MacArthur was the Commander-in-Chief, it was also a horrible defeat for him, the famous hero of the Pacific War.

MacArthur was an extraordinary man whose career was without example in US military history. Born in 1880, he graduated from the Military Academy at West Point, and was already promoted Brigadier General in 1918 when he fought in France during the First World War. After the war, he became the Commander of the Military Academy at West Point, later for five years US Chief-of-Staff and then Field Marshal of the Philippines. During the Second World War, he was Commander-in-Chief in the Southwest Pacific, where he brilliantly recaptured the islands occupied by Japanese forces and accepted the Japanese capitulation on the USS *Missouri* on 2 September 1945. He was then appointed Commander-in-Chief of the Allied Forces in Japan and ruled Japan from his office at the 5th floor of the building of the Dai-Ichi-Insurance Company in Tokyo. He had become something like a proconsul.

When the Five-Star-General (General of the Army) was given the military responsibility for the UN forces in Korea, he was already 70 years old. His victories and his merits had been exceptional. But he had a weakness: He had difficulties not being enthusiastic about himself. The people around him had developed a personality cult, part of which was the belief in the infallibility of the general. This cult had started during the Pacific War and intensified afterward. This attitude was dangerous because it encouraged a tendency to disregard facts. Facts, however, are obstinate as Lenin has allegedly said.

General Douglas MacArthur was no fan of the containment policy and its military equivalent, of the limited war. He argued more in political than in military terms. He felt it was high time to counter communism in an offensive way. He also thought that the Democratic administration focussed too much on Europe and neglected Asia where he expected the main future decisions of world politics to center. With his views, he was in perfect agreement with the Republicans, led by Senator Robert A. Taft.

The defeat at the Chongchon River had really hurt the General. He argued that he was only defeated by the restrictions he was instructed to observe. He requested authority to retaliate and attack military bases in China.[1] The Joint Chiefs instructed him on 29 December 1950 to use delaying tactics to defend the front in Korea and, if necessary, to evacuate his forces. On 30 December 1950, MacArthur summarized his suggestions about an extension of the war in a report to the Joint Chiefs-of-Staff. He sought permission to: "(1) blockade the coast of China; (2) destroy through naval gunfire and air bombardment on China's industrial capacity to wage war; (3) secure reinforcements from the Nationalist garrison on Formosa to strengthen our position in Korea if we decided to continue the fight for that peninsula; and (4) release existing restrictions upon the Formosan garrison for diversionary action, possibly leading to counter invasions against vulnerable areas of the Chinese mainland".[2] These suggestions which were unreasonable because they went much too far were rejected by his superiors. In the following discussions, the General argued that there was danger of his forces being annihilated. The crisis caused by this assertion resulted in the Joint Chiefs ignoring him and giving orders directly to the commanders in the field.

At this point, we have to turn to the considerations of the US political and military leadership of using nuclear weapons in the Korean War. Originally, it seemed that General MacArthur was not prominent among those who called for the use of nuclear weapons. Meanwhile it has been established that he was very much involved, yet that the political and military establishment was far

---

[1]Rees pp. 180 and 181, Spanier pp. 140 and 141.
[2]MacArthur pp. 378 and 379.

more involved and that orders were given to use atomic weapons under definite conditions.[3]

MacArthur asked twice in December 1950 to be given the authority to use nuclear weapons and specified the need for 34 atomic bombs. He also considered spreading a radioactive belt north of the Yalu. In view of the enormous destructive power of nuclear bombs, these demands were not only unreasonable, they were irresponsible.

The tone for corresponding considerations in Washington was set by President Truman. In a question and answer period during a press conference on 30 November 1950, President Truman answered in the affirmative to a question on whether the necessary steps to be taken to meet the military situation would include the atomic bomb.[4] Answering additional questions, he stated that there had been active consideration on the use of the atomic bomb, but that he did not want to see it used because it would hurt innocent people. He further said that the selection of targets was for the military authorities to decide. President Truman had used such surprisingly vague language that his press secretary issued a statement stressing that only the president could authorize the use of the atomic bomb and that no such authorization had been given. The generals got hold of the issue, and after long discussions, the Joint Chiefs-of-Staff ordered the use of atomic weapons against Chinese bases in Manchuria "if large numbers of new troops came into the fighting or, it appears, if bombers were launched against American assets from there".[5] As the other side did not escalate the war, these orders were not implemented. Thus nuclear weapons were not used.

Biological weapons were also not used during the war. The North Koreans, Chinese and Soviets accused UNC of having done so. Their charges reached a climax when the North Korean Foreign Minister Park Hon Yong, in a letter to the UN Secretariat dated 22 February 1952, claimed the US had carried out airdrops of infected insects bearing plague, cholera and other diseases over North Korean territory at the end of January 1952. The Chinese government even claimed that the US air force had made 955 sorties over northeast China to drop dangerous bacteria between 29 February and 31 March 1952. As we know from Soviet documents, these allegations had

[3] I rely in the following on Cumings (1997) pp. 288 ff.

[4] New York Times, 30 November/1 December 1950.

[5] Cumings (1997) p. 292.

no bases at all.[6] The evidence was fabricated in a clumsy way. Before an international commission arrived, fake areas of exposure were prepared with Chinese and Soviet assistance. In the post-Stalin period, the Soviet leadership made it clear that the charges were fraudulent. A resolution of the Presidium of Soviet Council of Ministers on 2 May 1953 was transmitted to Ambassador Kuznetsov in Beijing to tell Mao Zedong the following: "The Soviet government and the Central Committee of the CPSU were misled. The spread of information in the Press about the use by the Americans of bacteriological weapons in Korea was based on false information. The accusations against the Americans were fictitious".[7] So the allegations were false. The question remains, however, why the Soviet leadership dissociated itself in such a drastic way from a former common line of the three allies.

In the spring of 1951, MacArthur started to make his views on the expansion of the war publicly known. When the UN forces approached the 38th parallel, President Truman prepared an appeal for peace, in which he thought of suggesting the cessation of hostilities and the beginning of negotiations. This plan was counteracted by MacArthur who, on 24 March 1951, publicly discussed the possibility of expanding military operations to the coastal areas and bases of China. On the same day, Truman decided to dismiss the General who once again had exceeded the limits of his military responsibilities. Before Truman could do so, on 5 April 1951 Representative Joseph Martin read a letter dated 20 March 1951 in the House in which MacArthur supported the idea to use Chinese Nationalist troops in Korea and recommended massive counter force.[8] MacArthur had not only made unreasonable and irresponsible suggestions; by trying publicly to counteract the policy of his Commander-in-Chief, the President, he had again shown his unreliability. After thorough talks with his advisors and upon recommendation of the Joint Chiefs-of-Staff, President Truman relieved General MacArthur of all his posts on 11 April 1951. As the media were quicker than the telegraphic connections between the Pentagon and headquarters in Tokyo, MacArthur received the first information about his dismissal through radio.

[6]For details and documents see Milton Leitenberg, "New Russian Evidence on the Korean War Biological Warfare Allegations: Background and Analysis", in *Cold War International History Project Bulletin* 11, 03/99, (available via http://cwihp.si.edu/swhiplib.nsf/).

[7]Rees pp. 460 and 461.

[8]Text in Kaufman p. 150.

General Ridgway became MacArthur's successor. He was often praised for his leadership during the Korean War. We have to note, however, that he also suggested the use of atomic bombs in Korea, requesting 38 of them on May 1951.[9]

In the United States, a storm of indignation broke out which showed signs of hysteria. On the Democratic Administration, particularly on Truman, Acheson and Marshall, reproaches were heaped; for years under fire from the Republicans, there was even talk of an impeachment. MacArthur, on the other hand returned triumphantly to the US, addressed Congress on 19 April 1951 and was celebrated by a tickertape parade in New York on 20 April 1951. With the benefit of hindsight, we may call it topsy-turvy.

"There is no substitute for victory", General MacArthur had written in his letter to Representative Martin. This was the American tradition indeed; to wage a war as a crusade until the enemy was subjugated. MacArthur had participated in such a war just a couple of years ago, and when the Korean War began he was still occupied in re-educating the former enemy. He also wanted this type of war to be conducted in Korea: to subjugate North Korea, to reunite Korea under UN control, to weaken China by hitting its industrial and military bases and thus roll back the influence of China and its main ally, the Soviet Union. What he overlooked was that the world had changed and that such a policy entailed high risks. China was still weak but united, and it was more than questionable whether it made any sense to carry a war into a country of China's potential. Japan had not succeeded in subjugating China when it was weak. The main question, which preoccupied the US administration, was how the Soviet Union, which was China's ally, would react to a US attack on China. The administration, unlike MacArthur, was afraid of incalculable consequences for Asia and Europe if a US attack on China would give the Soviet Union a pretext to intervene.

"There was no doubt that we had reached a point where grave decision had to be made", wrote President Truman about the situation after the Chinese victory at the Chongchon River.[10] "If we chose to extend the war to China, we had to expect retaliation. Peiping and Moscow were allies, ideologically as well as by treaty. If we began to attack Communist China, we had to anticipate Russian intervention. Of course we wanted no war on any scale.

[9]Cumings (1997) p. 291.

[10]Truman p. 382.

But neither did the world or we want Communist slavery. And the question now was whether we had actually reached a point where this threaten us such that we had to move to the destruction of cities and killing of women and children".

The Truman administration considered these risks as too high. The Soviet Union was, as far as tactical weapons were concerned, inferior to the US; it had, however, emerged from the Second World War as a great power. The chances to fight Soviet communism militarily were — if they ever had existed — over; maintaining a balance was now the predominant aim. The containment policy took this aim into account. Thus, after the battle at the Chongchon River the administration returned to a policy of containment. The goal to conquer North Korea and subsequently unite Korea was given up; US policy focussed on preserving the Republic of Korea. The US administration accepted the preservation of its ally as substitute for victory.

Positional Warfare and Negotiations

From April 1951 until the end of the war in July 1953, the front between the two warring sides was running near the 38th parallel. Sometimes it moved south and other times north across the peninsula; the frequency of change progressively diminished. From the end of 1951, there were mainly encounters between the two lines of defense.

In the spring of 1951, the Chinese and North Korean forces, though having severely suffered from Ridgway's war of attrition, started two major offensives in order to conquer the South. Once again, the Chinese and North Korean divisions which were commanded by the Chinese General Peng Dehuai tried to make up for the lack of firepower and technical equipment, utilizing masses of soldiers. Under heavy casualties, they succeeded to push the southern line of defense approximately 50 km south, but they could not take Seoul once again. They were then pushed back approximately to the same positions from where they had started. In the summer of 1951, the front was running again somewhat north of the 38th parallel. Now, China and North Korea had no other possibility but to agree to negotiations. The Americans were — as we have seen — ready to just re-establish the status quo ante bellum. In the beginning of June 1951, Secretary of State Acheson made the return to this aim public.

Panmunjom is probably one of the best-known Korean place names. It is the name of a small hamlet 6 miles east of Kaesong, the capital of old Koryo and a couple of miles south of the 38th parallel. Panmunjom became famous because the negotiations on the armistice were held there. Today, the name Panmunjom is associated with the Joint Security Area, situated in the middle of the Demilitarized Zone and administered by the former warring parties, Chinese and North Koreans on the one side and the UN Command on the other side.

One can visit Panmunjom. Coming from Seoul, one needs just an hour to reach the Imjin River. Here, controls begin to get stricter. From a checkpoint of the US forces, one is transported by bus into the Demilitarized Zone and quickly reaches the Joint Security Area. When the visitors leave the bus, they are surrounded by US soldiers, and an officer who came along in the bus will mention something like "you have never been better protected in all your life". The guests visit the simple house where the Armistice Commission holds its meetings. The table in the room, covered by green baize, is divided in the middle by the Demarcation Line. Pennants mark its southern and northern parts. Visitors can also see the North Korean Freedom House and the South Korean Pavilion. Finally, the visitors are guided to an outpost from where they can have a look at North Korea which with its rice paddies and blue-green hills does not differ at all from the vistas during the trip from Seoul to Panmunjom. From the outpost, one can also see the "Bridge of No Return"; no North Korean prisoner of war who had crossed the bridge to the North had a chance to return to the South.

Panmunjom has also become the symbol of continuing tensions. Many incidents have occurred in the Joint Security Area. A particularly severe one took place on 18 August 1976. When a UN command was trimming a large poplar tree, two US officers were murdered by North Korean soldiers with axes.

Panmunjom is first of all a place of most difficult negotiations. The negotiations on the armistice did not start in Panmunjom but in a former teahouse near Kaesong in an area under Northern control. On 23 June 1951, the Soviet Ambassador to the United Nations Jacob Malik had indicated in a radio program in New York the willingness of the communist side to negotiate a cease-fire and a truce. This was a reply to Acheson's offer. After the two sides fighting in Korea had gotten in touch by radio, their negotiators met for the first time on 8 July 1951. The negotiations took much longer than the West had thought. It took two years to finish them.

The negotiations focussed on three issues:

— the fixing of a demarcation line for the cease-fire;
— the establishment of a framework to supervise the armistice;
— and the repatriation of the prisoners of war (POWs).

The negotiations continued in Panmunjom, that is to say in no man's land. At the end of November 1951, both sides agreed to choose a demarcation line which followed the actual front line. The Chinese and North Koreans gave up their original attempt to designate the 38th parallel as the demarcation line. In the discussions on the monitoring system, both sides showed a willingness to set up an Armistice Commission to supervise the Armistice Agreement and a Neutral Nations Supervisory Commission to supervise the prohibitions on reinforcements of military personnel and weapons in Korea. The toughest discussions centered on the questions of the repatriation of POWs; the North was not willing to accept the request of the UN to repatriate on the bases of voluntary decisions of the prisoners.

During the negotiations, the Northern side was represented by Major General Hsieh Fang, the Chief-of-Staff of the Chinese People's Volunteers, and General Nam Il, the Chief-of-Staff of the KPA. The United Nations Command was initially represented by Vice Admiral Turner Joy, but starting from the spring of 1952 it was by Lieutenant General William K. Harrison. The negotiations were arduous and unpleasant for the UN side. The Chinese and North Koreans seldom made own proposals, but waited for suggestions from the other side. Again and again, they introduced political issues into the negotiations which were supposed to be dealing with military questions. They used all sorts of tricks to delay the talks and abused and threatened the representatives from the UN. Often the meetings had to be interrupted. A ritual of hostilities developed which had its impact on the discussions within the Armistice Commission for years afterwards.

During the talks, the war continued. The blockade of North Korea was effective. Supplies for the Northern front had to be transported by land where they were exposed to American air bombardment. Weapons of mass destruction were, as we have seen, not used. Nevertheless, the air war was disastrous for North Korea. Even though the US air force was threatened by MIG-15-aircraft from the Chinese air force, it did incredible damage to North Korea's infrastructure as well as to many towns and villages by using napalm and huge bombs. Even irrigation dams were destroyed in that brutal air war. Many,

many people died in North Korea, out of which among them one million civilians according to an unofficial estimate.[11] Taking the suffering of the people into consideration, it sounds cynical to call the war a limited one. The supply to the front, however, was never cut off completely. Only operations of ground forces might have succeeded. The UN forces, meanwhile a huge machinery, started an offensive in the fall of 1951. Its scope was limited so as to put pressure on the communists. From November 1951 onwards, the UN forces just defended their front line, an operation resulting in many casualties. The Northern side misused the moments of decreasing pressure to delay the negotiations and to make anti-UN propaganda. They considered the negotiations on the armistice agreement as a continuation of the war by other means.

The Armistice Agreement

In view of the Chinese and North Korean intransigence, it was not surprising that the negotiations went on and on. In the spring of 1952, nonetheless, most of the questions were solved; only the question of the repatriation of the prisoners of war remained open. It had not been easy for the West to insist on the principle of voluntary return because the demand involved the risk of delaying the talks and thus burdening its prisoners in the North with longer captivity. In addition, it was quite difficult to find out which prisoners in Southern camps were willing to return to the North. Finally, it emerged that only 50% of the North Korean prisoners, the Chinese prisoners and the procommunist South Korean civilian internees were willing to return to the North.

The situation in the Prisoner Of War (POW) camps in the South was difficult. Many prisoners of war, approximately 150,000, were accommodated in an over-crowded complex on Koje Island, south of Pusan. There were strong tensions between pro- and anticommunist prisoners and civilian internees. The North Korean prisoners were even remotely controlled by North Korean agencies. The tensions resulted in all sorts of clashes and violent incidents, leaving many people dead. The US and the South Korean security forces had their hands full in trying to maintain order. In May 1952, a group of North

[11] See Chapter Five, note. 2.

Korean prisoners even seized the commandant of the camp, Brigadier General Dodd and held him hostage. He was released only after he, in an agreement with Brigadier General Colson who had filled in for him, had signed a confession that there had been "insistence of bloodshed where many POWs have been killed and wounded by UN Forces".[12] He promised humane treatment at the same time for the POWs in the future.

Both generals were reduced in rank to colonel because they had given North Korea and China a propaganda victory. The pattern that the North Koreans released captured American soldiers only against the confession of guilt was going to be repeated in 1968 when the crew of the *Pueblo* was freed and in December 1994 when a pilot of a helicopter which had been shot down over North Korea was released. In these cases, the confession of guilt was made upon instructions by the US Government. In 1952, however, a war was fought on the Korean peninsula and, therefore, a strict standard applied.

After the communists had revealed the numbers of their prisoners in the North at the end of 1951, the worries of the UN command increased. The new numbers were just a fraction of those communicated by the communists in March in the same year. This meant that many prisoners had died. The fate of UN soldiers taken prisoner by the North was horrible indeed. Approximately 38% of the American prisoners died in captivity.[13] The prisoners were also subjected to massive attempts of communist indoctrination.

For many years, the incoming Eisenhower administration was credited with having brought the armistice talks to a satisfactory conclusion by using the threat of employing nuclear weapons against Mainland China. The Republican candidate Dwight D. Eisenhower had won the presidential elections on 4 November 1952 after a bitter campaign which had focussed on the war in Korea. Eisenhower, a five-star-general, had increased his chances for winning the elections by promising to go to Korea himself. He went to Korea in the beginning of December 1952. He did not attempt to substitute the containment policy with a policy of liberation of which John Foster Dulles had talked so often about during the campaign. The new Republican administration aimed at achieving an armistice just as the preceding Truman administration had done. In a letter addressed to President Syngman Rhee on 6 June 1953, Eisenhower

[12]Roskey, p. 12.

[13]Rees p. 325.

explained: "But we do not intend to use war as an instrument to achieve the worldwide political solutions to which we subscribe and which we consider just".[14]

According to the official record, Secretary of State John Foster Dulles said to the Indian Prime Minister Nehru on 21 and 22 May 1953 "that if the armistice negotiations collapsed, the United States would probably make a stronger rather than a lesser military exertion and that his might well extend the area of conflict. (Note: I assumed this would be relayed.)".[15] This remark was often understood as an indirect threat to use nuclear weapons which contributed decisively to a quick end of the Korean war. However, it is not certain whether Nehru interpreted the remark in that way and whether he relayed it to Beijing. In addition, there was a development which called the significance of the Secretary's remark into question. The decision to whether and when to end the war was, as all other important decision regarding the war, taken by the Soviet leadership. As we can see from recently released documents, the Council of Ministers of the Soviet Union had already decided on 19 March 1953, more than two months before the Dulles-Nehru meeting, to take steps with the view "to secure the cessation of the war in Korea" and had informed Mao Zedong and Kim Il Sung accordingly.[16]

The decision in Moscow was taken two weeks after Stalin's death. Stalin had originally preferred to draw out the war because he believed that it would shake up the Truman administration and harm US military prestige as he told Mao Zedong in a telegram dated 5 June 1951.[17] He then agreed to raise the question of an armistice which was done by Ambassador Malik in New York on 23 June 1953.[18] Five months later, in another message to Mao, he advocated the pursuit of "a hard-line".[19] This did not really prove that he was the main obstacle for the conclusion of the armistice. Yet, it was obvious

[14]US Senate, *The United States and the Korean Problem. Documents 1943–1953*, Washington 1953, pp. 83 ff.

[15]US Department of State, Foreign Relations of the US. 1950, Vol. XV pp. 1068 ff.; Harold Stassen, who participated in the first meeting with Nehru, claims that Dulles and Nehru talked explicitly about an American threat with nuclear weapons (Harold Stassen and Marshall Houts, *Eisenhower: Turning the World Toward Peace*, St. Paul 1990, pp. 143 and 144).

[16]Wheathersby (1995/96) Document No. 112.

[17]Wheathersby (1995/96) Document No. 65.

[18]Wheathersby (1995/96) Document No. 73.

[19]Wheathersby (1995/96) Document No. 95.

that uncertainties caused by Stalin's death made the Soviet leadership revise the policy line with a view to get rid of the problem in the Far East.

The North Korean leadership was weary. The North Korean Foreign Minister Pak Hon Yong told the commander of the Chinese People's Volunteers Peng Dehuai on 16 January 1952 "that the Korean people throughout the country demand peace and do not want to continue the war"; Kim Il Sung had repeated the same in a message to Stalin on 16 July 1952.[20]

These various considerations and moves resulted in an approval of the principle of voluntary return of the POWs by North Korea and China. On 8 July 1953, it was agreed that those POWs who did not insist on being repatriated become civilians six month after the conclusion of the armistice agreement. During that period of time, the countries of origin were given a chance to change the prisoners' minds.

Before being in a position to sign the Armistice agreement, the US administration had to cope with difficulties caused by its main ally South Korea. With great stubbornness, President Syngman Rhee had insisted on his demand for Korea's unification. He had objected returning to a policy of containment after the defeat at the Chongchon River and had fought the start of the talks on a truce. He now tried to prevent the conclusion of the Armistice Agreement. In a letter addressed to President Eisenhower on 30 May 1953, he reacted to American pressure to not obstruct the conclusion of the truce. He stated that the Korean question should be solved by punishing the aggressor and by reuniting the country. This, he continued, would be honorable and just and would force the other side to abandon its efforts to conquer the world. He declared it unacceptable that Chinese communists remain on Korean soil and repeated — politely by asking permission — his threat to continue the fight with his South Korean forces. This threat was completely unrealistic as was illustrated by a Chinese attack in the middle part of the front in July 1953. This attack succeeded in inflicting heavy damage on several South Korean divisions and pushing them back considerably. It was not clear until the last moment whether Syngman Rhee would realize his threat to continue fighting.

President Syngman Rhee inconvenienced the Americans greatly by releasing many of the anticommunist POWs from prisons under South Korean custody. General Mark Clark, Ridgway's successor in Tokyo, finally reached an agreement with Rhee that although his government would not sign the

---

[20]Wheathersby (1995/96) Document No. 102 and 106.

Armistice Agreement it would, however, recognize it. Such a procedure was possible because according to international law, military commanders are authorized to conclude an armistice.[21] The US administration facilitated Rhee's decision to give up his obstruction by offering a mutual defense treaty, the reinforcement of South Korean forces and economic aid. The US administration had to pay to make President Rhee change his attitude, but it did not pay a high price. After the US government had become so deeply involved in Korean affairs, the Republic of Korea could be certain that the US would give assurances for the future. The US government did not repeat the mistake made when it left South Korea in 1949 without giving the South Korean government a guarantee to support it in case of an attack from the North.

The Armistice Agreement was signed on 27 June 1953, first by both heads of delegation, Lieutenant General Harrison and General Nam Il in Panmunjom, then by the Commander-in-Chief of the UN Command General Clark in Munsan and by the Supreme Commander of the KPA Kim Il Sung and the Commander of the Chinese People's Volunteers Peng Dehuai in Pyongyang. When the agreement entered into force at 10.00 p.m. on the same day, fighting ceased everywhere on the peninsula.

Besides arranging for the cease-fire, the Armistice Agreement provided for the following[22]:

— A Demarcation Line was fixed which followed the front line as it existed on the date of the conclusion of the Armistice Agreement. A Demilitarized Zone was established as a buffer zone; both sides had to move 2 km away from the Demarcation Line.

— An Armistice Commission was established, composed of five officers from each side, with the mission to supervise the Agreement and to settle disputes.

— A Neutral Nations Supervisory Commission was set up composed of officers from Sweden, Switzerland, Poland and Czechoslovakia. Its function was to supervise the prohibition to reinforce military personnel and weapons in Korea.

— The holding of a conference for the peaceful settlement of the Korean question was recommended.

---

[21]Seidl-Hohenveldern pp. 199 ff.

[22]Text in Rees pp. 462 ff.

— The release and repatriation of those POWs willing to return was agreed. The exchange was to be implemented in Panmunjom. Those prisoners who did not want to return were to be handed to a Neutral Nations Repatriation Commission, composed of representatives from Sweden, Switzerland, Czechoslovakia, Poland and India.

The exchange of the POWs willing to return was implemented in August 1953. Those POWs who were not willing to return, 22,000 Chinese and North Koreans and 359 members of the UN forces, were handed to the Repatriation Commission in September 1953. Since the conference for the settlement of the Korean question was not convened within six month after the Armistice Agreement was signed, these POWs were released at the end of January 1954.

The Result

The Korean War was a strange one. On the first day of the war, Radio Pyongyang claimed that South Korea had declared war but this claim was never confirmed. Thus, from the very beginning, the question of the participants was shrouded in mystery. The country which had the largest number of casualties among its forces, the People's Republic of China, did not officially participate in the war as calling its forces fighting in Korea "Chinese People's Volunteers". On the Southern side, the war was not only fought by individual states but by the United Nations which had imposed sanctions in favor of a non-member state and against a non-member state. Apart from these strange features, the war was a special one since the war theater was territorially strictly limited to the Korean Peninsula and since one side did not make use of its full arsenal of weapons. The preamble of the Armistice Agreement, therefore, used the term "the Korean conflict". This term was later used frequently, but played down the fact that the Korean War was a real one, a clash of armed forces with the aim to force political demands on the other side.

For the Democratic People's Republic of Korea, the war was no success at all. It did not achieve its goal to subjugate South Korea and to unite Korea under its leadership. Worse, North Korea was horribly devastated. The Republic of Korea succeeded in fighting off the attempt to destroy its integrity, however, only under heavy sacrifices and only with US support. Territorially, the *status quo ante bellum* was approximately restored. But more than a restoration had happened. It could not be overlooked that the division of the country, now determined by the Demarcation Line, had been hardened by the Armistice Agreement.

There was another aspect important for both Koreas. Civil wars are known for the bitterness with which they are fought. The war on the Korean peninsula was no exception to that rule. On the contrary, both sides fell upon each other in a brutal way. Both sides committed atrocities, the Northerners in the South, the Southerners against guerillas in the South and against North Koreans during their short stay in the North.[23] Koreans are a homogenous people, they speak the same language, share a common history, and enjoy the same culture. In 1919 under Japanese occupation, they seemed to have reinforced their national identity. So why did the Koreans fight each other in such a brutal way? It is difficult to understand.

Ideology was not really the main reason even though it looked like it. The North Korean leadership had at least an ideology. It wanted to introduce its socialist system in the South. Therefore, it revived the people's committees and started a land reform. However, the North Korean system was held together not by ideology but by police control. The South had no ideology to export. The Republic of Korea was ruled in an autocratic way. It could only export its police and its youth organizations, i.e. instruments of force. The core of the conflict was different: The leadership in both parts of the country wanted to rule the whole. The war was a struggle for power by the rulers. The references made to ideology were meant to camouflage power-politics. It seemed that the masses followed at random. As we have already seen, modern times had destroyed the social fabric. The old system with the aristocracy at the top had disappeared. The Confucian values were of no help because they had always stressed family values more then cohesion in the state. There had been no time to develop a new social order. A civil society and a network of organizations could have fostered cohesion but it was missing. Korean disunity, factionalism and fanaticism made things worse. Thus, the politics of Korea were those of a vortex, as Gregory Henderson has so aptly called them.

And the Korean War was a vortex of the worst kind. Its aftereffects were to influence relations between both parts of the country, but it could also be foreseen that it confronted the leadership in both Koreas with the problem of how to find a basis for governance within the strife-torn and amorphous society.

---

[23]For details see Cumings (1997) pp. 273 ff. and pp. 281 ff.; New York Times, 21 April 2000.

The People's Republic of China achieved its aim of asserting its traditional influence on the Korean peninsula and preventing the dissolution of its communist North Korean neighbor. The People's Republic of China did not succeed with its demand made during the armistice talks that all foreign troops withdraw from Korea. It could not promote the advance of communism in Asia but returned from the battlefield as a great power with which one had to reckon with in Asia. In spite of the horrendous casualties, the Chinese leadership insisted that wars were decided by men and not by weapons.

Through its participation in the Korean War, the People's Republic of China ran into a deep conflict with the United States, a conflict which was to continue for many years. This development was welcomed by the Soviet Union, but as already has been said, it goes too far to assume that the Soviet Union had steered toward that objective. For the Soviet Union, the war was costly and yet also instructive because it could observe the strength and perseverance of the West. These observations may have added to its willingness to adopt a policy of peaceful coexistence.

When the Chinese did an analysis of their first encounters with the Americans at the end of November 1950, they were surprised to find out that the American soldiers were afraid to die. The US military leadership had only done the obvious: to protect its soldiers as far as possible and to rely on the superior firepower of its forces. US casualties, however, were high. Altogether 142,000 soldiers were killed, wounded, missing in action or captured.[24] It was therefore not surprising that US politics suffered a heavy shock. The containment policy could be realized by the administration only with difficulties and on a winding path. This policy was brought to an end by the Republicans who had fought it vociferously when they were not yet in power. The subsequent policy of detente which succeeded in easing tensions between West and East could be interpreted as a justification of the policy of containment. By its intervention in Korea, the USA stopped communist expansions in East Asia. The Americans experienced a new situation; they fought a war which ended without a victory.

The United Nations had taken an extraordinary decision by imposing military sanctions against North Korea. The various UN bodies involved were also useful during the war by providing a meeting place for representatives from both sides. From the end of 1950, the UN promoted efforts for a cease-fire and

---

[24] Rees p. 461.

later for a solution to the questions on the fate of POWs. Since the real decisions were taken in Washington, the UN was accused of being an instrument of US politics.

None of the participants could really be satisfied with the results of the Korean War.

References

Eisenhower, Dwight D., *The White House Years, Mandate for Change, 1953–1956*, New York 1963.

Hermes, Walter G., *United States in the Korean War, Truce Tent and Fighting Front*, Office of the Chief of Military History, US Army, Washington 1966.

MacArthur, Douglas, *Reminiscences*, New York, Toronto, London 1964.

Roskey, William, *Koje Island: The 1952 Korean Hostage Crisis*, The Land Warfare Paper No. 19, September 1994.

PART III

Politics and Economics in the Republic of Korea

Chapter 7

Syngman Rhee's Korea

The First President of the Republic of Korea

In the first 15 years after liberation from Japanese rule, Syngman Rhee was the most prominent political personality in South Korea. His beginnings as a politician went back to his early youth, that is to say to the end of the Yi dynasty. Yi Sung Man, later known as Syngman Rhee, was born on 28 March 1875 into a *yangban* family which was distantly related to the royal family but had become impoverished and lost influence. He first enjoyed a traditional Confucian education, before becoming acquainted with Western learning at the Paejae (Paichai) Boys' School in Seoul, run by Henry G. Appenzeller, a Methodist missionary. From here, he found his way to the Independence Club of So Chae Pil which stood for democratic reforms. During the fight against incompetence and corruption at the royal court, Syngman Rhee's talent for agitation became obvious for the first time. When the Independence Club was dissolved, Syngman Rhee was arrested, tortured and sentenced to life-long imprisonment. During his time in prison, he converted to Christianity and wrote a paper under the title "The Spirit of Independence". Syngman Rhee began his political life as a revolutionary.

In August 1904, he was released from prison on the basis of an amnesty promoted by the Japanese at the moment when they set out to finally take control of Korea. That was a period which offered no chances for an independence fighter like Syngman Rhee. Therefore, a few months after his release from prison, he traveled to the United States. As a sort of self-appointed Korean envoy, he tried to induce the US government to intervene in favor of

Korea, but his efforts failed. Thanks to generous American support, he was able to complete his education in the years from 1905 to 1910. He studied first at George Washington University and later took courses in history and international relations at Harvard University. After having studied political science at Princeton University, he received a Ph.D. in 1910, his dissertation focused on the topic "Neutrality as Influenced by the United States". The foreigner from the Far East had come a long way rather quickly.

In the fall of 1910, Syngman Rhee returned to Korea but had no opportunities to engage in political activities since his country had become annexed by Japan. Since his personal security was not guaranteed, he returned to the US in 1912. From 1912 to 1919, Hawaii became his residence where he was active as an educator, as far as his restless life as a politician in exile allowed him.

His fight for Korea's independence found recognition when he became President of the Provisional Government in 1919. At the end of 1920, he traveled to Shanghai where the Provisional Government had its seat, but he did not succeed in tying together the opposing elements among the Koreans in exile. He stuck to his policies to try to achieve Korea's independence not by violence but by the support of Western countries. Therefore, he concentrated — and not without success — on finding support for Korea's independence in the United States. All attempts to persuade Western countries to recognize the Provisional Government failed, as well as the efforts to ask the League of Nations to intervene. During a visit at the League of Nations headquarters in Geneva from the end of 1932 to the beginning of 1933, he met his future wife, Francesca Donner, an Austrian citizen. His experiences as a politician in exile during the time periods between the two world wars were definitely bitter; he, nevertheless, continued to unshakably believe that the development in Asia would amount to a containment of Japan's aggressiveness, and thus entail automatically Korea's independence.

These hopes were greatly encouraged when the war between Japan and the United States got started. The Provisional Government declared war on Japan, but could not achieve diplomatic recognition by the US. Korea was liberated without the Provisional Government being able to make a substantial contribution.

When Syngman Rhee returned to Korea on 15 October 1945, he was 70 years of age with his body and mind in good shape. He had fought for Korea's independence for years, but had no administrative experiences to delegate functions he would never learn. He was well educated in political science, but lacked experience in actual politics within democratic institutions. He was, therefore, not used to compromise. As long as he was a politician in exile, he could afford to insist on his own ideas without taking other opinions into account because there was anyhow no chance for the realization of his ideas. Thus, he had no training in the art of the possible. During the long years of frustration, it had become a habit with him to demand the impossible. In Korean, this habit is called asking a tiger for meat.

His biographer Oliver certified that Syngman Rhee used to be optimistic. In reality, he often did not face the facts. In a letter dated 5 December 1942, addressed to the Chinese Undersecretary of State for Foreign Affairs Victor Hoo he pretended for example that a "military potential of the Korean nation" was available and at the disposal of the allies.[1] During the Korean War, he argued in a similar manner by pretending that there were large numbers of well-trained military personnel available which just needed to be equipped by the Americans; General Ridgway rejected these claims mentioning the poor leadership of the South Korean forces.

Syngman Rhee was overestimating his popularity when he had claimed that millions of Koreans were waiting for him to return. But he was a well known, perhaps even the most popular Korean politician. His excellent English was helpful during the many discussions with representatives from the US occupying power. But as one of his former ministers told me, Syngman Rhee, due to his long absence from Korea, lacked precise knowledge of the situation and the trends in Korea and was not particularly familiar with the other leading politicians. From the very beginning, he attempted to find a platform beyond party politics, but was unable to overcome the disunity among Korean politicians. This disunity was of indirect benefit for him. From early on, he argued to accept the establishment of a South Korean state since the founding of a united Korea would be obstructed by the Soviet Union. After the South Korean state, the Republic of Korea, had been established, Syngman Rhee was elected as its first President by the National Assembly on 20 July 1948.

The Constitutional Crises

The large majority by which Syngman Rhee had been elected president in 1948 — he received 180 of 195 valid votes — was deceptive; he was not really

---

[1]Oliver pp. 186 and 187.

generally appreciated. This was illustrated by the result of the elections for the 2nd National Assembly. His party, the National Association, received just 14 (8.7%) of the 210 seats, the Korean National Party and the Korean Youth Party, both his political allies, received a combined 34 seats (18.2%). The National Democratic Party, the party of the opposition, had 24 seats (11.4%); the remaining 80% of the seats had been won by independents. Syngman Rhee stubbornly believed that only he could rule Korea. In his speeches, often held in a dramatic style, he praised the blessings of democracy. In practice he disregarded the democratic institutions. "Why should we create anything between the president and the people" he is said to have stated.[2] This way of thinking could only lead to clashes with the National Assembly. His years in office are, therefore, characterized by numerous constitutional conflicts.

The first severe conflict between the President and the National Assembly occurred when Syngman Rhee's four-year term of office approached its end. Since there was no majority in the National Assembly for his re-election, he decided to introduce direct presidential elections by the people, thus making use of his popularity which had increased during the war. Since the end of 1951, he promoted a corresponding amendment to the constitution while, at the same time, pretending not to be interested in re-election. On 18 January 1952, the National Assembly rejected his proposal by 143 votes against 19 votes in favor. The Assembly suggested introducing a parliamentary system in which the prime minister, responsible to the Assembly, be the chief executive. In order to make the Assembly bend to his will, he exerted pressure on the members. He appealed to the people which he said to be entitled to recall their representatives if they object to the will of the people, a claim which did not find any basis in the current constitution. He instigated a campaign against the National Assembly, distributed brochures, made appeals, collected petitions and organized "spontaneous" demonstrations. Particularly helpful was Lee Bum Suk who had served as Prime Minister for only a few months but who as a leader within the youth organizations continued to play an important role in politics; he now became Minister of Interior. On 25 May 1952, under the pretext of fighting communist guerillas, martial law was imposed in Pusan which served as temporary capital during the war. Now the government had an instrument on hand

[2] Gibney, Frank, "Syngman Rhee: The Free Man's Burden", in *Harper's Magazine* Vol. 208, February 1954 p. 31.

which it could use to arrest numerous members of the National Assembly. The President disregarded the Assembly's resolution to repeal martial law. He heightened tensions by accusing his opponents of treacherous cooperation with the communists. In the beginning of July 1952, the government had all members brought to the National Assembly and locked them up. On 4 July 1952, the amendment introducing the direct form of presidential elections was approved. At the same time, a two-chamber system with a new upper house was introduced. Syngman Rhee never held elections for the upper house.

Although Syngman Rhee insisted that his own philosophy espoused liberal Jeffersonianism, he had behaved more like a descendent of the Taewongun by treating opponents roughly. This did not prevent him from declaring on 15 August 1952, ten days after his re-election, that "our democratic institutions and principles have been strengthened immeasurably".[3] In the West, another view prevailed: Syngman Rhee became the Free World's burden.

When the date for the next presidential elections approached, Syngman Rhee found another constitutional provision not to his liking, namely Art. 55 which permitted the re-election of a president "for one time only". On 5 September 1954, the Liberal Party introduced an amendment to abolish this provision. Voting took place on 27 November 1954: 135 members voted for the amendment, 60 against it, 7 abstained. This meant that one vote was missing for the necessary two-third majority of altogether 203 votes (= 135 1/3). Therefore, the Assembly's Vice Speaker, Choe Sun Jo, declared the amendment to have been rejected. The next day, the government published an opposing statement; fractions of votes, it argued, do not count. Now the Vice Speaker withdrew his earlier statement and declared the amendment to have been accepted. Syngman Rhee had again supplied evidence for his contempt of the law. By the same vote, additional amendments had been accepted which further strengthened the position of the president; the office of the prime minister was abolished.

In the presidential elections on 15 May 1955, Syngman Rhee had an easy job because his main opponent, the candidate for the Democratic Party Shin Ik Hui (P.H. Shinicky), had died just 10 days before the elections. Syngman Rhee gained 70% of all valid votes. The elections, however, were not altogether successful for the Liberal Party as its candidate for the office of

[3] Oliver p. 288.

the vice-president Lee Ki Poong (Lee Ki Bung), lost to the candidate of the Democratic Party, Chang Myun (Dr. John M. Chang), by a vote of 3.8 million to 4.0 million. Syngman Rhee treated his vice-president as not existing.

The next crisis approached quickly. In November 1958, the government introduced a law to tighten the provisions on national security. The law included for the future, that vaguely phrased criminal offenses like the violation of provisions on secrecy or of the prohibition of espionage, would entail draconian penalties. The Democratic Party, the opposition in the Assembly, which had won 79 (33.9%) of the 233 seats in the elections on 2 May 1958, was afraid the government might misuse this law against political opponents. These fears were definitely justified. The opposition held a sit-in in the chamber, but could not prevent that the law was passed. On 24 December 1958, the Liberal Party removed the members of the opposition from the hall and locked them in the Assembly basement. Then, the Liberal majority passed the amendment to the National Security Law along with 21 other important laws. One of these laws introduced restrictions to the Local Autonomy Law which had been passed in 1952 and had never been liked by the President; for the future mayors and local officials were to be appointed and not elected. President Syngman Rhee was only interested in securing his position through control and by placing loyalists into important positions.

Why was he allowed to manipulate constitutional provisions at will? This had a lot to do with the fact that people often did not realize the binding force of the constitution. The modern constitution had been introduced in a country where convictions, experiences and values differed from those in Western countries. Since Syngman Rhee needed the constitution as a basis for legitimacy, he had no other possibility but to pretend to be committed to constitutionalism. In later years, public opinion in Korea became increasingly aware of the impact of the constitution on the political process, a development which had not been completed until decades later.

The values which had shaped Korea's state ideology were those of Confucianism. Even though Confucianism was no longer the topic of state examinations nor the main subject for scholarly dedication, it continued to have its impact on the thinking and behavior of Koreans, however, with decreasing tendency. Confucianism continued to live by the virtue of tradition; it was the family which conveyed the Confucian values to the younger generation. Their effects are difficult to assess, but hierarchical structures and inequality were an obvious legacy of Confucianism.[4] In family relations, filial piety — respect and obedience of the son towards his parents which find their expression in numerous customs — embodied the central element. This meant that family relations were structured vertically. "...Set up filial piety, and it will fill the space from earth to heaven; spread it out, and it will extend over all the ground to the four seas; hand it down to future ages, and from morning to evening it will be observed; push it on the eastern sea, the western sea, the southern sea, and it will be (everywhere) the law for men and their obedience to it will be uniform. There will be a fulfillment of the words of the ode (III, I ode 10, 6), 'From west to east, from south to north, there was no unsubmissive thought' ".[5]

Since family relations are the model for the state, vertical structures also prevailed in the organization of government. It was not only a duty for the son to serve his parents, but a virtue for everybody to be content with one's own place in society. "1. The superior man does what is proper to the station in which he is; he does not desire to get beyond this. 2. In a position of wealth and honor, he does what is proper to a position of wealth and honor. In a poor and low position, he does what is proper to a poor and low position. Situated among barbarous tribes, he does what is proper to a situation among barbarous tribes. In a position of sorrow and difficulty, he does what is proper to a position of sorrow and difficulty. The superior man can find himself in no situation in which he is not himself".[6] Sensing and accepting the differences in society had been of the essence in Confucianist Korea. The continuation of these traditions facilitated autocratic rule such as the presidency of Syngman Rhee.

Political Parties

Since Syngman Rhee was in the center of political developments in Korea, criticism has mainly been directed at him. But he was not the only one responsible for politics taking a wrong turn.

---

[4] Juergen Kleiner (1980) pp. 321 ff.; Koh, Byong Ik, "Confucianism in Contemporary Korea", in Tu Wei-Ming (Editor) *Confucian Traditions in East Asian Modernity*, Cambridge 1996, pp. 191 ff.

[5] Li Chi, *Book of Rights*, Book XXI Section II 12, translated by James Legge, edited by Chu Chai and Winberg Chai, Vol. II, New York 1967, p. 227.

[6] *The Doctrine of the Mean*, Chapter XIV, by James Legge, *The Chinese Classics*, Vol. I Hongkong 1960, p. 395.

To establish a democratic state in a country which had been ruled until the turn of the century by an authoritarian monarch and his advisers and afterwards by occupying powers was a difficult undertaking. These difficulties were magnified as the social fabric had been destroyed and had also become amorphous as illustrated during the Korean War which had been a vortex of the worst kind. It was imperative, therefore, to develop a civil society in order to create cohesiveness. Political parties could greatly contribute to this development by enabling the people to convert their newly won sovereignty into practical politics.

Political parties were founded after the war but the results of the process were chaotic. In 1947, the US military government registered 354 political parties and social organizations. The political party system was poorly developed as illustrated by the success of independent candidates in the first three elections for the National Assembly: In 1948 Independents won 42.9% of the seats, in 1950 even 80% and in 1954 still 33%. Only in 1958 their number shrank to 11.8%.

Syngman Rhee, as already mentioned, had originally tried to find a platform beyond political parties. He did so by relying on the support of changing groups, the core of which was the National Association for the Rapid Realization of Korean Independence. When he discovered that there was no majority in the Assembly elected in 1950 for his re-election and he, therefore, decided to introduce the system of direct presidential elections he founded, at the same time, the Liberal Party which absorbed various groups. The Liberal Party which claimed to serve the interest of workers and farmers was attractive to all those who wanted their share in ruling the country. The Liberal Party did not focus on realizing political ideas but rather on monopolizing government authority. The Liberal Party presented candidates for the first time in 1954 and received 55.2% of the seats in the National Assembly. In 1958 its candidates won 54.1% of the seats. The Liberal Party remained the ruling party until the end of Syngman Rhee's era. Besides Syngman Rhee, Lee Ki Poong, who was the Speaker of the Assembly for many years, played an important role within the Liberal Party. He was a moderate man and had close ties with the family of Syngman Rhee; the President and his wife adopted the eldest son of Lee Ki Poong in 1957.

It was by chance that the Democrats became the opposition party of the Rhee era. The Korean Democratic Party of Kim Song Su and Song Chin U, the party of the well-to-do and the well-educated, was as conservative as

Syngman Rhee's National Association. The Democrats had voted for Syngman Rhee when he was elected President for the first time in 1948 hoping, that he would honor this support when he was forming his cabinet. But Syngman Rhee reacted otherwise, only his first minister of finance, Kim To Yon, was a leading Democrat. Kim Song Su, however, did not get an office. Disappointed, the Korean Democratic Party joined the opposition. In February 1949 it absorbed various groups and was renamed the Democratic National Party. In the new party Kim Song Su, Cho Byong Ok (Cho Pyong Ok) and Shin Ik Hui became the leaders. The election results of the new party were poor: In 1950 it won just 11.4% and in 1954 7.4% of the National Assembly seats. After having broadened its basis as a reaction to the constitutional conflict in 1954, the party became more successful. Its candidate, Chang Myun, was elected vice-president in 1955. In the 1958 election, the Democrats won 33.9% of the seats. The party's effectiveness had been badly spoiled by conflicts between the "old" faction of Shin Ik Hui and Cho Byong Ok, and the "new" faction of Chang Myun. Korean factionalism and disunity were alive and destructive.

There was no room for leftist groups in the Republic of Korea. The People's Republic and the People's Committees of Lyuh Woon Hyung had been banned by the American military government already in 1945. The left had boycotted the first elections of the National Assembly. The National Security Law passed by the National Assembly at the end of 1948 had been used against communists. The only considerable movement of the left was the Progressive Party of Cho Pong Am which adhered to socialist ideas, propagated a centrally planned economy, but rejected communist dictatorship. Cho Pong Am had originally been a communist, but had cut off relations in 1940. He achieved remarkable results in the presidential elections of 1952 and 1956. In 1958 he was indicted for having cooperated with the North Korean communists and sentenced to capital punishment on the basis of rather vague evidence. On 31 July 1959 he was executed. Ever since, no leftist political party has succeeded in the Republic of Korea. In a country where anti-communism had become a sort of state religion, socialists have always been condemned as fellow travelers of the communists.

The absence of a strong leftist party was only one of the deficiencies in the development of the political parties in South Korea. It was also of a disadvantage that personalities were more important than programs. The parties were not associations of like-minded people trying to realize common ideas but loose groupings of personalities and their followers. Clan chiefs gathered followers in their regions. Therefore, the Korean sickness of factionalism continued to exist. Factionalism was stronger in the opposition parties than in the ruling party, because the ruling party was led by the President of the Republic who held all the power in the country. As the parties did not fight in order to realize ideas, groups and their leading personalities were subjected to frequent changes. Syngman Rhee's chief of police, Cho Byong Ok, and his Prime Minister, Chang Myun, became leading oppositionists later. Cho Pong Am, the leader of the Progressive Party, was originally a trusted lieutenant of Syngman Rhee and served as his first Minister of Agriculture. Political parties had neither a broad basis nor a satisfactory organization. As their programs were of a general and vague character, there were neither actual alternatives nor a dialogue between ruling and opposition parties. Altogether, the political party system was much to weak to fulfill its role within the framework of a democratic institution.

Domestic Politics

The Republic of Korea, although showing the attributes of a democratic institution, was an autocratically ruled country; the president held unrestricted government authority at his disposal. Syngman Rhee was able to turn his attention to many questions at the same time, but he could not manage to handle all major government operations himself. He appointed, therefore, his followers as government officials and threatened his ministers with dismissal. In the twelve years of his rule, he went through 8 prime ministers and approximately 100 ministers, among them 20 ministers of interior. He tried to undermine the independence of judges, provided for in Art. 77 of the Constitution, by influencing their appointments massively. His manipulations were not without success, as illustrated by the trial against Cho Pong Am.

After a long life of agitation, Syngman Rhee knew the importance of a government propaganda machine. He showed particular interest in the Office of Public Information which he had founded. Newspapers risked being banned from time to time. There was, however, a critical press and public discussions which illustrated that Syngman Rhee's Korea was not organized in a way which could be called totalitarian.[7] In order to seize complete hold of the individual,

[7]The CIA accused Syngman Rhee in a report in 1950 of using totalitarian tactics; quoted by Cumings pp. 340 and 341 with note 6.

an ideology beyond just anti-communism would have been necessary. Syngman Rhee's "one people principle" (*il minchui*) aimed at creating national unity in thinking and in action, but this philosophy was too simple and shallow to be attractive.[8]

One of the factors which hindered democratic development was corruption. It was an old evil and very dangerous because the Korean society was used to accepting it as unavoidable. Even public affairs contain private favors, a Korean proverb says. The miserable salaries of government officials, the difficult economic situation as well as the general atmosphere of manipulation facilitated corruption.

Economically, the Republic of Korea faced difficulties indeed. During the Japanese rule, the regions of Korea had been developed in a different way, as was already mentioned. This had disastrous consequences after Korea had been divided. The South had developed predominantly as an agrarian country with only some light industries. Most of the heavy industries as well as all of the power generation was located in the North. The situation in the South deteriorated when the Japanese experts withdrew and when later many refugees arrived from the North. During the war, many factories were destroyed. Inflation was tremendous, amounting to 81.9% in 1955. Only thanks to US aid, South Korea could slowly recover. What was missing was a consistent economic policy which promoted investments and expanded infrastructure.

Being an agrarian country, one of the most urgent issues of the Republic of Korea was land reform. Already in 1948, the US military government had distributed most of the former Japanese-held lands to Korean farmers. Art. 86 of the Constitution provided that farmland would be distributed to self-tilling farmers, and in 1949, the Assembly determined the method of distribution by law. Leased land was purchased by the state which sold it to the tenants who had to pay in kind. The aim to convert former tenants and agricultural laborers into independent farmers was achieved only to a certain extent. The tenants who had to purchase the land often got into debt which sometimes resulted in a new tenant-landlord relationship. At the end of the Rhee era, leased land had emerged on a large scale. The land tax had to be paid in kind as in the past.

The expansion of the educational system was also urgent. First of all, illiteracy had to be fought because at the end of the Japanese era, less than

[8]Henderson pp. 284 and 285.

half of all Korean children had attended elementary school. Elementary education was made compulsory by Art. 16 of the Constitution and was by and by realized with the result that most of those born after 1945 received school education. In the beginning of the 1950s, illiteracy stood at 10% because not all of those belonging to the older generation had a chance to make up their schooling later. This figure should not be deceiving. Koreans have an extreme thirst for education. Korean families have always sacrificed to give their children a good education. The respect for education, originating from Confucian thinking, broke through as soon as ample opportunities were offered to receiving education.

The Fundamentals of Foreign Relations

After the US administration had corrected its disengagement policy under great sacrifices and had saved the integrity of the Republic of Korea during the Korean War, there was no danger that the mistakes of 1949, when US forces were withdrawn would be repeated. Soon after the Armistice Agreement was signed, Secretary of State John Foster Dulles came to Seoul in order to discuss a bilateral defense treaty. In Art. III of the US-Korean Mutual Defense Treaty, signed on 1 October 1953, each side recognized "that an armed attack in the Pacific area on either of the parties in territories now under their respective administrative control, or hereafter recognized by one of the parties as lawfully brought under the administrative control of the other, would be dangerous for its own peace and safety and declares that it would act to meet the common danger in accordance with its constitutional process".[9] The reservation meant that the US would not be automatically involved in hostilities on the Korean peninsula. But another, far more effective automatism existed. Because American forces remained in South Korea and some units were deployed close to the Demilitarized Zone, US troops would be inevitably involved in any hostilities. This was and is a fact to be taken into consideration by North Korea. This trip wire effect has been the key element of deterrence. The US government can react very quickly in case North Korean forces attack and also involve US forces into the hostilities. In such an emergency, in case of an attack on US forces, the President is authorized by the War Powers

[9] Text in Chung Kyung Cho (1956) pp. 313 and 314.

Resolution of 1973 to introduce US Armed Forces into hostilities without declaration of war or specific authorization.[10] When the Mutual Defense Treaty entered into force on 17 November 1954, Agreed Minutes were signed in which South Korea expressed its intention to "Retain Republic of Korea forces under the operational control of the United Nations Command while that Command has responsibilities for the defense of the Republic of Korea, unless after consultation it is agreed that our mutual and individual interest would best be served by a change".[11] Thus the South Korean forces remained, as they had during the war, under the US operational control. Operational control gives command only in case of a military action. However, one has to be prepared for that situation. Thus, the American protector had received an instrument to counteract South Korean's unpredictability.

The defense treaty with the United States was the basis of South Korea's security. Syngman Rhee's foreign policy focused one-sidedly on the US. The American government supported the South Korean economy. The Joint Statement issued after Dulles' visit on 7 August 1953 figured that the aid program for the Korean economy needed approximately 1 billion dollars of funds for a period of 3 to 4 years.[12] However, the US invested far more funds over a much longer period of time. In spite of the generosity of the US, relations between the two allies were not free of tension. Syngman Rhee continued to remind the US administration of its policy of liberation; he warned against the dangers of coexistence and recommended a policy of strength against the communists. He also demanded to equip the South Korean forces with nuclear artillery. He remained an ally difficult to influence.

The Armistice Agreement had recommended holding a conference in order to insure the peaceful settlement of the Korean question. A resolution of the UN General Assembly (A/Res. 711 (VIII)) on 28 August 1953 supported that recommendation. As the preparatory talks between both sides in Panmunjom did not produce any results, the conference could not be held within the allotted three month after the signing of the Armistice Agreement as had been envisaged by the Armistice Agreement. The foreign ministers of the Big Four agreed, however, during their conference in Berlin in

---

[10]Larry A. Niksch, *South Korea: US Defense Obligations*, Congressional Research Service, The Library of Congress, 1 April 1994.

[11]United Nations Treaty Series No. 3635.

[12]Kim Se-Jin, (1976) p. 184.

February 1954 to meet in Geneva to discuss two important issues, Korea and Indochina. The conference began its work on 25 April 1954. On the Eastern side, the Soviet Union, the PRC and the DPRK, represented by their foreign ministers Molotov, Zhou Enlai and Nam Il, participated. On the Western side, all countries which had provided forces to the UN Command (with the exception of South Africa) were present. Among the representatives of the 15 Western countries, Secretary of State Dulles, the US Undersecretary of State Walter Beddell Smith, the British Foreign Minister Anthony Eden and the South Korean Foreign Minister Pyun Yung Tai were leading the way.

The crucial question was on how to bring about the unification of Korea for which everybody was speaking up. In his first statement on 27 April 1954, the South Korean Foreign Minister chose a simplistic approach.[13] He demanded that since free elections had already been held in the South, now free elections had to follow in the North in order to fill the hundred seats left vacant in the South Korean National Assembly. Later, he agreed that the elections could be held in both the North and the South, and supervised by the UN. The latter condition was unacceptable for the communist side because it considered the involvement of the UN in the Korean War illegal. The communists suggested that the elections should be prepared by an all-Korean commission composed of equal numbers of representatives from the North and the South; the supervision of the elections would be done by the Neutral Nations Supervisory Commission established by the Armistice Agreement. These were clever suggestions; as in both commissions East/North and West/South would have the same number of votes, an automatic communist veto was in-built. Also, regarding the question on the withdrawal of troops, no agreement could be reached. On 15 July 1954, the Western countries broke off negotiations because they were in vain. The Republic of Korea and the DPRK was only interested in a solution which would enable each of them to incorporate the other part of the country. Thus, it was not surprising that no common basis for an agreement could be found. Since no agreement for a peaceful settlement had been reached, the Armistice Agreement remained in effect according to its paragraph 62.

After the failure of the Geneva Conference, it was the United Nations' turn again to address the Korean question. On 11 December 1954, the General

[13]Text in Pyun Yung Tai, *Korea. My Country*, Seoul 1954, pp. 32 ff.

Assembly approved the report on the Geneva Conference and confirmed that it was the aim of the UN to establish, by peaceful means, a united, independent and democratic Korea with a representative form of government and to restore world peace and security in the area (A/Res. 811 (IX)). By overwhelming majorities, the General Assembly also confirmed these aims in the following years. The UN remained present in Korea through the UN Command and the UN Commission for the Unification and Rehabilitation of Korea (UNCURK) which had succeeded UNCOK at the end of 1950 (A/Res. 376 (V) on 7 October 1950).

The Armistice Agreement came under heavy attack by the South Korean government. They argued that a truce had to be followed either by a peace treaty or by the resumption of hostilities. As the Geneva Conference had not achieved any success, the South Korean government would have preferred massive actions, even a preemptive strike, if it had not been stopped by the Americans. It now focussed on the removal of the Armistice Agreement. Even when the Chinese withdrew their troops from North Korea in 1958,the South Korean government was unwilling to show leniency. It raised sharp criticism against the Neutral Nations Supervisory Commission. Things had gone wrong because of the obstructive attitude of the representatives of Poland and Czechoslovakia. Reaching decisions was impossible as both sides had the same number of votes. It would have been important that the Commission functioned, because North Korea violated the prohibition to reinforce its weapons by expanding its airforce and its artillery. The UN Command reacted on 31 May 1956 by forbidding the members of the Commission from any activities in the South. In August 1957, the UN Command declared itself to be relieved of the obligations not to reinforce its weapons in Korea (UN Doc. A/3631, dated 13 August 1957). The members of the Neutral Nations Supervisory Commission, the representatives of Sweden, Switzerland, Poland and Czechoslovakia continued to meet at Panmunjom, but had no chance to fulfill their functions of supervising the prohibition of the Armistice Agreement to reinforce weapons and military personnel.[14]

Syngman Rhee's foreign policy was extremely anticommunist. Communism was considered to be a deadly disease, a satanic religion. Negotiations with the "reds", particularly with the "puppets" in Pyongyang were inconceivable, even contacts with the North were considered treason. This attitude excluded any progress in the relations with the North.

---

[14]For an analysis of the Swiss position, see Neue Züricher Zeitung, 27/28 December 1986.

South Korea and Japan

During the 1950s, one could hear the question in Seoul whom Syngman Rhee hated more, the communists or the Japanese. The South Korean President was definitely no friend of the Japanese and did not demonstrate diplomatic skills in the negotiations with the former colonial power which began at the end of 1951. It is, however, an exaggeration to only blame him for the stagnation of South Korean–Japanese relations. It was a difficult task to normalize relations with the former rulers who had left so many bad memories in Korea. Also, the Japanese government was to be blamed because its intransigence made progress impossible in the many South Korean–Japanese conferences. Controversies centered on fishery questions, financial demands and the fate of Koreans residing in Japan.

Since Japan declined to enter into negotiations concerning fisheries, South Korea took the initiative. In a Proclamation of Sovereignty over Adjacent Seas, dated 18 January 1952, President Syngman Rhee fixed the so-called peace line which was running between 20 to 200 nautical miles away from the coast.[15] The South Korean government claimed sovereignty inside this area for the purpose of exploration of the natural resources on the continental shelf and for fishery conservation. This line, called the Rhee line in Japan, was anything but a peace line. South Korea started seizing vessels found within the line and sentenced the Japanese fishermen. In the period from 1952 to 1954, a total of 232 Japanese vessels were seized and 2784 fishermen were sentenced to prison terms.[16] Japan's fishing industry was considerably hurt by the South Korean measures. The Japanese government considered the Rhee line illegal and evoked the freedom of fishing on the high seas. It argued that according to international law, coastal waters were only three nautical miles deep. South Korea, at that time, was not alone in its attempt to expand its sovereignty along its coasts. Many years later, in 1982, the Law of the Sea Convention enabled coastal states to establish an exclusive economic zone of 200 nautical miles away from the base line.[17]

---

[15] Park Jong Sung, "An Analysis of the Korea Japan Fishery Dispute", in *Koreana Quarterly* Vol. 5 No. 2 (Summer 1963) pp. 65 ff.

[16] Kim Kwang Bong p. 60.

[17] Ignaz Seidl-Hohenveldern, *Völkerrecht*, 9th edition, Köln 1997, pp. 223 ff.

The considerable Japanese property in South Korea had been confiscated by the US military government and later transferred to the Republic of Korea. In Art. 4 of the US–Japanese Peace Treaty on 8 September 1951, Japan had recognized the validity of these dispositions.[18] During the normalization talks with South Korea, Japan took an opposite view, claiming that it had not waived its original rights and claims to property in Korea.[19] Japan compared its claims with the South Korean claims for restitution of losses suffered during the Japanese rule. Both sides claimed huge amounts of money. Only at the end of 1957 did Japan, under US pressure, renounce its property claims against Korea.

At the end of the Pacific War, approximately 2 million Koreans resided in Japan; many of them had come as forced laborers. After the war, most of them returned home, but 600,000 Koreans remained in Japan, primarily for economic reasons. The status of the Koreans in Japan was not precisely fixed. In the first years after the war, they had enjoyed privileges as they were members of a country liberated from Japanese rule. Later, they had been registered as foreigners and had become subject to all sorts of discrimination. This development had pushed quite a number of them (1955: 180,000) in the arms of Chosen Soren (Chongryon in Korean), the procommunist organization of Koreans in Japan. The pro-South Korea residents were organized in the Mindan. The South Korean government tried to improve the status of the Koreans residing in Japan during the course of its talks with the Japanese government. The Japanese were somewhat receptive to this issue but found it difficult to decide whether it should consider the Koreans in Japan as citizens of North Korea or of South Korea. From the end of 1959, the Japanese government started repatriating Koreans residing in Japan to North Korea if they wished to move there. The South Korean government protested against this policy even though it had not undertaken any remarkable efforts to repatriate the Koreans living in Japan to the South. Attracted by promises of economic advantages, a great number of Koreans — by 1955 approximately 85,000 — moved from Japan to North Korea.[20] This development brought the South

[18]Text in: *Documents on American Foreign Relations* Vol. XIII January 1–December 31, 1951, published for World Peace Foundation, New York 1953, pp. 470 ff.

[19]Lee Jin Won, "Brief Survey of Korean–Japanese Relations (Post-War Period)", in *Koreana Quarterly* Vol. 1 No. 1 (Summer 1959) p. 76.

[20]Kim Kwan Bong p. 52.

Korean–Japanese talks to a standstill. The fate of Japanese wives who accompanied their Korean husbands on their moves to the DPRK has remained an important political issue in Japan over the years.

More important than the specific problems was the question of the basis on relations between the two countries. The question had not been sufficiently answered by the US–Japanese Peace Treaty in which Japan had recognized Korea's independence. In order to get the relations between the two countries organized, a new foundation had to be found. It seemed natural to the Koreans that the process had to be started by easing the strains of the past. The Korean government, therefore, insisted that Japan apologized for its misdeeds and declared the treaties which had led to the subjugation of Korea as invalid *ex tunc* (from the beginning). From the South Korean perspective, the agreement to be concluded with Japan was to be something like a peace treaty. The Koreans tried to join the victors of the war; this was understandable but disregarded the fact that Korea's liberation had not been the result of Korean efforts.

The Japanese government disagreed strongly. It insisted that Japan had not been at war with Korea, and was only willing to find an arrangement for future relations. The Japanese attitude was expressed in a statement by the head of the Japanese delegation, Kanichiro Kubota in October 1953. Of this statement, which was only read and not mentioned in the minutes, various accounts are given. It appears undisputed that he said that the Japanese rule had brought benefits to Korea, and that, therefore, Japan was entitled to pursue property claims. According to Korean sources, Kubota further stated[21]:

— It was a violation of international law that Japanese territories and properties were disposed of prior to the conclusion of a peace treaty.
— The repatriation of Japanese nationals from Korea to Japan violated international law.
— The reference to the enslavement of the Korean people in the Cairo Declaration was an expression of wartime hysteria.

It was surprising how quickly the Japanese had found a way back to an attitude of self-confidence mixed with arrogance. Later, the Japanese government

[21]Kim Kwan Bong p. 48; Lee Chin Won op. cit. pp. 78 and 79; Oliver, "Korean–Japanese Discord", In *Korean Quarterly* Vol. 6 No. 5 (May 1957) p. 5; paper of the South Korean Ministry of Foreign Affairs (undated) in the author's possession.

withdrew Kubota's statement officially, but any progress in the relations between both countries was out of reach.

The Student Uprising on 19 April 1960

Manipulation was the signature tune in the Republic of Korea during the era of Syngman Rhee. This was clearly illustrated during elections when the government tried all sorts of tricks to rig them. The government distributed favors before elections. It also made clear that those constituencies which tended toward the opposition had to expect disadvantages. Its most important instrument used in rigging the elections was the police which transmitted the government's wishes to the remotest corners of the country.

Supporting the candidates of the Liberal Party and obstructing the activities of the oppositionists were some of the missions of the police. If necessary, gangs were hired in order to scare the oppositionists. There were also other tactics used to distort election results.[22] There was, for example, the "owl ballot": The votes were counted at dusk — a power failure would come in handy — by people with perspicacity who "discovered" far more votes for the ruling side than for the opposition. Government manipulations of elections differed, but elections were never free in Rhee's Korea.

Rigging of elections reached their peak in the presidential elections on 15 March 1960. Since the government was not sure whether it would win, Minister of Home Affairs Choe In Kyu had recommended that government officials take extraordinary measures and not mind laws and rules.[23] The government gave instructions

- to insert 40% of the ballots into the boxes before voting;
- to group voters into nine- or three-man units for the purpose of mutual supervision;
- to provide arm bands to party supporters in order to exert psychological pressure upon opposition voters;
- to keep election supervisors of the opposition parties out of balloting places by means of threat or bribery.

[22] Hahn Ki Shik, "Underlying Factors in Political Party Organization and Elections", in Wright pp. 92 ff; pyonchanui p. 472.

[23] Hahn Ki Shik op. cit. p. 94.

Those methods showed fantasy, but were ugly and unmistakably denied the democratic process. The political process in Syngman Rhee's Korea had reached a low.

The preparations and manipulations would not have been necessary to secure Syngman Rhee's reelection. Exactly four years ago, his opponent — the Democratic Party had nominated Cho Byong Ok from the "old" faction — died shortly before the elections. Thus, Rhee's reelection was assured. But the preparations had their impact on the election of the vice president. This time Lee Ki Poong from the Liberals won against Chang Myun from the Democrats. Lee Ki Poong won 8,337,059 (79.2%) of the 10,527,445 votes, Chang Myun won only 1,843,750 (17.5%). Lee Ki Poong will have felt assured to take a decisive step to become the successor of Syngman Rhee who was meanwhile 85 years old.

The Democratic Party, the Opposition in the National Assembly, protested against the rigging of the elections and tried to have them declared null and void. But it did not seem that the protest would have any consequences.

Demonstration protesting the rigging of the elections in Masan, a southern seaport, had serious consequences. Bloody clashes with the police occurred. On 11 April 1960, the dead body of Kim Chu Yol, a student, was found in the harbor with grenade fragments in his eye socket. This not only ignited large demonstrations by the students in Masan, but the event set off protests in many big cities throughout the country. A development was set in motion which was violent, chaotic and uncontrollable. On 18 April 1960, 3,000 students from Korea University demonstrated peacefully in Seoul against the violence of the police and for the cancellation of the presidential elections. On their return from the downtown area, they were attacked by gangs hired by the government; many were hurt. The news of this incident spread rapidly. The result was a huge demonstration the next day in Seoul. The students marched first to the National Assembly building and then to the presidential palace Kyungmudae. When the masses came closer to the palace, police opened fire. Many students were injured, more than one hundred killed. Emotions increased. Police boxes and other buildings were set on fire.

The ruler in Kyungmudae reacted, as he had always done, by violence and cunning. He imposed martial law and called in troops. He closed schools and universities and censored the press. He also tried to lessen tensions. He announced that he would leave the Liberal Party and change his cabinet. But this time, his method did not work. He should have considered it a bad omen that his old friends, the Americans, turned away.[24] After the Korean Ambassador in Washington had been called in by the Secretary of State, the US announced, among other things: "The Secretary suggested that the Korean government should, in its own best interest and in order to restore public confidence, take necessary and effective action aimed at protecting democratic rights of speech, of assembly and of the press, as well as preserving the secrecy of the ballot and preventing unfair discrimination against political opponents of a party in power".[25] That was good advice which should have been given much earlier, at least before the elections. By this time, it only meant that the US administration was letting Syngman Rhee down.

Calls for Syngman Rhee's resignation spread rapidly. On 25 April 1960, the opposition asked for it in the National Assembly. Professors of many universities, supported by huge crowds, did the same on the streets of Seoul. The military, commanded by Lieutenant General Song Yo Chang, a thoughtful man, sympathized with the protestors and did not step in. Left alone, Syngman Rhee announced on 26 April 1960 his willingness to resign if the people so desired. On 27 April 1960 he resigned officially. His presumptive heir Lee Ki Poong committed suicide on 28 April 1960 together with his wife and his two sons.[26]

The uprising in April 1960 was more than just a revolt. It was neither planned nor organized, but broke out spontaneously. The Rhee regime had taught the students the technique of "spontaneous" demonstrations when, for example, it had organized demonstrations against the repatriation of Koreans from Japan to the DPRK. The April uprising was a movement of the intellectuals, brought about by students and professors, who were supported by the urban population in Seoul and other big cities. The younger generation, which had been educated with Western ideas, realized the conflict between democratic ideas and the Korean reality, a conflict which had been illustrated once again by the rigged elections on 15 April 1960. The younger generation turned against Rhee's police state and stood for a fair system. The ruling elite did not feel strong enough to fight the new development. The police had shot at the students, but the military did not, yet the military was the only force left which could have secured the survival of Syngman Rhee's Liberals.

[24] For details see Cumings pp. 344 ff.

[25] Kim Se-Jin, (1976) p. 259.

[26] Details in Korea Times, 7 April 1985.

Approximately one third of the Liberals had left their parliamentary group on 25 April 1960 already and had joined the opposition.

Syngman Rhee, who had started his career as a revolutionary, was toppled by a revolution. When he left for Hawaii on 29 May 1960, he did so as an unloved despot whom the people had got rid of. Today he is nearly forgotten in South Korea. A memorial statue stands in Hawaii where he died on 19 July 1965, but not in South Korea.[27] Only his widow surviving him for many years and his relatives tried to keep his memory alive. A broader public might perhaps appreciate his contribution to save the integrity of South Korea when he had fought resolutely against the attack from the North.

A Period of Transition

Syngman Rhee had been toppled, the old system was dissolving, but by whom and in which way should the country be governed? The supporters of the April revolution, the students, were not prepared for such a task. Something strange happened: The transition took place within the framework of the old constitution and by representatives of the old establishment.

As Chang Myun had resigned as vice president in order to protest against the Rhee regime, it was up to the highest ranking member of the State Council (Art. 52 of the Constitution), i.e. to the Foreign Minister, to act for the President. Thus, Huh Chung (Ho Chong) who had just been appointed Foreign Minister by Syngman Rhee became the Acting President. Huh Chong had been a close friend of Rhee as they had already worked together in the US. In the early years of the Republic, he had held several cabinet posts and had become mayor of Seoul at the end of the 1950s. He had been a founding member of the Korean Democratic Party, but joined neither the Democratic nor the Liberal Party later. Since he was considered to be rather independent, he was accepted as chief executive. He was a cautious man and had only limited success in implementing the revolution by non-revolutionary means.

To create the framework for a democratic beginning, the old constitution had to be amended. The Amendments were passed by the old Assembly elected in 1958 and were promulgated on 15 June 1960. The new provisions tried to prevent authoritarian developments. The parliamentary form of government

---

[27]Korea Herald, 17 August 1985.

was introduced: A cabinet presided by the prime minister as chief executive was responsible to the lower house (House of Representatives). The president, who was to be elected by the House of Representatives and the upper house (House of Councilors), was given only ceremonial functions. The rights of the citizens were no longer subjected to statutory limitations.

Elections for the National Assembly followed on 29 July 1960. They were really free and brought victory for the Democratic Party which won 175 (75.1%) of the 233 seats of the Lower House and 31 (53.4%) seats of the Upper House. The leftist parties were too divided to rally enough voters behind their programs. The Socialist Mass Party, the largest leftist party, won only 4 seats (6% of the votes) in the Lower House.

The result was remarkable. The Democratic Party had been an opposition party in the First Republic, but had not actively taken part in the uprising against the ancient regime. Its victory was due to the fact that it was the only larger party left after the Liberal Party had been dissolved when Syngman Rhee had left. The Democratic Party, though belonging to the establishment of the First Republic, was now left handling the heritage of the April revolution, a rather impossible mission.

There were other difficulties too. Within the Democratic Party, there were conflicts between its two factions resulting mainly from personal animosities. The election of Yun Po Sun, a descendent of a wealthy *yangban* family for President, went well. The election of the Prime Minister, however, did not. Kim To Yon from the "old" faction, who had been nominated by Yun Po Sun, did not receive the necessary majority votes in the Assembly. Thus Chang Myun, the leader of the "new" faction, became Prime Minister. Chang Myun who had already been Prime Minister under Syngman Rhee was a cautious man, a democrat and a person of integrity, but did not live up to the expectations of a strong and dynamic leader. After Yun Po Sun and Chang Myun had assumed office on 23 August 1960, the Second Republic finally started working.

The task ahead for the Chang Myun administration was not easy. The post-revolutionary atmosphere demanded that the representatives of the old system account for their misdeeds. Already under the Huh Chung government, various people who were responsible for the rigging of the elections and for the killing of demonstrators had been indicted. The "revolutionaries" considered the sentences passed on 48 defendants by the Seoul District Court on 8 October 1960 as too lenient. Students staged demonstrations to protest; some of them intruded into the chamber of the House of Representatives and interrupted the session. According to the demands of the students who were supported by the press, two laws were passed to punish "anti-democratic criminals". At the same time, the constitutional provision prohibiting retroactive punishment was abolished. The new laws were used to remove government officials, from the Rhee era, from their posts. The laws were applied to approximately 2,500 policemen. Since the Chang Myun government had already dismissed several thousand policemen earlier — the April uprising was finally caused by the violence of the police — the police force, completely demoralized, ceased to function. Therefore, public order and security were endangered, criminality increased.

Numerous, nearly daily demonstrations for very different reasons occurred during the first six months of the Second Republic. The system was denounced as a "government by demonstrations" or a "government of the unknown student". Radical groups emerged which disliked the considerate approach of the Chang Myun government. The parties of the left and the National Students' Federation for National Unification (Mintong) favored contacts with North Korea and the neutralization of Korea. A proposal of the Students' Federation in May 1961 to hold a conference of students from South and North in Panmunjom was also supported by an organization of teachers. Now the right reacted and staged demonstrations. The government failed to restrict the wild demonstrations and procommunist activities. The leniency of the Chang Myun government towards the demands of the radicals was caused by its lack of revolutionary legitimacy of which it was very conscious, "conscious to a fault" as Henderson has put it.[28]

Conflicts within the ruling party added to the general instability. In November 1960, the Democratic Party split. The "old" faction of Yun Po Sun formed the New Democratic Party with Kim To Yon as party chief. While the fight against Syngman Rhee had held the two factions together, they were now falling apart in pursuit of power and influence. Since Chang Myun also lost support of the younger members of his own faction, he lost his parliamentary majority. Chang Myun had to change the members of his cabinet several times, thus giving rise to the feeling that the chief executive lacked determination. His position was further undermined when he had to impose unpopular measures, a devaluation of the Korean currency, the Hwan, and a reduction in the defense budget. Even when it mattered, Korean politicians were unable to stand together.

---

[28]Henderson p. 180.

The political leadership from the Syngman Rhee era belonged to the bourgeoisie, to the class of landlords, businessmen and government officials. Most of them have had a university degree and many of them had been active as civil servants or educators before entering politics. The political leadership of the Second Republic had a similar background, except that the percentage of the well educated was even higher. The student revolution had toppled Syngman Rhee, Lee Ki Poong and other Liberals. But those who tried a new beginning had belonged to the old elite. The general consensus, which had been so overwhelming in April 1960, did not last when daily, ordinary and extraordinary problems had to be solved. Chang Myun could not satisfy the demands of the radical groups which pretended to be the heirs of the revolution. He also lost the support of the administrative machinery. To the Korean citizens, who were used to being ruled from above, the Second Republic looked chaotic.

References

Sources:

Documents on Korean–American Relations 1943–1976, edited by Kim Se Jin, Research Center for Peace and Unification, Seoul 1976.

The Korean Problem at the Geneva Conference, April 26, June 15, 1954, Department of State Publication 5609, Washington, October 1954.

Where Korea Stands, Office of Public Information, Republic of Korea, Seoul 1955.

Allen, Richard C., *Korea's Syngman Rhee. An Unauthorized Portrait*, Ruttland and Tokyo, 1960.

Douglas, William A., "Korean Students and Politics", in *Asian Survey* Vol. III No. 12 (December 1963) pp. 584 ff.

Hahn, Bae Ho and Kim, Kyu Taik, "Korean Political Leaders (1952–1962): Their Social Origins and Skills", in *Asian Survey* Vol. III No. 7 (July 1963) pp. 305 ff.

Lee, Hwa Soo, "*An Analysis of the April Revolution in Korea*", in *Koreana Quarterly* Vol. 8 No. 2 (Summer 1966) pp. 96 ff.

Lee, Young Ho, "The Politics of Democratic Experiment. 1984–1974", in Wright pp. 13 ff.

Stone, Allan, "The Korean Student Revolution: A Political Analysis", in James, B. Palais, *Occasional Papers on Korea*, No. 2, March 1974, pp. 132 ff.

Pyonchanui, *Minju hankuk sawol hyokmyong sa* (*Publishing Committee, History of the April Revolution for a Democratic Korea*) Seoul 1960.

Chapter 8

The Rise of Park Chung Hee

The Putsch

When a policeman, who had fallen asleep in his station, was awakened by soldiers in the early morning hours on 16 May 1961 in Seoul, he got up — and so the story goes — and shouted: "Long live the People's Army". He thought the North Koreans had again invaded the South. He was mistaken. The soldiers in front of him were South Koreans. They belonged to a small group composed of approximately 3,600 men from various units, including marines, paratroops, artillery and infantry whose officers had started a revolt against the Chang Myun government. Since they did not meet much resistance, they had already seized the strategically important points — the government building, the city hall, police stations, power plants, radio stations — all before the first light of dawn. At 5.00 a.m., the rebels appealed to the public by radio to support the military revolution. During the same day when martial law was proclaimed, the National Assembly was dissolved and all political activities were prohibited.

Incredible but true: The government did not attempt to resist these developments. After the news of the revolt had reached Prime Minister Chang Myun in his suite in the Bando Hotel, he went into hiding. Though the rebels did not face much resistance in the provinces, they had not yet achieved their goals. It was imperative to persuade the military commanders, who held key positions, that a military takeover was inevitable and to win their support if possible. The key military commanders were the Commander, First Army, Lieutenant General Lee Han Lim, the Army Chief-of-Staff Chang Do Young and the Commander-in-Chief of the National Armed Forces, President Yun Po Sun. It was a strange revolt. The rebels did not do much shooting but rather a lot of negotiating.

The most urgent problem was to reach an understanding with Lieutenant General Lee Han Lim. Since he commanded the 20 divisions of the First Army, which were in a state of readiness for battle, his intervention on behalf of the government would be highly dangerous for the rebels. Lee Han Lim was not supportive of a putsch, but did not take any measures to quell it. For the moment, this was enough for the rebels. A couple of days later, after the success of the rebels was assured, Lee Han Lim was arrested. Lieutenant General Chang Do Young had been appointed Army Chief-of-Staff just three months ago by the Chang Myun government, an event which had caused a storm of indignation in the National Assembly because of his close relations to Lee Ki Poong. He reacted hesitantly to the demands of the rebels. They did not consider this as sufficient and tried to win the country's most influential military officer over. In the afternoon of 16 May 1961, he finally accepted the chairmanship of the newly formed Military Revolutionary Committee.

The President considered the administration of Chang Myun with whom he was on bad terms as weak and unpopular. Therefore Yun Po Sun, who had taken an oath to observe the constitution, accepted the breach of the constitutional order. He declined American suggestions to deploy troops against the rebels. The Americans were talking about supporting the legally constituted government but remained inactive. Following the demands of the rebels, President Yun Po Sun warned the Corps Commanders against bloodshed, sanctioned the proclamation of martial law and asked the cabinet ministers to come out of hiding. Yun Po Sun even remained in office as President, thus conveying the impression of constitutional continuity.

The South Koreans accepted the insurrection since they had seen enough chaos during the Second Republic. They also did not have much reason to respect their politicians who were calling themselves democrats, yet were adopting the patriarchal and arrogant attitudes of the former ruling class. The estimate of the rebels had been correct. After Chang Myun had resigned as Prime Minister on 18 May 1961, the leaders of the putsch, Major General Park Chung Hee, Major General (retd.) Kim Dong Ha and Colonel (retd.) Kim Jong Pil began to consolidate their position. Koreans would find out quickly that the new leaders were aiming at a radical change of politics.

Military Rule

The new rulers changed the government structure indeed and promulgated a law to enact the change on 6 June 1961.[1] A Supreme Council for National Reconstruction was established which exercised the powers of the government as well as of the legislature and had far-reaching influence on the judiciary. The Council was composed of 20 to 32 officers on active duty. Members were chosen by co-option. The constitution of the Second Republic was not completely repealed, but was subjected to the law that was passed on 6 June 1961. Regardless, the Republic of Korea had become a military dictatorship.

Another agency was founded which would prove to be one of the most important and durable instruments of the Park era, the Central Intelligence Agency (*chungang chongpo pu*, abbr. *chung chon pu*), mostly called the Korean CIA. It was created by one of the masterminds of the insurrection, Colonel (retd.) Kim Jong Pil. He succeeded quickly in founding a machinery which would fulfil its most important task to prevent imitations of the insurrection on 16 May 1961. From the beginning, the KCIA was a controversial and dreaded agency which became known for its use of manipulations and violence. Though the KCIA was under the control of the Supreme Council, it became a state in the state and even persecuted members of the Supreme Council. One of the KCIA's first victims was Chang Do Young. He had first become Chairman of the Supreme Council and later became Prime Minister. But in the beginning of July 1961, he lost all his posts, was indicted for attempted insurrection and was sentenced to death. He was later pardoned and went into exile.

Now the head of the rebels, Major General Park Chung Hee assumed the chairmanship of the Supreme Council. Lieutenant General (retd.) Song Yo Chang, who had prevented more bloodshed on the last day of the First Republic, became Prime Minister. Another former officer, Lieutenant General (retd.) Kim Hong Il, who had been an officer with the Chinese Army, President of the Korean Military Academy and Ambassador in Taiwan, was appointed Foreign Minister.

Like military regimes everywhere, the new Korean rulers loved cleanliness and order. They tackled chaos and corruption. Spectacular crackdowns on hooligans, street toughs and smugglers were initiated. Businessmen who were suspected of having acquired assets illegally were checked. In the army and

---

[1]Text in Military Revolution pp. 149 ff.

the civil service, many thousands were purged. In the period from the end of July 1961 till the beginning of May 1962, a Revolutionary Court tried 679 persons of whom 15 were sentenced to death; 8 of them were executed.[2] Of the 1,573 newspapers, news services and other periodicals, 1,170 were closed.[3] These measures were supposed to "root out the old evils", but were also well suited to silence oppositionists. More than 4,000 politicians were blacklisted. Alleged communists were severely persecuted. Anti-communism was one of the two main arguments with which the military tried to legitimize its rule. The first of the Six Points announced on the first day of the insurrection stated: "Upholding anti-Communism as our foremost national policy, we will revitalize our anti-Communist stand which had heretofore been mere formality empty words".[4]

The other main argument used by the junta to supply legitimacy was its readiness for an economic reconstruction of the country. They said in their Six Points: "By swiftly relieving the destitution of the people on the verge of despair and starvation, we will concentrate on establishing a self-supporting economy".[5] And indeed the military regime started quickly to realize this idea. It introduced the first five-year plan for the period from 1962 to 1966 which focused on securing sources of energy, on improving mining and infrastructure, on increasing farm productivity and on improving the trade balance. Gross national product already grew considerably during the first five-year period. A successful development was started which was marked by rapid growth.

The Background

The units which staged the coup on 16 May 1961 were just a small force of 3,600 men. The rebels claimed that their group included 250 officers, their numbers were probably even smaller.[6] In an article on 16 May 1965, i.e. four years later, the Chosun Ilbo lists 94 key figures. In any case, it was just a tiny minority within the 600,000 men of the armed forces which had started the unrest. The unrest thus began as a revolt within the military.

---

[2]Korea Annual 1966 p. 285.

[3]Military Revolution p. 29.

[4]ibidem p. 202.

[5]ibidem p. 202.

[6]ibidem p. 17.

The rebels were headed by Major General Park Chung Hee who was known as an officer with leadership qualities who hated corruption. In the period from 1950 to 1961, he had been transferred 25 times and had finally become Deputy Commander of the Second Army. He had no reason to be particularly satisfied with his advancement. The same was true for the number two man of the rebels, Kim Dong Ha. He, a tough officer, had only made it to Brigadier General in the Marine Corps. When he had demanded to dismiss his allegedly corrupt superior in June 1960, he had been retired and promoted to Major General. Thanks to his participation, the rebel forces included marines. The mastermind of the revolt was the former intelligence officer Kim Jong Pil who was leading a group of dissatisfied colonels and who was a nephew of Park Chung Hee by marriage.

From the first hours, the rebels tried to transform their revolt into one of "the military". They succeeded in doing so. They convinced the Army Chief-of-Staff Chang Do Young to support them. They made the chiefs of the other services — Lieutenant General Kim Shin (Airforce), Vice Admiral Lee Sung Ho (Navy), Lieutenant General Kim Sung Eun (Marine Corps) and the Chairman Chiefs-of-Staff Lieutenant General Kim Chong Oh — members of the Supreme Council. The revolt had quickly been transformed into a coup d'état of the armed forces.

The officers were not a homogenous group, but divided into factions — the usual picture in Korea.[7] The factions were built along the lines of career and regional affiliations and were fighting each other. This continued even after the coup had resulted in frequent changes within the leadership. Officers who had belonged to the original small circle of conspirators were later removed from the seats of power; eight of them even ended up in jail. Officers who had originally been opposed to the putsch were awarded high and influential positions. Only Park Chung Hee survived and remained at the center of events.

The rebels called their action "a sort of medical operation"[8] in order to revive democracy and the transitory period "administrative democracy".[9] But these were just phrases. What Park Chung Hee and his followers actually did was something different. They substituted a representative democratic system by military dictatorship and a policy of energetic administration. They had

---

[7] Kim Se-Jin (1971) p. 61.

[8] Military Revolution p. 211.

[9] Kim Se-Jin (1971) p. 109.

learned to know this type of policy during the Japanese era. Park Chung Hee, Kim Dong Ha and other leading officers of the coup had served in the Manchurian army which had been set up and trained by the Japanese. That the Japanese model of a strict administration in the absence of politics was revived by the Korean officers illustrated the continuing impact of Japanese colonialism on developments in Korea.

In the beginning of the 1960s, many third world countries were ruled by military governments. But why did this also happen in South Korea, a country in which soldiers were traditionally inferior to civil servants? Various factors came together to encourage such a development.

During the Korean War, the South Korean armed forces had expanded tremendously. They amounted to 600,000 men and were supported by a huge defense budget. The armed forces had a strict discipline, were equipped with modern weapons, and had their own supplies and infrastructure. The initial stages of becoming a state within a state had already been passed.

Syngman Rhee had not contributed much to South Korea's modernization. He had not left functioning political institutions. The Korean society continued to lack cohesion. Syngman Rhee had personally manipulated and dominated the military, but civil control of the military through institutions had not been achieved. He had even misused the military to promote his personal ambitions, for example when he had imposed martial law over Pusan in 1952 and over Seoul in 1960. The political leadership of the Second Republic had intensified tensions between politicians and officers when it frequently reassigned the ministers of defense and the generals holding top military positions.

These developments paved the way for a coup d'état, they did not trigger it. The direct reason was a military one. Since the South Korean armed forces had been built into a huge machinery in a short period of time, the officers were unusually young.[10] In 1960, the average age of the altogether 15 3- and 4-star generals was 35 years. This meant that promotions were blocked for colonels and lieutenant colonels. They were particularly unhappy with this development as they considered many of their superiors, some of whom had only had a limited education and a short training, as not very capable and corrupted by the Rhee administration. Encouraged by the student revolution in 1960, the younger officers, particularly those of the 8th class, started from May 1960 on purification campaigns. They met, however, only limited success, and some of

[10]Kim Se-Jin (1971) pp. 56 ff.

their leaders, including Kim Jong Pil, had to retire. The younger dissatisfied officers made up the majority of the rebels in May 1960. Among the 94 officers mentioned in the Chosun Ilbo were 72 colonels and lieutenant colonels of whom 36 belonged to the 8th class of the military academy. The young officers had decided to look after their own interests. This made them rebels.

They called their action a revolution. That was just a way of speaking as the revolt occurred from above and not from below. The coup had, however, revolutionary traces as it resulted in an exchange within the ruling classes. The young officers, who now composed the pool for top government positions, did not originate from the bourgeoisie as the leadership of the First and Second Republic. Most of them came from a modest background. They had been trained in the natural sciences and technology and were known for their determination. They belonged to a profession which had just recently gained the respect of the Korean people.

The Start of the Third Republic

In the last of their Six Points, announced on 16 May 1961, the rebels had said that after completion of their mission, they would return the control of government to civilians. Three months later, in August 1961, Park Chung Hee declared that the transfer of power to a civilian government would be implemented in the summer of 1963. This pledge was repeated in the Joint Communiqué issued after the visit of Park Chung Hee to Washington and talks with President John F. Kennedy on 14 November 1961.[11] The restoration of a civilian government in Korea was a matter of great concern to the US administration.

The first stage of this process, the drafting and adopting of a new constitution did not present any problems. The amended constitution was accepted by a national referendum on 17 December 1962 with 78.8% of the votes cast. The new constitution brought fundamental changes.[12] The presidential system was reintroduced. The president was to be elected directly by the people and would hold the position of head of state, chief executive and commander-in-chief of the armed forces. The president would be able to issue emergency ordinances,

[11] Kim Se-Jin (1976) pp. 271 and 272.

[12] Text in Chung Kyung Cho (1971) pp. 231 ff.

whenever necessary, either for military reasons or for the maintenance of public safety and order. The National Assembly would have one chamber. Only members of political parties, and not independents, could become candidates for the National Assembly. If the Assembly would advise the president to remove a cabinet member, the president would not necessarily have to follow the advice. Decisions of the Assembly regarding the budget would be limited. If the Assembly chooses not to adopt a budget within thirty days before the beginning of the fiscal year, the executive can disburse expenditures in conforming with the budget of the preceding year. The new constitution gave the president a strong position and the Assembly a weak one, exactly what the first constitution had done. This approach implied the possibility to continue the traditional autocratic rule under the new constitution. The militaries just stood for administrative effectiveness.

The next stage was more problematic. It had to be decided as to how to breathe life into the constitution and — first of all — who should occupy the top positions. The militaries had to decide on whether they would return to the barracks, as they had announced earlier, or whether they would stay in politics after having tasted governmental power. They would also have to decide on whether to allow former politicians, whose activities had been banned since the coup, to return to the political stage.

There was no unanimity among the rulers on how to proceed. Song Yo Chang, who had been removed from the post as Prime Minister in June 1962, was arguing against the continuation of military rule. Others favored the founding of a pan-national political party, an idea which Park Chung Hee also liked momentarily. There were, however, a number of officers suggesting to found an own political party which would enable the new rulers to cooperate and hopefully dominate within the new constitutional system. The brains behind these ideas was the head of the KCIA Kim Jong Pil. He had already started preparing for the founding of a party of the "new generation" in summer 1962, long before political activities were allowed again. His ideas prevailed, and in the beginning of 1963 the Democratic Republican Party (DRP) was organized. The controversies between the military, the inclusion of civilian politicians from the First and Second Republic and the lack of a program based on an ideology had their impact on the new party which had suffered from factionalism from the very start.

After the ban of political activities had been lifted, in the beginning of 1963, civilian politicians also started to get organized. Many of them were, however, still excluded since they could only be admitted into political activities after having been acquitted by a committee of the Supreme Council. Efforts were undertaken to unite the adversaries of the military regime. They failed due to the old controversies. Once again, when unity mattered, the politicians were unable to overcome their disunity. Thus, Park's opponents were spread over various political parties. Yun Po Sun had founded the Civil Rule Party as a successor to the New Democratic Party of the Second Republic. Also the Democratic Party was revived, now led by Mrs. Park Sun Chun. Yun Po Sun had stepped down as President in March 1962 protesting the Political Activities Purification Act.

The rearrangement of the political party system was accompanied by severe turbulence. Park Chung Hee was less worried by the attacks of his opponents but was more worried about the power play among his followers. Kim Dong Ha, one of the leaders of the coup, left the Supreme Council and the preparatory committee of the DRP in January 1963 because he was convinced that the DRP was going to be an instrument of his competitor Kim Jong Pil. In March 1963, he was arrested by the KCIA under suspicion for an attempted coup and was later court-martialed. Kim Jong Pil who was not only strongly disliked but also held responsible for illegal methods of raising funds — the so-called Four Major Cases of Grave Suspicion — had to go into exile.[13]

In these months, Park Chung Hee did not steer a straight course, thus adding to the general instability. On 18 February 1963, he indicated that he might give up his nomination for the office of president if particular conditions would be fulfilled, if, first of all, all political disputes stopped.[14] As this announcement surprised even his followers, it seemed to be serious. Yet, the in-fighting continued to increase in spite of promises by politicians and officers to cease their conflicts. Park Chung Hee proposed to continue the military rule for another four years and to have the people vote on the continuation or termination of military rule. Friends and foes protested, and also the Americans. In response, Park Chung Hee revised his course again and returned to his original position. He declared the envisaged referendum postponed and on 27 July 1963, he formally announced that government authority would be transferred to civilians within a year. Park Chung Hee began to waver, but he still managed to maintain his dominant position.

---

[13] Kim Se-Jin (1971) pp. 115 and 116.

[14] Korea Times, 19 February 1963.

In the following election campaign, Park Chung Hee, who was the candidate of the DRP, had to face several competitors; Yun Po Sun, the candidate for the Civil Rule Party was the most important. Yun tried to discredit Park by associating him with the communists.[15] On 15 October 1963, Park Chung Hee was declared the winner with 46.6% of the valid votes, Yun Po Sun received 45.1%. The DRP won the National Assembly elections on 26 November 1963 although it had only won 33.6% of the votes. It gained 110 (62.8%) of the 175 seats, thanks to a system of proportional representation. The Civil Rule Party won 41 seats, and the Democratic Party won 13.

The high marks, which the elections received from UNCURK, were exaggerated. An atmosphere of manipulation, well known from the old days of the First Republic, prevailed. The starting position for the DRP on the one side and the other parties on the other side was different since the DRP was the instrument of the ruling officers and could get prepared for the elections much earlier. Financing was far more difficult for the opposition parties. The campaigns of some of the members of the opposition had been disturbed. Song Yo Chan, the presidential candidate of the Liberal Democratic Party, had to campaign from his prison cell before he withdrew from the presidential race. The Central Election Committee registered numerous violations of the election law, 701 for the presidential elections and 1064 for the Assembly elections.

On 17 December 1963, the National Assembly held its first session. On the same day, Park Chung Hee took his oath as President. South Korea had its Third Republic. The rebels of the May coup in 1961 continued to control the government.

The Normalization Treaties with Japan

Relations between South Korea and Japan had not improved. The normalization between the Republic of Korea and its only like-minded neighbor was overdue. The high demand for foreign capital during the first five-year plan made it even more urgent to reach an understanding with Japan. Japan had an interest in the developing Korean market. In Japan, opinions were voiced that a stable Korea was of strategic importance for Japan's security. American pressure on Japan was aimed in the same direction. The US administration,

[15]Kim Se-Jin (1971) p. 135 note 26.

increasingly burdened by the war in Vietnam, was in favor of an understanding between its main allies in the Far East and of promoting Japanese cooperation in the economic restoration of South Korea. The American position was well represented in a Joint Statement issued in Seoul after talks between the Korean Foreign Minister and US Assistant Secretary of State Bundy on 3 October 1964: "The Foreign Minister and Mr. Bundy agreed that normalization of relations between Korea and Japan would be an important contribution to the cause of peace in Asia and expressed the hope that public opinion in Korea would recognize the national interest on a supra-partisan basis. They expressed the hope that negotiations for normalization of those relations could be resumed at an early date. Mr. Bundy repeated earlier US expressions of willingness to assist in appropriate ways to bring about a successful conclusion of this long-standing problem".[16]

Progress was achieved when KCIA director Kim Jong Pil and the Japanese Foreign Minister Masayoshi Ohira agreed on the settlement of the important and so far controversial property claims in November 1962. This paved the way to further settle the other open issues during the 7th round of negotiations which began in December 1964. When Foreign Minister Etsusaburo Shiina came to Seoul on 17 February 1965, he expressed regret with regards to the unhappy past. He used the following words: "It is most regrettable and we reflect on the fact that there was an unhappy period in the long history of our two countries".[17] The South Koreans could interpret this formula as an apology in disguise. During Shiina's visit, the Treaty on Basic Relations between the Republic of Korea and Japan was initialed.[18] The treaty and various agreements were signed on 22 June 1965 and entered into force on 18 December 1965.

The South Korean government achieved its main goals. The treaty confirmed that the Japanese–Korean treaties and agreements signed on or before the annexation "are already null and void". Though the treaty did not expressly declare the treaties as void from the beginning, such an interpretation was possible. The treaty furthermore acknowledged "that the Republic of Korea is the only lawful government in Korea as specified in the Resolution 195 (III) of the United Nations General Assembly". This wording went much further than the Resolution had done by implying the recognition of South

[16]Kim Se-Jin (1976) p. 285.

[17]Korea Annual 1966 p. 74.

[18]Text in Korea Annual 1966 pp. 382 and 383.

Korea as the sole representative of the whole of Korea. The South Korean government had good reasons to be pleased with the results.

Japan promised grants of 300 million US dollars and capital assistance of 200 million US dollars; 300 million US dollars the form of commercial credits were envisaged. The fisheries agreement did not mention the peace line (Rhee line) but brought a solution of the practical problem by recognizing the right of both sides to extend their fishery zones to twelve nautical miles. The Koreans living in Japan since the end of the Pacific War were given the right to reside there permanently.

Although the urgency to reach a settlement with Japan was obvious and the result met the South Korean demands, the negotiations with Japan resulted in a severe domestic crisis in South Korea. Opposition parties, students, church leaders, intellectuals attacked the normalization agreements vehemently. Inspired by their traditional mistrust towards Japan, they claimed the conclusions of the agreements were humiliating, disadvantageous and well-suited to allow for Japanese economic aggression. On 24 March 1964, 3 years after the putsch, South Korea again witnessed the beginning of large student demonstrations. According to estimates, altogether 3.5 million people participated in anti-Japanese demonstrations over a period of one and a half years.[19] The government could quell the unrest only by deploying police and military forces and even imposing martial law temporarily.

Starting in June 1965, the conflict moved from the streets and into the National Assembly. The opposition was temporarily united in the Mass Party under the leadership of Mrs. Park Sun Chun, reconstituting the old Democratic Party from the second half of the 1950s. The Mass Party waged an extreme fight against the agreements. Its lawmakers tried to block deliberations in the Assembly and threatened to resign if they failed to achieve their aims. The resistance against the agreements was not only nurtured by animosities against Japan but also by an aversion against the Park Chung Hee administration, which the opposition considered to be illegitimate. Numerous scandals had tainted the reputation of the government. It was, therefore, not surprising that the opposition demanded the resignation of President Park Chung Hee.

Park Chung Hee did not enjoy much support from his followers because under the pressure of the conflict, the various factions had started in-fighting. In May 1964, Park Chung Hee replaced the cabinet of the independent Prime

[19] Kim Kwan Bong p. 116.

Minister Choi Doo Sun with the Chung Il Kwon cabinet in which 8 DRP ministers were included. He had to let Kim Jong Pil down, who had paved the way for the Korean-Japanese settlement once again. After Kim Jong Pil had resigned from the DRP chairmanship, he was sent abroad for the second time.

The members of the ruling party had accepted the agreements in the Assembly's Special Committee on 11 August 1965 in less than one minute. The members of the opposition did not participate in the voting in the plenary. On 14 August 1965, the agreements were approved by a vote of the DRP members. The legal basis for the normalization of relations between South Korea and Japan had been settled. By the beginning of 1966, both countries exchanged ambassadors.

The foreign policy of Park Chung Hee had achieved success; he had finally normalized relations with Japan under acceptable conditions. Also in domestic politics, he had prevailed over his adversaries. It was obvious, however, that the Third Republic was unstable. The fierceness of the conflict had added to the country's instability.

Foreign Policy Issues

The Park Chung Hee administration did not only succeed in normalizing relations with Japan but also achieved progress in improving relations with other foreign partners.

The original tensions between the new rulers in Seoul and the US administration could be overcome quickly as both sides had overriding interests in continuing the close cooperation. The US government could not let its ally down although it behaved in a strange way. The South Korean government depended completely on US support for its security and economic restoration. An increasing exchange of visitors illustrated the restored harmony. President Park Chung Hee came to see President Kennedy in November 1961, President Johnson in May 1965 and April 1968 and President Nixon in 1969; President Lyndon B. Johnson came to Korea in the fall of 1966. On 9 July 1966, the Agreement "Regarding Facilities and Areas and the Status of United States Armed Forces in the Republic of Korea" — called Status of Forces Agreement, SOFA — was signed.[20] The conclusion of that agreement had been overdue. Until now, based on an understanding reached during the Korean War, the

[20]Text in Korea Annual 1967 pp. 361 ff.

US had "exclusive jurisdiction over members of the US military establishment in Korea".[21] The new agreement, in accordance with demands of the South Korean government and public, gave Korean civil courts the jurisdiction to try members of the US forces for crimes not committed in the performance of official duty.

South Korea participated in the war in Vietnam in order to support the American ally. In spite of fierce controversies in Korea, the Korean government despatched combat troops to South Vietnam, altogether a total of 50,000 men. In addition, 20,000 Korean civilians were working in South Vietnam. The Park Chung Hee government hoped to contribute to promoting stability in Asia and to enhance its own influence.

In order to improve South Korea's image, the country took up diplomatic relations with non-aligned countries and promoted regional cooperation. Upon a South Korean initiative, the Asia and Pacific Council (ASPAC) held its first Ministerial Meeting in Seoul in June 1966. The Council was a forum of loose cooperation between pro-American countries in the region (South Korea, Australia, Republic of China, Japan, Malaysia, New Zealand, The Philippines, Thailand and South Vietnam). Although the Council did not develop into an instrument for political or military cooperation, it gave the South Korean government the chance to offer proof of its readiness for international cooperation. Openness and flexibility of the foreign policy of Park Chung Hee differed favorably from isolationism and immobility of the Rhee era.

A Hectic Period

The domestic situation remained unstable even after the end of the conflict concerning the normalization agreements with Japan. Political life in the Third Republic was livelier and more colorful as compared to during the military dictatorship. Newspapers and student activities contributed in shaping public opinion and were not shy in criticizing the government. The National Assembly was used as a forum for discussing politics. The constitutional framework for dealing with political conflicts was, however, violated time after time by the executive branch. Its traditional predominance also prevailed during the Third Republic.

[21]Korea Annual 1966 pp. 379 and 380.

Park Chung Hee could rely on the military and the government machinery. He saw to it that many key positions in the government were filled with former officers. He, furthermore, had two instruments at his disposal to achieve his goals, his secretariat and the KCIA. His secretariat functioned like a military staff and had developed into a sort of second cabinet under the leadership of Lee Hu Rak. The KCIA with its far-reaching powers was directly responsible to the president. The National Security Act of 1960 and the Anti-Communist Act of 1961 had remained in force in the new constitutional system. The vague provisions of the Anti-Communist Act could be interpreted as imposing penalties on all kinds of anti-state activities thus giving the government easy access to persecute oppositionists. To give an example: Kim Chae Hwan, a candidate for the opposition, was arrested by the KCIA shortly before the National Assembly elections on 6 June 1967 under the charge of having received money from communist sources in Japan. The KCIA used this pretext to sack the office of the new Democratic Party to which Kim Chae Hwan belonged. The press was a frequent victim of government interventions. In the summer of 1968, journalists of the Dongyang press agency were charged with leaking military secrets. A couple of days later, the Dong A Ilbo fell victim to the KCIA because the daily had exposed abuses in connection with the distribution of foreign credits. When the students demonstrated in July 1969 to denounce the DRP for attempting to revise the constitution, newspapers were not allowed to report about the event. The constitutional rights and freedom of citizens were disregarded. Extreme measures such as closings of universities and the imposition of martial law added to the feeling of the citizens to be ruled arbitrarily. South Korea had an authoritarian form of government as in the Syngman Rhee era.

But something was different, namely the vigorous way with which the Park Chung Hee government tackled economic problems. As already mentioned, the first five-year plan had been introduced for the period from 1962 to 1966. A second one followed for the period from 1967 to 1971 which aimed at improving domestic capital formation and the trade balance and in fighting unemployment and inflation. An impressive growth of the Korean economy based on export oriented industrialization began: Between 1962 and 1966, GNP grew by 7.8% whereas in the period from 1967 to 1971 by 10.5%. At the same time, the contribution of manufacturing to GNP rose significantly, from 12% in 1961 to 21.2% in the period 1967 to 1971. The contribution of agriculture decreased in the same period from 44.1% to 30.1%. The contribution of exports to GNP increased during the same period from 3.2% to 12.8%. Employment also improved, while the fight against inflation had only limited success during the period of rapid growth. However, price increases which had amounted to an average of 16.7% in the period from 1962 to 1966 dropped to 7.8% in the period from 1967 to 1971.

It was the government which took the main decisions on the economic policy. The government laid down the economic aims and controlled their implementation, primarily by means of its lending and financial policies. A system of close cooperation between the government and private business developed. The entrepreneurs, particularly the big conglomerates, the *chaebol*, took up the goals fixed by the government, transferred them into business operations and made their profits. The process resulted in strengthening the business groups, and enabling them to influence the fixing of economic priorities. Important instruments of transmission were the large business organizations, the Federation of Korean Industries (FKI) and the Chamber of Commerce and Industry in the first place. A perfect system of synchronization developed. Cohesion among those dominating economy and business improved as many civil servants, politicians and officers went over to the private sector guaranteeing their new employers access to important government agencies. Those belonging to this class often had their education together in high schools, universities or in the military academy and shared basic views and values.

According to Art. 7 paragraph 2 of the Constitution, "political parties should have necessary organizational arrangements to enable the people to participate in the formation of the political will". This provision was inspired by a similar provision of the German constitution, the Basic Law. But political parties did not develop in such a way that they could meet this obligation. Park Chung Hee leaned on the DRP of which he was the President. The chairmen of the DRP who were subordinate to the party president and who changed from time to time had to do the daily work. The DRP was Park's political arm, particularly in the National Assembly. Often Park Chung Hee could make the DRP implement his goals in the Assembly, but not always, as tensions caused by factionalism also appeared in the ruling party. A common ideology that might have eased tensions was missing.

There was some progress on the opposition side when a new attempt to unite the forces of the opposition into a single party was successful. The New Democratic Party, founded in February 1967 and led by Yu Chin O, a scholar of constitutional law and former president of the prestigious Korea University, was and remained the center of the opposition. The new party resorted to extreme measures, including a boycott of the session of the Assembly, to a sleep-in in the chamber, to erecting barricades from chairs around the rostrum. Since the DRP hit back, parliamentary democracy fell by the wayside. This was illustrated when the adoption of the budget on 28 December 1967 in the Assembly was accompanied by fist-fighting of its members.

The elections in 1967 brought victory for Park Chung Hee and his party, the DRP. Park Chung Chee, who had propagated the modernization of the fatherland during the election campaign, received 51.4% of the valid votes (1963: 46.6%) in the elections on 3 May 1967. Yun Po Sun, who as the candidate for the New Democratic Party, was again the main competitor and had conducted a passionate campaign. He gained 40.9% of the votes (1963: 45.1%). Since Park Chung Hee, who have had an impressive record of economic progress and of successes in foreign policy, achieved a clear but not overwhelming victory, the judgment that this had been an honest election appears to be correct. Unlike the presidential elections, the National Assembly elections on 8 June 1967 were rigged. Even the government had to admit irregularities. The DRP won 129 of the 175 seats, the New Democratic Party 45.

Park Chung Hee continues

The political fate of Kim Jong Pil, who had already been in exile twice, took yet another turn. On 30 May 1969, he announced his resignation from the chairmanship of the DRP and from the National Assembly. He did so in order to protest the purge of his close follower Kim Yong Tae. Kim Yong Tae had been ousted from the DRP because he had tried to promote Kim Jong Pil as a candidate for the 1971 presidential elections. These efforts made sense. Since the constitution just permitted the reelection of a president for one more term (Art. 69 paragraph 3), Park Chung Hee could not run a third time. Kim Jong Pil was considered to be the number two man in Korea as he was the mastermind of the coup in 1961, founder of the KCIA and the DRP, chairman of the DRP and chief negotiator with the Japanese government. But he had overlooked that Park Chung Hee was not ready to relinquish power.

Park Chung Hee did not talk much in public about his plans. Suggestions of his followers to continue in order to assure "public stability and economic progress" and to enable him to run again by amending the constitution will have been most welcome.[22] The discussion of a constitutional amendment resulted in another dramatic crisis. The NDP reacted in an extreme way. First, it expelled 43 party lawmakers who thus became independent members of the National Assembly. Second, on 10 September 1969 the party dissolved with the result that three party members, who had not been expelled, lost their seats in the Assembly. That was exactly the idea behind the trick, to deprive the three legislators of their parliamentary membership because they had indicated to vote for the amendment.

On 13 September 1969, the amendment was pushed through. In the early morning hours of that Sunday, 122 supporters of the President entered the National Assembly building through a backdoor, met in a committee room and within half an hour approved the amendment. The members of the opposition had not been informed about the meeting. This was another low in South Korea's parliamentary history.

The necessary referendum followed on 17 October 1969. The constitutional amendment was approved by a two-thirds majority. In the absence of any alternative, the passage of this amendment was not surprising. Park had given himself another chance to stay at the top.

He won the presidential elections on 27 April 1971 with 53.2% of the valid votes. These elections would not have been noteworthy if the candidate for the opposition, Kim Dae Jung, had not done so well by receiving 45.3% of the votes. Kim Dae Jung, a young civilian and a relatively unknown politician, had presented new ideas in his campaign, attracting large crowds. He argued for social reforms and for greater flexibility towards the communist countries. He suggested taking up diplomatic relations with East European countries. He also proposed to seek assurances from the four powers, from China, the Soviet Union, the United States and Japan, for the security of the two Koreas in order to prepare for the easing of tensions of the peninsula. Many Koreans I have talked to were convinced that Kim Dae Jung would have won if the government had not used direct and indirect means to influence the outcome of the elections. For Park Chung Hee, the good results of his opponent will have been a shock.

In the National Assembly elections on 25 May 1971, the opposition achieved good results by winning 69 of the 204 seats. The DRP no longer enjoyed a

[22] Chung Kyung Cho (1971) p. 54.

two-thirds majority as before (1967: 73.7%), but they still held a majority of 113 seats (55.4%).

During and after the campaign, Park Chung Hee had so often been described as a strong man, a dictator, and a "generalissimo".[23] He was, however, in those years forced to be very flexible. Since his opponents within and outside his own camp were fighting vigorously, he could not be sure whether he would reach the necessary two-thirds majority for the constitutional amendment. He had to make concessions and had no chance to steer a straight course. Important changes of key associates occurred. In October 1969 Park dismissed his chief secretary, Lee Hu Rak, and the KCIA director, Kim Hyung Wook. Lee Hu Rak returned quickly: He was appointed Director of the KCIA in December 1970. Kim Jong Pil, who had been called back in fall 1969 in order to assist Park in winning the referendum, was appointed Prime Minister after the National Assembly elections in 1971. The changes were many, but Park Chung Hee managed to remain on top. He did not take the democratic principle seriously such that leaders in high offices should only be elected for a certain length of time. On the contrary, he and his followers, who just had in mind to secure their positions, did everything possible to narrow the chances for a change at the top of the government. They even prevented a transition of the office of the president to one of their own men. Park Chung Hee and his followers made the mistake in believing that only they alone, the saviors of the Republic of Korea, were in a position to lead the country successfully.

References

Briggs, Walter, "The Military Revolution in Korea; on its Leader and Achievements", in *Koreana Quarterly* Vol. 5 No. 2 (Summer 1963) S. 17 ff.

Douglas, William A., "South Korea's Search for Leadership", in *Pacific Affairs* Vol. XXXVII No. 1 (Spring 1964) S. 20 ff.

Kim, Chong Shin, *Seven Years with Korea's Park Chung Hee*, Seoul 1964.

The Central Election, Management Committee, *Korean Constitution, Election and Political Party Laws*, Seoul 1964.

The Secretariat, Supreme, Council for National Reconstruction, *Military Revolution in Korea*, Seoul November 1961.

[23]By Kim Dae Jung, quoted in Chung Kyung Cho (1971) p. 73.

Chapter 9

The Yushin System

A Turbulent Year

On Christmas in 1971, the fire sirens wailed in Seoul. The 21-story Taeyongak Hotel in the capital's center had caught fire. Fire engines rushed to the scene but could not deliver water above the 9th floor. Helicopters were used in an effort to rescue guests and employees. A number of people, totally desperate, jumped to the ground. According to official sources, 165 people perished in the fire.[1]

Unrest at the universities continued even after the presidential and National Assembly elections in the spring of 1971. The students fought against the compulsory military training program which had been introduced at the universities in 1969. The unrest became so severe that the government did not know how to cope with it and, in a desperate move, had the campuses of the seven most important universities in Seoul occupied by troops. At the same time, pressure on an unruly press was increased, for example by temporary arrests of journalists. That the judges also rebelled was surprising. By the end of July 1971, the Seoul district prosecution sought writs of arrest for two judges charged with taking bribes from a defense lawyer in a trial of violation of the National Security Act. During the following days, more than one third of the judges turned in their resignations. They suspected that the prosecution had acted in retaliation against acquittals by the district court in cases involving alleged violations of the Anti-Communist Act. For the first time, the judges

[1]Korea Annual 1972 p. 42.

were fighting against pressure and for their independence. However, they stood up only after two of their colleagues had got into trouble. Their protests were successful; the prosecution dropped the charges against the two judges.

Violence erupted during various times in 1971. In August, more than 20,000 people demonstrated in one of Seoul's suburban districts against having been displaced by force. They attacked the police station and burned police cars. In mid-September, a few hundred workers assaulted the building of Hanjin Trading to emphasize their demands for immediate payment of overdue salaries. And even a mutiny occurred. Personnel from a special airforce unit, who were trained for missions against North Korea on Silmi Island off Inchon, broke out of their compound and hurried to Seoul by boat and bus. They probably wanted to plead with higher authorities for better treatment. Before reaching Seoul, they were stopped. 37 people died in the shoot-out.

The political parties did not show any signs of consolidation. The NDP suffered from one of its usual leadership crises; Yu Chin San, who had become the party chief at the beginning of 1970, was forced to resign and was succeeded by Kim Hong Il in May 1971. Disunity within the DRP was worse. A no-confidence vote, moved by the NDP in the Assembly against the Minister of Home Affairs Oh Chi Song, found a majority in the voting on 2 October 1971 because DRP members had also supported the move of the opposition. They had done so against strict orders from the Blue House. A massive purge followed; one of its victims was Kil Chae Ho who belonged to the rebels of May 1961 and who had been the DRP's Secretary General for many years.

But it was Park Chung Hee who was responsible for the greatest sensation in the fateful year 1971. On 6 December 1971, he declared a state of national emergency arguing that this action was taken "with a view to awakening the people to the realities facing them ...".[2] It was announced that the freedoms of the people would be even more restricted than before. The government could not cite a legal basis for this surprising measure. In a statement in the National Assembly on 7 December 1971, Minister of Justice Shin Shik Su mentioned vaguely the constitutional rights of the president to protect the national security during a time of crisis. The alleged critical situation of national security could not, however, justify the declaration of an emergency. According to Art. 75 of the Constitution of the Third Republic, the proclamation of an emergency was only possible when there was a military necessity or

[2]Text in Korea Annual 1972 p. 21.

when it was necessary to maintain public safety and order by the mobilization of the armed forces.

Moreover, justifying the emergency measures by claiming a danger to the national security was not very convincing. Certainly, tensions on the peninsula continued to exist. The withdrawal of the Seventh US Division from Korea, which had been completed in June 1971, had burdened the South Korean Armed Forces with greater responsibilities. The government of the People's Republic of China had succeeded in being recognized within the UN system as the only representative of China, and it was too early to judge which impact this development would have on politics in Asia. But — and that was new and important — the thaw had spread to the Korean peninsula. For the first time in many years, South and North talked to each other. Since 20 August 1971, the Red Cross Societies of both Koreas had contacts in Panmunjom with the aim to facilitate the fate of the family members separated between the two parts of the country since 1945. Thus, the first cautious steps in the direction of normalization were taken. Park's emergency measures had no other aim but to give him additional tools to remain in control of the country.

The government introduced a "Special Measures Law on National Defense" in the Assembly which was meant to empower the president to proclaim an emergency when it was necessary to counter a great threat to the national security or to maintain social peace and order.[3] The law was also given retroactive effect to cover the emergency proclamation on 6 December 1971 which illustrated the bad conscience of the government. In the early morning hours of 27 December 1971, the DRP members of the Assembly passed the law in absence of the NDP–members which reminds us of the adoption of the constitutional amendment in 1969. Constitutionally and legally, nothing was gained. The far-reaching authorization of the president as provided for in the Special Measures Law on National Defense could only have been enacted by an amendment to the constitution. But legal questions did not matter in Park's Korea.

The October Reforms

If the Koreans had thought an end had been reached by the introduction of extraordinary measures, they were mistaken. A year later, Park Chung Hee

[3] Text in Korea Annual 1972 pp. 361 ff.

demonstrated that he could go one step further. On 17 October 1972 the President declared martial law, dissolved the National Assembly and banned all political activities. He did not try to find legal justification for his measures. This would have been impossible because the measures of 17 October 1972 were an attack against the constitution. Park Chung Hee had plotted against his own constitution.

South Korea quickly returned to a constitutional system, even though it was an unconventional one. On 27 October 1972, just 10 days later, the cabinet, acting as Extraordinary State Council, proposed amendments which changed the constitution considerably. The new system restricted the authority of the Assembly and blew up the authority of the president. This system was to be achieved by establishing a new body, the National Conference for Unification. A national referendum on 21 November 1972 approved the new constitution. The great support achieved (91.5%) did not mean much. The vote had been taken when martial law was still in force; there was neither an alternative nor even a chance for discussions.

The 2,359 members of the National Conference for Unification were elected on 15 December 1972. The Conference elected Park Chung Hee for President with all but 2 of the 2,359 votes. His earlier promise not to run again had been forgotten. The new constitution permitted unlimited reelection; the term of office was now 6 years. On 27 December 1972 Park Chung Hee was sworn in; at the same time the new constitution entered into force. South Korea had its Fourth Republic.

The elections for the National Assembly on 27 February 1973 lacked the usual electrifying effects since they were of no real importance. The results confirmed the position of the two large parties. The DRP received 73, the NDP 52 of the 146 seats awarded by a direct vote. The additional 73 members were elected by the National Conference upon proposal by the president. The lawmakers, nominated by the Conference, formed a separate parliamentary group, the Political Association for the Reforms (*yushin jonguhoe* or *yujonghoe*).

Park Chung Hee called the measures on October 1972 "revitalizing reforms".[4] The Korean term *yushin* can also just be described by reforms or renewal. It definitely recalls the Meiji reforms (*issin*) showing once again the impact of the Japanese model. Ever since the end of the Pacific War, anti-Japanese feeling have found their strong expression in South Korea. It

[4]Korea Annual 1973 p. 371.

was taboo to argue against anti-Japanese attitudes. Park Chung Hee did not care. He admired the Meiji-reforms, called the transformation of Japan by the Meiji reforms a "miracle" and said: "At any rate, though the age and people are different from then, the case of the Meiji imperial restoration will be of great help to the performance of our own revolution. My interest in this direction remains strong and constant."[5] Whatever our Korean friends may want to make us believe, South Korea under Park Chung Hee tried to imitate the example of Japan. The Yushin system Park introduced differed fundamentally from the constitutional systems South Korea had known since 1948.

The establishment of the National Conference for Reunification — a highly imaginative invention — was an attempt to raise the position of the president even more and make his authority unchallengeable. The National Conference is a supreme body — "the depository of the national sovereignty" (Art. 35) — and above party politics, chaired by the president. Its members are directly elected and cannot be affiliated with a political party or be members of the National Assembly. The Conference has the function to elect the president, to elect one third of the lawmakers, and to confirm amendments to the constitution. As proved by the results of the presidential elections on 23 December 1972, the government exercised firm control on the composition of the National Conference. The president will no longer be afraid of obstruction by the National Assembly as one third of the members owe their position which is rewarding to him. The National Conference can accept or reject the president's suggestions only *in toto*. The president also has the authority to dissolve the National Assembly which has annual sessions of not more than 150 days.

The president has additional far-reaching powers. In case he anticipates a threat to national security or public safety, he has the power to take the necessary emergency measures "in the whole range of state affairs" (Art. 53). In the case of an emergency, the freedoms and rights of the people can be suspended; they are anyway subject to statutory limitation. That means that the protection provided by them for the citizens is weak.

It fits into the picture that the independence of the judges was weakened by an act promulgated during the martial law period in January 1973. The new law empowered the president to appoint and dismiss all judges. For

[5]Park Chung Hee, The Country, *The Revolution and I*, pp. 117 and 120.

the appointment of the Chief Justice, the president needs the consent of the National Assembly, for all other appointments he needs a proposal by the Chief Justice. Taken together, these changes meant a departure from the democratic system of separation of powers. South Korea had achieved something special, a constitution which legalized authoritarian rule.

When Park Chung Hee defended the reforms, he argued that they were necessary in order to gain a position of strength for the dialogue with the North. This argument was not totally invalid. The talks with the North had continued. On 4 July 1972, the sensational Joint Communiqué had been issued in which the governments of both Korean states had announced joint efforts to achieve reunification. Domestic politics in South Korea had continued to be unbalanced, due to the turbulence of 1971. The National Assembly could not perform any serious work since the DRP blocked all attempts by the NDP to discuss the emergency measures taken in 1971. Factionalism had become so strong within the NDP that the party split into two. The two factions held two separate party congresses and neither party could decide who the party chairman was. Park Chung Hee felt more strongly than ever that party politics was bad. "The irresponsible political parties lost the sense of national mission and the representative institution was made the scapegoat of their political struggle. What could we really expect from these political parties and from the representative institution?", he said when he proclaimed the extraordinary measures on 17 October 1972.[6]

He reacted — the circumstances were favorable due to the sensational contacts with the North — by introducing a governmental system tailored for him. It was supposed to be the framework for an undisturbed, energetic and effective administration which had always been his ideal. While the system of the transitory period was called an "administrative democracy" and the ruling party later propagated "nationalist democracy", the Yushin system was defended as a Korean form of democracy. The new form, adapted to Korean realities, was confronted with the liberal democracy which, it was argued, had been introduced though the basic prerequisites were missing in Korea. In the words of Park Chung Hee: "It is commonly recognized that democracy as practiced in the United States, France or England, is not suited to Korea. Needless to say, a real democracy can only be set up on a healthy economic foundation. The fact remains that Korea is suffering from an unbalanced

[6] Korea Annual 1973 p. 370.

economy — jarred and shaken by disruption, black dealings between politicians and businessmen, the resultant rise of political tycoons, a sharp difference between have and have-not. A healthy democracy stands for, and is built upon a firm foundation of sincerity, honesty, and law. In Korea, however, deceit, exaggeration, corruption, incompetence and dogmatism have produce a mask of democracy".[7] Therefore, he argued, the country has to go through the stages of a national revolution. At least, he did not try to pretend to follow a democratic path.

In later years, Park Chung Hee tried to bring the Yushin idea to life. He initiated the New Community or New Village Movement (*saemaul undong*).[8] This movement aimed at improving infrastructure and income in rural areas. It concentrated on creating a cooperative spirit among farmers, even though no comprehensive ideology ever developed. The New Spiritual Movement (*saemaum undong*), an effort to reform the thinking pattern of people, remained vague and ineffective.[9]

The Policy of Repression

The introduction of the Yushin system did not completely extinguish the resistance against Park. But under the nearly unrestricted rule, which the new system allowed, it had become even more difficult to voice different views. The dissidents had to determine how far they could go with their criticisms. They generally shared the President's basic view that the tension on the Korean peninsula demanded special efforts. Now and then, the government believed they had discovered communist subversive activities. The dissidents, however, were mostly good Korean patriots with conservative views. They had difficulties in reaching agreement among themselves to determine what was necessary and feasible. Nevertheless, they united for larger campaigns which came in the form of explosions as the pressure was stronger than ever and as the dissidents were ever more excluded from the regular political process.

Criticisms centered on the Yushin reforms which formed the basis of the system. At the end of 1973 and the beginning of 1974, the dissidents collected

---

[7]Park Chung Hee op. cit. pp. 184 and 185.

[8]Korean Overseas Information Service, *Saemaul Undong (New Community Movement)* Seoul, December 1937.

[9]Korea Herald, 21 January 1977.

signatures for an appeal to abolish the Yushin constitution and to reestablish democratic institutions. The same demands were made in a declaration issued at the end of a mass, held at the Catholic cathedral in the Myongdong district in Seoul on 1 March 1976, the 57th anniversary of the Samil declaration. Among those who demanded the restoration of a parliamentary system and the guarantee of human rights were the former President Yun Po Sun and Kim Dae Jung.

The government reacted to these and other expressions of resistance with pressure and tricks. On several occasions, the students were given early vacations. Universities were closed. The campus of Korea University was occupied by troops in the spring of 1975. Professors were intimidated by a law which demanded that their contracts had to be renewed by 1 March 1976. This made it easy to get rid of unwanted professors. The press was put under heavy pressure. At times, the press could not cover actions of opposition circles or could do so only much later or indirectly. The prestigious daily Dong A Ilbo was hit hard. From the end of 1974 to the middle of 1975, all of their important customers had withdrawn their ads with the result that the paper got into financial trouble. The fate of other publications was worse; they lost their licenses. From time to time, however, the press dared to come out with criticism. Even under the Yushin system not every government action was taboo, as I have witnessed myself during the period under discussion. It was a question of trial and error to discover which subjects were not totally taboo. The attitude of the government towards the press found its equivalent expression in a statement by Lee Suk Jae who had been one of the leaders of the putsch in 1961 and had later held important posts. When he left his last job as Director of the Board of Audit and Inspection in August 1976, he told reporters: "You did not report what I did not want to be reported. It's good cooperation too".[10]

The resistance moved more and more towards circles of the churches. Active minorities within the Catholic Church and the Protestant churches who are often led by their priests and pastors, spoke up for human rights. The government tried to have clergymen restricted only to performing their pastoral duties and to refrain from partaking in any political activities. Government repression did not stop even for a bishop. Daniel Chi (Chi Hak Sun), the bishop of the diocese of Wonju, was jailed in the summer of 1974. But those

[10]Korea Times, 6 August 1976.

priests and pastors, who saw the political deficiencies of the system, were not ready to allow the government to push them into a neutral corner. Kang Won Yong, a Presbyterian pastor and Director of the Christian Academy in Seoul stated: "We are called upon to fight the forces enslaving us because they drive us directly into hell".[11]

Protests by Christians were joined by personalities from other camps. The churches could give some sort of cover as the government with a view to the many contacts of the churches with churches in foreign countries hesitated to be accused of suppressing the freedom of religion. As has already been mentioned, Yon Po Sun and Kim Dae Jung, experienced politicians of the opposition, had been involved in the protest on 1 March 1976 at the Myondong cathedral. Kim Chi Ha, a polemic and satirical poet, who had become Catholic, met with a good response among Christians. His concise and caustic criticisms of abuses made him also well known among intellectuals. In his famous poem "The Five Bandits" published in 1970, he castigates the protagonists of the authoritarian regime. He was repeatedly arrested, sentenced and released. On 31 December 1976, he was sentenced to a prison term for violating the Anti-Communist Act. Due to an amnesty, his sentence was reduced at the end of 1978; in December 1980 he was freed.

The NDP had no chance to play the part of a real opposition by contributing to control the government's activities. The National Assembly was deprived of power and was dominated by the ruling party. In spite of the serious situation, the infighting within the NDP continued. When the party leaders — from August 1974 to June 1976 Kim Young Sam, since summer 1976 Lee Chul Seung — tried to follow a moderate course which included occasional cooperation with the government, they had to face mistrust of their followers.

Kim Dae Jung was the oppositionist with the greatest charisma, yet he had not found any central role in the party since his successful presidential campaign in 1971. He had remained the leader of a faction, the faction of the politicians from the Cholla provinces. In the fall of 1972 he went into exile. On 8 August 1973, he was kidnapped in a hotel in Tokyo by the KCIA and brought to Seoul where he was placed under house-arrest. When the arrest was suspended at the end of October 1973, he declared that he had no intentions of becoming politically active again. South Korean–Japanese relations were so

[11]Kang Won Yong, *Zwischen Tiger und Schlange*; *Beiträge aus Korea zu Christentum, Entwicklung und Politik*, Erlangen 1975 p. 116 (translation from German by the author).

strained by this incident that the South Korean government had no other choice but to convey its apologies to the Japanese government. Kim Dae Jung was indicted on the basis of statements he had made during the election campaign in 1971 and was later arrested in a trial for his participation in the Myongdong declaration. At the end of 1976, he was sentenced to five years in prison for making untrue claims about the Republic. That meant: He was withdrawn from politics. In a statement he made on 15 August 1975, on the occasion of the 30th anniversary of Korea's liberation, he repeated the demands he had made in the election campaign.[12] He suggested again to realize a four–power peace guarantee for the Korean peninsula and to promote economic reforms. He came out again as one of the few, if not the only one, to voice social concerns. He proposed "to systemize the participation in management by labor as has been done in West Germany". And he stated: "Without guaranteeing freedom, bread and justice, our future is entirely without hope." Kim Dae Jung had become a martyr for democracy.

Since the Yushin constitution was tailor-made for Park Chung Hee, he felt that the demands to amend the constitution were aimed at him personally. His reaction was, therefore, violent. Based on the emergency provisions of the constitution, he issued two Emergency Measures on 6 January 1974. Emergency Measure No. 1 made every attempt to amend the constitution a punishable offense; Emergency Measure No. 2 established Special Courts Martial to try those crimes. Emergency Measure No. 4 followed on 3 April 1974 and was directed against revolting students, and provided even for capital punishment. After the assassination attempt on Park Chung Hee by a Korean from Japan, which ended up killing his wife during a celebration of the national holiday in the National Theatre on 15 August 1974, Park Chung Hee gained more sympathy. This enabled him to withdraw the Measures Nos. 1 and 4 by the end of August 1974. When the unrest returned, he issued Emergency Measure No. 9 which, in an even more radical way, not only penalized demands to amend the constitution but also nearly every criticism of the government. In the Assembly's Legislature/Judiciary Committee, Justice Minister Hwang San Duk explained on 19 March 1976 that the demand to abolish the Yushin constitution was a denial of the Yushin constitution and, therefore, a violation of Emergency Measure No. 9.[13] In other words, Park Chung Hee not only

[12] A copy of the text is in the author's possession.

[13] Chung Ang Ilbo, 20 March 1976.

attempted to perpetuate the Yushin constitution but also his government by decree. The realization of this concept resulted in many trials. According to official statistics, 203 persons were tried for violating Emergency Measures Nos. 1 and 4; most of them were released later.

The KCIA was more than just an agency used for collecting intelligence on foreign countries. Since its inception it had another main function, a domestic function, namely to fight against the government's foes. It had become the main instrument of repression. In a system which did not respect the freedom of its citizens and in which checks and controls of government authorities were cut down, the KCIA could operate at will. In the 1960s and 1970s, charges with regards to the KCIA methods were mostly leveled only in private, but sometimes the newspapers picked up such stories. In February and March of 1975, South Korean newspapers reported that students claimed to have been tortured. The NDP took up the issue in the National Assembly. The government denied the accusation. Two representatives from Amnesty International came to South Korea, checked the claims and found them to be true. The mission, which ended its work on 9 April 1975, found: "Torture is frequently used by law-enforcement agencies both in an attempt to extract false confessions, and as a means of intimidation".[14] Since then, more details about tortures have become known.[15] But already in the 1970s, Western intelligence agencies would have had good reason not to call the KCIA a partner.

Times of repression were followed by times of relaxation. At times, the government gave the opposition leeway and, at other times, intercepted them by countermoves. But whatever the Park Chung Hee administration did, the domestic situation remained tense.

The System of Rule

Although domestic tensions continued and Park Chung Hee had to survive a crisis repeatedly, his system of rule worked. He achieved his aim to administer the country effectively. The presidential secretariat and the KCIA continued to be his most trusted instruments. The military remained loyal.

---

[14] Amnesty International, *Report of the Mission to the Republic of Korea, 27 March–9 April 1975*, (A copy in the author's possession).

[15] See, for example, Cumings (1997) pp. 366 and 367.

He, however, could not prevent struggles for power among the people close to him. In the spring of 1973, one of the rebels of May 1961, member of the 8th class of the Military Academy and now commander of the Capitol Garrison Command, Major General Yoon Pil Yong, fell victim to that type of feud. In the beginning of December 1973, after Kim Dae Jung had been kidnapped, the President dismissed KCIA Director Lee Hu Rak who had been considered as irreplaceable. And on 19 December 1975, Choi Kyu Hah, a diplomat and former foreign minister took the place of Kim Jong Pil as Prime Minister. Of the 94 key figures of the putsch in 1961, only one third were mentioned in the Who's Who chapter of the Hapdong News Agency's Annual 1976.

Handling of Parliament was much easier than before for the President. On 8 October 1975, Mrs. Kim Ok Sun, a member of the opposition, attacked the administration and the President sharply by saying that Park was a dictator who tried to cover his administration's mistakes under the guise of national security. She had to pay the price for this statement and lost her seat. Under the Yushin system, the National Assembly increasingly developed into an enforcement agency of the government. Attempts to regain control were seldom. That the new building for the Assembly inaugurated in fall 1975 was located on an island in the Han River, far away from the political centers of the capital, could be considered as symbolic. The fall of parliamentary democracy meant that the influence of the ruling party, the DRP, headed by the former speaker Rhee Hyo Sang, decreased. The DRP, additionally exposed to the competition of the *yujonghoe*, tried to activate its one million members of whom only 20% paid their fees. But his could not stop the fall of the party's influence.

Park's system of rule differed from Syngman Rhee's as it aimed at achieving substantive political goals. The Park Chung Hee administration was in a position to make basic political decisions and to implement them. In its foreign policy, it remained flexible by adapting to the policy of détente in Asia without neglecting security. It succeeded in promoting the independence of the armed forces and in improving their equipment. The economic policy of an export — oriented industrialization was continued and met with great success. The government machinery, filled with many former officers, implemented the decisions of the President and the cabinet. If necessary, the machinery was modified. An example: The Economic Planning Board was established in order to draft and control the five-year economic plans. A new bureaucracy developed which was defined by Kim Sang Hyop, President of Korea University, in a speech on the occasion of a commencement ceremony on 25 February 1975 as "a clever machinery for forced implementation of modernization programs in an underdeveloped society".[16]

In order to improve the reliability of the administration, the government tried to fight corruption. On March 1975, another anti-corruption campaign was started. Within one year 22,000 officials were checked and 4,190 were dismissed.[17] The drive to weed out corrupt officials continued. In 1976, punitive measures against more than 15,000 officials were taken, 1,439 of them were fired, 4,886 had their salaries reduced.[18] The government also tried fighting corruption by increasing the salaries of officials. It seems that the success was limited. During a committee meeting of the National Assembly on 25 November 1975, Prime Minister Kim Jong Pil had said the following: "We tried to uproot absurdities after the May 16 revolution, but we realized that society was not so simple as we believed it then".[19]

As the resistance against the Yushin constitution continued, Park Chung Hee and his followers were called upon to defend the system. When Kim Jong Pil defended the government's repressive measures in the spring of 1975, he said that the South Korean government respected human rights in its own way. Choi Kyu Hah, not a man of action, denied that the government was repressive and said it was pursuing "a democracy of survival".[20] More articulate advocates of the system like the former Minister of Education, Min Kwan Shik, stressed that Korea never had a functioning democracy, that therefore there was no democracy to be restored and that Koreans were still on a long and arduous road to democracy.[21] He could, however, not indicate a starting point to secure personal freedom and the citizens' participation in the formation of the political will. The truth was that by the end of the 1970s, the basic requirements of democratic government — representative democracy, division of power, rule of law, guarantee of basic rights — were conspicuous by their absence.

---

[16]Copy of the text in the author's possession.

[17]Dong A Ilbo, 23 March 1976, Korea Times, 23 April 1976.

[18]Korea Times, 28 January 1977.

[19]Chosun Ilbo, 26 November 1975.

[20]Korea Times, 1 July 1976.

[21]Min Kwan Shik, "Personal Reflections on Democracy in Korea", in *Korea Journal* Vol. 15 No. 8 (August 1975) pp. 55 ff.

Stormy Winds

In 1978, Park Chung Hee wanted to prepare the second stage of the Yushin system. He had a good start. Though his term of office expired only on 26 December 1976, he had his reelection held on 6 July. The early election was supposed to have demonstrated his determination and ability to act. The National Conference for Reunification, elected only a few months before, justified its reputation as a body of acclamation. It reelected Park Chung Hee with 2,577 out of 2,578 votes.

This election did not contribute to domestic pacification. Scandals occurred like the apartment building scandal which exposed hundreds of leading personalities who had made a lot of money by buying luxury apartments in an irregular way. There were demonstrations against the Yushin system. But even worse for the regime were economic difficulties which were felt by a broad public. Though the general economic development had been on an upswing in Park's Korea, there were stages of difficulties. By the end of the 1960s and into the early 1970s, South Korea faced major problems of resource management. The heavy investments required to sustain Korea's rapid growth were well beyond Korea's own saving capabilities, as the World Bank stated later.[22] Thus, the reliance on external sources was tremendous. Since many firms did not succeed in managing external loans, they went bankrupt. Now, in 1978 and 1979, people were enraged by the inflation (1978: 11.6%; 1979: 18.8%). A higher tax burden resulting from the value-added tax introduced on 1 July 1977 contributed to aggravating the situation.

The NDP made a lot of profit from this development. In the National Assembly elections on 12 December 1978, the opposition party gained 32.8% of the votes, the DRP only 31.7%. Only thanks to the tricky system that one third of the members were to be elected by the National Conference upon suggestion of the President, Park Chung Hee had a majority in the Assembly. He, however, no longer considered Parliament as a partner in the political process.

The concerns of the people found a much better expression after Kim Young Sam had replaced Lee Chul Seung as Chairman of the NDP at the end of May 1979. Kim Young Sam had succeeded in being elected because Kim Dae Jung had supported him. Kim Dae Jung had been included in an amnesty

---

[22]World Bank, Report No. 1387-KO, *Growth and Prospects of the Korean Economy*, 23 February 1977 pp. 12 ff.

granted to 5,378 prisoners on 27 December 1978 due to the occasion of the inauguration of President Park Chung Hee. His prison-term was suspended and he was allowed to leave the hospital in which he had been admitted the year before. He continued to have influence in the NDP through his followers. The newly elected party chairman Kim Young Sam called for more opposition, for democratic change and for Park's resignation. Thus, since for many years it was a politician who directed the resistance against the Park Chung Hee regime.

It was the unsolved social question which started a development that led to Park's downfall. We are talking about the Y. H. Case.[23] On 7 August 1979, the owner of Y. H. Industrial Co. shut down his factory and dismissed all workers, approximately 350 poorly paid young women, and fled to the US. The factory had originally produced wigs and later ski suits but had gotten into trouble. The women wanted their jobs back and demonstrated for that goal. Kim Young Sam allowed the protestors to gather at party headquarters. On 11 August, the police intervened, attacked the NDP headquarters and forcibly took the protestors away. Some were hurt; one 21-year-old woman committed suicide by jumping out of a window. The workers had contacts with the Urban Industrial Mission, a Protestant American-Korean labor group, which the government had tried to suppress for quite some time calling it a communist organization. The incident was ugly. Finally, big brother broke his silence on human rights violations in South Korea. On 13 August 1979, a spokesman of the State Department called the action "excessive and brutal" on 13 August 1979.[24] Park Chung Hee should have interpreted that statement as a bad omen.

Government repression focused now on Kim Young Sam. He had been quoted by the New York Times on 16 September 1979 saying: "The time has come for the United States to make a clear choice between a basically dictatorial regime, increasingly alienated from the people, and the majority who aspire to democracy". He had also repeated his earlier demands to the US government to use public and direct pressure on Park Chung Hee. His statements were interpreted as being detrimental for the Republic. Therefore, the majority of the ruling party deprived him of his seat in the Assembly by a vote on 4 October 1979. This act was, even in South Korea's parliamentary history which knows so many strange incidents, something special. At a time when the party chairman needed the support from his party members, he had to face internal

---

[23]New York Times, 15 August 1979.

[24]New York Times, 15 August 1979.

opposition. Party members filed a petition to declare his election as party chairman void; the Seoul District Court did so by a temporary injunction on 8 September 1979, a decision Kim Young Sam and the majority of the NDP did not accept. It was really a difficult job to head a political party in South Korea.

On 16 October 1979 in Pusan, the party chairman's hometown, several thousand students protested against the expulsion of Kim Young Sam from the National Assembly. The demonstrations were supported by many citizens. The government imposed martial law on 18 October 1979 and suppressed the demonstration by sending in troops. The military also intervened in Masan and Changwon, towns to which the unrest had spread. Large demonstration all around the country were expected on 29 October 1979. Nobody really knew how to continue.

The man in the Blue House had become lonely. After he had dissociated himself from the DRP, he lacked an instrument to gather broad support and many supporters. He now relied exclusively on his closest advisers. They apparently gave him bad advice. When he had the police and military brought into action in the summer and fall of 1979 to quell the unrest, he had lost his sense of proportions. He also overlooked the fact that the deterioration of the economic situation had negatively effected one of the pillars which had supplied legitimacy to his regime. The signs of danger were visible at the wall. Park's eldest daughter Park Keun Hae, who had filled in as First Lady after her mother was murdered in 1974, saw the signs. In an interview 10 years after her father's death, she revealed that she had recommended to her father to replace CIA Director Kim Jae Kyu and the Director of the Presidential Protective Force Cha Chi Chol.[25] But Park Chung Hee who did not see the writing on the wall did not listen to his daughter.

The Assassination of Park Chung Hee

On 26 October 1979, President Park Chung Hee had dinner with some of his faithfuls.[26] The dinner was held in a building owned by the KCIA in Kungjong-dong — a district close to the Blue House — just opposite the

[25]Korea Post Vol. 2 No. 12 (December 1988) pp. 50 ff.

[26]Report of Major General Chun Doo Hwan, in Korea Herald 6 November 1979; indictment of Kim Jae Kyu in Korea Annual 1980 pp. 393 ff.; judgement of the Court Martial of 20 December 1979 in Korea Annual 1980 pp. 398 ff.; Ilyo Sinmun, 24 April 1988.

premises of the Apostolic Delegation. KCIA Director Kim Jae Kyu, an old friend of the President, also belonging to the 2nd class of the Military Academy, later Lieutenant General, was the host. The Chief Secretary of the Blue House Kim Kae Won, also an old friend of the President, and a former Army Chief-of-Staff and KCIA director, was one of the guests. The other guest was Cha Chi Chol, the Director of the Presidential Protective Force. And two waitresses were present.

What the men have discussed is not quite clear. But it can be true that they discussed events in Pusan and Masan which gave reason to concern and that Cha criticized KCIA Director Kim Jae Kyu because of having misjudged the situation. It is clear that there had been a long-standing conflict between Cha Chi Chol, who shielded the President and was known for rude manners, and Kim Jae Kyu and other henchmen of the President. That was the reason why Park Keun Hae, the President's eldest daughter, had recommended that her father replace Cha and Kim Jae Kyu. As she has further stated, Cha Chi Chol and Kim Jae Kyu felt uncertain about their futures.[27]

Kim Jae Kyu left the dining room several times, but finally returned with a pistol, shot down Cha Chi Chol and then the President. When his weapon jammed, he grabbed a new pistol from one of his subordinates waiting outside and fired again at Cha Chi Chol and President Park Chung Hee. His subordinates outside killed the bodyguard, driver and two members of the protective force of the President.

And then something strange happened: Kim Jae Kyu went to an annex building where his deputy and the Army Chief-of-Staff, Chung Seung Hwa, waited for him. He had asked both to come there for dinner. He told both men, who must have heard the shots, that something awful had happened and pushed both men into a car with which he wanted to head for KCIA headquarters. General Chung Seung Hwa, however, gave orders to drive to army headquarters. This was a preliminary decision for the post-Park era against the KCIA and for the military.

Kim Kae Won had not intervened during the fighting. It is not clear whether he was in agreement with the murderer. He brought Park Chung Hee to a nearby hospital which could only confirm the President's death. On 3 November 1979, the murdered President was laid to rest. He was buried by the side of his wife at the National Cemetery in Seoul.

[27]See note 25.

Park Chung Hee

Park Chung Hee was not an unpleasant man. The picture Koreans have seen so often in their newspapers of a stoic, grim face with the chin moved forward was just a pose. Photos from the mid-1960s showed him smiling among the members of his family and laughing among visitors. He was an earnest man, but not lacking in humor, and reports tell us that he could even show warm-heartedness. He was full of emotions as his dramatic style of speaking and writing revealed. In public, the small and frail man acted in a very formal way. He was not interested in becoming cosmopolitan, he hoped that his example would be effective.

Park Chung Hee was a diligent president who loved details. When inspecting ministries in the beginning of the year and travelling across the country, he always embarrassed officials by his questions. It fits well into this picture that he took his duties very seriously. He, however, determined the maxims of his actions himself. He remained modest; the Blue House was not transformed into a luxurious palace. He stayed away from nepotism. His interests and passions had other aims: the country and the power.

Park Chung Hee did not come from the upper class nor did he enjoy an university education. He was born on 30 September 1917 as the son of a poor farmer at a small village close to Kumi in the North Kyongsang province. After having attended school, Boku Shoki — thus his name was pronounced in Japanese — became a teacher in villages in his home province from 1937 to 1940. He then began a military career at the Military Academy in Manchuria. After having finished his training there, he attended the Military Academy in Tokyo. At the end of the war, he was a first Lieutenant of the Imperial Army in northern China. In 1945, he joined the South Korean armed forces and belonged to the 2nd class of the Military Academy. After the revolt in Yosu, he got into serious difficulties. He had joined the rebels and was arrested. This was the reason why, after 1961, he had repeatedly been accused of being a communist — though he was definitely a strongly anti–communist president. How he got free is not quite clear. There are assertions that it was Chung Il Kwon who, at that time already Brigadier General, later Army Chief-of-Staff, Prime Minister and Speaker, saved him.[28] I feel that this might be true.

[28]Yang Song Chol, *pundaiun chongchi* (*Policy of Division*) Seoul 1987 pp. 74 ff., see also Cumings (1997) p. 350.

After the beginning of the Korean War, he was readmitted to the military as a captain. By the end of the war, he had become Brigadier General and could only add one more star in the following years. A lack of abilities could not have been the reason although he revealed his talents only after having entered politics.

His rise to power illustrated that he was strong-willed and, though being of firm principles, flexible enough to survive in politics. He was a great master of playing one person off against another. He was obsessed with the idea that the community came first. This explained, although it did not justify, why he so often disregarded the rights of individuals. In his book "Our Nations Path" published in 1962, he wrote: "Now is the time for each individual to place his hand upon his heart, reflect upon our shameful past, and resolve to regenerate himself as a loyal and patriotic member of the national community. All the anti-national, unpatriotic poisons lurking in our hearts must be rooted out and burned away by our passionate love of the country. When the dried-up spring of patriotism gushes forth again and the wilted national consciousness regains its former vigor, then there will be light in this land, the first torch of a National revolution, a People's Revolution".[29]

Park Chung Hee was mainly driven by patriotism. He wanted to free Korea from poverty and heteronomy, which he had experienced as a young man. He worked with all his strength to achieve these aims. He felt that the greatest obstacle in Korea's path to modernization was the Korean disunity. This explained his aversion against party politics. As an admirer of the Meiji reforms in Japan, he had tried to renew Korea by energetic administration which replaced politics. It was not too difficult to find recognition for this system since Korea had always been ruled in an authoritarian way by a small class. His self-confidence was strengthened when he alone survived in the center of power. By and by, he came to believe that only he was capable to show Korea the path to modernization. He did not realize that institutions were more important than people. He did not develop any feeling of the importance of the legality of government; in so far he remained a revolutionary. His opponents' arguments that Korea had never had a constitutional transfer of power of the office of chief executive did not impress him. The man, whose task was to protect him against a coup, killed him: Park Chung Hee was swallowed up by his own system.

[29]Park Chung Hee, *Our Nation's Path*, pp. 21 and 22.

After his death, Park Chung Hee seemed to be forgotten. His brutality and ruthlessness had made him the villain of South Korean history.[30] His name was seldom mentioned in South Korea. Only his eldest daughter Park Keun Hae, with the support of some of the faithful, tried to keep his memory alive. Ten years after her father's death, all of a sudden she met a better response. On the occasion of the 10th anniversary of the former president's death, the Chung Ang Ilbo published the result of a poll on 25 October 1989 with surprising results. 63.7% of those asked considered Park Chung Hee the most outstanding national leader since Korea's liberation. 61% thought that his merits had outshone his mistakes. Only 13.7% were of the opposite view. The majority of Koreans consider him the engineer of Korea's economic rise. Again ten years later, even Kim Dae Jung, now one of the successors of Park Chung Hee, praised the murdered president for his economic accomplishments.[31]

References

Informationsministerium der Republik Korea, *Park Chung Hee, Staatspräsident der Republik Korea*, Seoul 1967.

Kal, Bong Keun, "Characteristics of the New Constitution", in *Koreana Quarterly* Vol. XIV No. 4 (Winter 1972–73) pp. 52 ff.

Lee, Chae Jin, "South Korea: The Politics of Domestic-Foreign Linkage" in *Asian Survey* Vol. XIII No. 1 (January 1973) pp. 94 ff.

Park, Chung Hee, *Our Nation's Path*, 2nd edition, Seoul 1962.

Park, Chung Hee, *The Country, The Revolution and I*, 2nd edition, Seoul 1970.

Park, Chung Hee, *To build a nation*, Washington 1971.

---

[30] International Herald Tribune, 25–26 November 1995.

[31] Korea Times, 16 May 1999.

Chapter 10

Steps to Power

The Shots of Kungjong-dong Reverberate

The shots in Kungjong-dong which had killed President Park Chung Hee made the remaining powerful stay awake all night. The meeting place on 26 October 1979 was the army headquarters in Seoul's Yongsan district. General Chung Seung Hwa, the Army Chief-of-Staff, had directed the car in which he traveled together with KCIA Director Kim Jae Kyu to army headquarters. Upon the General's request, the Minister of Defense and the most important commanders came. Later the top civilian officials, Prime Minister Choi Kyu Hah, the Minister of Home Affairs, the Minister of Justice, the Foreign Minister also arrived. They had been alarmed by Kim Kae Won, the Secretary General of the presidential secretariat. After some time, Kim Kae Won, who had witnessed the murder, revealed that KCIA Director Kim Jae Kyu was the assassin. Kim Jae Kyu was arrested. On 29 October 1979, Kim Kae Won was also arrested. After the cabinet members had convinced themselves that President Park Chung Hee had been killed, they decided to impose martial law over the country (with the exception of Cheju Island) starting at 4.00 a.m. on 27 October 1979. General Chung Seung Hwa was made martial law commander. Troops were deployed. When a spokesman announced the decision of the cabinet, he informed the Korean public that Prime Minister Choi Kyu Hah was acting as President as provided in Art. 48 of the constitution.

The die was cast: The proclamation of martial law put the control of the government in the hands of the military. The situation was not easy, no doubt, but an emergency which could only be overcome by engaging troops did not exist. Why the US administration considered the measures taken by the South Korean government as moderate is a mystery. As the rights of the executive as well as of the judiciary were placed at the disposal of the martial law administration, the Choi Kyu Hah government was weakened. Choi was also not a man of determination; it was difficult to believe that Park Chung Hee, as his daughter reported,[1] had him in mind as his successor. The KCIA, another pillar of Park's rule, had been weakened by the bloody deed of its director and had no chance to participate in the power struggle. Already on 27 October 1979, all heads of department of the KCIA were arrested by the military. Lieutenant General Lee Hui Sung became KCIA Director.

In the following months, two main developments could be observed. On the one hand, civilian politicians tried to normalize and democratize the country. On the other hand, there was an infighting within the military and a step-by-step advancement of a group of generals within the government.

Civilian Developments

One could have the impression that the crisis was managed according to the constitution. Its provision (Art. 45) that, in case of a vacancy in the office of the president, the successor shall be elected within three months was kept. On 6 December 1979, Choi Kyu Ha was elected President by the National Conference for Unification; there had been no rival candidate. He immediately repealed Emergency Measure No. 9 which had penalized criticizing the government and had made the Yushin system unchallengeable. Thus, one barrier which had made democratic activities close to impossible was removed. President Choi Kyu Hah formed a new cabinet headed by Shin Hyun Hwack, a capable economic and administrative expert. On 28 February 1980, the President restored the civil rights of 687 dissidents, including Kim Dae Jung and Yun Po Sun.

Already before his election, Choi Kyu Hah had announced that the new president ought not to exhaust the full tenure of office, but should revise the constitution and hold elections according to the new constitution. This was well meant, but Choi Kyu Hah by making himself an interim president weakened his position considerably. A committee of the National Assembly

[1]Korea Post Vol. 2 No. 12, December 1989 p. 50.

started working on a revision of the constitution hoping to finish the preparations by May 1980. On March 1980, the government set up a Constitution Deliberation Council. However, private efforts to draft a constitution had been faster. Already on January 1980, experts presented a draft which envisaged direct elections of the president and the Parliament, a strengthened position of the prime minister, increased controlling functions of Parliament and an improved division of powers.[2]

Although a new constitution did not yet exist, political groups were formed in view of the next presidential elections. As possible candidates, the "three Kims" were mentioned. The career of Kim Jong Pil, Park's old friend and competitor took another turn. On 12 November 1979, he was elected president of the DRP and thus became its candidate for the next presidential elections; to make it to the top had been his aim for so many years. Within the opposition party, NDP Kim Young Sam, the party boss, called the shots. The third Kim, Kim Dae Jung, faced a difficult situation; he could enter the political stage only at the beginning of March 1980, after his civil rights had been restored. He could not reach agreement with Kim Young Sam and felt that the NDP's judgment of developments after Park's death was too optimistic. He therefore, had already urged the US on 2 November 1975 to assure the neutrality of the generals during the succession process.[3]

Many Koreans felt that progress did not come quick enough. And as so many times before, it was the students who gave expressions to these feelings. After they had demonstrated since mid-March 1980 for academic reforms and for the abolition of the military training program, they now demanded political reforms. They demanded to repeal martial law and to introduce democratic reforms. From the 13th to the 15th of May 1980, Korea was once again upset by large student demonstrations.

Somewhat earlier, in April 1980, it had become obvious again that social problems had to be solved. In Sabuk, a small place in Kangwon province, miners had demanded wage increases and the resignation of their union leader whom they considered to be too close to the management.[4] They had rioted and brought the place under their control for a number of days. The fighting between the miners and the police was brutal, and was a reminder of the

---

[2]Dong A Ilbo, 17 January 1980.

[3]New York Times, 3 November 1979.

[4]Hanguk Ilbo, 24 and 25 April 1980.

brutalities the Koreans had committed against each other during the Korean War. After the governor of the province had stepped in, the conflict could be solved by a compromise.

Another Rebellion within the Military

The proclamation of martial law had put the military leadership at the center of Korean politics. Within the military, there was no unanimity which political structures were desirable and how far the military should participate in filling them.

Major General Chun Doo Hwan had gathered a group of younger generals around him. Most of them belonged to the 11th class of the military academy and at the same time, to a private organization called *hanahoe* (one mind society) organized by Chun. These generals stood for a conservative course and were opposed to a liberalization of politics. At the time of the murder of President Park Chung Hee, his close follower Chun Doo Hwan had been in a strategically favorable position. He was the Commander of the Defense Security Command (*kukkun boan saryongbu*, better known as *boansa*) which was the reconnaissance and counterintelligence branch of the armed forces. Because of his function, he was made the head of a team which was charged with investigating the murder of Park Chung Hee. In this capacity, he gathered a lot of information and became deeply involved in events after Park's murder.

On 12 December 1979, the generals around Chun Doo Hwan launched their attack.[5] Why they chose that day is not absolutely clear. A couple of days ago, General Chung Seung Hwa had proposed to transfer Chun Doo Hwan to a less influential post on the East Coast. It was perhaps this fact which made Chun's group move quickly. In the evening of 12 December 1979, the group around Chun Doo Hwan met at the 30th unit camp of the Capitol Garrison Command located in the area of the Kyongbok Palace in the heart of the capital. The officers involved who showed up at the 30th camp unit seemed to have been a small group. The Seoul District Prosecution Office named 9

[5] *Background Details of December 12 Incident*, distributed by the Ministry of Foreign Affairs in January 1980 (a copy is in the author's possession); Far Eastern Economic Review, 22 August 1980 pp. 8 and 9; Kim Myong Shik in Korea Times, 15 November 1987; Interview with Roh Tae Woo in Korea Times, 13 November 1987.

officers on 29 October 1994.[6] Yoo Hak Seong, Assistant Minister of Defense for Logistics, one of the conspirators and, therefore, someone who knew had earlier mentioned 6 generals.[7] The key figures were besides himself and the group's head Chun Doo Hwan: Major General Roh Tae Woo, commander of the 9th division, Lieutenant General Cha Kyu Hon, commander of the Capital Defense Corps, Major General Park Jun Byung, commander of the 20th division and Lieutenant General Hwang Young Shi, commander of the 1st Corps. These generals decided to arrest the Army Chief-of-Staff and Martial Law Commander General Chung Seung Hwa by accusing him of having played a role in the assassination. They accused their boss of being a suspect because during the murder, he was close to the scene of the crime and because he was opposed to the investigation of his own participation. A team was sent which arrested General Chung Seung Hwa. The first casualties occurred. When commanders, who were loyal to the Army Chief-of-Staff, mobilized troops, the conspirators also moved the units they commanded. Additional casualties occurred. The rebels succeeded quickly, but tension prevailed in the capital.

On that fateful day, 12 December 1979, Major General Chun Doo Hwan had tried to reach President Choi's consent to arrest General Chung Seung Hwa, but the President had rejected the request. Only after the rebels had taken their decisive steps did the President agree in the early morning hours of 13 December 1979. What happened on 12 December 1979 — called in those years the December 12 incident — was more than a conflict within the military; it was a rebellion. Subordinate officers removed jointly and without endorsement by the civilian leadership their commander-in-chief. As all participants later moved to leading positions, it was obvious that they set out in the night of 12 December 1979 to seize power, not just in the military but in the state. In the terms of the South Korean Criminal Code, this was an insurrection.

Developments followed the pattern of events in May 1961. If the rebels wished to succeed, they had to fill the most important military position, that of the Army Chief-of-Staff. After General Chung Seung Hwa had been arrested, General Lee Hui Sung became Army Chief-of-Staff and Martial Law Commander. Chun Doo Hwan and his accomplices refrained from taking top positions immediately. Chun Doo Hwan, Lieutenant General since 1 March 1980, was made Acting Director of the KCIA. Since he, at the same time, continued to

---

[6] Korea Times, 30 October 1994.

[7] Korea Times, 12 September 1987.

serve as Commander of the Defense Security Command, he was in charge of civilian and military intelligence. Prime Minister Shin Hyun Hwak opposed the accumulation of posts, but his resistance was in vain. The number two man of the rebels Roh Tae Woo was appointed Commander of Capital Security Command.

Kwangju — The Beginning of a Trauma

On 17 May 1980, martial law was extended to Cheju Island and was tightened. A new decree on the same day banned all kinds of political activities, closed all colleges and universities and subjected the media to censorship.

Troops moved into the capital guarding all strategically important points. Leading politicians of the DRP and the opposition were arrested under the charge of having made money illegally and having instigated unrest. Kim Jong Pil, the president of the DRP, and Kim Dae Jung were arrested. Kim Young Sam was put under house arrest on 20 May 1980. The National Assembly and the offices of the larger political parties were closed.

President Choi Kyu Hah justified these measures with the necessity to react to "an anarchic situation".[8] This argument was shallow, however, as the unrest had just died down. Therefore, the National Assembly intended to take a decision on rescinding martial law during its session scheduled for 22 May 1980. The truth was that Chun Doo Hwan and his followers wanted to stop the efforts to democratize the institutions which would have excluded them from politics. Chun and his group succeeded. The new measures were in no way sufficient to ease tensions and to calm down discontent. On the contrary, the country was going to face the most severe shock for many years.

Serious clashes between students and workers on the one side and the military on the other side occurred on Sunday 18 May 1980 in Kwangju, the capital of the South Cholla province. On the next day, even more people took to the streets. The military — martial law troops — reacted in a massive way. Parachutists and Special Forces attacked the demonstrators with fixed bayonets and drove into the crowd with armored carriers. A leaflet distributed by the Committee of the Chosun University stated that the soldiers

---

[8]Korea Annual 1980 p. 404; see also the statement of Prime Minister Shin Hyun Hwack in Korea Times, 7 December 1988.

had stabbed at people as if they were pumpkins.[9] It was a day of destruction and devastation, leaving many people killed or injured. It was a day of brutalities which also affected innocent people. This caused many people to show solidarity with the demonstrators. On 21 May 1980, the conflict spread from Kwangju to the two Cholla provinces showing the ingredients of a civil war. As the demonstrators succeeded to get hold of military vehicles, weapons and ammunition, the clash became even more violent. From 22 May 1980, Kwangju was in the hands of the rebels. Committees took over the administration of the city trying to fight chaos. Firing continued but there were also discussions between representatives from the population and the martial law commander.

Meanwhile, the military had deployed enough troops and encircled Kwangju with 25,000 men.[10] The troops deployed belonged to the 31st reserve division stationed in Kwangju, to the 3rd, 7th and 11th airborne brigade of the Special Forces and to parts of the 20th infantry division. In the early hours of 27 May 1980, Kwangju was conquered by troops in an assault like in times of war. The troops proceeded in a brutal way.

The precise figure of casualties was never established. On 31 May 1980, General Lee Hui Sung, Martial Law Commander, stated that the casualties amounted to 170 people killed (144 civilians, 22 soldiers and 4 policemen) and 380 people injured.[11] The figures were later corrected to 191 people killed (164 civilians, 23 soldiers and 4 policemen) and 852 injured.[12] These figures were confirmed by Minister of Defense Yoo Song Min before the Defense Committee of the National Assembly many years later, on 7 June 1985.[13] He rejected the charges that 2,000 people were killed. The government, however, had difficulties to explain why the Kwangju annual report of statistics of 1980 listed the total number of persons who died in the city in June 1980

[9] Leaflet of the Committee of Chosun University for the Fight for Democracy of 22 or 23 May 1980 (A translation is in the author's possession).

[10] Report of Minister of Defense Yoon, Sung Min to the National Assembly in Korea Herald, 8 June 1985; statement of Chung, Ho Yong, Commander of the Special Warfare Command during the Kwangju uprising, before a Special Committee of the National Assembly in Korea Times, 8 December 1988; statement of Park, Jun Byung, Commander of the 20th infantry division before the same committee in Korea Times, 22 December 1988.

[11] Korea Annual 1981 p. 9.

[12] See Korea Herald, 8 and 15 June 1985, 3 July 1985.

[13] Korea Herald, 8 June 1985.

at 2,627. It argued that "a clerical error" was responsible for that figure and had the official-in-charge punished.[14] Kim Dae Jung, who would have known, mentioned to me the figure of approximately 1,000 persons killed in Kwangju in May 1980.

What were the intentions of the people fighting in Kwangju? They fought against a military dictatorship which had found its expression in the tightened rule of martial law. They demanded to dismiss Lieutenant General Chun Doo Hwan whom they considered to be the key figure of the martial law system. And they demanded the release of Kim Dae Jung who was from South Cholla and whom they considered as belonging to them. They had no intention to permanently seize state authority. Only the brutal intervention of the military had caused the demonstrations to develop into an uprising. This was even later admitted by some of the military leaders. Lee Hui Sung, Army Chief-of-Staff and Martial Law Commander during the uprising, stated in 1988: "There were many factors for the Kwangju incident. But a direct cause was the martial law forces' excessive action in putting down the demonstrations".[15] Major General Chong Ung, division commander in Kwangju, tried to oppose the drastic measures; he was, therefore, dismissed. In 1988, he claimed that the events in Kwangju had been methodically planned by the military leaders.[16] Inevitably, Chun Doo Hwan and his supporters, the rulers of the country, had to take the responsibility for the events in Kwangju. They never recovered politically, as the bloody uprising in Kwangju questioned the legitimacy of their rule permanently.

New Political Structures

After the uprising in Kwangju was quelled, a new agency was established on 31st May 1980 called the Special Committee for National Security Measures (SCNSM).[17] It had altogether 24 members, among them the most important ministers and 14 generals. The committee's task was allegedly to

[14]Korea Herald, 8 June 1985.

[15]Korea Herald, 10 February 1988.

[16]A copy of the statement (in handwriting) is in the author's possession.

[17]Announcement by Government Spokesman Lee Kwang Pyo, Minister of Culture and Information on the *Establishment of the Special Committee for National Security Measures*, 6 June 1980, distributed type-written by KOIS.

coordinate between the cabinet and the martial law administration. But in reality the SCNSM, which was the invention of the all-powerful Defense Security Command, seized state control. It is interesting to note that the Minister of Defense Choo Young Bock was briefed by Kwon Jung Dal, the Deputy of Chun Doo Hwan in the Defense Security Command, already on 17 May 1980 about the plans to establish the Special Committee for National Security Measures.[18] Among the 24 members of the committee were the six key figures of the insurrection mentioned above. Chun Doo Hwan chaired the SCNSM's Standing Committee which became the central core of the new structure. Chun Doo Hwan and his accomplices had taken another step towards seizing power.

The new rulers wanted to restore public order, and that was the real justification for their intervention. But what else did they have in mind? We get some information from an interview that Chun Doo Hwan had given to Time Magazine before the Kwangju uprising, which was, however, published only on 26 May 1980. Chun listed three reasons for the military rule: guaranteeing national security against the danger from the North, building up the economy and developing a political system compatible with Korean conditions. After reading this interview, one might have had the impression that Park Chung Hee was speaking, and Chun used the opportunity to express his admiration for the murdered president by calling him "a leader almost without parallel in our history". But he added a new tone when he said: "What we need now is creative nationalism". He apparently had in mind developing Park's patriotism into nationalism.

In later statements, he took up the same issues developing them a bit further. He elaborated on his ideas concerning Korea's economic development in his inaugural address on 1 September 1980 by demanding to "construct a genuinely democratic welfare state".[19] He then suggested to increase job opportunities through increased public investments, to improve working conditions, to close the wage gap, to provide economic security for workers and to improve labor management cooperation.

The way the generals proceeded in the spring of 1980 to seize control of the government reminds us of the similar actions of the military in the spring

---

[18]See Yoo's statement before a Special Committee of the National Assembly, Korea Herald, 20 November 1988.

[19]Korea Annual 1981 p. 389.

of 1961. At that time, a Supreme Council for National Reconstruction assumed executive as well as judicial functions. But there was one important difference. Park Chung Hee and his followers called their revolt a revolution. As the revolt came from above, the term coup d'état would have been more fitting. Regardless of the term, Park's group did not deny that they destroyed the existing form of government. Chun's group acted in another way: They pretended to have come to power in a legal way. The organization of the Special Committee for National Security Measures was based on provisions of the Martial Law Act. However this act, though giving far-reaching powers, did not authorize the change of the constitutional system. The military had made use of the opportunity offered to them by martial law to abolish the Yushin constitution.

The SCNSM had been set up by President Choi Kyu Hah. By accepting the office of President and by staying in office after having been sidelined, Choi Kyu Hah contributed even more than Yun Po Sun had done in 1961 to give some sort of legality to the military regime. Choi Kyu Hah resigned on 16 August 1980 and his last speech also contained false emotions. Justifying his decision to step down he said: "My purpose is to provide a historic turning point for the building of a new happy community of stability, morality and prosperity which is the demand of our times".[20] The reality was different: As he was no longer needed, he had to go.

The next steps were quickly taken by the military. Chun Doo Hwan had resigned from the office as KCIA Director on 2 June 1980 and was promoted to four-star general on 6 August 1980. On 27 August 1980, he was elected President by the National Conference for Reunification which had been reactivated even though the Yushin constitution was obsolete. This election did not count for much since it was held when martial law was still in force. The government quickly presented a draft for the amendment of the constitution which was accepted by a referendum with 91.6% of the votes (turnout 95.5%) on 22 October 1980. Also, this referendum did not count for much because martial law was still in force. There was no chance to quickly discuss the provisions of the new constitution; this situation was a reminder of the way the Yushin constitution was introduced at the end of 1972. According to the provisions of the new constitution, a Legislative Council for National Security was formed replacing the Special Committee for National

[20]Text in Korea Annual 1981 pp. 409 ff.

Security Measures. The Legislative Council had the functions of an interim Parliament. Its members, however, were not elected but appointed by the President.

The Legislative Council worked hard and passed 189 laws altogether.[21] Many of the laws were aimed at restoring that kind of public order which to guarantee the new rulers had in mind.

Purges had already started when people were arrested on 17 May 1980 and continued throughout the summer.[22] Many thousands of officials fell victim to the purges. More than 50,000 alleged criminals were rounded up. Nearly 40,000 people were sent to military reeducation camps, called Samchong camps. 50 of them died, a fact which the Korean public came to know only in 1988.[23] The "purification" measures were finished by a Special Measures Act of Renovation of the Political Climate on 3 November 1980 which provided that those people who were responsible for corruption and confusion were excluded from political activities. The activities of more than 500 politicians, among them Kim Jong Pil, Chung Il Kwon, Kim Young Sam, Lee Chul Seung and Kim Dae Jung were banned.[24]

Other laws restricted the activities of the already weak trade unions. Bargaining was confined to the individual enterprise level; the unions were not permitted to get involved in labor conflicts. A Press Law on 26 December 1980 imposed strict government controls on all media. Since July 1980, 700 journalists had been dismissed, numerous papers and magazines had been closed down or merged, and publishing companies had been closed.[25] The Defense Security Command had implemented these measures. Only two TV stations, KBS and MBC, and one press agency, Yonhap, survived.

The Legislative Council also passed various laws to fix new political structures. It passed laws on the Presidential and National Assembly elections and on political parties. The stage was set for the Fifth Republic.

---

[21] Airgram of the US Embassy in Seoul, dated 30 May 1981 (unclassified).

[22] Korea Annual 1981 pp. 25 ff.

[23] Hankook Ilbo, 21 December 1988; Korea Times, 27 June and 1 October 1988, Far Eastern Economic Review, 20 October 1988.

[24] Far Eastern Economic Review, 21 November 1980.

[25] See the statement before a Committee of the National Assembly in Korea Times, 23 November 1988, and the statement of Kwon Jung Dal before the Seoul Prosecution in Korea Times, 13 May 1990.

The Trial of Kim Dae Jung

The military junta had already disposed of quite a number of opponents. Kim Jae Kyu was sentenced to death on 20 December 1979 for murdering Park Chung Hee and was executed on 24 May 1980. The death sentence against Kim Kae Won was commuted into life-long imprisonment on 29 January 1980. General Chung Seung Haw, after having been tortured by his former subordinates, was sentenced to ten years in prison for assisting Kim Jae Kyu in attempted sedition.[26] The boss of the DRP Kim Jong Pil had to relinquish all his public posts on 24 June 1980. Kim Young Sam also retired from politics on 12 August 1980.

The only decision missing was what to do with Kim Dae Jung whom the junta considered as their most dangerous opponent. What charges should the junta level against him?

A statement by the martial law administration on 22 May 1980 indicated the direction.[27] Two charges were leveled against Kim Dae Jung. Firstly, he was said to have instigated students to demonstrate in order to create chaos, to overthrow the government and to seize power. To prepare these moves, he was said to have created private organizations. He was further accused of having scheduled the uprising at Kwangju on 22 May 1979. Secondly, he was charged with having earlier organized pro-North Korean Koreans and other anti-state elements in Japan and the USA. He allegedly had been involved when Hanmintong was founded, an organization which had been designated as an anti-state organization by the Supreme Court in 1978. And he was suspected to have been involved in procommunist activities until recently. That was the aim of the military: to push Kim Dae Jung into the communist corner and to label him as a communist.

When the martial law administration published the results of its investigations, it went a step further.[28] Kim Dae Jung was not only charged with having planned a putsch but also of having played the decisive role in the Kwangju uprising. He was accused of being the mastermind of events and of having controlled the student's street demonstrations from behind the scene. It was further said that the investigation had brought to light that he was a communist and had participated in leftist activities in 1945.

---

[26] See his statement in Dong A Ilbo, 19 November 1987.

[27] Korea Herald, 23 May 1980.

[28] Korea Herald, 5 July 1980.

The indictment — a miserable paper which did not even mention the applicable provisions of laws — turned the arguments around.[29] Kim Dae Jung was accused first of having acted as a communist and only second of having planned the putsch. His alleged connections to the events in Kwangju were only briefly mentioned. To indict Kim Dae Jung because of alleged procommunist activities during his stay in Japan in 1972 and 1973 violated a South Korean–Japanese agreement by which both governments had tried to settle the abduction case in 1973.

The general court martial, presided over by Major General Mun Ung Shik, sentenced Kim Dae Jung to death on charges of anti-state activities and preparations of an insurrection on 17 September 1980.[30] The verdict was pronounced and explained verbally in just six minutes. As Kim Dae Jung told me, he had never received the verdict in writing. It is, therefore, difficult to ascertain the reasons for the verdict in detail. They will have been the following: The death sentence was justified with violations of the Anti-Communist Law and the National Security Act, the main argument being that he was a communist. The preparation of an insurrection was only punishable by imprisonment, not by death (Art. 87 and 90 of the Criminal Code). If it was the intention to sentence him to death, it was indispensable to evoke the Anti-Communist and National Security Laws. The appeals were in vain. The trial was finished which had been marked by hatred. When the prosecutor demanded the death penalty for Kim Dae Jung on 11 September 1980, he had said that "deceitful, opportunistic and demagogic politicians" like Kim Dae Jung should disappear from Korea forever.[31] Eighteen years later, Kim Dae Jung was President of the Republic of Korea.

Kim Dae Jung was and is not a communist as I can witness on the basis of many talks I have had with him. He is a democrat and one of the few South Korean politicians who started voicing social concern early on. He is also not an atheist but a Christian, a Catholic believer. To call him a communist and sentence him under this charge was absurd. In the eyes of Western observers, he had become a martyr for democracy. Accordingly, the death sentence caused a storm of indignation in the West. It affected negatively the relations to South Korea's friends who were already disturbed by the events following the

[29]Korea Times, 15 August 1980.

[30]Korea Times, 18 September 1980.

[31]Korea Times, 12 September 1980.

murder of Park Chung Hee. Many governments, organizations, politicians and individuals fought for the life of Kim Dae Jung. To intervene in favor of Kim Dae Jung was the main task of many embassies in Seoul in the months following the death sentence. The German Embassy, for example, made a dozen démarches with high government officials of the host country. The answer was always the same: The South Korean government rejected these representations as interference in the domestic affairs. The pressure, however, had an effect.

What really counted was the attitude of the US administration.[32] Since the murder of Park Chung Hee, the US government was concerned about the developments in Korea. The US tried to foster efforts to give South Korea a more liberal constitution, but had to also take South Korean and its own security interests into consideration. It became even more concerned by the insurrection of Chun Doo Hwan and his followers on 12 December 1979. The US agencies in South Korea were taken by surprise and the US Ambassador William Gleysteen and the Commander-in-Chief, United Nations Command, General John Wickham spent a frustrating night in a military bunker in Yongsan, unable to influence developments.[33] General Wickham had an additional reason to be upset; the Chun group had moved units which were under the operational control of the Combined Forces Command without — as stipulated — informing the general in advance that they were removing units from CFC operational control. This night might have presented the only chance for a military intervention of loyal Korean forces assisted by the US. Since General Wickham was afraid of clashes between army units, he urged the Ministry of Defense to suspend movements of forces loyal to the Ministry of Defense until dawn.[34] Six weeks later, senior military officers approached the US Embassy in search of support for a counter-coup which the embassy declined. The risks involved in initiating a fight between various factions of the Korean armed forces were too high.[35] At the end of January 1981, it was much too late to start overthrowing the Chun regime.

---

[32]Oberdorfer p. 133 with many details; *United States Government Statement on the Events in Kwangju*, Republic of Korea, in May 1980, Backgrounder of the US Embassy, Seoul, dated 19 June 1988; GIST, *South Korea: Recent Developments*, published by the Department of State, May 1980; *For the Record*, Press Release of the US Embassy Seoul, 18 June 1980.

[33]Wickham pp. 57–66, Gleysteen pp. 78–82.

[34]Wickham p. 59.

[35]Gleysteen pp. 93–97.

The question of US operational control of the South Korean forces developed into a political problem which was to haunt the US government for years. The reason was Kwangju. In this event, the military junta had followed established procedures. On 16 May 1980, military authorities notified the Combined Forces Command of their intent to remove some units of the 20th division from CFC operational control. The CFC acknowledged the release notification. So far, all was good.

It was at this point that the Americans made a serious mistake. Although none of the forces deployed at Kwangju — the special forces anyway and the units of the 20th division not any longer — was under the control of any American authority, General Wickham and Ambassador Gleysteen involved themselves into discussions about the actions to be taken in Kwangju.[36] Following the interpretation by the US government, US officials "reluctantly accepted" to replace Special Forces units with elements of the 20th division because these had been trained for riot control duty.[37] As we learned from Ambassador Gleysteen, the Americans actually went a step further: they approved the use of the 20th division in Kwangju.[38] This was meant well but it could have been misused by the Chun group to insinuate that the US government was collaborating to quell the uprising at Kwangju. The junta did not hesitate to do so. However, the contrary was true. US government agencies in Washington and Seoul pressed desperately for a political solution and against a military. They, however, again found out what they had experienced during the days of Park's coup d'état in May 1961, namely that their leverage on South Korean politics was marginal. In the words of Ambassador Gleysteen: "We knew that Korea was going through a momentously important event, yet for the most part we were held to the sidelines".[39] Unfortunately, the US agencies involved did not succeed in correcting the South Korean distortions. Thus, there were already ill feelings on the American side when Kim Dae Jung was sentenced to death.

Now the US administration stepped in energetically. Its intervention, prepared by President Jimmy Carter and continued by the incoming President Ronald Reagan, saved the life of Kim Dae Jung. President Reagan invited

---

[36] Wickham pp. 127–149, Gleysteen pp. 131–141.

[37] Backgrounder p. 3; see also Journal Commerce, 27 February 1996 (via LEXIS-NEXIS).

[38] Gleysteen p. 133.

[39] Gleysteen p. 139.

President Chun Doo Hwan to come to Washington as his first official guest in January 1981. Before Chun left Korea on 23 January 1981, he commuted the death penalty to life imprisonment. That was part of a deal which made Chun's visit in Washington possible.[40] In his remarks during Chun's visit, President Reagan went far. At a luncheon on 2 February 1981, he said: "We share your commitment to freedom. If there is one message that I have for the Korean people today, it is this: Our special bond of freedom and friendship is as strong today as it was in that meeting thirty years ago"[41] (General MacArthur gave the liberated capital Seoul back to the Korean government). State interests sometimes call for self-denial. But to invoke a commitment to freedom of someone who so far had ruled by suppression was an unnecessary exaggeration.

The courageous man in prison thanked God. In a letter addressed to his children, dated 29 January 1981, he wrote: "I am reflecting now on God's endless love, which once more has saved my life. Especially when I consider that His blessing has delivered me from certain death four times, I can feel only unbounded rejoicing and gratitude".[42]

The Betrayal

The trial and the arguments used against Kim Dae Jung shed light on the background of political events after the murder of Park Chung Hee.

Kim Dae Jung was charged with having planned a coup d'état. Indeed, he aimed at abolishing the Yushin constitution, removing martial law and introducing a democratic constitution. Since he was free to move only at the beginning of March 1980, he was still in a process of propagating his ideas and gathering followers. The notion that he had instigated the uprising at Kwangju, and thus had played with fire, was incorrect. His confession that he had given money to Chong Tong Nyon, a leader of a student council in Kwangju, was false; it was forced out of him by torture.[43] Kim Dae Jung had heard of the Kwangju uprising only in July 1980 when he was still in prison.

[40]US Ambassador Walker in Korea Herald, 1 July 1989; see also Washington Post, 14 December 1980 and 27 January 1981.

[41]Oberdorfer pp. 136 and 137.

[42]Kim, Dae Jung, *Prison Writings*, Berkeley 1987 p. 20.

[43]Kim, Dae Jung before the National Assembly on 18 November 1988, Korea Herald 19 November 1988.

Others were unscrupulous. Chun Doo Hwan and the generals around him took one step after another to achieve power. They started with the insurrection on 12 December 1979, used the tightened martial law on 17 May 1980, and formally seized government authority through the Standing Committee at the end of May 1980. On 27 August 1980, Chun Doo Hwan made himself President. It was not Kim Dae Jung but Chun Doo Hwan and his followers who destroyed the existing constitutional order. They had good luck because they could hide behind the broad shoulders of President Choi Kyu Hah who endorsed their action.

Kim Dae Jung was imprisoned under charges of having prepared an insurrection. To sentence him as a communist meant to defame him. Yet Kim Dae Jung had to be happy to stay alive. Chun Doo Hwan and his generals on the other hand filled the top positions in a state that they had shaped.

Radical political changes are only possible when the old system is betrayed. That had happened. But why? The new rulers had to prove that they had more in mind than just the restoration of law and order.

References

Lee, Hyun Bok, "ship iguk ihu ibaehil — in durama (The 200 days drama after 26 October)" in *Chonggyong munhwa* 1985 No. 6 pp. 178 ff.

Chapter 11

No Better Country?

Consolidation of Power

Civilian normalcy would only return after martial law had been lifted and a political machinery had been set up. Martial law was lifted on 24 January 1981. Political parties were needed to fill the structures created by the new constitution. Since the new rulers who had reached the top in such an arduous way and had no intention of returning to the barracks, it was indispensable that they formed their own political party. On 15 January 1981, they inaugurated the Democratic Justice Party (DJP); Chun Doo Hwan became the party president. A former member of the opposition, Lee Chai Hyung, became party chairman. The kingpin was Kwon Jung Dal who had been Chun's deputy at the Defense Security Command. He now became Secretary General of the DJP. He succeeded in winning many public figures, including former officers, businessmen, scholars, government officials, journalists and former politicians. This was not surprising. The party platform was based upon building a just society by means of persistent reforms in all spheres of life. This, however, was not the main idea which attracted followers.[1] The new party was supposed to be the organization for seizing and maintaining power by the new rulers in the new constitutional system. A lot of people did not want to miss that chance.

On 17 January 1981, the successor party for the Democratic Party and the New Democratic Party was inaugurated under the name of Democratic Korea Party (DKP). Yu Chi Song, who had played a leading role in the NDP, was

[1] Korea Annual 1982 p. 59.

elected chairman of the DKP. This party stood for a parliamentary democracy, the protection of civil rights and an independent judiciary. Its destiny was the opposition.

Former members of the Democratic Republican Party and the Yujonghoe formed the Korea National Party (KNP) on 23 January 1981. Their aim was to preserve the heritage of the Park Chung Hee era. They stated in their party program that it was their goal to use the wisdom and experience they had accumulated in the drive to modernize South Korea and construct a welfare society during the past two decades.[2] A former member of the National Assembly and wealthy businessman, Kim Chong Chul, was elected as party president.

The new constitution provided for an indirect election of the president. He was to be elected by an Electoral College which resembled the National Conference for Reunification. When this body was elected on 11 February 1981, candidates of the DJP gained 69.6% of the seats (turnout: 78%). On 25 February 1981, the Electoral College elected Chun Doo Hwan as President for a seven-year term. He received 4,755 votes out of 5,271 votes (90% of the votes). The DJP had passed the first exam.

The next test followed a month later when National Assembly elections were held. The Democratic Justice Party captured only 35.6% of the votes cast, but thanks to a tricky electoral procedure 151 (54.7%) of the 276 seats.[3] The electoral system was organizod in the following way: Two thirds of the lawmakers, i.e. 184, were elected directly, 2 in each of the 92 constituencies. One third, a total of 92 seats, were allocated according to a proportional representation system; of these 92 seats, two thirds were given to the party which had gained the majority in the direct elections. The system worked. The DRP received 61 seats in addition to the 90 directly-won seats. The Democratic Korea Party won 81 seats, the Korea National Party won 25 seats. Chun Doo Hwan could hope that he would have an obedient Assembly in the years to come.

The first National Assembly election of the Fifth Republic was not held in a democratic way.[4] The majority of the leaders of the opposition were

[2]Korea Annual 1982 p. 61.

[3]Central Election Management Committee: *Korean National Assembly Members Election Act*, Seoul 1983.

[4]Far Eastern Economic Review, 3 April 1981.

still barred from running. Thus, only 94 former politicians were elected. The election campaign had been rigorously restricted. At rallies, the candidates could only campaign together and candidates were given only half an hour to appeal for votes. These strange performances were staged only a couple of times. The government-controlled press backed the DJP candidates; money and gifts were also helpful. In view of these circumstances, the result of 35.6% for the DJP was not convincing.

Trouble Ahead

If Chun Doo Hwan wanted to be successful, he had to tackle the country's economic crisis caused by the political development of 1980. He had made Nam Duck Woo, the father of the economic miracle under President Park Chung Hee, Prime Minister and appointed other technocrats as ministers. He then introduced a new five-year-plan. Economic success followed rather quickly.

For the South Korean economy, the year 1980 was a year of recession and inflation, caused not only by the political turbulence but also by the second oil crisis.[5] GNP growth was negative (−4.8%), and inflation of wholesale prices stood at 39%. As wage increases were well below the rate of inflation, workers had to face real wage losses. 1981 brought no change although growth picked up. In 1982, the situation improved as real wages increased. 1983 made a great leap forward: GNP growth rose to 12.6%, and inflation fell to almost zero (wholesale prices: 0.2%). Chun Doo Hwan had good reasons to hope that the Koreans would credit him with this success.

Although Chun's economic policy aimed not only at expansion but also at a balanced growth, the second take-off of the South Korean economy was somewhat bumpy. This was illustrated by financial scandals in 1982 and 1983, one of which had a lasting effect. For many years, a curb market existed in South Korea. This was a market where private loans were available.[6] This market was controlled by housewives. The interest rates were high since the risks were high. To secure their loans, moneylenders took promissory notes from borrowers. There was one lady in particular who was very active on

[5]Economic Planning Board, *Korea Statistical Yearbook 1986*, Seoul 1986 pp. 459 ff. and 409 ff. *Business Korea Yearbook 1986*, Seoul 1986 pp. 16 ff.

[6]New Züricher Zeitung, 23/24 May 1982; Clifford pp. 194 ff.

the curb market, Mrs. Chang Yong Ja. She misused the system by lending money against moderate interest rates and requesting notes in an amount far surpassing the loan. She then put the promissory notes into circulation by selling them at a discount and accepting, nevertheless, repayment from the borrowers. It was called the curb market, but it was big business involving hundreds of millions of US dollars. Large companies, which were often short of cash, also borrowed money from "Madame Chang". She even borrowed money from the banks and lent it against higher interest rates to her customers. On May 1982, when borrowers had found out that their promissory notes were still in circulation even though they had repaid their debt, the scheme collapsed. Important companies like Ilssin and Kongyung Construction went bankrupt; some banks and insurance companies ran into difficulties. It was an unparalleled scandal.

How could it have been that Mrs Chang could conduct that kind of business? There was a technical side to the business. Capital was a scarce commodity in South Korea. If companies, mostly owned by families, needed capital, they did not turn to the stock market by going public or issuing bonds but rather looked for loans. If they could not get loans from the banks, they turned to the curb market. And there was also a political side of Mrs. Chang's business. She was married to Lee Chol Hee, a former intelligence officer. Both of them had boasted in their dealings about their connection to the Blue House. The names of relatives of Lee Soon Ja, the wife of President Chun Doo Hwan, were mentioned. Her father Lee Kyu Dong and her uncle Lee Kyu Kwang were investigated. Cabinet members and DJP members tendered their resignation. Kwon Jung Dal, who had been instrumental in founding the DJP, lost his job as Secretary General of the party. The scandal was disastrous for Chun Doo Hwan because it left behind a lingering suspicion of corruption. During his term of office, Chun Doo Hwan could never get rid of this suspicion.

"I Order You to Destroy the Target"

In the early morning of Thursday 1 September 1983, many people waited at Kimpo Airport in Seoul for relatives, friends and guests who were supposed to arrive on flight KE 007 of Korean Air Lines. The aircraft, a Boeing 747, had started in New York, refueled in Anchorage and was scheduled to arrive in Seoul at 6:05 a.m. The scheduled time of arrival passed, but the airplane did not come. Korean Air Lines and the airport authorities made various announcements on why KE 007 was overdue. People began to feel uneasy. At 10:45 a.m. a national TV station, KBS, reported that the aircraft had been forced to land on Sakhalin. This report was based on a misunderstanding. Japanese authorities had discussed with the Korean Embassy in Tokyo on various alternatives to why flight KE 007 had not yet arrived.[7] When the Embassy had passed on this information to the Korean Ministry of Foreign Affairs, the other alternatives got lost and the officials thought to have understood that the aircraft had landed in Sakhalin. Most of those waiting for flight KE 007 were relieved when they heard the news and returned home.

Some Koreans may have remembered a similar incident which had occurred 5 years and 4 months earlier when Soviet fighter aircrafts had forces KE 902 which had lost direction and crossed the Kola Peninsula to land. The pilot had managed to land his Boeing 707 on a frozen lake south of Murmansk. When the plane had been fired upon in midair by the Soviet fighters, two passengers had been killed and thirteen wounded. Perhaps, some of those waiting for flight KE 007 had a premonition of impending disaster.

In the afternoon, the arrival lounge at Kimpo Airport was filled again because rumors had it that the aircraft had been shot down. People became extremely excited. A brother and his sister lost consciousness when they heard the terrible news. At 19:30 p.m. the Minister of Culture and Information, Lee Jin Hie, confirmed that it was rather sure that KE 007 had been gunned down by a third country. The next day the Korean media, quoting US Secretary of State George P. Shultz and Japanese sources, reported the nearly unbelievable news that the airliner had been shot down by Soviet fighters.[8] 269 people on board, 240 passengers from 15 countries and 29 crewmembers (6 of them not on duty), had been killed. President Chun Doo Hwan condemned the Soviet attack and said that he shared the sorrow and indignation over the incident.

The indignation of the Soviet attack was worldwide. An international conflict developed in which the South Koreans, who were mainly affected, played only a minor role. The main role was played by the US administration,

[7] Interview with an official of the Ministry of Foreign Affairs by the author on 21 March 1990.

[8] Alexander Dallin, *Black Box, KAL 007 and the Superpowers*, Berkley 1985; R. W. Johnson, *Shootdown Flight 007 and the American Connection*, Scranton 1986; Murray Sale, "KE 007. A Conspiracy of Circumstances", in *The New York Review* Vol. 32, 25 April 1985; Seymour M. Hersh, *The Target is destroyed*, New York 1987; Korea Times, 23 November 1984; Die Zeit, 19 April 1985.

not only because there were Americans among the victims, but because the US considered the Northern Pacific Ocean as an American Ocean. Additionally, they considered the incident to be a national security issue. In a televised speech on 5 September 1983, President Reagan called the downing of flight KE 007 a "massacre".[9] Statesmen of other countries followed with similar statements. Diplomatic activities ran at full speed. The UN Security Council became the main forum of accusations. On 6 September the US Ambassador to the UN, Mrs. Jean Kirkpatrick, had played parts of the radio communications between the Soviet Air Defense Command Centers and the pilots of three fighter jets which followed and shot 007 down. The communications had been monitored by Japanese agencies. The parts produced in the Security Council were, however, faulty due to omissions and mistakes, as was found out later.[10] The International Civil Aviation Organization (ICAO) made an investigation and published its findings.[11]

At first, the Soviet Union tried to deny the incident and used it to spread suspicion of an US involvement in what the Soviet government called a spy flight. But the West could provide too much evidence against this allegation. Later on, the Soviet Union had to admit that flight KE 007 was shot down by a Soviet fighter. Years later, in a rather unusual press conference on 9 September 1988, Marshal Orgakow, Soviet Military Chief-of-Staff, in the presence of Deputy Foreign Minister Kornienko and the head of the International Department of the Communist Party Central Committee Zamyatin presented the Soviet version.[12] Orgakov admitted that flight KE 007 had been shot down by heat-seeking missiles. He insisted, however, that the aircraft, which had intruded deeply into Soviet airspace, had been a reconnaissance plane.

What had really happened?[13] On August 1983 around 10:00 p.m., Korean time flight KE 007 departed from Anchorage.[14] The flight was to proceed on route R 20 in the North Pacific, the most northern route of the five routes from

---

[9]New York Times, 6 September 1983.

[10]Dallin pp. 17 ff.

[11]ICAO Document C-WP/7764 of 2 December 1983 and C-WP/7809 of February 1984.

[12]Washington Post, 10 September 1988.

[13]On the basis of the final ICAO report: Letter LE 4/19.4–93/68, 16 July 1993 with Attachments A to D (quoted as Attachment); see also Murray Sayle, "Closing the File on Flight 007", in The New Yorker, 13 December 1993 pp. 90 ff.

[14]All dates and times in the text are Korean dates and times.

Anchorage to Japan. Soon after the aircraft deviated from its assigned track in a northerly direction. This meant KE 007 was flying towards the Soviet Union. Although KE 007 had deviated from its course, it reported passing reporting points NABIE and NEEVA. These reports were related to Anchorage Air Control by flight KE 015 which had departed from Anchorage fourteen minutes after flight KE 007 and was also flying to Seoul. Another aircraft was cruising in the airspace above the Northern Pacific that night. It was an American reconnaissance aircraft, a RC-135, a modified Boeing 707 which had four engines just like the Boeing 747 of flight KE 007. KE 007 crossed the track of the RC-135. At 2.00 a.m. KE 007 reported passing NIPPI to Radio Tokyo, but was in reality flying much further north crossing Kamchatka — a military sensitive area. The Soviet air defense command had noticed the intruder aircraft; interceptor aircraft scrambled. Flight KE 007, however, reached the Sea of Okhotsh and thus international airspace.

At 3.15 a.m., KE 007 contacted Tokyo Radio again and requested to climb to 35,000 feet. The clearance was given. Meanwhile, KE 007 had deviated approximately 500 km north of its assigned track and had again intruded into Soviet airspace, this time flying over the island of Sakhalin, another military sensitive area. The Soviet interceptors found the intruders. When flight KE 007 communicated with Tokyo at 3:15 a.m., it was followed by several Soviet fighters; one of them, a SU-15, the pilot of which had number 805. At the same time General Kornukov, who was in command, gave the following order: "I order you to destroy the target".[15] This order was relayed to the pilot Osipovich in his SU-15. At 3:27 he fired two deadly missiles. The dialogue with ground control went as follows: "805, did you launch one missile"? "Launched both". "Roger, well done".[16] It was not well done, Osipovich had shot down a civil airliner. The last words of the crew of flight KE 007 monitored by the ground control in Tokyo were: "Korean Air 007 rapid are ... we are ... rapid compressions descend to one zero thousand".[17]

There were some people who saw the disaster. Servicemen of the Japanese air force saw on their radar screens an unidentified aircraft over Sakhalin between 3:10 and 3:30. They saw that the plane was approached by Soviet interceptors and then quickly, lose altitude before finally disappearing from

[15]Attachment C p. 126.
[16]Attachment C p. 73.
[17]Attachment C p. 39.

the radar screen. Flight KE 007 had crashed into the sea. One stops breathing making oneself aware of this sequence of events and thinking of the people in the aircraft.

A Mystery Solved

Many questions remained open, and they remained open for many years. Three questions in particular needed to be answered. Why did flight KE 007 deviate so much to the north of its track? Why did the Soviet Air Defense Command proceed so rigorously? Did anybody have the chance to alert the 007 crew of the impending danger?

Since not enough information was available, speculations abounded. The intrigue of spy cases made people willing to listen to speculations that KE 007 was flying a secret mission. Thus the Soviet Union met with good response when it propagated its version that flight KE 007 was a reconnaissance plane. Many, however, tried to find out the truth. Such efforts were also made in Russia and the daily Izvestiya published a series about the incident in 1991. One day the truth came to light. The Russian government produced the black boxes which it had already recovered from the seabed a few weeks after the incident. In late 1992, the Russian government handed a copy of the Cockpit Voice Recorder (CVR) and the Digital Flight Data Recorder (DFDR) containers to the Korean government. In January 1993, it presented the original tapes to the ICAO office in Paris. The French government examined the tapes for the ICAO, and in June 1993 the ICAO presented its final report.[18] The ICAO also made use of additional material handed over by the Russian government. These included tapes of ground-to-ground and ground-to-air recordings of the Soviet Armed Forces and of transcripts of such recordings. The ICAO report finally resolved most of the mysteries.

The report confirmed that flight KE 007, soon after departure from Anchorage, deviated to the north of its assigned track. It maintained a constant magnetic heading of 246 degrees. This path was so accurate that it must have been controlled by the autopilot. There were no system failures or malfunctions on the airplane. Therefore, the pilot was responsible for the course. Today airliners are generally navigated by the Inertial-Navigation-System (INS). KE

[18]See note 13.

007 had three separate INS systems on board, but the flight was not controlled by the INS. The crew should have engaged the INS as soon as they were sure they were on the right track. Normally they receive confirmation by a radio beam, called Very High Frequency Omnidirectional Radio Range (VOR); the VOR at Anchorage was, however, shut down that night for maintenance. Therefore, the crew had to use other means, provided by their instruments, to fly close to the programmed route so that it could engage the INS; it could capture the right track only if it was not less than 7.5 nautical miles away from it. Captain Chun Byung In, an experienced pilot of excellent reputation who was crossing the North Pacific for the 84th time, came within one mile of the programmed route; he did not engage the INS but switched his auto pilot to a compass heading of 246 degrees. Thus, the compass and not the INS was controlling the autopilot. Why he did this is not clear. He might have been trying to confirm his route at Bethel, a small place 380 nautical miles west of Anchorage which had an operating VOR system. But already at that point, KE 007 had deviated so much from its course that it was outside the corridor where it could capture the track. If the crew had believed to have VOR confirmation at Bethel and then engaged the INS, it was of no effect; the aircraft continued to cruise on the compass course. Another possible explanation for the fact that the aircraft was travelling on the magnetic course could have been that the crew had simply forgotten to switch on the INS.[19] Whatever the crew had thought, they were never aware during the more than five hours of the flight, that they were off-course. So they definitely had no bad intentions; they did not intend to violate Soviet airspace. This was not a reconnaissance mission, nor did the crew want to take a shortcut to Seoul. As can be heard from their conversation, the members of the crew had been somewhat weary. They are ultimately responsible for the extraordinary navigation mistake.

What about the mistakes on the Soviet side? For the Soviet air defense units, the incident started with confusion. When they had originally spotted the US RC-135 reconnaissance aircraft, and then later detected flight KE 007 they mistook it to have been the same aircraft. Thus, they maintained track number 60-65 for KE 007 which had originally been allocated to the RC-135. The Soviet rules were strict; their air defense forces were to shoot down any intruders.[20] But some of the officers involved had doubts to whether the

[19]Sayle p. 93.

[20]Sayle p. 95.

aircraft was a RC-135 and tried to identify it. The question was considered on whether it might be a Soviet aircraft. Other officers felt it might be a civilian aircraft. Colonel Maistrenko, the operations duty officer of the combat control center, said at 3.15 a.m.: "... may (be) a passenger (aircraft). All necessary steps must be taken to identify it".[21] The pilots were ordered to check on whether the unidentified aircraft was flying with navigation lights on; if the lights were not on, they felt it could not be a civilian aircraft. General Anatoli Kornukov, the commander of air defenses on Sakhalin Island, was also worried about the type of aircraft this was. General Kamenski, the Commander of the Far Eastern Military District Air Force, had the same concern. "We must find out, maybe it is some civilian craft or god knows who", he said at 3:14 a.m.[22] Even after General Kornukov had given the order to destroy the target at 3:17 a.m., he continued to ask whether the aircraft, which was followed by Gennadi Osipovich in his SU-15, was flying with its navigation lights on. A minute later, he received the information as to what they were on. He then gave the order to warn the unidentified aircraft by firing warning bursts and rocking the wings so as to force the airliner to land at Sokol. Then, he returned to his original order to destroy the target. The question, however, on what type of aircraft the target had been, haunted him. When he had the first chance to talk to the pilot after he had returned to the airfield 26 minutes after the missiles were fired, he asked whether Osipovich could more or less determine the type from the outline. Osipovich answered: "(I could) see a large aeroplane, because it was descending ... the navigation lights were on".[23] Ironically, General Kornukov was appointed Russian air force chief in January 1998 by President Yeltsin.[24]

The impression one gets from reading the transcripts is that of incredible confusion on the ground. One is tempted to ask how the Soviet air defenses would react in case of a real military attack. Confusion, however, was not the main factor which made quick decisions necessary. It was the fact that KE 007 was soon to leave Soviet airspace.

Before the officers in charge had the unidentified aircraft shot down, they had already known that the aircraft had its navigation lights on. This made

---

[21] Attachment C p. 86.
[22] Attachment C p. 103.
[23] Attachment C p. 207.
[24] International Herald Tribune, 24/25 January 1998.

it unlikely that it was a reconnaissance plane. They should have thoroughly checked the plane's identity. That they did not do so and that they followed the strict rule to shoot down the intruder is inexcusable.

It was also a violation of international rules. Paragraph 7.1 of the Attachment A of Annex 2 to the Convention on International Civil Aviation, to which the Soviet Union was a party at the time of the incident,[25] recommended: "Intercepting aircraft should refrain from the use of weapons in all cases of interception of civil aircraft".[26]

Did anybody have the chance to alert the crew in the cockpit of flight KE 007 of the impending danger? Shortly behind flight KE 007 was flight KE 015 with Captain Park Yong Man in command. The crews of both planes had contact with each other. It was KE 015 which had forwarded the reports of KE 007 to pass points NABIE and NEEVA to Anchorage Air Control. In an interview given years later, in December 1986, he mentioned that he was taken aback when he heard the estimate of KE 007 for reaching NEEVA because KE 007 would be five minutes late.[27] A discussion, he said, had developed between the copilots about the wind situation. Ten minutes later, he claimed, he had asked Captain Chun Byung In himself for the reason of the delay. Chun also mentioned strong headwind. Thereafter there were no contacts between the two aircrafts. That the two captains talked with each other is not confirmed by the transcripts of the cockpit's voice recorder published by the ICAO. There was, however, a discussion about the wind situation between KE 015 and the first officer of KE 007 which started at 3:03 a.m., 23 minutes before the disaster.[28] The crews compared the times at which they would reach the reporting point NOKKA, and it became clear that KE 015 would reach that point only 4 minutes after KE 007. It was obvious that KE007 was later than expected. The KE 015 crew mentioned that they had an unexpected strong tailwind while KE 007 mentioned having headwind. Since the two planes were thought to be only 4 minutes apart from each other, it could not have been true that one aircraft had a tailwind and the other a headwind. It made

[25]According to information from the ICAO Secretariat, the Soviet Union adhered to the Convention on 15 October 1970.

[26]International Civil Aviation Organization, International Standards. Rules of the Air, Annex 2 to the Convention on International Civil Aviation, 7th edition, July 1981.

[27]Cho, Kap Che, "*KAL 007 choikuni mok hyokcha* (*KAL 007; The Last Witness*)" in *Wolgan Chosun*, December 1986, pp. 396 ff.

[28]Attachment C pp. 5–8.

the crew in the cockpit of KE 007 think and they inquired as to how strong the tailwind that KE 015 experienced was and from which direction it came. A discussion among the crewmembers of KE 007 about the speed of KE 015 followed, but no consequences were drawn. It is apparent that even now, the crew of flight KE 007 was not aware that something was wrong. Captain Park's impression that the crew in the cockpit of KE 007 was confused and panicked was not correct. It is difficult to understand why Captain Park Yong Man who was alarmed by the delay of KE 007 did not attempt to suggest to Captain Chun Byong In on checking the reason for his delay more thoroughly. As he was senior to Chun ever since the time when both of them had been airforce officers, he could have easily done so, but he remained quiet.

Japanese military installations had seen an aircraft flying over Sakhalin into Soviet airspace on their radar screens. It is plausible, as the Japanese government stated that the Japanese officers were not aware that it was an off-track civil aircraft.[29] These military installations were not a part of the civil ground control system, so they had no real chance of intervening.

The question remains whether the US military installations which had observed the flight of KE 007 had noticed the deviation and could have warned Captain Chun and his crew. Since the US considered the North Pacific a militarily sensitive area, it monitored the air traffic in that region.[30] The US government informed the ICAO that it had been unable to uncover relevant radar information from the flight of KE 007, but there was the RC-135 in the air. Did the RC-135 notice or even observe KE 007? The US government further stated that the RC-135 had monitored the airspace around it for protection only.[31] One could be content with this answer if there had not been nearly inaudible and unintelligible words recorded by Anchorage ground control at 11.34 p.m., interpreted in 1985 to have said "persons should warn them".[32] After having listened to the tape, the ICAO investigation concluded that it was not possible to determine what had been said. Nevertheless, at least a question remains open.

For the Korean nation, nothing was left but mourning. On 7 September 1983, the flags were held at half-mast and a minute's silence was taken

---

[29] Attachment B. p. 61.

[30] Sayle (1993) p. 101.

[31] Attachment B. p. 49.

[32] Attachment B. pp. 35 and 36.

everywhere in the country. A memorial service was conducted at the stadium in Seoul. In his speech held one hour before the service, President Chun Doo Hwan attacked the Soviet Union vehemently and asked to reveal the truth and assume responsibility for the incident.[33] "A nation that does not fight against violence and injustice is a nation without life," he said. Therefore, Korea must build a strong and powerful nation. If all citizens unite with one resolve, the aim could be achieved. The appeal to unity during a crisis was successful. Solidarity with the government was the consequence. Chun Doo Hwan had capitalized on the horrible incident.

Terror in Rangoon

On the second day of his state visit to Burma, on 9 October 1983 at 10:30 a.m. President Chun Doo Hwan was supposed to lay a wreath at the Martyrs' Mausoleum in Rangoon. The mausoleum dedicated in the memory of Aung San, the father of Burma's independence, and to his fellow officers is situated north of the Shwedagon Pagoda, the capital's most famous landmark, and consists of an open hall. Before the South Korean President was to arrive, his most important ministers and government officials had already gathered at the mausoleum and were waiting on a red carpet as photo shows. At 10:25 a.m. an enormous detonation shook the mausoleum, killing sixteen Koreans and four Burmese and injuring seventeen Koreans and thirty-two Burmese.[34] Among the dead were Deputy Prime Minister So Sok Joon, Foreign Minister Lee Bum Suk, Minister of Energy Suh Sang Chul, Minister of Commerce and Industry Kim Dong Whie, Chun's two main advisors in the Blue House, Secretary of Economic Affairs Kim Jae Ik, and Chief of the Presidential Secretariat and former Ambassador to the US Hahn Pyong Choon, and the Korean Ambassador to Burma Lee Kae Chul.

President Chun Doo Hwan, the target of the attack, had good luck. When the bomb had exploded, he was still traveling to the mausoleum with the Burmese Foreign Minister. He cancelled the rest of his trip, which was to have included visits to India, Sri Lanka, Australia, New Zealand and Brunei, and

[33] Text in Korea Annual 1984 pp. 377 ff.

[34] Far Eastern Economic Review, 27 October 1983; Korea Times, Special Edition, 10 October 1983; Korea Times, 11 October 1983.

returned to Seoul. After his return, he ventured the idea that North Korea was behind the attempt. He was proven correct.

A few days after the incident, Burmese security forces arrested two foreigners in different locations in the vicinity of the capital. They had tried to kill themselves by detonating grenades, but were seriously wounded. A third suspect was killed in a shoot-out. It was quickly found out that these three men were North Korean agents: Major Zin Mo, Captain Kang Min Chul and Captain Shin Ki Chul. The two surviving officers, Kang and Zin, were tried before a Rangoon court. Upon Kang's confession, it was possible to establish the course of events.[35]

The three North Korean officers received an order by a commander of a special unit stationed in Kaesong to assassinate Chun Doo Hwan. The assassins reached Rangoon aboard the freighter *Tong Gon* at the end of September 1983. There they were assisted by members of the North Korean Embassy and succeeded in transporting their equipment ashore. During the night of 6 October 1983, they went into the mausoleum and installed two remote-controlled bombs between the ceiling and the roof. The placement of the bombs was exactly above the place where the visiting dignitaries were to stand. On 9 October 1983 at 10.25 a.m. Major Zin Mo, the leader of the trio, who was observing events from a place 400 to 500 meters away, detonated the bomb by remote control.

Why he detonated the bomb too early, that is to say before President Chun Doo Hwan had reached the mausoleum, is not quite clear. It is generally believed that he mistook the South Korean Ambassador's car for the President's car.[36] Another factor might have played a role; Zin's watch, which was seized by the Burmese authorities, was 5 minutes faster. But, indeed, the Ambassador's car flying the Korean flag, and escorted by motorcycles could easily have been mistaken for the President's car. It is said that a bugle had been blown. After the bombs had exploded, the North Koreans tried to reach their ship in the Rangoon River 30 km south of the capital. But the Burmese security forces were quicker. At the end of the trial on 9 December 1983, Zin Mo and Kang Min Chul were sentenced to death, to life imprisonment and to imprisonment for three years. Their appeals were unsuccessful.

[35]For details of Kang's confession, see Korea Annual 1984 pp. 22; excerpts of the Burmese report of the incident to the UN in Korea Annual 1985 pp. 385 ff.

[36]Clifford p. 214; Oberdorfer p. 141.

On 4 November 1983, the Burmese government had announced that the explosion had been the work "of saboteurs sent by the Democratic People's Republic of Korea".[37] Burma severed diplomatic relations with North Korea. The terminology used by the Burmese government was somewhat strange as they stated "to derecognize the diplomatic status of the government of Democratic People's Republic of Korea". What it meant was what the Vienna Convention on Diplomatic Relations of 1961 (Art. 45) calls breaking off diplomatic relations.

After this incident, North Korea became listed as a terrorist state. An international debate developed in the 6th Committee of the UN General Assembly. Unlike in the Korean Airlines incident, the two big powers, the USA and the USSR, did not get involved. Many other countries considered the conflict to be solely a Korean one. Regardless, there was no chance to take effective measures against a secluded country like North Korea. Why North Korea dared to attempt an assassination of the South Korean Head of State, one can only speculate. It is likely that Pyongyang wanted to hit Seoul's successful policy in the Third World which had been promoted when South Korea was chosen to organize the 1986 Asian Games and the 1988 Olympic Games. Chun's trip to Burma was intended to strengthen relations with a country which had close contacts with North Korea. The inclusion of Rangoon in Chun's trip had not been uncontested at home. An official in the Ministry of Foreign Affairs who had followed the preparations of the trip told me in March 1990 that Foreign Minister Lee Bum Suk had doubts about the trip. The Foreign Ministry's officials were sure that the Burmese government would not agree to a visit of Chun. When the South Korean Embassy was instructed to sound out the Burmese reaction, the Ministry added that the answer "no" would be okay. Much to the surprise of the Ministry, the Burmese government agreed to a visit by the South Korean President. Foreign Minister Lee Bum Suk, however, was reluctant to fly to Burma even in the evening before the departure.

The North Korean government denied having anything to do with the incident at the mausoleum. It tried to turn the tables and claimed that one of the men arrested had confessed in the presence of ambassadors of third countries that he originated from South Korea and had attended school and university in Seoul.[38] A few weeks after the memorial service for the victims of flight KE

[37]Text in Korea Annual 1984 pp. 383 and 384.
[38]UN Doc. A/38/355/Add. 3.

007, the South Korean nation was mourning again. On 13 October 1983, one million Koreans participated in a funeral service at Yoido Plaza. It was left to Prime Minister Kim Sang Hyup to give a speech. President Chun Doo Hwan was again not present.

There is no clear answer as to who was responsible for not preventing the attack at the mausoleum. Perhaps, both the Burmese and the South Korean security agencies were confident that there would be no danger at the venerable site. Or it may be true, as the South Koreans claim, that their request to inspect the site was rejected by the Burmese authorities? Security arrangements for visits of President Chun Doo Hwan thereafter became a trial for host countries as I have experienced myself. It was also not of real importance to detect the reasons for the deficiencies of the security arrangements. It was sufficient that somebody took the blame. It was Chun's cabinet which did so by resigning on 14 November 1983. Chun Doo Hwan had already lost some of his best advisors at Rangoon. After the resignation, he lost his Prime Minister, Kim Sang Hyup. Kim Sang Hyup, a nephew of Kim Song Su, the founder of the Dong A Ilbo and Korea University, was a respected scholar and democrat. He had been President of Korea University for many years. Many were surprised that a man of his background had accepted becoming Chun's Prime Minister. "What is going on, Your Magnificence"? the Wolgan Chosun had written on 11 July 1982 while expressing the hope that with Kim Sang Hyup, "a wind of freedom" would come to South Korea. Since he was Prime Minister for such a short period of time, he had no chance to fulfill these expectations.

Chun Doo Hwan had capitalized on the horrible incident over Sakhalin. It was impossible to do the same with Rangoon. He had tried a dashing attack into socialist territory, but returned home a shattered man. South Koreans began to doubt his leadership qualities.

The Test

A visitor, who knew South Korea from the mid-1970s and returned 10 years later to the land of the "morning freshness", was pleasantly surprised that the curfew had disappeared. The curfew from midnight to 4.00 a.m., introduced by the US military government more than 36 years before, had been lifted on 5 January 1982. The curfew had brought many parties to a standstill as guests hurried to catch taxis as their fares went up when midnight approached.

The curfew and with it, the atmosphere of tension during the nighttime had disappeared. The visitor also observed that life on the schoolyards was more colorful than before. Since 1983, the students were no longer obliged to wear school uniforms. After having become accustomed to life in Korea again, the returning visitor could not avoid observing that the friendly impressions were misleading. The governmental system of Chun Doo Hwan resembled that of the authoritarian regime of Park Chun Hee even though this resemblance was seldom discussed.

State authority emanated from the Blue House, the official residence of the president; the executive branch of government had become all-powerful. Control mechanisms were poorly developed. The government maintained a reliable majority in the National Assembly, while many politicians of the opposition were still banned from political activities, and many dissidents were in jail. The media was under the strong influence of the government. The government leaned on the military from which it had originated, on the bureaucracy and on private business which depended on close cooperation with the administration because it was determining the basic framework for economic activities. The instruments of control had not changed. Only the name of the KCIA had changed. Since 1 January 1981, the KCIA was called Agency for National Security Planning, better known as *ankipu* (*kukka anchon kihoik pu*). Institutions, which had to make suggestions, develop policies and determine the goals, that is to say political parties and groups of the civil society, were weak while the institutions responsible for the implementation of the policies like the bureaucracy and the military were strong. In other words, the input-organizations were much weaker than the output-organizations. The practice, exaggerating the danger from the North, continued in order to discipline the population. Corruption also continued to be practiced. A number of scandals weakened public's trust in a government which had originally taken office claiming to fight "irregularities". In the summer of 1984 Jung Nae Hiuk, the Chairman of the DJP and a former Speaker, was forced to retire because he was suspected to have misused his posts to make money. Han Sung Joo has accurately called the Korean politics of that period "basically authoritarian with a certain degree of effectiveness".[39]

One must add that the political climate was chillier than during the Park era. One of the reasons for this was the spreading of a dull nationalism. Chun's

[39]Han Sung-Joo (1985) p. 173.

idea of a creative nationalism had proved to be meaningless. What, however, developed was an arrogance which partly stemmed from instability, partly from enthusiasm about the economic rise, and partly from the successful competition with the North. A statement made by Chun Doo Hwan is unmatched. In February 1986 he said: "Since my inauguration in 1980, I have visited many countries for summit talks. Each time I travel abroad, I feel more greatly confident that our country is better than any other nation in the world".[40] Traveling educates people.

From time to time, particularly in 1984, some relaxation could be observed. Professors who had lost their jobs were allowed to return to the universities. Students who had been expelled could register once again. Journalists could return to their editorial offices. The police left the campuses of the universities which were granted more autonomy. Since 1981, one amnesty for political prisoners followed after another, but a general amnesty was never granted. The last amnesty, called an act of leniency, left only 15 people on the old black list; among them were the three Kims.[41] Although the various amnesties were conducive to a more liberal atmosphere they indicated, nevertheless, that something was wrong in the state of Chun Doo Hwan.

This modest relaxation was sufficient for enabling opposition forces to organize resistance movements against Chun's rigid rule. Chun had either overestimated the consolidation of his power or he had wanted — with a view to the forthcoming National Assembly elections in 1985 — to allow to let steam off. In 1984, students once again staged many protests and the usual clashes between rock-throwing students and teargas-firing policemen were observed.[42] The students, realizing the gap between claims and reality, demanded democratization, freedom of the press and social justice. In October 1984, unrest at Seoul National University reached such a high level that for a few days, 6,400 policemen controlled the access to the university. The resistance movement against Chun Doo Hwan became organized finally when a number of politicians from the opposition joined forces. In the summer of 1984, they founded the Consultative Committee for the Promotion of Democracy Kim Young Sam and Kim Dae Jung became co-chairmen of this Committee although they were still banned from political activities. The

[40]Korea Herald, 23 February 1986.

[41]Korea Newsreview, 8 December 1984.

[42]New York Times, 6 May 1984.

government restricted the activities of the Council but did not suppress them completely.

Kim Young Sam tried to return to politics in a press conference on 14 August 1984 when he demanded real liberalization. Kim Dae Jung had no chance of directly interfering in Korean politics since he was still in exile in the US. His fate had been somewhat more favorable since the death penalty had been commuted into imprisonment for life in January 1981. This penalty was later commuted to imprisonment for 20 years. In December 1982, the sentence was suspended and he was allowed to travel to the US for medical treatment. In an interview by Newsweek a couple of weeks later, he rejected the assertion that the South Korean government had forced him into exile.[43] Korean public pressure to release him had been too strong, he argued. Was it also public pressure which caused the Korean government to comply with Kim's wish to return to Korea? Hardly. It was the US administration which had exercised pressure by insisting that Kim Dae Jung return home without serving the rest of his sentence. During his stay in the US, he had apparently succeeded in winning the support of prominent American personalities. On 8 February 1985, a few days before the National Assembly elections, Kim Dae Jung arrived in Seoul. He was accompanied by two members of Congress, many followers and journalists. The government took so-called security measures. Chun Doo Hwan seemed to feel that the risk to domestic politics, which might be caused by the return of the famous dissident, was low.

For the National Assembly elections to be held on 12 February 1985, not only did the DJP, the DKP and the KNP file for candidates but so did a new opposition party, the New Korean Democratic Party (NKDP). This party was formed on 18 January 1985 with the old campaigner Lee Min Woo as chairman. It was the creation of the Consultative Committee for the Promotion of Democracy. In its platform, the new party advocated democracy and direct presidential elections. It did well in the election gaining 28.6% of the votes and 67 of the 276 seats in the Assembly. Some members of the DKP, which had only won 35 seats, and some of the KNP, which had won 20 seats, joined the NKDP; consequently the new party had a strong parliamentary group of 103 members. The Democratic Justice Party won only 34.9% of the votes, but thanks to the tricky election system 148 seats. The result of just one-third of the votes, even a little less than in the elections four years before (35.6%), was

[43]Newsweek, 31 January 1983.

a defeat for Chun Doo Hwan. He had not passed the test after four years of civilian rule.

References

Han, Sung-Joo, "Prospects for Korean Policies", in *Korea in the Year 2000*, ed. by Han Sung Joo Seoul 1985 pp. 173 ff.

Kodo, Takeo, *ce okonghwakuh, ku kunpu inmaek* (*The Fifth Republic and its Person al Military Connections*), Seoul 1987.

Chapter 12

"Down with Military Dictatorship"

Molotov Cocktails and Sit-ins

The results of the National Assembly elections of 12 February 1985 illustrated that the ruling party, the Democratic Justice Party, and its president, Chun Doo Hwan, lacked broad support from Korean citizens. The President's opponents interpreted this as a sign of weakness. They saw their chances and started to enhance their resistance. The next two and a half years were to be the most turbulent period since 1980 when Chun Doo Hwan had fought his way to the top.

The students revolted, and unrest at the country's universities increased rapidly during 1985. The students opposed the military's interference in politics and spoke up for freedom of expression, of the press and of association.[1] They also advocated the autonomy of universities. They condemned Korea's foreign debt, fought for a new system of presidential elections and sought to bridge the gap between the rich and the poor. In the course of time, the students focused more and more on democratic reforms. From the beginning, student activities had an anti-American slant which found its expression through numerous attacks on US installations. These attacks occurred at the US Cultural Center in Seoul (23 May 1985), at the office of the American Chamber of Commerce (21 May 1985), at the US Cultural Center in Kwangju (2 December 1985), and at the US Cultural Center in Pusan (21 May 1986). The students

[1]The Sung Kyun Times (The newspaper of Sung Kyun Kwan University), 25 November 1985.

asked for an explanation of the American role when the uprising in Kwangju was quelled in May 1980. The students demonstrated on campuses, and on the streets. They also made use of satirical plays. In the spring of 1986, students staged a play at the campus of Seoul National University.[2] The play satirized candidates who were trying to be elected. They had interesting names: Candidate one was called Ku Dae Ta (coup d'état), candidate two Ki Man Hae (cheat) and candidate three, also a joke character, was called Han Min Jung (the Korean people). When Ku Dae Ta entered the stage, he shouted: "Why an election, I shall be president anyway". Additionally, the students distributed flyers and brochures and used banners with their slogans. They often organized behind the university's main gate and then marched on the street where they were awaited by the riot police. They threw stones and Molotov cocktails. They occupied university buildings, attacked police stations, and set fire to police buses. Some students poured gasoline over their clothes, set fire to themselves and died in the fire. Times were bad indeed.

As figures had proven, the student's movement had broad support. According to a report by the Ministry of Home Affairs, 1,371 demonstrations and 448 sit-ins, in which 650,000 students participated, occurred in the first 10 months of 1985. 1,603 students were picked up, and 304 were arrested. The unrest had spread from the capital to the majority of the country's institutes of higher learning.

In the spring of 1986, the students gained support from their professors. In a joint declaration, several hundred professors demanded amending the constitution by introducing the direct election of the president. In separate moves, Protestants and Catholics called for democratic and social justice. Buddhist monks also staged demonstrations against the government. In the fall of 1986, for example 2,000 Buddhist monks from all parts of the country participated in a demonstration at the Hain monastery, a famous monastery northwest of Taegu. A few days later, I talked to one of the participants at Hain-sa and learned that the monks had been protesting against the government for not respecting the freedom of faith and trying to misuse religion for political purposes. And the monks opposed the advance, supported by the government, of what my interlocutor called a materialistic and mechanistic culture. Many dissident groups also organized. Mintonyon, led by Pastor Mun Ik Hwan, became well-known.

[2]Dong A Ilbo, 23 May 1986.

In the Assembly, the government had to face an aggressive opposition all of a sudden since a number of the leaders from the extra-parliamentary opposition had been elected for the NKDP. The parliamentary group of the NKDP tried everything, even staging sit-ins in the Assembly chamber. Time and again, turbulence hindered the work of the Assembly. The NKDP focused on demanding and achieving the direct election of the president by the people. "Let us elect the president by our own hands", was their slogan. The opposition had post-Chun arrangements in mind. Its leaders believed that one of them could only stand a chance of seizing power if he became a candidate in direct elections. Consequently, the NKDP demanded setting up a special Assembly committee for amending the constitution. When the NKDP did not receive positive reaction from the government, it started a campaign to collect signatures in Seoul on 12 February 1986. They carried out this campaign throughout Korea in spite of police intervention. This was a bold initiative.

The NKDP could have been more successful if it had not been frustrated with factionalism. Adding to the difficulties was the fact that the leaders of the main factions, Kim Young Sam and Kim Dae Jung, were still outside the party structure. Kim Young Sam was in a better position. When the ban on blacklisted politicians was lifted on 6 March 1985, he could again become politically active. Kim Dae Jung, on the other hand, suffered from restrictions. The suspension of his prison sentence was interpreted by the government in such a way that he was neither entitled nor eligible to vote and could not be a member of a political party. Kim Young Sam made use of his advantage over Kim Dae Jung and became a member of the NKDP in February 1986. By and by, he assumed the leadership of the party.

The proposal to introduce direct presidential elections had meanwhile become the core issue of political conflict. Originally, Chun Doo Hwan and his party rejected this idea and also the proposal to establish a special committee in the Assembly for the preparation of a corresponding amendment. Under pressure, however, their attitude changed. By the end of 1985, the DJP offered setting up a parliamentary committee "to study" the constitution. This was rejected by the NKDP. In the beginning of 1986, Chun Doo Hwan went a step further. He agreed to establish an Assembly committee if its task was to prepare a new system of presidential elections for the period after 1989; the next presidential elections were going to be held in 1988. In June 1986, he suddenly favored an amendment which was to be effective already for the election of his successor. The Special Committee took up its work at the end of July 1986. The DJP presented surprising suggestions, demanding the introduction of a parliamentary system in which a prime minister, elected by the Assembly, would be the Chief executive and the president would only be a symbol. As the prime minister was to be elected by Parliament, the system of an indirect election of the most powerful government official would be maintained. Apparently, the DJP had come to the conclusion that its candidate stood no chance of winning direct elections.

A Wavering President

Chun Doo Hwan had not only lost direction in the question of constitutional reform. After the National Assembly elections, in February 1985, he gave the impression that he was following a softer course. The lifting of the ban on politicians and the abolition of the military training program at universities in March 1985 seemed to indicate a new policy. The reshuffle of the cabinet directly after the elections and the appointment of Lho Shin Yong, a moderate, as Prime Minister could also be interpreted in the same way. But when the changes of the cabinet, the leadership of the government party, and the presidential secretariat occurred increasingly more often — three additional changes until the end of 1986 —, one could detect signs of a lack of self-confidence which Chun Doo Hwan had not displayed before. He mostly just reacted.

In the summer of 1985, the government tried to introduce a law, the so-called Campus Stabilization Law, which provided that the students who took part in riots would be reeducated in camps. Decisions to send students to these camps would be taken by a commission to be appointed by the Ministry of Education, and not by law courts. Protests against this proposed law were so vehement that the government could not realize their plan. There were, anyway, a number of possibilities used to clamp down on students. Students were checked and arrested, and demonstrations were fought by clouds of teargas. The disagreeable smell of teargas which irritates the eyes, nose and throat could be found not only on the campuses but also in downtown Seoul. The engagement of the police against the students culminated in an assault on Konguk University where more than 1,000 students from twenty-seven universities had gathered. After having sealed off the campus for a few days, the police stormed the university on 31 October, even to the point of using helicopters. 1,195 students were arrested.[3]

The NKDP also suffered from the repressive politics of the government. The government party, the DJP, unilaterally passed the budgets for 1986 and 1987. Efforts by the NKDP to block the final budget debate failed. Members of the opposition were harassed by the government and the government party. The movements of Kim Young Sam and Kim Dae Jung were restricted once again.

The government tried vigorously to suppress the opposition's signature-gathering campaign for direct presidential elections. The opposition and dissidents had called upon citizens to form a large rally at the former Seoul High School on Saturday, 29 November 1986. When I talked to Kim Young Sam before that date, he was absolutely confident that one million people would show up. But the police, employing 70,000 men, knew how to prevent the event. Policemen controlled the access to the capital, blocked off important junctions in downtown Seoul, sealed off subway exits, protected public buildings, and imposed house arrests on oppositionists. People were scared and thus only small demonstrations took place. The government's policy prevailed, although at the expense of transforming the Republic more and more into a police state.

The worsening of events was also underscored by an increasing number of political prisoners. In the spring of 1985, there were 115 political prisoners. A little more than a year later, in July 1986, the government released a figure of 1,000. By the end of 1986, the figure had more than doubled and stood approximately at 2,400.

The Crisis of Legitimacy

In 1985 and 1986, the Republic of Korea was a functioning polity. The country was administered effectively, infrastructure had improved rapidly, and the economy was thriving. Large international gatherings like the meeting of the World Bank and the International Monetary Fund in the autumn of 1985 and the Asian Games in the summer of 1986 were successfully organized in Seoul. Everyday life was now and then disturbed when conflicts between the government and its foes were fought on the streets.

---

[3]Korean Annual 1987 p. 11.

Chun Doo Hwan found it increasingly hard to cope with his foes. This was underlined by the fact that the press, in spite of the government's many censorship type interventions, had became bolder daring to criticize the rulers in a harsh way. For example, on 20 February 1986 the Chosun Ilbo published an editorial under the heading "How long shall the contradictory situation last?" The editorial criticized "the incredibly miserable complacency of the politicians", and demanded that both sides give in. During 1986, Chun Doo Hwan lost control. He could fend off his enemies only by force.

The idea that the strongest cannot rule by force for any length of time but must achieve a basic agreement with the ruled was also well known to East Asian thinking. Confucius expressed this idea as follows: "1. Tsze-kung asked about government. The Master said, 'The requisites of government are that there be sufficiency of food, sufficiency of military equipment, and the confidence of the people in their ruler.' 2. Tsze-kung said, 'If it cannot be helped, and one of these must be dispensed with, which of the three should be foregone first?' 'The military equipment,' said the Master. 3. Tsze-kung again asked, 'If it cannot be helped and one of the remaining two must be dispensed with, which of them should be foregone?' The Master answered, 'Part with the food. From of old, death has been the lot of all men; but if the people have no faith in their rulers, there is no standing for the State' ".[4]

To win the confidence of the people was of a particular urgency for Chun Doo Hwan as he had seized power by a putsch. Koreans could not recognize the various steps which had brought him to the top. But the traces of blood at Kwangju indicated clearly enough that force had been used. Chun Doo Hwan never admitted publicly that he had come into the Blue House by way of a coup d'état. Only Huh Moon Doh, one of his close assistants, was courageous enough to admit belatedly that Chun's takeover had been a "revolution."[5] Chun Doo Hwan knew very well that he had a legitimacy problem. In a speech at the National Press Club in Washington on 3 February 1981, he said: "But I also know too well that genuine stability can be achieved only when the majority of the people accept the legitimacy of the government and support its decisions."[6] When he gave a reception for members of the

[4] *Confucian Analects* Book 12 Chapter 7 in James Legge, *The Chinese Classics*, Vol. 1, Hongkong 1970 p. 254.

[5] Korea Times, 22 November 1988.

[6] Korea Annual 1981 p. 398.

DJP on 7 May 1986, he argued against a tough course because of the risk of losing the people's confidence. Chun Doo Hwan was neither stupid nor did he lack understanding, yet it would have been easier for him if he was able to communicate with the Korean people. Unfortunately for him, he had no charisma.

Chun Doo Hwan was born on 18 January 1931 in Naechon-Ri, a place in South Kyongsan province, a province from which Park Chung Hee had also come. He had chosen a career as an officer and belonged to the 11th class of the Military Academy. He had his first taste of politics when he was appointed secretary of the Supreme Council for National Reconstruction, the decisive institution for the beginning of the Park era. Chun Doo Hwan was a man who could react quickly, and a man with guts who could also make unpleasant decisions. When he was confronted with criticism by foreign dignitaries, he kept his posture and defended himself in a clever way, as I have witnessed various times. It was not too difficult to see him as a regimental commander in the war in Vietnam where he was posted for one year. He preferred black-and-white solutions, and did not favor nuances. His political maneuvers were often somewhat clumsy. Unlike Park Chung Hee, he ruled with a pompous style. He always appeared to be cool, if not cold. Nobody around him radiated warmth. Since the financial scandal in May of 1982, the first couple was suspected of being corrupt. How could such a president hope to be accepted as an example and to win followers?

From the very start, Chun Doo Hwan tried to legitimize his rule by reaching goals which he himself had mapped out.[7] But which of his aims was meant to convince his countrymen?

He had assumed office to restore public security and order. The arbitrary way in which he pursued those aims in 1980 scared the Koreans and did not instill them with confidence. He had further promised to protect South Korea against the dangers from the North. Most Koreans were willing to agree that this agenda was indispensable, but it had been misused too often to really be convincing. He had also pledged continuing economic development. This was an important aim which had made many Koreans accept Chun for a while. But it was a mistake to hope that a positive economic development would be enough to satisfy people. His attempt to acquire legitimacy by performance was rejected by many Koreans.

---

[7]See, for example, his Address on 3 March 1981 in Korea Annual 1981 pp. 393 ff.

For many Koreans, economic progress alone was no longer sufficient. Koreans were well-educated. Since liberation, the young generation had used that opportunity to familiarize themselves with Western democratic ideas and had been infected with them. Western values had found their way into Korean political culture which had been shaped by Confucianism for so many centuries. Such values as trust in others, equality, tolerance, and upholding of civil rights had become an important way of thinking for the young (those under 40 years of age), the urban population and the new middle class.[8] For them, the new values had become more important than the traditional Confucian ones. An increasing number of Koreans wished to see the realization of these values come to fruition. They demanded greater autonomy, that is to say they wanted to determine their own political future. They demanded, as the Chosun Ilbo said in the editorial on 20 February 1986, to return to parliamentary democracy and to follow the rules. They strived for more security of the legal system and a better guarantee of civil rights. More and more people got upset by their President's hypocrisy which promised democracy but did not stick to its principles. Finally, Chun Doo Hwan reduced the concept of democracy to a peaceful transfer of power at the end of his term in 1988. In his inauguration address on 1 September 1980, he had promised to serve for one term as president and had repeated this promise so often that nobody would listen any longer.[9] He could not convince his fellow countrymen that such a reduced concept of democracy was sufficient.

A Breath of Revolution

The South Korean police had always been accused not only of spying on people, searching their homes, confiscating their property and detaining them, but also of torture. Such charges were repeatedly brought up by the opposition in the National Assembly.[10] The government always rejected them. On 19 January 1987, a reliable witness showed up. The Director of the National Police informed the Korean public that a student, Park Chong Chol, had died of torture when he was questioned by the police. This statement was preceded by

[8]Han Bae Ho, *The Korean Political Culture: Four Cultural Cleavages and Polarizing Trends in Political Alignment, Korea University*, Seoul 1985.

[9]Text in Korea Annual 1981 pp. 388 ff.

[10]Korea Times, 9 November 1985.

the usual denials, but a physician who had been called by the police to examine the student and a relative of the student who had witnessed the autopsy had verified the torture and informed the newspapers. The government tried not to reveal the complete truth and even tried to cover events up, but the truth had come to light.[11]

Park Chong Chol, a linguistics student at Seoul National University, was arrested by several policemen on 14 January 1987 and brought to a police station. The police questioned him about the whereabouts of another student, one of Park's friends. Park Chong Chol refused to answer the questions. Five policemen were involved. They started beating him with their fists and pushed Park's head three or four times into a bath-tub filled with water, pressing his head hard against the bath-tub rim. The young man suffocated. He preferred death to betrayal.

The Korean public was horrified. The worst accusations against the Chun government had proven to be true. The human rights movement gained momentum from the incident. The movement was lead by the newspapers which succeeded in shaking off government control increasingly and had become vocal in criticizing governmental abuses. The Lawyer's Association held a hearing on 23 January 1987 when people began reporting on how they had been tortured. In his sermon during a mass for the murdered student on 26 January 1987, Stephan Cardinal Kim commented the agencies' excuses that the policemen had been overeager by saying: "These are Cain's answers". There were many, even among the members of the government and its party, who felt that the murder of Park Chong Chol was a turning point.

Chun Doo Hwan did not share this view, of course. Since the police succeeded in restricting the general public's participation in the two memorial services for Park Chong Chol held on 7 February and 3 March 1987, he believed he was in command. He felt assured of that view when he noted the complete disunity of the opposition. In a period where unity was of the essence, the members of the opposition were busy fighting against each other. Kim Young Sam and Kim Dae Jung had decided to split from the NKDP and form a new party. Chun Doo Hwan thought he could make good use of a chance when on 13 April 1987, he declared the discussion about a constitutional reform, which he had initiated the year before, finished. His successor, he said, would be elected in 1987 according to the existing indirect system. On 6 September,

---

[11]Chosun Ilbo, 30 May 1987; Korea Times, 25 January, 22, 24 and 30 May 1987.

he went one step further. He recommended to a small group of DJP loyalists that Roh Tae Woo be his successor. Roh was the chairman of the DJP since February 1985 and the number two in South Korea. Chun certainly had in mind finding a successor from whom he would have nothing to fear after leaving office. A national convention of the DJP-nominated Roh Tae Woo as the party's candidate for the next presidential elections. Everything seemed to go according to Chun's plan. When the guests of Roh's victory celebration, held in the evening of 10 June 1987 at the Hilton Hotel in Seoul, had to cope with teargas even inside the Hotel, they felt that not all was set.

Chun Doo Hwan had misjudged the situation. From 10 to 26 June 1987, South Korea experienced its worst demonstrations since 1980. Demonstrations not only occurred in Seoul but also in many other cities, including Pusan, Taegu, Taejon, Kwangju, Chinju, and Inchon. They not only took place on university campuses but also on the streets. Many demonstrations became violent. The police used clouds of teargas. During those days when I had to reach my office at Namdaemun, I could not avoid crossing the battle lines; I caught so much teargas that I had a problem with my left eye for weeks and can attest that the teargas used by the police was a particularly unpleasant one. In the period from 10 to 20 June 1987, 9,578 persons were arrested, 300 taken into custody, and 53 injured by teargas.

The demonstrations were initially staged by students who had translated their vague ideas about democratization into the slogan: "Down with military dictatorship". For the democratic movement to succeed, it was crucial that the students received support from many sides.[12] Passersby did not only applaud the students but also got involved. The students found sympathy and support by professors, lawyers, physicians, brokers, taxi drivers, monks, priests and pastors. Thanks to the economic progress, the middle class had expanded tremendously. In 1987, 65% percent of South Koreans considered themselves to be members of the middle class.[13] They could afford a better life, education, and access to information and communication. They were taking part in creating the components of a civil society, thus strengthening pluralism. For Chun Doo Hwan, it was a sad story. The economic growth which he — and Park Chung Hee — had promoted so vigorously had produced the enemies

[12]Kwon, Tai Hwan, "Perceptions of the Quality of Life and Social Conflicts", in *Korea Journal* Vol. 28 No. 9, September 1989 pp. 10 ff.

[13]Han and Chung p. 216.

of authoritarianism. By mid-1987, the moment had come when for a part of the middle-class, the satisfaction with their economic development no longer outweighed their dissatisfaction with the political developments. An opinion survey, carried out by the daily Hanguk Ilbo in May 1987 and published on 9 June 1987, revealed that 85.7% of the self-identified middle-class respondents agreed with the following statement: "We should promote human rights even if it delays economic growth".[14] They did not only want personal changes among those who held power, but they also wanted democratization.

The National Coalition for a Democratic Constitution had called for peace rallies to be undertaken on Friday 26 June 1987. Many were scared, yet many participated. Demonstrations took place in Seoul and in thirty-two other cities. The police coped relatively easily with the demonstration, nevertheless a breath of revolution was in the air.

Change of Course

On 29 June 1987, Roh Tae Woo issued an eight-point declaration revising thoroughly the policy of government and its party.[15] He demanded the direct election of the president; a change of the election law; amnesty and restoration of civil rights for dissidents including Kim Dae Jung; a better protection of human rights; freedom of the press; local government administration and autonomy for universities; protection of activities of the political parties and drastic social reforms.

One could hardly believe it. Were these not the demands of the oppositionists and dissidents? Indeed, Roh Tae Woo had changed course. The turn-about was the obvious thing to do; how else could the crisis have been overcome? After parts of the middle class supported the move for democratization, it could no longer be contained by way of police force. Whoever played with the idea to impose martial law and to engage troops had to come to a negative result.[16] Many countries would have found the imposition of martial law appalling and might have cancelled their participation in the 1988 Summer Olympic Games. This danger was made clear to the South Korean

[14]Hanguk Ilbo, 9 June 1987.

[15]Text in Korea Newsreview, 4 July 1987.

[16]Oberdorfer pp. 169 ff.

government through interventions of diplomatic representatives from various countries. The names of other cities which might fill in for Seoul were already talked about.

Talks held by US Assistant Secretary of State Gaston Sigur in Seoul from 23 to 25 June 1987 have pointed in the same direction. He made it clear that the US security guarantee was valid only as long as the South Korean government did not use the military to put down the unrest. Some days earlier, President Chun Doo Hwan had received a letter from President Reagan arguing cautiously for a political solution of the crisis.[17] Finally, the US administration had taken a stand in a South Korean domestic crisis and argued for moderation. Its intervention will have been helpful. I found, however, — and I was during the whole period under discussion in Seoul — that the solution was as endogenous Korean as the movement for democratization.

It has often been discussed whether Roh Tae Woo had reached an advanced agreement on his sensational declaration with Chun Doo Hwan. Chun even spread the news via his assistants that he was the author of the declaration; a view later confirmed by his former press secretary[18] and by his wife.[19] The declaration reflected indeed more of the courage and decisiveness of Chun. It was Roh Tae Woo, however, who made the announcement for the change of course. This announcement had revitalized his candidature for the presidency after he had nearly been written off. And that was exactly the point of the exercise.

The Koreans reacted positively, partly enthusiastically to Rho's declaration. A coffee shop owner fixed a notice on the window saying "Today is a joyous day and coffee and tea are free of charge".[20] Aftershocks from the unrest of June were felt on 9 July 1987 when many hundreds of thousands of people escorted the coffin of Lee Han Yol who had been killed by a teargas grenade. The procession had started at Yonsei University and peacefully proceeded to city hall. 40,000 to 50,000 participants had stayed on the city hall plaza and then tried to march to the Blue House. The police succeeded in blocking the march. Also, in the following period extreme student groups, mostly radical idealists, and sometimes communists, were active.[21]

[17]Oberdorfer pp. 168 and 169.

[18]Wolgan Chosun, January 1992.

[19]Korea Times, 19 December 1996.

[20]Korea Herald, 30 June 1987.

[21]Far Eastern Economic Review, 6 August 1987.

Immediately after Roh's declaration, the implementation of his proposals got started. On 6 July 1987, 177 people in detention were released, and on 8 July 1987, 357 political prisoners were also released.[22] On 9 July 1987, the civil rights of 2,335 persons including Kim Dae Jung were restored. The National Assembly passed an amendment to the constitution on 12 October 1987 by which the direct election of the president and constitutional jurisdiction were introduced and the protection of human rights improved. The carelessness of changing the constitution so often illustrated that the constitution and the institutions set up by it did not count for much in South Korea. The new constitution was approved in a referendum on 28 October 1987 by 93.3% of the votes cast (turnout: 78%). Finally, everybody was waiting for the presidential elections.

As election day on 16th of December 1987 approached, only six candidates were left: besides Roh Tae Woo, there were also the three Kims. Roh Tae Woo was busy campaigning and traveling across the country where he was always supported by a well-lubricated campaign machinery. He was happy with his new role as a champion of democratic reforms. Although many Koreans may have doubted whether he had seen the light, his message to continue economic progress accompanied with more freedom was well-received. As a poll showed, voters felt that his competence in the economic and social field surpassed that of his two main competitors.[23] The campaign changed him. The former general, used to issuing orders, had to learn to face discussions and conflicts. He even had to tolerate an attack on his life on 10 December 1987 in Kunsan. Several explosive devices were thrown at him, and he had to cancel a rally in Chonju slated for the same day.[24] Even years later, he complained, as he put it, about this "violation of his human rights".

Kim Jong Pil had emerged again, gathering old comrades and reviving the Democratic Republican Party (DRP) which he had once founded during the Park Chung Hee era. His efforts focused on the Chungchong provinces from where he came. His image as an experienced and smart politician as well as his talent for public speaking worked in his favor.

Since Kim Young Sam was the Chairman of the Party for Reunification and Democracy, which had been formed on 1 May 1987, he easily became a

[22] Korea Times, 9 July 1987.

[23] Chungan Ilbo, 22 September 1987.

[24] Korea Times, 11 December 1987.

presidential candidate. The days when the government tried to harass the new party by calling it pro-Communist were over. Kim Young Sam presented himself as a middle-of-the-roader and a moderate man and tried to win over those who had revolted during the last months. Relentlessly he demanded: "Down with military dictatorship".

It became obvious at an early stage that Kim Dae Jung would also be a candidate. After having suffered sixteen years of many hardships, he could not resist the temptation to try and reach his goal of becoming the president of the Republic. To the contrary, he swept aside earlier statements. It took him, however, quite some time to get started. In order to become a candidate, he needed the nomination by a party. Therefore, he founded the Party for Peace and Democracy. He became the candidate for the progressive camp. He appealed directly to the people and was the people's tribune. On a cold day with blue skies, on 29 November 1987 he attracted approximately one million people to his rally at Yoido. He also made good use of TV broadcasts.

On election day, the majority voted for Roh Tae Woo as could have been expected. He gained 36.6% of the votes, Kim Young Sam 28%, Kim Dae Jung 27.1% and Kim Jong Pil 8.1%.

Neither Kim Young Sam nor Kim Dae Jung had overcome regionalism. Kim Young Sam had a strong showing in Pusan and the neighboring South Kyongsan province; Kim Dae Jung showed favorably in Kwangju and the two Cholla provinces. Both, however, lacked sufficient support outside their home provinces. Roh Tae Woo, on the other hand, had a strong showing in Taegu and North Kyongsan and had also found support in all other parts of the country except the two Cholla provinces. He also did well in Seoul where one quarter of Koreans live; he gained 30% of the votes, Kim Dae Jung 32% and Kim Young Sam 29.1%. Roh Tae Woo thus became the winner.

After the elections, much was said about election fraud. For weeks, Kim Dae Jung could not discuss any other subject. Rigging had happened.[25] But since Roh Tae Woo was leading by 2 million votes, the rigging became irrelevant. This was at least the view of the Korean public which disregarded the question of election fraud.

Kim Dae Jung and Kim Young Sam have often been accused of spoiling the victory for the opposition by opposing each other in the election. If only

[25]Sunday Telegraph, 20 December 1987; The Joint Christian Committee of National Coalition for Democracy, *Election Watch*, December 1987.

one of them had been a candidate, it was argued, the opposition would have won. This theory, however, was dubious. If only one of the two Kims had run, only a part of the followers of the other Kim would have voted for him, since the animosities between the regions were too strong. A common candidate of the opposition might have gained one-third of the votes, thus endangering Roh's position. These were just intellectual games. The next President of the Republic of Korea was Roh Tae Woo.

References

Han, Sung-Joo, "South Korean Domestic Politics and Inter-Korean Relations", in *East and West Studies* Series 9, Seoul 1989 pp. 147 ff.

Han, Sung-Joo and Chung, Oknim, "South Korea: Economic Management and Democratization", in James W. Morley (editor), *Driven by Growth, Political Change in the Asia Pacific Region*, Revised Edition, Armonk 1999, pp. 197–223.

Chapter 13

The Beginnings of Democratic Rule

A Surprising Result

The 25th of February, 1988 was a really cold winter day in Seoul. The ceremony by which Roh Tae Woo was introduced into the high office of President of the Republic of Korea was nevertheless held outdoors, in front of the National Assembly building. The event, attended by 25,000 guests, had been organized in such a way that the outgoing President, Chun Doo Hwan, did not pass his office on to the new President — Roh Tae Woo. In his inaugural address, Roh Tae Woo referred to the demands he had made in his speech on 29 June 1987. Koreans were happy to hear their new leader say the following: "The day when freedom and human rights could be slighted in the name of economic growth and national security has ended".[1] From the very start, the new President tried to dissociate himself from his predecessor.

On the day Roh Tae Woo assumed office, the constitution of the 6th Republic entered into force. The constitution provided for the election of a new National Assembly.[2] Before elections could be held, however, a new election law had to be passed. On 8 March 1988, the ruling party, the Democratic Justice Party, used its majority to adopt a new election law which introduced important changes.[3] The number of constituencies, from each of which one member of the National Assembly was to be elected, increased to 224; the

---

[1] Inaugural address by President Roh Tae Woo, 25 February 1988, edited by KOIS, Seoul.

[2] Text in Korea Annual 1989 pp. 349–362.

[3] Korea Annual 1989 p. 144.

number of proportional seats was fixed to 75. The election campaign was dull, with the heroes still being tired from the presidential elections. Therefore, participation was weak (75.8%). The result, however, woke up many. The Democratic Justice Party of Roh Tae Woo received 33.96% of the votes and 125 (41.8%) of the 299 seats, thus missing the majority mark by 150 seats. The three opposition parties achieved a majority of 165 seats: the Party for Peace and Democracy received 70 seats, the Party for Reunification and Democracy received 59 seats and the New Democratic Republican Party received 35 seats. The opposition parties were thus in a position to dominate parliamentary politics. The President, directly elected by the people, had to get along with a Parliament dominated by the opposition. It was not easy to start the process of democratization by *cohabitation*, as this form of government is called in France.

In order to succeed with his policies, the President tried to reach agreements with the opposition parties. If the opposition passed laws with which he disagreed, he used the veto power attributed to him by the constitution (Art. 53). However, as he was not pleased with the way of co-operation between the executive and legislative branch of government, he looked out for another solution. And he found one.

On 22 January 1990, the President announced that he had reached an agreement with Kim Young Sam and Kim Jong Pil to join forces and merge the Democratic Justice Party, the Party for Reunification and Democracy and the New Democratic Republican Party into a new Democratic Liberal Party. Quick actions followed. The three old parties were dissolved, and on 10 February 1990, the new party was founded under the joint chairmanship of Roh Tae Woo, Kim Young Sam and Kim Jong Pil. The Koreans had difficulties believing what they were told. Had not Kim Young Sam recently fought against Roh Tae Woo and his party under the slogan "Down with military dictatorship"? The history of the system of political parties in South Korea abounds in reformations and party changes by single politicians. The merger of a government party with an opposition party like the Party for Reunification and Democracy, which was the successor of the old Democratic Party, was something new. It did, however, make sense. The new Party, the DLP, had a two-thirds majority in the National Assembly. Therefore, Roh Tae Woo would not face too much future trouble in Parliament. This was a step taken to overcome regionalism which had been the greatest problem of the party system in the 6th Republic.

For decades, voting had been dominated by the division between rural and urban elements.[4] Governing parties were mainly supported by rural voters, and opposition parties were mainly supported by voters in the urban centers. This behavior of the voters changed during the presidential elections in 1987 and the National Assembly elections in 1988. Three aspects of voter behavior became dominant. Firstly, the difference between the generations was important; the younger voters preferred the two opposition parties of Kim Young Sam and Kim Dae Jung. Secondly, a cleavage based on occupation developed; farmers voted mostly for the ruling party; the middle class showed a preference for the Party for Reunification and Democracy; and the laborers and employees in the service sector did not identify with any particular party. Thirdly, regionalism was important.[5] The DJP had achieved its best results in Taegu as well as in the provinces of North Kyongsang and Kangwon; the Party for Reunification and Democracy of Kim Young Sam had its best results in Pusan and in the neighboring province South Kyongsang; the Party for Peace and Democracy of Kim Dae Jung conquered all seats but one in the two provinces of North and South Cholla; the New Democratic Republican Party of Kim Jong Pil got more than half of its direct seats in the two Chungchong provinces. In Seoul, the three big parties were not far apart from each other with the party of Kim Dae Jung in the lead.

Korea's published opinion and, to a certain extent, it's public opinion never had any difficulty considering Kim Dae Jung as a smart and clever politician and Kim Young Sam a boring, if not dull, one. This time it was, however, Kim Young Sam who was quick to draw lessons from regionalism in elections. In order to overcome regionalism, he joined forces with representatives from the old authoritarian regime. While he thought he might lose some of his democratic credibility, he also believed that he would gain more votes if he could make it to the top of the new party.

There was another prerequisite. It remained to be seen whether the new DLP would succeed in getting the votes of its three predecessors in their home provinces. If so, the DLP would be by far the strongest political force throughout the country, with the exception of the two Cholla provinces. A deficiency of the new system was that it left out exactly that part of the country where

---

[4]For details see Han Bae Ho (1989) pp. 6 ff.

[5]See also: Chung Ang Ilbo, 28 April 1988, Korea Times, 28 April 1988.

the inhabitants had always felt badly treated. Thus, the DLP did not attempt to completely overcome regionalism.

First Attempts to Come to Terms with the Past

Roh Tae Woo was a President directly elected by the people. The National Assembly had also been directly elected by the people, but the country continued to be ruled by the forces of the old authoritarian regime, and the military continued to be influential. Democratic forces were knocking at the door, trying to open it. When the Olympic Games in Seoul were over (17 September to 2 October 1988) and the new DLP not yet formed, the democratic forces succeeded in reviewing and checking the history and particularly, the irregularities of the 5th Republic.

The constitution of the 6th Republic accorded the National Assembly the right to "inspect affairs of state or investigate specific matters of state affairs", and to "demand the production of documents directly related thereto, the appearance of a witness in person and the furnishing of testimony or statement of opinions" (Art. 61 §1). The Assembly made use of its rights and inspected hundreds of government institutions, including powerful agencies such as the Office of the President, the Agency for National Security Planning, the Military Security Command and the Army Intelligence Command.[6] The investigations remained incomplete but brought a number of irregularities to light. The most shocking news was the one revealing that 50 trainees were beaten and/or shot to death in re-education camps run by the military in 1981.

Two special committees of the National Assembly tried to deal with the past; a committee chaired by Lee Ki Taek was to discover the irregularities during the 5th Republic, and a second committee chaired by Moon Tong Hwan was formed to check the repression of the rebellion in Kwangju in May 1980. In front of the two special committees, many VIPs from the Korean establishment had to answer for their actions. This included ministers and generals as well as leading personalities from the media and big business. Many of the meetings were broadcast live on TV. Many ugly details were revealed. The Korean public came to know details about the rebellion within the military on 12 December 1979, about the brutal actions of the military in Kwangju

[6] Korea Times, 9 and 26 October 1988.

in May 1980, about the purge of the media in 1980 and about the many cases of corruption during Chun's term of office as President. To hear about the irregularities revolving around the Ilhae Foundation particularly infuriated the Koreans. The Foundation had originally been established to grant financial assistance to the children of officials who had been killed during the assault in Rangoon on 9 October 1983. It was later changed into an instrument for Chun Doo Hwan. He intended to use it as a power base after retirement. Korean companies had been forced by Chong Wa Dae officials to provide large amounts of cash for the foundation. The budget was administered by the Chief of the Presidential Security Force.

The investigations by the two special committees were not legal procedures to establish the truth. Rather, they were political disputes fought with high emotions, often offensive and not always objective. They served as a catharsis, a purifying exercise which was considered indispensable by the Korean public. The Koreans were glued to their chairs in front of their TV sets. Even some of the transmissions had higher viewing rates than the Olympic games.[7] Democracy was set into motion. *Glasnost* showed its first results.

Some of the results were quite concrete after the judiciary stepped in. When the prosecution called an end to its investigations of crimes committed by politicians during the 5th Republic, it mentioned that it had arrested 47 leading personalities.[8] Eleven members of the family of Chun Doo Hwan had been imprisoned. Among the powerful people jailed were the former mayor of the City of Seoul, Yum Bo Hyun, and the former head of the Presidential Security Force and later Chief of the Agency for National Security Planning, Chang Se Tong.[9]

The public wrath focused on Chun Doo Hwan.[10] He tried to avoid it. In a televised address he said, "I apologize sincerely to all the Korean people", and promised on 23 November 1988 to turn over all his personal assets to the state.[11] After having delivered that statement, he withdrew together with his crying wife to the Buddhist temple Paektam in the Sorak Mountains.

The opposition parties then focused on requesting criminal investigations against six prominent politicians from the 5th Republic. Among those was

---

[7]Korea Times, 10 November 1988.

[8]Korea Annual 1989 pp. 169 and 170.

[9]Korea Times, 19 October 1988 and 28 January 1989.

[10]Survey by KBS, reported in Handbook Ilbo, 25 November 1988.

[11]Korea Annual 1989 p. 52.

Chung Ho Young, a former general and minister, who had survived as a member of the National Assembly. The opposition parties also insisted that they would hear the former Presidents, Choi Kyu Ha and Chun Doo Hwan, as witnesses before the two special committees.

These efforts were only partly successful. Chung Ho Yong who, in his capacity as commander of the Special Forces, was considered the main culprit in the massacre at Kwangju in May 1980, was forced to give up his seat in Parliament. He did so on 29 December 1989 only under strong pressure from his own party.

Chun Doo Hwan, more than one year after he had retired to the mountains, had another scene in public albeit an embarrassing one.[12] He was reading his answers to 125 questions during a joint session of the two special committees and was denying his involvement in oppressing the rebellion in Kwangju. When he tried justifying the actions of the forces by invoking the right of self-defense, the outcry became so intense that the session had to be interrupted. Chun Doo Hwan did not return to the committee room, and read the rest of his answers during a press conference. No action followed.

It had, however, been humiliating for him. In the eyes of the Koreans, it was he who had been responsible for the irregularities of the 5th Republic. This was a great relief for his friend, colleague and successor Roh Tae Woo, who could avoid being nailed down. Roh in return protected his friend from more serious actions. After having come to terms with Kim Young Sam and Kim Jong Pil, President Roh Tae Woo could declare the discussions about the 5th Republic finished at the beginning of 1990. Enjoying the support of the large new DLP, he could hope to bring his term as president to a peaceful end.

Light and Shade

During the last years of his term of office, Roh Tae Woo focused on foreign policy, particularly on summit diplomacy. He met President George Bush several times by paying a state visit to the US in July 1991 and also received the American President twice — in February 1989 and in January 1992. He also met the Japanese Prime Ministers Toshiki Kaifu (January 1991) and Miyazava (January 1992); and paid visits to Canada in July 1991, and to Mexico in

---

[12] Korea Times, 1 January 1990.

September 1991. He also made use of the changes in the Soviet Union. He met President Mikhail Gorbachev three times — in June 1990 in San Francisco, in December 1990 in Moscow, and in April 1991 on Cheju Island. He then established diplomatic relations with Russia on 30 September 1991. This was a breakthrough since the Republic of Korea had never had official relations with the Soviet Union/Russia, which had always actively supported North Korea. By normalizing relations with Russia, Roh Tae Woo paved the way for South Korea and North Korea to become full members of the United Nations on 17 September 1991. He even succeeded in establishing diplomatic relations with China on 24 August 1992. In domestic politics, Roh Tae Woo was not similarly successful.

In 1989, the Korean economy grew by 6.7%. This was not a bad result, but Koreans who were used to having a two-digit growth in the preceding years (1986: 12.9%, 1987: 12.8%, 1988: 12.4%) considered it alarming. The government resorted to the traditional instruments: it asked business to once again increase exports and curb imports by advocating an austerity program. This contradicted the efforts of the Uruguay Round of GATT-negotiations, which aimed at the liberalization of world trade. Consequently, the Korean government argued for a cautious policy, trying particularly to keep agriculture out of future regulations.[13] As growth improved in the following years (1990: 9.3%, 1991: 8.4%, 1992: 4.7%), no effort was made to tackle the basic problems of the Korean economy even though they were known to the experts. The Korea Development Institute (KDI) listed some of the problems[14]: structural imbalances, the preference of the conglomerates, the neglect of the masses, and a high dependence on foreign countries. There was someone who attacked the government because of its alleged incompetence and economic mismanagement.[15] It was nobody to be overlooked. It was Chung Ju Yung, the founder of the Hyundai conglomerate, who since the fall of 1991, was involved in a tough conflict with the government. The Hyundai group at that time had 43 member companies with sales totaling 45 billion US $. The government descended on Chung Ju Yung, the Hyundai companies and its management with claims of

[13]Statement by Park Pil Su, Minister of Trade and Industry, on 4 December 1990 in Brussels, Korea Annual 1991 pp. 449 and 450.

[14]Clifford p. 310 with note 23.

[15]International Herald Tribune, 17 April 1992 and 12/13 December 1992, Frankfurter Allgemeine Zeiung, 24 April 1992.

tax evasions. Access to short term credit was blocked. Hyundai executives and one of the sons of Chung Ju Yung were arrested. Chung Ju Yung, a self-made man of extreme wealth, was not afraid. In January 1992 he founded a political party, the United Peoples Party (UPP). He revealed that he had given Roh Tae Woo a huge amount of secret donations. This was not only embarrassing for the President, it also made clear that corruption continued. This was the first one-sided notice of the existing synchronization between business and government made by someone who had profited from that relationship.

In 1991 and 1992, the Korean voters had to go to the polls three times, for local, National Assembly and presidential elections. Elected bodies on the local level had been abolished by President Park Chung Hee in 1961. For many years, Koreans had called for the reestablishment of elected councils with the aim of strengthening participation and democracy. The constitution of the 6th Republic provided for the election of local councils. Necessary laws were passed and the re-establishment of local government realized in two steps. On 26 March 1991, elections were held in small cities, counties and municipal wards; political parties were forbidden to field candidates for these elections. They were, however, allowed to do so for the council elections held on 20 June 1991 in the large cities (Seoul, Pusan, Taegu, Inchon, Kwangju, Taejon) and in the nine provinces. Of the 866 seats, the DLP won 564, the New Democratic Party of Kim Dae Jung won 165, the Democratic Party of Lee Ki Taek won 21, the People's Party of Korea (PPK) organized by dissidents won 1, and Independents won 115.[16] The new system created by the DLP seemed to work; the DLP got a huge share of the seats (65%). The party of Kim Dae Jung, renamed the New Democratic Party, remained a regional party for the country's Southwest area and did poorly in Seoul where it only received 21 of the 132 seats.

This trend was not repeated in the National Assembly elections held on 24 March 1992. Much to the displeasure of the government, the DLP received only 149 of the 299 seats.[17] It later was able to win over independents in order to command a majority in the Assembly, but the days when it ruled with a majority of 215 seats were gone. The opposition parties did well. The Democratic Party of Kim Dae Jung and Lee Ki Taek received 97 seats, including 25 of the 42 seats in Seoul, and the UPP of Chung Ju Yung received 31 seats.

---

[16]Korea Annual 1991 pp. 107–110.

[17]Korea Annual 1992 pp. 106–109.

The UPP apparently gained many DLP votes, thus promoting victories for the DP in several constituencies. All of the three factions within the DLP lost, particularly the faction of Kim Jong Pil. The result was also a defeat for Roh Tae Woo, the chairman of the DLP.

Now the difficult question of who would win the prize in the presidential elections scheduled for 18 December 1992 became even more fascinating. First of all, candidates had to be nominated. It was certain that Kim Dae Jung would run; probably greatly encouraged by the results of the last National Assembly elections. Chung Ju Yung would also run. The decision that remained was whom the DLP would field. Kim Young Sam considered himself to be the DLP's natural candidate as he was the acting president of the party. One does not do injustice to him if it is assumed that it had been his aim ,when he agreed to the party merger in 1990, to finally win the support of the new party for his candidacy. He used to deny that suggestion, arguing that he had agreed to the party merger in order to avoid a deep crisis in domestic Korean politics. This, however, seemed unconvincing. It was quite a fight for Kim Young Sam to reach the party's nomination, a fight which already started one and a half years before the election. Roh Tae Woo supported his candidacy, but Kim Young Sam met tough resistance from members of the former DJP. He did have the good luck, however, that their faction within the DLP was divided into two subgroups which were unable to agree on a convincing candidate. On 19 May 1992, Kim Young Sam was finally nominated as the DLP's presidential candidate by a majority of the party convention.

The election campaign was tough and unpleasant. The candidates leveled criminal charges against each other, and attacks on party headquarters took place. The conflict between the government and Chung Ju Yung continued. The government claimed that Chung had received financial support from various companies of the Hyundai conglomerate although the election laws forbid private companies to finance politicians. Kim Dae Jung joined Chung Ju Yung in protesting the activities of the government against the UPP, apparently hoping that he would benefit from Chung's cutting into the electorate of the DLP. The result of the presidential elections held on 18 December 1992 was clear: Kim Young Sam won 42% of the votes, Kim Dae Jung followed with 33.8%, Chung Ju Yong won 16.3% and Park Chan Jong won 6.3%.[18] In real numbers, the difference between the two Kims was nearly two million votes.

[18]Korea Annual 1993 pp. 60–63.

Kim Dae Jung had found no way to overcome regionalism. Therefore, it was understandable that he was deeply disappointed. He abruptly decided to end his political career, and resigned as a member of the National Assembly. He left for Oxford in January 1993.

After more than 30 years, the Republic of Korea again had a civilian president. The Koreans had to give Roh Tae Woo credit for this achievement and for guiding the country along a rocky path in the direction of democracy. A revolutionary breeze could be felt in the summer of 1987, but no revolution had followed, since the political personal had not been exchanged. Although free elections had been held at various times and at various levels, the same people who had served in top positions during the rule of military authoritarianism generally continued to occupy key positions in the institutions of the 6th Republic. Roh Tae Woo, a former general and a rebel together with Chun Doo Hwan, was the most obvious example. The influence of the military continued to exist as well, but was contained by their former colleague who had become their Commander-in-Chief. The Agency for National Security Planning was still very much alive. Hence, the overwhelming power of the executive branch of government, which denied a clear separation of power, survived. Parliament made efforts of purification, and the judiciary had attempted to do the same, but the attempts were half-hearted and lacked consequence. Corruption had also outlasted democratic attempts, as Chung Ju Yung made clear beyond doubt, when he had revealed that he had given Roh Tae Woo a huge amount of secret donations. Still, much had to be done in establishing democratic institutions, democratic patterns and democratic behavior in the Republic of Korea.

References

Cotton, James, (editor) *Korea under Roh Tae Woo: Democratization, Northern Policy, and Inter-Korean Relations*, Canberra 1993.

Han, Bae Ho, *The Korean Politics in Transition: The Emerging Pattern of Cleavages, Conflict, and Party Alignment*, Seoul 1989 (typewritten).

Lee, Manwoo, "Domestic Politics and Unification: Seoul's Perspective", in Kihl pp. 167–188.

Lee, Manwoo, *The Odyssey of Korean Democracy. Korean Politics 1987–1990*, New York, Westport, London 1990.

Chapter 14

Civilian Leadership

The Reformer

Kim Young Sam, the first civilian head of state for more than 30 years, set out to initiate change and reform. He wanted to transform the country into a "New Korea". In his inaugural address on 25 February 1993, he stated: "The 'New Korea' will be a freer and more mature society. Justice will flow like a river throughout this land. This 'New Korea' will be a sharing community, working and living together in harmony. A higher quality of life will flourish and the dignity of the individual will be upheld. The divided Korean people will become one and live in peace in a unified land".[1]

The new president had impeccable democratic credentials for the task before him. Born on 20 December 1927 on Koje Island near Pusan, he had been a politician all his life. In 1954, he became the youngest elected member of the National Assembly, and when he was elected President in December 1992, he was the longest serving member of the Assembly. He had fought bravely and courageously against authoritarian and military rule and for freedom and democracy. He had to suffer from being harassed by military governments. In 1951, he served as Secretary to the Prime Minister. Apart from that brief interlude, he had had no chance of gaining experience in the administration of his country.

After he had moved to the traditional seat of power, the Blue House (Chong Wa Dae), he launched one reform project after the other. He attempted to

[1]Korea Annual 1993 p. 391.

strengthen democracy, and to create a democratic society. He did so by fighting corruption and establishing civilian control over the military. He spoke of overcoming regional animosities. He preached the message of sweat and tears, but promised at the same time that a revitalized economy would help to double the per capita income of Koreans by the time he finished his five-year term. He propagated a "New Diplomacy" which, as he said in an address on 24 May 1993, gave emphasis to universal values such as democracy, liberty, welfare, and human rights, based on morality.[2] He later stressed the importance of globalization (*segye hwa*) for Korea, asking his countrymen to catch up with the international trend of competition and co-operation. In varying terms, he spoke of Korea's unification. He mentioned a commonwealth with the North, a federation, but what he really had in mind was a gradual approach. In a few brief words, Kim Young Sam set out to overhaul and improve politics in nearly every field.

Kim Young Sam interpreted Korea's history in his own way. He established a connection between the Provisional Government in Shanghai of 1919, the students' rebellion against Syngman Rhee on 19 April 1960, the fight of the people against the military in Kwangju in May 1980, the uprising against military dictatorship which started on 10 June 1987, and his own rule.[3] In other words, he argued that his government had inherited the positive tradition of Korea's history. He condemned the dark incidences in Korea's past. He termed the overthrow of Prime Minister Chang Myun on 16 May 1961 by Park Chung Hee a "coup d'état" and the rebellion within the military on 12 December 1979, which brought Chun Doo Hwan to power a "coup d'état-like incident".[4] To do away with the colonial past, he decided to dismantle the building of the presidential office and the National Museum, because both had been built in the mid-1920s as residence and office for the Japanese Governor General. The spire on the dome of the National Museum building was cut and lowered in a ceremony celebrating the 50th anniversary of Korea's liberation, on 15 August 1995.

It is neither new nor exceptional that governments make use of their own interpretation of history to serve their purposes. The best-known example of this

---

[2]Korea Annual 1993 p. 394.

[3]See his speech before the National Assembly on 21 September 1993, Korea Annual 1994 p. 345.

[4]Korea Annual 1994 pp. 60 and 61.

in East Asia was the efforts of the Japanese government to whitewash wartime history in textbooks. But why did Kim Young Sam try to redefine history?

He spoke of the "legitimacy of the Republic of Korea".[5] Yet, states do not need legitimacy, nor do people. Governments, however, need it badly, and that was apparently what he had in mind. Kim Young Sam was in no need of additional legitimacy. His legitimacy was supplied by his election by the people. Therefore, he was overdoing it when he invoked the heritage of the independence and democratic movements.

The authoritarian shadows of his predecessors were still with him. Politicians and government officials who had been successful during the old regime were still around, within his party and the government. He would have to fight against them if he intended to foster democratic ideas and behavior. It was not sufficient to redefine ugly authoritarian incidents and leave "these problems to the judgement of history".[6] Here he did not go far enough, at least at the outset of his administration.

The building which Kim Young Sam had ordered to be demolished was a landmark in the center of Seoul. After Korea had been liberated from Japanese rule, the building was first used by the US military government and then from 1948 onwards, as a main government building called "Capitol" until it was transformed into the National Museum in the late summer of 1986. It was unnecessary to seek the advice of geomancy to understand the importance of this site chosen by the Japanese. The building was placed directly before the Kyongbok Palace, the palace of the kings and therefore, the traditional seat of power. Its floor plan had the shape of the first character for Japan. The uneasy feelings of many Koreans towards that landmark were understandable, but was it really necessary to invest a large sum of money in demolishing the building? One could have argued that it was the old Capitol where the first Korean constitution had been discussed and decided upon, and where the Republic of Korea came into existence on 15 August 1948 when the US military government transferred power to the first Korean president, Syngman Rhee. The decision of Kim Young Sam to demolish the building demonstrated his exaggerated preference for symbolic actions.

There was one more intriguing aspect of the handling of history by Kim Young Sam. It was his intention to mobilize the Korean public, but it could

---

[5]Korea Annual 1994 p. 345.

[6]Korea Annual 1993 p. 70.

not be overlooked that the redefinition of history was done by decisions of the head of state. It seemed that the old habit of ruling from above had not died.

Mr. Clean

The most important and visible part of the President's reform measures was his drive against corruption. If he wanted to be successful, he had to act against those who received and gave bribes. He was thus, fighting against corrupt government officials and business, particularly big business. The close synchronization between government planning and business activities, which had contributed so much to Korea's economic rise, had been more and more lubricated with money. The Chairman of the LG International Corporation, Koo Pyong Hwoi, used a nice formula to describe the system. When he was asked by President Kim Young Sam on 29 May 1993 whether politicians continued requesting money from businessmen, he answered "No politician calls for money, but we are rather afraid of not giving any money".[7] The system had worked in a quiet and efficient way. It was exactly this collusion between government and business which had to be broken up.

Kim Young Sam started his anti-corruption campaign with a simple but effective step: he disclosed his personal assets and asked high-ranking officials and members of the DLP to do the same between 6 March and 6 April 1993. This action had a stunning effect. Three ministers, the mayor of Seoul, five vice-ministers, 242 other officials, five members of the National Assembly and four bank presidents lost their jobs because they were found to be corrupt. Many more were to follow.

The President then supported his anti-corruption drive with legislative measures. The existing Ethics Laws for Public Servants was revised in May 1993 and punishment was introduced for those who registered false personal assets. In August 1993, the President introduced the Real Name Financial Transaction System by an Emergency Order. It was unanimously approved by the National Assembly a few days later. The new law stated that all financial transactions must be concluded under the name and registration number shown on the personal identification cards or under the name of a business license and the number of the tax registration of a corporation. This law came close to causing

[7] Korea Annual 1993 p. 69.

a revolution in a country where up till then, any name could have been used for opening a bank account and for financial transactions. This practice had made it easy to hide assets. As the sums of the black money, also called "faceless" money, were considered to be huge — estimated by some observers to amount to US $37 billion — grace periods and exceptions were granted in order to limit the negative impact on the national economy.[8] Bonds were offered, granting investors exemption from tax investigations, a measure meant to absorb part of the black money. Nevertheless, the money supply increased considerably. Small businesses suffered. As they could no longer rely on private moneylenders, many went bankrupt. Even after the introduction of the new system, old practices seemed to continue.

From the start of the President's anti-corruption campaign, one case followed another. Many politicians, high government officials, and business leaders were investigated, arrested, indicted and tried. Among them were quite a number of individuals who had wielded much power in the past, including Park Chul Un, a former minister, and Park Tae Joon, the former Posco Chairman and Chairman of the DJP; both had been intra-party competitors for Kim Young Sam during the 1992 presidential elections. Big businesses was hit as well. In December 1994 for instance, three tycoons, the chairmen of Daewoo, Dong A and Samsung Engineering were sentenced for bribery; the court, however, showed leniency and suspended their sentences, because of the convicts' contributions to Korea's economy.[9]

The anti-corruption drive hit mainly figures from the past. This was the obvious group of affected individuals because only they had the opportunity to be involved in corruption. At the same time, the anti-corruption drive eliminated many of the President's enemies. This came in handy for Kim Young Sam. The question remains as to whether he made use of the anti-corruption drive with the intention of getting rid of enemies within the government and his party. Some authors felt that the trials were politically motivated.[10]

The proceedings against Chung Ju Yung, the founder of the Hyundai business group and contender in the presidential elections of 1992, may invite such an interpretation. Less than two months after the elections, in the beginning of February 1993, the prosecution charged Chung Ju Yung with embezzling

[8]International Herald Tribune, 24 August 1993.

[9]International Herald Tribune, 7 December 1994.

[10]Clifford pp. 334–338.

millions of Won in company funds to aid his campaign.[11] This forced Chung Ju Yung to retire as Chairman of the UPP and from politics altogether. At the end of 1993, he was sentenced to three years in prison. However, the sentence was suspended because the convict was 77 years old. Chung Ju Yung had already indicated several months earlier that he had got the message. In an interview, he stated that he did not believe in the accusations of corruption which he had leveled against the DLP and Kim Young Sam, but that he had just tried to fight the huge tax bill. And he added, "I have to do what I am supposed to do. I have to go back to my place in the business world".[12] That was exactly the message. He should leave politics, economic politics included, to the politicians and government officials, and mind his own private business. Chung's statement was too unambiguous to be overlooked. That he would lose the battle was foreseeable, particularly for Chung Ju Yung, who had so very much been a part of the old system. Why he still tried to tackle the establishment is difficult to understand. Perhaps he did so because of his frustration, for in spite of all his wealth, he would never belong to those who make the rules. It was a kind of rebellion against the old system, a rebellion coming from private businesses.[13]

The prosecution which investigated his case, as well as all the other cases of corruption, was under the direction of the Minister of Justice (Art. 14 Public Prosecutor's Office Act); that is to say the prosecution was part of the government. The prosecution had become very active under the administration of Kim Young Sam.

The Trial of the Century

The past caught up with Chun Doo Hwan and Roh Tae Woo. Both former presidents were arrested, tried and convicted for military insurrection, treason and corruption. The trial against the two former presidents was something special even in a country which abounds in dramatic events. Therefore, the term "trial of the century" became popular.

There were rumors and charges that the two presidents had amassed fortunes while being in office. There had also been demands to hold them

---

[11]International Herald Tribune, 10 February and 7 April 1993.

[12]International Herald Tribune, 5 March 1993, Kirk pp. 331 and 332.

[13]Kirk, pp. 316 ff.

accountable for suppressing the uprising of the citizens in Kwangju and for their rebellion after the death of Park Chung Hee. The Seoul District Prosecutor's Office had carried out investigations concerning the events after the death of President Park Chung Hee, but had decided that it could not investigate the uprising in Kwangju because it was a "high-powered political activity".[14] It had similarly declared on 29 October 1994 not to indict the two ex-presidents, because it was "feared to revive national divisiveness and confrontation in the course of legal disputes over the past, and what is taken into account is that they have already been judged by the people through parliamentary hearings on the 5th Republic (irregularities)".[15] Thus, the prosecution surrendered to politics.

Now, in the fall of 1995, developments were set in motion by a remark made by Park Kye Dong of the Democratic Party during a session of the National Assembly on 19 October 1995. He stated that Roh Tae Woo, when stepping down as president, had deposited 400 billion Won in slush funds at numerous city banks. Park Kye Dong even publicly showed a copy of the bank accounts. This time, the prosecution stepped in energetically, and one detail after another came to light. In a televised address on 27 October 1995, Roh Tae Woo confessed that he had indeed kept a secret fund of 500 billion Won (US $667 million), 170 billion (US $227 million) of which were still available, the rest having been given to the DLP and to "people who work for the country".[16] He tearfully apologized to the Korean people. This did not stop the proceedings against him. On 16 November 1995, he was arrested. Those who had assisted him and those businessmen who had given him money were charged as well. On 18 December 1995, the trial for corruption began at the Seoul District Court.

Proceedings against his friend, colleague and predecessor, Chun Doo Hwan, followed. There was, however, a decisive difference. From the very beginning, Chun Doo Hwan was charged with corruption and also with crimes committed in relation to the military rebellion in December 1979 and the suppression of the citizens uprising in Kwangju in May 1980. These charges were far more serious, not only because they could lead to capital punishment, but also because they would deny legitimacy to Chun's administration and dishonor him even further. On 3 December 1995, Chun was arrested. His trial began on

[14]Korea Times, 19 July 1995.

[15]Korea Times, 30 October 1994.

[16]International Herald Tribune, 28/29 October 1995.

26 February 1996, also before the Seoul District Court, centering on the graft charges. His former assistants were also indicted.

A legal battle followed.[17] It was hotly contested as to whether the crimes committed in December 1979 and May 1980 by Chun Doo Hwan and Roh Tae Woo had already fallen under the statutes of limitation (Art. 249 Code of Criminal Procedure). There was no unanimity of views of the time at which the crimes were committed and when the period of limitation started to run, and whether limitations for some of the crimes had been suspended during the former presidents' term of office, since they enjoyed an immunity from prosecution, except for insurrection and treason (Art. 84 of the Constitution). The view prevailed that additional legislation suspending the statutes of limitation was necessary. This was done hastily by the National Assembly which passed two acts on 19 December 1995: Act on Non-Applicability of Statutes of Limitations to Crimes Destructive of the Constitutional Order and a Special Law on the May 18 Democratization Movement. Article 2 of the Special Law stated that for the crime of military insurrection and treason of December 12 and May 18, the tolling of the period of limitation for the prosecution would be suspended until 24 February 1993.[18] In other words, the period of limitation for these crimes started running only from the moment when Tae Woo had completed his term of office as President. On the day the two Acts were promulgated, i.e. on 21 December 1995, Chun and Roh were also indicted on mutiny and treason charges. The same charges were leveled against a number of those officers who had supported Chun and Rho in December 1979 and May 1980. Chun Doo Hwan and four generals were additionally charged with having committed homicide during the Kwangju incident. On 28 February 1996, all these cases were turned over to the Seoul District Court.

The legal obstacles had not yet been overcome completely. Serious arguments against the validity of the Special Law were leveled and brought before the Constitutional Court[19]: that the Special Law was for individual cases, that it was retroactive and that it was against the principle of prohibition for double jeopardy. The Constitutional Court rejected the petition, on doubtful grounds, however. It acknowledged that the Special Law contained legislation

---

[17]For details, see James M. West, "Martial Lawlessness: The Legal Aftermath of Kwangju", in *Pacific Rim Law and Policy Journal*, January 1997.

[18]Kyodo News International, 25 December 1995.

[19]C Court.go.kr/english/case 44, dated 16 February 1996.

for individual cases which might violate the principle of equal protection. Nevertheless, it justified the law because of the strong national request for cleaning past stains, and for the purpose of establishing a legitimate government. On the question of retro-activity, some judges argued that it could be justified because the prosecution could not be expected to act against men in charge of the national power and that the crimes committed were too undemocratic and brutal. Five of the nine judges, however, considered the Special Law unconstitutional. This did not make the Special Law void, because at least six votes were necessary to declare a law unconstitutional (Art. 113 Constitution). One could not avoid the impression that the Court's arguments were influenced by the public debate.

In any case, the trials could proceed. It was quite a spectacle to watch 2 former presidents, 14 former generals and 11 tycoons, standing in prison garb before the court answering its questions. As far as the funds were concerned, they were termed by the defendants as election campaign funds or ruling funds made up of routine contributions and not honored by granting favors. As far as the two incidents under investigation were concerned, Chun Doo Hwan and Roh Tae Woo used evasive tactics if they did not prefer not to answer at all. The defense followed the line of arguing that the military upheaval and the crackdown had been necessary for a thorough investigation of the assassination of Park Chung Hee and to restore public order. Roh Tae Woo termed the events of 12 December 1997, particularly the arrest of General Chung Seung Hwa, the Army Chief of Staff, as an accidental incident that occurred during the investigation of Park's assassination.[20] Chun argued that he should be held responsible for Chung's arrest.[21] The extension of martial law on 17 May 1980 was defended by Roh Tae Woo as a measure taken against a prominent threat from the North.[22] Both ex-presidents did not show any repentance; Chun Doo Hwan, the tougher of the two, spoke of "a trial of political retaliation".[23]

On 26 August 1996, the Seoul District Court pronounced the sentences.[24] Chun Doo Hwan received capital punishment for military insurrection, treason and corruption, and Roh Tae Woo received twenty-two and a half years in

[20]Dawn (Karatchi), 5 December 1995.

[21]The Muslim (Islamabad), 26 March 1996.

[22]International Herald Tribune, 2 April 1996.

[23]The Muslim (Islamabad), 8 August 1996.

[24]Korea Times, 27 August 1996; Kyodo News Service, 26 August 1996; Los Angeles Times, 26 and 27 August 1996; International Herald Tribune, 27 August 1996.

prison on the same charges. Roh receive a lighter sentence as the court took into account the fact that he had been an elected president, and had many achievements such as South Korea's entry into the United Nations. Both ex-presidents were also fined large sums of money. 13 former generals were also convicted (only Park Joon Byung was acquitted), as well as 9 business executives and 9 former senior government officials.

On 16 December 1996, the Court of Appeal converted the sentences for Chun Doo Hwan into lifelong imprisonment and for Roh Taw Woo, into imprisonment for seventeen years. The Court took into account the convicts' efforts to foster the Korean economy and to transfer power peacefully through direct presidential elections.[25] The Supreme Court upheld this decision on 17 April 1997.[26]

President Kim Young Sam had given a helping hand so that the trials could get started. It was he who had asked his party on 24 November 1995 to enact the Special Law for the May 18 Democratization Movement. It had been his government which directed the prosecution.[27] It was the President who saw to it that only the masterminds of the two incidents were tried.[28] In a statement on 13 December 1995, he called the behavior of his two predecessors during the investigation as "shameless".[29] Why did President Kim Young Sam give up his earlier attitude of letting bygones be bygones?

When the question of prosecuting Chun Doo Hwan and Roh Tae Woo became an important issue of public discussions in 1994 and 1995, Kim Young Sam tried to stick to his original policy to let history judge. When Seo Seok Chae, Minister of Government Administration, mentioned in an interview on 9 August 1965 that a former president had 400 billion Won in slush funds hidden at numerous banks, the President fired him immediately. This reaction was not just the result of the President's wish to keep in line with his principle to which he had publicly subscribed. One has no difficulty in suspecting that it was motivated by political expediency. When the forces of the old regime, led by Chun Doo Hwan and Roh Tae Woo, admitted him to their club in 1990, they had it in mind to make sure that he would not prosecute them for past events.

---

[25]Los Angeles Times, 16 December 1996; Financial Times, 17 December 1996.

[26]New York Times, 18 April 1997.

[27]International Herald Tribune, 26 November 1995.

[28]Korea Herald, 26 November 1995.

[29]International Herald Tribune, 13 December 1995.

There may have been a deal, the details of which are not known. However, Chun Doo Hwan, in his statement on 2 December 1995, lifted the veil a bit.[30] He mentioned that in December 1989 Roh Tae Woo, Kim Young Sam, Kim Dae Jung and Kim Jong Pil had decided to conclude "the case" in return for his testimony at a National Assembly public hearing. This explanation seemed plausible.

It was political expediency which made Kim Young Sam change his mind in the fall of 1995. At that time, public calls to try Chun Doo Hwan and Roh Tae Woo had increased.[31] More than 5000 faculty members from Korean universities called for the punishing of the former presidents. 120,000 Catholics signed a petition asking for the same. Students boycotted classes and joined protests. The President's resistance against the mounting pressure appeared to weaken public support for him which he, as an elected president, was more dependent upon than his predecessors. This development, at the same time, may have weakened the position of his allies in the forthcoming National Assembly elections. In reaction, he changed his course and turned against those who had made it possible for him to become president. The remarks of Park Kye Dong in the Assembly on 19 October 1995 about Roh's slush funds resembled those which Minister Seo Seok Chae had made some weeks earlier. Park's remarks gave Kim Young Sam the opportunity to publicize his new policy which he termed as "righting the wrongs of history".[32]

Had the trials really been helpful in righting the wrongs of history? Historical events and historical facts cannot be changed in retrospect. They can be discovered, revealed, put together and presented to the public. This goal was achieved only to a certain extent. The courts did not succeed in establishing many new facts. This was partly due to their inability to convince former President Choi Kyu Hah to provide evidence. The Seoul High Court had arranged to bring him to the court, but Choi Kyu Hah would not answer any questions. Although these proceedings did not bring important facts to light, they did, however, give the Korean public the opportunity to become informed about what had happened in 1979 and 1980. Views on historical facts can be changed. A whole nation may be called upon to look back and revise earlier assessments of past events. Koreans had been made to believe that Chun Doo

[30] Korea Annual 1996 p. 50.

[31] West, footnotes 119–121.

[32] Address on National Policies on 6 January 1996, Korea Annual 1996, p. 551.

Hwan and Roh Tae Woo were their legitimate leaders. Now they knew that this had not been the case, that these leaders had committed severe crimes, military insurrection, treason and that they were corrupt. Koreans experienced that the rule of law also was applied to those who had been most powerful in the past. What was achieved by the trials was very well put by a father whose son was tortured to death in 1987; he said "It is progress towards democracy, it is now unavoidable that they will be judged by history".[33]

What had Kim Young Sam gained politically? Not much. His inconsistency in dealing with the events in December 1979 and the uprising in Kwangju in 1980 had been much too obvious and had contributed to legal confusion. He insisted that he had followed the same principles from the very beginning, but in fact, he had changed his course. He had reacted in a pragmatic way.

Democratization Efforts

It was remarkable that the generals on active duty did not come to the rescue of their former commanders-in-chief and colleagues before or during the trials. This happened for various reasons. From the start of his presidency, Kim Young Sam had curbed the influence of the military and subjected it to civilian rule. He had started by reshuffling the chiefs-of-staff and most of the commanders. He banned private organizations within the military like *hanahoe* (one mind society), an association organized by Chun Doo Hwan. By and by, he dismissed all members of *hanahoe*. The anti-corruption drive was also helpful in getting rid of officers. Officers who had accepted bribes for promoting their subordinates or in connection with defense projects or with the purchase of arms were arrested and indicted. President Kim Young Sam continued to remain in control of the military. After a North Korean submarine had invaded South Korean territorial waters without being noticed in September 1996, the President reprimanded a number of officers. The younger officers who took top positions under Kim Young Sam were of a different type than their predecessors. They were military technocrats who focused on their duty to defend the country. This duty was an important one as the tensions with North Korea continued to exist. In their own field of security related politics, the generals continued to exert strong influence.

[33] Los Angeles Times, 26 August 1996.

With a view to national reconciliation, President Kim Young Sam on 6 March 1993 granted amnesty to thousands of people convicted for public security-related crimes. Among them was the Reverend Moon Ik Hwan, the chairman of *mintongnyon*, who had been jailed because he had illegally visited North Korea. Many thousands had their honor restored. Teachers who had been fired because they tried to organize a trade union were rehired. Students who had been expelled from universities because of anti-government activities were readmitted. Additional amnesties followed.

An institution which deserved the President's special attention was the country's intelligence agency, the Agency for National Security Planning (ANSP), because it had been used as an instrument of suppression. Kim Young Sam made changes in the ANSP. He reshuffled the staff and appointed Kim Deok, a professor of law and politics, to be director of the agency. As tensions with North Korea increased during the nuclear crisis, Kim Young Sam became reluctant to weaken the agency further. At the end of 1996, the government party passed a law which revived the Agency's right to interrogate and arrest pro-North Korean citizens.[34]

This act, together with an extremely controversial labor law, was adopted by 155 assembly members from the ruling party under the chairmanship of the Deputy Speaker. It was passed in the absence of opposition parties within 6 minutes on 26 December 1996. This procedure reminds one of similar events during the Park Chung Hee era, when on 13 September 1969 the government party adopted an amendment to the constitution allowing for the re-election of Park Chung Hee, and when on 27 December 1971 the government party adopted a bill justifying emergency measures retroactively. There were other instances of severe clashes between the government party and the opposition parties in the National Assembly, some of them provoked by a radical attitude of the opposition. It became obvious that the traditional attitude of confrontation was still alive in Parliament. However, compromises were also achieved. For instance, compromises were found on the reformation of the Election Law, the Political Fund Law and the Local Election Law.

In the developing democratic atmosphere, political parties had become more important than ever. They had to get prepared for the local elections scheduled for 27 June 1995 and the National Assembly elections scheduled for 11 April 1996. Within the government party, the DLP, factional fighting

[34]Korea News Review, 4 January 1997.

continued. The fights resulted in Kim Jong Pil leaving the party of which he was Chairman. He took along his followers and founded a new party, the United Liberal Democrats (ULD). It was Kim Young Sam who had let Kim Jong Pil down by asking him, on 10 January 1995, to retire from the leadership of the DLP. To lose one of the three factions which had established the DLP proved to be a fatal mistake. In the local elections on 27 June 1995, the weakened DLP suffered a setback, while the ULD did astonishingly well as did the DP.

In these elections, the heads and councils of the five big cities and the ten provinces, the mayors and commissioners of small cities, counties and wards of big cities and the councils of these units had to be elected. With the exception of the small unit council's elections, political parties were allowed to participate. Of the heads of the five big cities and the ten provinces, only five went to the DLP, four each went to the ULD and the DP, and two went to independents. Particularly saddening for the DLP were the results in Seoul. The candidate for the DP, Cho Soon, won while the candidate for the DLP reached only third place. Of the 133 council members in Seoul the DP gained 122, and the DLP only 11. Of the 25 ward chiefs in Seoul, the DP received 23. In other parts of the country, including Pusan, Inchon, the two Kyongsang provinces and in the Kyongi Province the DLP did better.

Not only was the emergence of a separate political party headed by Kim Jong Pil important, but more so was the return of Kim Dae Jung to politics. After having actively supported the DP's candidates during the local elections and seeing their success, he announced his return on 13 July 1995. In September 1995, he once again founded a political party, the National Congress of New Politics (NCNP). He gathered his old followers, who had previously found shelter in the DP under the new party. He also tried to include personalities from outside into the new party. With Kim Dae Jung back on the political stage, the opposition, all of a sudden, had a spokesman who could not be overlooked and to whom the President had to pay attention. The ULD and the NCNP had one common goal; the introduction of a parliamentary cabinet system. The DLP reacted to its defeat by adopting a new name, New Korea Party, and reshuffling its leadership.

The National Assembly elections on 11 April 1996 were held during the turbulence created by the great trials. They brought a satisfactory result for the NKP and Kim Young Sam, winning 139 out of 299 seats. The ULD with Kim Jong Pil was the real winner with 50 seats. The NCNP with Kim Dae Jung missed its goal of 100 seats by winning just 79 seats; its failure was due to a poor performance in Seoul where it won only 18 of the 45 seats. The DP, with only 15 seats, failed to gain the necessary numbers to form a parliamentary group. All in all regional rivalry had again shown its dominating power.

The Sad End

The labor laws, railroaded through the National Assembly on 26 December 1996, contained the first revision of the traditional labor law system. They tried to tackle various problems[35]: the increasing lack of competitiveness of Korean companies due to permanent wage increases since 1987, the limited opportunities for workers to organize themselves and the rigid system of working hours. The new laws were greeted with massive strikes organized by the officially recognized FKTU (Federation of Korean Trade Unions) and by the still unrecognized KCTU (Korean Confederation of Trade Unions). It took quite some time until a compromise was reached on 10 March 1997. The December amendments repealed and new laws were passed by the Assembly.[36] Companies were enabled to dismiss workers under certain conditions; however, a two-year grace period was fixed. In the future, several trade unions were allowed in one company. This meant the recognition of the KCTU. A more flexible work hour system was also allowed in order to promote competitiveness. President Kim Young Sam had been unable to control the strike. He had needed the assistance of the opposition. As the dark clouds of future economic difficulties could already be seen, the reform should have gone much further. Less than a year later, the economic crisis made it necessary, for example, to abolish the grace period for worker dismissals.

The efforts made by President Kim Young Sam to control the government and politics sometimes looked desperate. Under him, the turnover in political personnel was as frequent as that under his predecessors, or was worse. He needed, for example, five prime ministers, six ministers of national unification, four ministers of interior and four ministers of foreign affairs. The lack of consistency might have been forgiven by people, but worse was yet to come — the Hanbo scandal.

---

[35]Donggyun Shin, "Labor Market Reform" in *Korea Economy 1999*, Vol. 15 published by Korea Economic Institute of America pp. 39 ff.

[36]Financial Times, 11 March 1997 (BBC Summary of World Broadcasts, 11 March 1997).

In January 1997, the Hanbo group, a chaebol focusing on steel production, went bankrupt with 5,8 billion US$ in liabilities, most of which was not recovered. Hanbo had expanded during the Kim Young Sam administration and received huge credits for which it could not provide any security. Investigations were undertaken by Parliament and the prosecution. The second son of Kim Young Sam, Kim Hyun Chul, had to appear before the National Assembly and to answer questions as a witness. He denied any involvement in the scandal. The investigations by the prosecution revealed that Hanbo had bribed many government officials and politicians in order to buy influence. In May 1997, Kim Hyun Chul was arrested on charges of corruption and tax evasion. In October 1997, the Seoul District Court sentenced him to three years of imprisonment and a high fine. After the Supreme Court had returned the case to the Seoul High Court because of problems in court proceedings, the Seoul High Court sentenced him to two years in jail on 23 June 1999.[37]

The proceeding in the National Assembly and before the court did not answer the question of whether Kim Young Sam had received money for the election campaign in 1992. Kim Dae Jung admitted in October 1995 that he had received a large amount of money from Roh Tae Woo for his election campaign. Kim Young Sam insisted that he was clean: "I have never, however, received a single Won that came with a string attached or that was tied to business interests".[38] That his family was involved in corruption which he had started to fight made many people suspicious. In February 1997, Kim Young Sam, in a public apology to the Korean people, had taken responsibility as a father.

By the end of 1997, the Korean economy went into a severe crisis due to a collapse of export prices and an inability to substitute short-term external debt. Kim Young Sam's successor as President, Kim Dae Jung, had to step in to agree on a bailout mechanism with the World Bank and bilateral donors. Kim Young Sam, who had started his office with such high hopes and promises, left humiliated. He was right when he once said that reforms were more difficult than a revolution. History, which he had invoked so often, will credit him with a substantial contribution to Korea's democratization.[39]

---

[37] Korea Times, 24 June 1999.

[38] Address on 6 January 1996, Korea Annual 1996 p. 352.

[39] See also Hahn, Bae Ho (1997) pp. 1 ff.; Doh, C. Shin pp. 218–220.

Kim Dae Jung before the Doors to Power

When the date for the next presidential elections approached in 1997, the splits in the government party, NKP, became obvious once again. It seemed close to impossible to agree on a candidate for the elections. In November 1997, the NKP merged with the DP to become the Grand National Party (GNP). Cho Soon, who had been the presidential candidate for the DP, became the president of the new party; Lee Han Dong, who had tried to be a presidential candidate, became the chairman of the new party; and Lee Hoi Chang, with the support of Kim Young Sam, became the party's presidential candidate. Lee Hoi Chang had been a former judge and was briefly, for 123 days, Prime Minister under Kim Young Sam; he was a typical representative of the establishment. As time went by he tried to dissociate himself from Kim Young Sam, whose image continued to worsen in view of the economic crisis.

One of the contenders for the presidential candidacy within the NKP was Rhee In Je, the governor of the Kyonggi province. He left the NKP to found a party called New Party by the People (NPP), which nominated him for president.

Kim Dae Jung was doing quite well in the polls, but he knew that he could not make it if he was only supported by southwest Korea and Seoul. So, in October 1997, he formed an alliance with the ULD of Kim Jong Pil. Kim Dae Jung became the joint candidate for both parties, Kim Jong Pil was assured to become Prime Minister with larger responsibilities if Kim Dae Jung would win; and Kim Dae Jung promised to introduce later a parliamentary system. It was quite astonishing to see Kim Dae Jung cooperating with the remnants of the Park Chung Hee era. It had been Kim Jong Pil who had founded the KCIA, and it had been the KCIA which had persecuted Kim Dae Jung. However, if Kim Dae Jung wanted to be successful, he had to overcome regional rivalry as Kim Young Sam had done five years before. There was only the ULD left as a possible partner. Thus Kim Dae Jung had no choice but to seek the support of Kim Jong Pil. The campaign was rather dirty with charges between the candidates centering on allegations of using illegal funds. None of the candidates made really clear how they would proceed to overcome the economic crisis, even though most of them promised to co-operate with the IMF.

The calculations of Kim Dae Jung had been correct. On 18 December 1997, Kim Dae Jung received 39.61% of the votes, Lee Hoi Chang 38.0% and Rhee In Je 18.96%. Kim Dae Jung succeeded not only in the two Cholla Provinces but also in Seoul, and he considerably improved his margins in Taejon and the South Chungchon Province. Many Koreans probably felt that in a severe crisis, a man with the stature, intelligence and courage of Kim Dae Jung would be needed.

Before having officially entered the Blue House, Kim Dae Jung took part in important decisions of the government. As was mentioned, he gave his agreement to the negotiations with the IMF, and he also agreed with Kim Young Sam to pardon Chun Doo Hwan and Roh Tae Woo. On 22 December 1977, the two ex-presidents were freed and had their civil rights restored. Very soon, it was up to President Kim Dae Jung, who had fought so hard and for such a long time to become the head of state, to guide his country through the crisis.

The Domestic Policies of President Kim Dae Jung

The inauguration of Kim Dae Jung took place on 25 February 1998. The country's best-known dissident was now its president. This was a quite a change. Kim Dae Jung is no supporter of the "Asian Values" theory which propagates an enlightened authoritarianism. He stands for Western democracy. In his inaugural address he suggested putting participatory democracy into practice.[40] At a later occasion, he also mentioned that he wanted to be remembered as a champion of democracy, human rights, inter-Korean peace and a prosperous Korea.[41]

Before he could realize his reforms, he had to set up the necessary government machinery. This was not easy, as he had to deal with a National Assembly in which the opposition party, the GNP, had a majority. This was still the Assembly elected in 1996. When Kim Dae Jung became President, the distribution of 299 seats was as follows: GNP 161, NCNP 78, ULD 43, NPP 8, Independents 4; for five seats by-elections were necessary.[42]

The opposition made immediate use of its majority power when the President asked the Assembly to agree to his choice of having Kim Jong Pil as Prime Minister. On 25 February 1998, the opposition prevented parliamentary approval by boycotting the session. Another attempt on 2 March 1998 to make

[40]Type written text, date 25 February 1998 (in the author's possession).

[41]Korea Times, 30 April 1999.

[42]Dormels, Rainer, "Das erste Kabinett der Regierung Kim Dae Jung", in Patrick Koellner (editor), *Korea 1988*, Institut fuer Asienkunde, Hamburg 1998, p. 126.

the Assembly agree to the President's choice went down in tumultuous clashes between government and opposition parties. Kim Dae Jung could only succeed in keeping his promise from the election campaign by a trick. On 3 March 1998, he appointed Kim Jung Pil as "Acting" Prime Minister and put together his cabinet, a cabinet of politicians. On 17 August 1998 the Assembly confirmed the appointment of Kim Jong Pil as Prime Minister.

Later, the situation for the government in the Assembly improved. By mid-1999, the two ruling parties had a majority of 160 seats (NCNP 105, UDP 55 seats) thanks to crossovers.[43] However, the legislative process remained difficult. Many sessions of the Assembly were disrupted by violence. Again and again, the Speaker was prevented by the GNP from presiding over a session. It was as in the old authoritarian days. Another bad practice was also revived: the "railroading" of laws through the National Assembly. That is to say, the passing of laws against the protest of the opposition in an unconventional, sometimes unlawful way. Now, it happened with reversed roles. This time, it was the NCNP which "railroaded" bills through the Assembly; it did so in January and May 1999. This was a practice against which the NCNP had fought as long as it had been in the opposition. During the first two years of his administration, Kim Dae Jung did not succeed in finding a way to cooperate with the parliamentary opposition. The results of reforms by law were, therefore, modest. The President was aware of this and declared in his New Year's press conference on 26 January 2000 that he would make efforts to reform politics.[44]

Kim Dae Jung contributed to the spirit of reconciliation by granting amnesty to 74 political prisoners and 11 labor activists at the beginning of his presidency.[45] He also curbed the influence of the Agency for National Security Planning by appointing Lee Jong Chan as the new director, by dismissing many of its officials and restricting the Agency's work on collecting overseas information and monitoring events in North Korea. The agency had launched a smear campaign before the presidential elections, linking Kim Dae Jung with North Korea. Since January 1999, the agency is called National Intelligence Service.

President Kim Dae Jung was proud that the South Korean press enjoyed absolute freedom.[46] The arrest of Hong Seok Hyun, the publisher of the daily

[43]Serge Berthier, "The Political Chaos", in *Asian Affairs* No. 8, Summer 1999 p. 20.

[44]Korea Times, 26 January 2000.

[45]International Herald Tribune, 14–15 March 1998.

[46]New York Times, 20 February 2000.

Chung Ang Ilbo, at the beginning of October 1999 called that assertion into question. Hong was arrested for alleged tax evasion. As his paper, affiliated with the powerful Samsung group, was one of the most vocal critics of the Kim Dae Jung administration, the opposition denounced the action as a press-taming bid.[47]

In his inaugural address, Kim Dae Jung had condemned corruption. He tried to fight it. The most prominent case was the so-called tax scandal. It was asserted that during the election campaign in 1997, GNP politicians had used the Office of National Tax Administration (ONTA) to collect funds. Lee Hoi Sung, the younger brother of the leader of the opposition, Lee Hoi Chang, was indicted in this connection. This incident partly explained the enmity of Lee Hoi Chung against the Kim Dae Jung administration, which he labeled a dictatorship.[48] It was a setback for the judiciary when the National Assembly voted down the motion to permit the arrest of Representative Suh Sung Mok, one of the key figures in the scandal.

The President was embarrassed that corruption continued to occur among his followers.[49] In June 1999, he had to ask two of his ministers to resign. Mrs. So Sook, an actress, had to quit as Environment Minister because she had accepted US $20,000 "encouragement money" from businessmen. Shortly before, Justice Minister Kim Dae Young was fired. The reasons given referred to his prior activities as prosecutor when, in 1998, he had plotted to tame unionists; he had been under pressure to resign because his wife was involved in the "dress scandal". Wives of former and present cabinet members had allegedly accepted luxurious dresses and coats which were paid by business circles. Governor Lim Chang Yul and the Mayor of Inchon Choi Ki Sung, both followers of Kim Dae Jung, were charged with having accepted bribes in the summer of 1999. As the scandals were tarnishing the administration's reputation, Kim Dae Jung offered a public apology on 25 June 1999. Three months later, the President established an anti-corruption panel charged to request investigations and make policy recommendations. It was only too obvious: the goodwill of the chief executive alone could not remove deep-rooted practices.

Since the end of 1999, South Korean politicians started focusing on the National Assembly elections on 13 April 2000. Since Kim Dae Jung had not

[47]Korea Times, 3 October 1999.

[48]Korea Times, 4 May 1999.

[49]International Herald Tribune, 9 August 1999.

kept his promise of introducing a parliamentary system which would strengthen the authority of the prime minister, Kim Jong Pil resigned as Prime Minister on 6 December 1999. His post was filled by Park Tae Joon, the President of the ULD. By the end of February 2000, the ULD decided to terminate the coalition with the party of Kim Dae Jung, renamed Millennium Democratic Party.

The results of the elections were disappointing for Kim Dae Jung.[50] His Millenium Democratic Party received only 35.9% of the votes and 115 of the Assembly's seats. His former coalition partner, the ULD, suffered a severe setback, receiving only 17 seats. The GNP, the main opposition party, won 133 seats and thus remained the strongest parliamentary group. Small parties and independents won a total of eight seats. Regionalism had reappeared. The MDP won an overwhelming victory in the ChollaCholla provinces. The GNP won almost all seats in the Kyongsang provinces.

President Kim Dae Jung needs support from other parties in the Assembly to go ahead with his policy of reforms. He will probably muddle through, but it will be difficult for him to live up to his people's expectations.

References

Han, Bae Ho, "Assessing Kim Young Sam Administration's First Four Years", in *Korea Focus* 1997, Vol. 5 No. 2.

Kirk Donald, *Korean Dynasty, Hyundai and Chung Ju Yung*, Hongkong 1994.

Paik, Young Chul, "Political Reform and Democratic Consolidation in Korea", in *Korea and World Affairs* Vol. 18 No. 4 (Winter 1994) pp. 730–748.

[50]Korea Herald, 15 April 2000.

Chapter 15

The Economy

The Miracle at the Han River

At the beginning of the 1960s, the leaders of developing countries aimed at bringing their economies to the level achieved by industrialized countries. In 1962 Kwame Nkrumah, the leader of Ghana, put it in the following way[1]: "The peoples of the colonies know precisely what they want. They wish ... to be unrestricted to attain an advancement that will put them on a par with other technically advanced nations of the world." In other words, the developing countries wanted to catch up with the industrialized countries. Many tried, most of them failed. The Republic of Korea, however, succeeded.

Per capita GNP in South Korea rose from US $87 in 1962 to US $3,145 in 1988, and to US $10,543 in 1996. Koreans only needed the period of one generation to transform their country from an impoverished, agrarian, developing state, destroyed by the Korean War, into a modern industrialized society which entered into the ranks of the large trading nations. South Korea's advanced status was recognized, when in December 1996, it became a member of the OECD, the "club" of the industrialized countries. The Republic of Korea's figures was calculated to be 30 on the Human Development Index in the 1998 report of UNDP.[2] It is understandable that Koreans used to talk about the "miracle at the Han River", although only until 1997.

Setting up modern industrial structures together with improvements in living conditions preceded South Korea's political progress towards

[1]Nkrumah, Kwame, *Revolutionary Path*, London 1973, p. 40.

[2]*Human Development Report 1998*, published by UNDP, New York 1998, p. 128.

democratization. Park Chung Hee and Chun Doo Hwan ruled in an authoritarian way, and the door to liberty was only opened in 1987. That was the moment when the economic changes had resulted in changes of the society, and produced a middle class which demanded a government ruled by the people.

Due to the fact that in many countries development assistance result in reducing the prosperity gap, donors became impatient and reviewed the system. Donors felt that the political system had to be changed if aid was to be successful. Since the beginning of the 1990s, it has become popular to lay down political criteria for the evaluation of framework conditions in developing countries. Germany, an important donor country, for example, made it known that it would take into account the following criteria: respect for human rights; participation of the people in the political process; the guarantee of security under the law; the creation of a market-oriented economy; and development-oriented domestic politics.[3] Had these criteria been used and strictly applied by Germany and like-minded donors from the 1960s to the 1980s, South Korea would not have been granted development aid. South Korea did, however, receive assistance from Germany (DM 500 million financial assistance, DM 190 million technical cooperation in the period form 1961 to 1982), which contributed to the country's economic progress. The political take-off followed the economic take-off. The flag followed trade. This fact should not be overlooked.

The growth of South Korea's GNP reflects its quick economic development. During the period from 1962 to 1981, the average growth rate was 8.8%. From 1982 to 1988, GNP grew by an average of 10.6%; South Korea experienced an economic boom. From 1989 on, growth slowed down, but reached a remarkable 7.5% in the period from 1989 to 1996. The focus on growth, and the obsession with expansion by government and business made the Koreans neglect the inherent dangers, dangers which made the Korean economy collapse at the end of 1997.

Rapid Growth

The driving force behind the expansion of the Korean economy was its export oriented industrialization, called the "export-push strategy" by the

[3]Press and Information Office of the Federal Government: *Facts About Germany*, Frankfurt 1998 p. 239.

World Bank.[4] South Korea was transformed from an agrarian state into an industrialized country. Accordingly, the composition of the GNP changed. The contribution of agriculture (forestry and fishing included) to GNP decreased from 37.6% in 1965 to 12.8% in 1985, and 7.0% in 1995. At the same time, manufacturing and mining rose from 19.9% in 1965 to 31.3% in 1985, and 27.2% in 1995, demonstrating the extent to which manufacturing was the dynamic part of the Korean economy.[5] The tertiary sector had also expanded.

The rapid growth of the Korean economy since the 1960s was something extraordinary, particularly since the situation at the beginning was unfavorable. The Japanese colonial power had promoted the development of modern economic structures in Korea, albeit in its own interest, and by including Korea into the Japanese market. The various regions had been developed in a different way. The South, which had always served as the country's granary, produced 60% of the food. Most of the heavy industry as well as the power plants were based in the North. This had dramatic consequences when the country was divided. The withdrawal of the Japanese experts and the many refugees from the North added to the collapse of economic structures in the South. Before South Korea's economy could be built up, the Korean War caused another setback. Because of the destruction of the war, output declined and due to the huge defense budget money supply increased with the consequence of a tremendous inflation. South Korea only recovered slowly from this disaster and only thanks to massive economic assistance by the US. Since the American aid was not determined by specific plans for the development of the Korean economy, it could only partly reach the aim to contribute to setting up independent economic structures. Nevertheless, South Korea's economy recorded some progress. In the period from 1957 to 1961, GNP grew by 4.7%.

South Korea's economic rise was based on long term development plans, five-year plans, introduced and thoroughly implemented by the military government of Park Chung Hee. Already, the first five-year plan for the period of 1962 to 1966 was a success, since it resulted in a growth of GNP by a yearly average of 7.8%. Park Chung Hee had talked of the principle of "maximum competition and minimum planning". However, there was strong guidance by

[4] *The East Asian Miracle.* A World Bank Policy Research Report, Oxford 1993, p. 123.
[5] Suh Moon Gi p. 17, Kim Kiheung pp. 70 ff.

the government. The model Park Chung Hee followed was not that of the command economies of the East, but that of the Meiji reforms in Japan which had focused on growth by industrialization.[6] Markets were important, but functioned within the framework of goals laid down in the plans by the government. Since 1962, one five-year plan followed the other. They were drawn by the Economic Planning Board which had been established by the military. The guidance by the government continued invalidating the functioning of free markets in various areas.

The rise of the Korean economy could be attributed to various reasons. Export-oriented industrialization proved to be the right recipe. The South Korean governments were strong enough to get their plans put through and flexible enough to review the plans if necessary. However credit must not be given only to the government, but also to business. There were many entrepreneurs willing to comply with the administration's plans and to take risks. The synchronization of the government's planning objectives and the activities of private business was pretty well organized, however, as already mentioned, it was severely damaged by corruption.

The country's greatest potential during the period of economic progress was its well-educated and well-trained workers. As soon as the educational system started functioning after the Second World War, Koreans poured into the schools and universities. The extreme readiness for education has Confucian roots; to become educated was a prerequisite for all those who wanted to develop their human qualities according to Confucian rules. The goals changed; the students and their families which made education possible, often with great sacrifices, had success and advancement in mind. Many entrepreneurs succeeded in creating bonds of loyalty between workers and their company. The trade unions were weak, and wages low. Thus, the comparative advantage of costs for the Korean industry was, for 25 years, rather high.

At the beginning of the modernization process, the poor developing country, South Korea, lacked capital. Capital did, however, come from abroad, particularly from the USA and later also from Japan. The United States granted South Korea development assistance (without military assistance) with the amount of US $5.7 billion in the period from 1946 to 1973. During the duration of the first five-year plan, grants from the US counted for the largest part of South Korea's foreign capital. Later, the foreign public assistance was more

[6]Former Prime Minister Yoo Chang Soon, quoted by Clifford p. 50 and note 13.

and more substituted by private capital. Since the mid-sixties, the Japanese financial commitment in South Korea played an increasing role. The basis of this was the normalization treaty of 1965, by which Japan pledged grants in the amount of US $300 million, loans in the amount of US $200 million, and private investments in the amount of US $300 million. A pattern developed. The US assisted with public and commercial credits, and Japan helped with commercial credits and private investments. The World Bank, (together with the International Development Organization) became an important donor too. In 1988, its share of South Korea's external debt was 18%.

Since South Korea needed much foreign capital for its development, its external debt accumulated. It reached US $47 billion in 1988, but was reduced as the trade balance showed a surplus since 1986. When expansion of the economy again became the main focus of government and business in the mid-nineties, the external debt bounced upwards,[7] reaching US $88.7 billion in 1994 and US $119.7 billion in 1995. In 1996, South Korea's external debt stood at US $157.5 billion, US $100 billion of which were short-term. The debt-GDP ratio had risen to 32.5%.

Foreign Trade

Since South Korea's economic progress was based on exports, a study of the country's foreign trade is indispensable. Statistics underline the decisive impact of exports for the political economy. In 1961, exports contributed only 3.2% to GDP, in 1988 however, they contributed 42%. In absolute terms: South Korea's exports totaled US $5 billion in 1975, US $11 billion in 1977, US $20 billion in 1981, US $60 billion in 1988, and US $136 billion in 1997.

In its first 30 years, the South Korean export industry experienced structural changes.[8] Three phases can be distinguished. During the first stage starting from 1962 on, those industries which already existed were improved for exports, i.e. the light industry. Goods with the highest labor content such as textiles, clothing, wigs and plywood dominated South Korea's exports. During the second phase from the mid-seventies onwards, goods which had until that

[7] Aiyer p. 25.

[8] Eckart Dege, "Die Industrialisierung Südkoreas", in *Geographische Rundschau* 38 (1986) pp. 522 ff.

time been manufactured for import substitution by the heavy industry, were now improved and also exported, particularly cement, steel, chemicals and ships. Ten years later, a third phase occurred. Exports were extended to electronic goods and cars which had already been manufactured before for the domestic market.

Export statistics reflect these changes.[9] In 1997, products from the third phase dominate exports: Electronics 31%, cars 7.9%. Products from the second phase were also important: Steel 5%, petrochemicals and petroleum products 8.9%, ships 4.8%. Textiles still weighed heavily, amounting to 20% of the exports.

South Korea is a country with few raw materials. Some coal, lead, zinc, tungsten and iron ore are mined, but the country depends on the import of raw materials. In 1997, raw material accounted for more than half of its imports (52%). Expenditures for crude oil contained in that percentage accounted for 12%. The imports of consumer goods (11%) had surpassed those of machinery (9%). The affluent Korean middle class apparently excelled in preferring foreign goods.

For more than 20 years, all efforts focusing on improving export profits did not succeed in overcoming the trade balance deficit.[10] Then it happened in 1986, for the first time South Korea's trade balance was showing a surplus of US $4.2 billion. Also, the current account balance was in the black with US $4.6 billion. This trend continued for three more years, having its peak in 1988, the year of the Seoul Olympic Games. At that time, the surplus of the trade balance amounted to US $11.5 billion. From 1990 onwards, the trade balance was negative again, with the exception of 1993 when there was a small surplus of US $1.8 billion. The gap between import and export continued to grow, amounting to a deficit of US $15.3 billion in 1996. The reasons were manifold. The South Korean currency, the Won, was evaluated against the US Dollar and the Japanese Yen. Constant wage increases since 1987 had effected the competitiveness of Korean goods, and the terms of trade worsened. The South Korean economy depended too much on exports of only certain goods, such as semiconductors and steel, which were sold on sensitive and quickly changing markets. In addition, since 1967, the recession in parts of Asia took its toll on the Korean economy.

[9]Kim Kiheung pp. 70 and 71.

[10]Song Byung Nak pp. 60 and 61.

It has often been criticized that Korea's foreign trade was too much focused on two partners, the USA and Japan. Indeed in 1985, 50.5% of Korea's exports went to these two countries; 35.5% to the US, 15% to Japan.[11] In that same year, 45.1% of Korea's imports came from the same two countries; 24.3% from Japan, 20.8% from the US. In those years, Koreans were advised to diversify their foreign trade regionally. This was done. The markets in China, Hong Kong, Taiwan and the ASEAN countries became increasingly important for South Korea's exports. By 1997, exports to the US and Japan were nearly halved; their share of Korea's total exports was down 26% (USA 15.9%, Japan 10.8%). Imports from these two trading partners remained high. In 1997, they stood at 40.1% (Japan 17.8%, USA 21.4%). Exports to East Asian markets (Japan excluded) had risen from 11% in 1985 to 30.1% in 1997. Imports from the same countries showed only a small increase from 12.9% to 17.9%. This development made South Korean exports sensitive to economic fluctuations in East Asia.

Prices and Employment

The economic development of the Republic of Korea after the Korean War was unbalanced. The current account showed a deficit, inflation was tremendous reaching 81.9% in 1955, and unemployment was high. Since the beginning of the 1960s, the focus of economic development was on growth only, neglecting the aspects of a balanced growth.

The 1960s and 1970s continued to be periods of high inflation. Wholesale prices (at an annual average)[12] increased from 1962 to 1969 by 12%, and from 1970 to 1979, by 15.9%. The inflation rate was the result of a rapid expansion originally financed by large budget and refinanced by central bank money. The increase of the money supply had an inflationary effect. The huge increase of prices for crude oil and for grain since 1974 strengthened this trend. Wholesale prices soared to 42.1% in 1974. In 1980, as a result of the second oil crisis and the political turmoil after the assassination of President Park Chung Hee, inflation reached another peak at 38.9%.

---

[11] Kim Kiheung pp. 72 ff.

[12] *Major Statistics of Korean Economy 1984 and 1987*, Korea Annual 1989 to 1996.

Since the mid-1980s, this trend changed. From 1983 to 1987, wholesale prices were stable, and inflation remained below 1%. Various factors came together to bring about this result. Import prices for crude oil and oil products dropped. The Chun Doo Hwan administration insisted on containing wage increases. Therefore, nominal wage increases reached just 10% in the period from 1983 to 1987.

Inflationary trends showed up again in 1988, favored by increases in nominal wages and the prices of raw materials. From 1988 to 1994, wholesale prices increased annually by an average of 3%. Inflation was continuing and Koreans were complaining, but in reality, the inflation was modest. In the years before the collapse of the South Korean economy, at the end of 1997, inflation remained in the single digit range (6.9% in October 1997). Therefore, inflation was not a reason for major concern.

Statistics for unemployment reflect an important aspect of Korea's economic development. It moved via the creation of human capital from high unemployment to labor shortages. At the start of economic reforms in 1963, unemployment stood at 8.2%. Since then, the rate dropped. From 1980 to 1988 for instance, it dropped from 5.2% to 2.5%. In the nineties, unemployment remained about 2.5%, at the same time, nominal wages increased annually by 13%.[13] The hitherto unknown influx of foreign workers was a clear signal that labor shortages existed. Unemployment was not the problem of the Korean economy in the 1990s, but slow increase in productivity was.

Distribution of Income and Wealth

A foreign visitor who knew the Republic of Korea from the mid-1970s and returned at the end of the 1980s was in for a pleasant surprise. It was quite obvious that the living conditions of Koreans had improved tremendously. Koreans had much better accommodation than before. Private persons could now afford cars with the result that Seoul, as well as the country's other big cities, suffered from heavy traffic. In 1985, there were just 1 million cars in the whole country but in 1989, nearly 1 million cars were registered in Seoul alone.[14] Koreans were travelling in their country in huge numbers. Goods offered on

[13]Song Byung Nak pp. 60 and 61.

[14]*Korea Statistical Yearbook 1989*, p. 294, Korea Times, 17 January 1990.

the markets had considerably improved. Department stores displayed a rich choice of quality goods, including imported ones. Koreans had profited from their hard work, no doubt.

Koreans, however, did not share the impression of the foreign visitor. According to a survey done by the KDI in 1988, the majority of citizens felt that they had become poorer compared with the average citizen five years before.[15] This was strongly felt by industrial workers and farmers. Employers, self-employed people and professionals on the other hand, felt that they were at least as rich as the five years prior. What is important is the "felt inequality" of income distribution; the conviction of the majority of Koreans that they had not participated in the general economic progress.

Available statistics contradict these feelings of Koreans: income inequality was declining. In 1980, 1985 and 1988, the Bureau of Statistics undertook household income surveys. These surveys showed that the ratio of the income shares of the lowest 40% of all households over the income shares of the highest 20% of all households improved from 35% in 1980 to 47% in 1987.[16] This tendency continued; in 1993, the ratio had risen to 52%.[17] That means that income had improved. This was true for urban as well as rural households.

If the Koreans' feelings that their economic inequality deteriorated had focused on the distribution of wealth, they were correct, as a study undertaken by the KDI in 1988 demonstrates. The upper 10% held 43% of the total wealth, while the bottom 10% held only 0.5%. The greatest disparity was found in real estate ownership[18]: The upper 10% owned 76.9% of the total private land. Much real estate was in the hands of the conglomerates and/or their owner family members. Reforms to fight the inequality of wealth distribution and particularly, real estate ownership, had been necessary for many years. The extension of the "real name financial transaction system" to real estate was a step in that direction.

At the beginning of the 1990s, the World Bank was so impressed by the progress of various Asian countries that it published a study on "The East Asian Miracle". The study discusses the economic performances of Japan,

[15]Kwon Soowon, *Income, Distribution and Government Initiatives to Reduce Disparities*, KDI March 1990 p. 31.

[16]Kwon pp. 3–5.

[17]Suh Moon Gi p. 26, Song Byung Nak p. 173.

[18]Kwon pp. 18 and 19.

Korea, Hong Kong, Taiwan, Singapore, Thailand, Indonesia, Malaysia and China, which it termed the "high performing Asian economies". The World Bank argued that among other factors, the declining level of inequality during rapid growth was one of the virtues of economic development. A relation was established between per capita real GDP growth, and the ratio of the income share of the richest fifth of the population to the poorest, for the period between 1965 to 1989. It confirmed that the Republic of Korea occupied a top position among countries combining high growth with declining income inequality.[19]

The Economic Debacle

As was already mentioned, the South Korean trade balance closed the year of 1996 with a huge deficit of US $15.3 billion. With both its two largest trading partners, Japan and the US, Korea's trade balance showed a deficit (of US $15.7 billion and 11.6 billion respectively).[20] Increased expenditures for foreign travel, payment on interests and transport added to the misery, as they resulted in a deficit on services of US $7.7 billion. The current account balance for 1996 reached a deficit of US $22.9 billion.[21] These trends could not be overcome in 1997; exports rose modestly, imports caused a gap in the merchandise account of US $8.4 billion. The deficit of the current account balance reached US $13.8 billion. Additional borrowing during this period was necessary, driving the external debt to US $120 billion in September 1997.

More difficulties were to come. The bankruptcy of Hanbo Iron and Steel in January 1997 proved to be just the beginning of many collapses of South Korean companies. Various other companies had to ask for financial assistance or to file for protection or bankruptcy because they were unable to service their debt. Affiliates of well-known conglomerates were affected: Sammi, Jinro, Dainong, Ssangyong, and Kia among others.

An additional development aggravated the situation for Korea. Since mid-1997, the currencies and financial markets in certain South East Asian countries had come under pressure. The process started in Thailand where the country's currency depreciated rapidly because investors felt that the Thai Bath was

[19] *The East Asian Miracle* (see note 4) pp. 29 to 32.

[20] Henseleit p. 113.

[21] Henseleit p. 115.

overvalued, and the Thai economy overheated. Their lack of confidence spread to Indonesia, Malaysia, the Philippines, and finally reached the Republic of Korea. Here, the situation was dramatic. Of the country's external debt of US $154.4 billion in 1997, more than 40% US $68.4 billion was short-term, of which US $20 billion was due before the end of the year.[22] The roll over of short-term debt had been no problem in the past. With the South East Asian crises and the deteriorating situation in Korea, investors lost confidence and were not willing to extend new credits. The half-hearted support measures of the Kim Young Sam administration could not change investors' mistrust.

Consequently, many companies had to pay back their foreign debt and a run on the US Dollar and Japanese Yen followed. Foreign currencies became more and more expensive, and the Korean currency started falling. At first, the Korean government and the Bank of Korea tried to defend the Won. After they had lost significant reserves, they stopped intervening. Between late November and 11 December 1997, the Won lost half of its value against the US Dollar. The Bank of Korea had only enough reserves left to cover two weeks of imports. Hence, there was also a liquidity crisis. The South Korean government had no other choice but to turn to the IMF and other multilateral and bilateral donors for assistance. This was done in late November. On 4 December 1997, the IMF approved a standby arrangement of US $21 billion for three years, hoping that altogether, US $51 billion would be made available from various international sources. The economy of the Republic of Korea, once the pride of Koreans and the envy of many other countries, was in a shambles. What had gone wrong?

Since 1994, South Korea's terms of trade declined rapidly and considerably. The deterioration of the relative prices of Korean exports cannot only be excused with the negative impact of the depreciation of the Japanese Yen. It was mainly the result of a decline of productivity which was first of all caused by wages outstripping labor productivity gains.[23] The advantage of competitive prices had disappeared. As South Korea continued to import, it had to pay relatively more in terms of its own exports. It would have been the task of business to avoid such a development.

The extreme dependence on short-term credits and the unwillingness of investors to roll them over was the second main reason for the collapse of

---

[22]Aiyer p. 25.

[23]Sakong Il p. 179 with note 19.

the Korean economy. The impact of a declining confidence of investors was immediately felt. This vulnerability had been neglected by government as well as by businesses.

A decisive role was played by the banks. They were not free in their lending policies; they were under pressure from the conglomerates, which had the expansion of their capacities in mind, as well as from governments which considered expansion a remedy against the diseases of the Korean economy. Government really counted, because it directed parts of bank lending. Bankers and businessmen, seeing the risks of lending and borrowing money without sufficient securities, found consolation in the idea that government would bail them out if they encountered difficulties. Government, banks and conglomerates acted in a reckless and irresponsible way. Korean banks, mainly Korea First for example, gave large credits to Hanbo, which had a debt-to-equity ratio of 1.600%.

The conglomerates, which had been so much in the center of Korea's economic achievements, had their share of the downfall. Some of the conglomerates were too big and powerful. Only four of them, Samsung, Hyundai, Daewoo and LG, accounted for half of Korea's exports, and one third of Korea's domestic sales. In many areas such as cars, electronics, steel, ship building, they were fighting against each other and trying to outdo each other. The conglomerates were big, and their profit margins were increasingly small. Many of the *chaebol* continued to be run by the founder families, some of them with management problems. The various companies of one group were often not only connected by family ties but also by cross share holding which lacked transparency. The *chaebol* of old had outlived their use.

Given these problems, it was not surprising at all that the IMF, the World Bank and other donors, which had been willing to support Korea with liquidity in order to stabilize the exchange rate and re-establish confidence of the financial markets, insisted on reforms of the financial sector and the labor market. South Korea's government was involved in various ways. It had to see to it that the reforms were really implemented. It had to insist that the debacle was home made and not an "IMF crisis" as it had been called by some who did not want to admit the Koreans' own mistakes. The government also had to change its overall attitude towards the national economy. Guided capitalism has to be substituted by the guidance of the markets. It was good luck for the Republic of Korea that exactly at the peak of the crisis, a new President was elected, who had not been involved with the old practices and who understood the inner relations between democracy and market economy.

A Recovery?

The incoming administration of President Kim Dae Jung energetically tackled the challenges of overcoming the economic crisis. It attempted to consolidate the financial sector, to reform corporate governance, to attract foreign direct investments and to promote industrial peace.

The South Korean banks had suffered tremendous amounts of losses in 1998, the banks as well as their assets had to be restructured. An institutional framework was set up and the authority of the Financial Supervisory Commission was strengthened. Banks were either closed, merged or taken over by government. 64 trillion Won (US $53.3 billion) were set aside to re-capitalize the banks. Although the consolidation of the banks is often considered to be the most successful of the necessary reforms of the Korean economy, doubts remain. Many banks still have considerable non-performing loans. It is not very likely hat the old habits, particularly the collusion between the banks, the government elites and the conglomerates, together with their neglect of risks and returns, have disappeared. In this context, it must be noted that state intervention in the financial sector had become stronger than ever during the rescue operation, even though it is aiming to expose the Korean banks to the markets. A new generation of professional managers, focusing on independent decision-making about allocating credits, will be necessary to finally establish a well functioning financial system in South Korea.[24]

Since the conglomerates, the *chaebol*, had their share in the downfall of the South Korean economy, it was indispensable to reform them. They were asked by the Kim Dae Jung administration to reduce their debt with the aim of reaching a debt-to-equity ratio of under 200%. Some of the conglomerates, particularly the top four, Hyundai, Samsung, SK (formerly Sunkyung) and LG (formerly Lucky Goldstar), have come close to that goal. However, if this was done by buying shares with domestic funds in disguise, i.e. with offshore funds, the improvement of the debt-to-equity ratio was caused by manipulation.[25] The

[24]Mann pp. 57–59.

[25]See Korea Herald, 9 November 1999.

government further requested the conglomerates to concentrate on core activities and sell non-profitable operations. In some cases, large groups were asked to buy failing companies. Thus, for example, Hyundai acquired the car manufacturer Kia, but needed additional credits in order to finance the deal. And then the government promoted the so-called "big deals"; it asked the large *chaebol* to consolidate production by swapping business assets. For example, the aerospace activities of Samsung, Daewoo and Hyundai were merged. Whether these mergers resulted in sufficient effects of synergy is not clear. They, however, produced concentration and restricted competition. What the government probably had in mind was to keep as many factory operational as possible, thus avoiding lay-offs.

The government also insisted on more transparency and accountability of the corporations. There was a feeling of uneasiness as to whether the large conglomerates were willing to comply with these policies. Daewoo, at least, did not do so; the group increased its total debt and, as a result, collapsed in mid-1999. The government stepped in and announced that it would dismember the group.[26] The more than US $50 billion debt of Daewoo is a reminder that the crisis of the *chaebol* is not yet over.

In order to reestablish foreign trust in the South Korean economy, the government facilitated foreign direct investment through the Foreign Investment Promotion Act, passed in November 1998. Foreign exchange control was also liberalized as well as land ownership. Nothing symbolizes the changes more than the fact that foreigners can begin to own real estate in the Republic of Korea.

If the interventions of the government were not far reaching enough to expose the South Korean economy thoroughly to the markets, they at least helped to keep the economy going in 1998, and make it return to some sort of normalcy in 1999. In 1999, private consumption expanded tremendously and also investments picked up. South Korea had also good luck. Its major export markets in Asia and the US continued to absorb Korean goods. In 1998, the surplus of the trade account reached US $41 billion; in 1999 it will be approximately half of that because imports have risen. The result is astonishing: While the Korean economy contracted in 1998 by 5.8%, it picked up growth in 1999, reaching 12.3% in the third quarter. As the sharp down fall was followed by a rapid recovery, the development is called a "V-shaped recovery". Koreans

[26] International Herald Tribune, 17–19 August 1999.

have good reasons to feel relieved, President Kim Dae Jung had won on the economic front.

The most obvious sign of the downsizing of factories and offices was the increasing unemployment. It went from 2.3% before the crisis (June 1997) to 8.7% in February 1999. It was a catastrophe for all those who lost their jobs and was an embarrassment for the government. It was, perhaps, the greatest success of Kim Dae Jung thus far that social unrest could be kept at a low level. Helpful was the tripartite committee of labor, management and government. This committee was originally meant to be an advisory committee, but has meanwhile become a legal entity. The committee was set up to promote industrial peace.[27] The fact that Kim Dae Jung had been the only important politician who articulated social issues and, therefore, enjoyed the trust of labor had played a decisive role.[28]

The fact that the South Korean economy recovered so quickly was one of the surprises Koreans offer the world from time to time. Complacency is, however, premature since much more has to be done to guide the South Korean economy to the markets. It would be detrimental if Korean companies concentrated again on expansion. In spite of the present success, the question remains as to whether the recovery will be sustainable.

References

Sources for the: figures for the period until 1990; *Korea Statistical Yearbook 1975, 1984, 1987, 1989. Monthly Statistics of Korea 1990 No. 2. Social Indicators in Korea 1989. Major Statistics of Korean Economy 1978*; All edited by the Economic Planning Board; *The Korean Economy, Review and Prospects*, 9th edition, by Korea Exchange Bank 1989; figures since 1990, *Korea's Economy 1999*, Korea Economic Institute of America, edited by Joseph A. B. Winder, *Monthly Statistical Bulletin December 1998*, edited by the Bank of Korea *Korea Inside*, Vol. 1 No. 9 (December 1999), Korea Economic Institute of America.

Aiyer, Sri-Ram, "The Search for a New Development Paradigm", in *Joint Us–Korea Academic Studies* Vol. 9, 1999 pp. 21 ff.

Graham, Edward M., "The Reform of the Chebol Since the Outset of Financial Crisis", in *Joint US–Korea Academic Studies* Vol. 10, 2000, pp. 83–104.

---

[27] Korea Times, 5 May 1999.

[28] Peter M. Beck, "Building a New Economy", in Korea Times, 24 February 2000.

Henseleit, Rainer, "Südkorea: Wirtschaftslehre zur Jahresmitte 1997", in Patrick Koellner: *Korea 1997*, Institut für Asienkunde, Hamburg 1997, pp. 94–116.

Kim, Kiheung, "Korea's External Economic Relations", in *Korea's Economy 1999* pp. 69 ff.

Mann, Catherine L., "Korea and the Brave New World Finance", in *Joint US–Korea Academic Studies* Vol. 10, 2000, pp. 55–68.

Sakong, Il, *Korea in World Economy*, Washington 1993.

Song, Byung Nak, *The Rise of the Korean Economy*, 2nd edition, Oxford 1997.

Suh, Moon Gi, *Developmental Transformation in South Korea*, Westport 1998.

PART IV

The Democratic People's Republic of Korea

Chapter 16

The State of Kim Il Sung

Kim Il Sung Superstar

From the moment he chaired the Provisional People's Committee for North Korea in February 1946 until his death on 8 July 1994 Kim Il Sung has been the dominating politician in North Korea. In the first phase, his bid for power was not unchallenged; later he became larger than life.

Larger than life is his statue, which reaches a height of 75 feet and stands before the revolutionary museum in the North Korean capital Pyongyang. His busts are everywhere, as are his pictures, and his face adorns the badges worn by everybody. He was not only the country's ruler but also its teacher. He was in possession of the truth. Therefore, everyone has to read his publications. The veneration which he enjoyed included his family. At his native place, Nam-ri, today known as Mangyong-dae, a museum has been built in his honor which every North Korean has to visit. Objects which he has touched are kept like relics. Many of the thousands of presents he received are exhibited in the House of International Friendship.

He was seldom just called comrade; he was mostly referred to with embellishments.[1] For quite some time, he was called the "beloved and great leader comrade Kim Il Sung". Later, he became the "respected leader", the "outstanding leader of the Korean people", a "prominent activist of the international communist movement and the working class", an "unshakable anti-imperialist peace fighter" and an "ardent revolutionary" or "the great leader".

[1]North Korea Quarterly No. 54 (1998) pp. 108 ff. and No. 55 (1989) p. 152.

Even after his death, his personality looms large. In February 1998, he was made the DPRK's "eternal President" by an amendment to the constitution.[2] North Korea has a President, but one who is dead.

The personality cult around Kim Il Sung and its exaggerations looked ridiculous to the western eye, but fulfilled their aims. This cult was intended to supply legitimacy to "the great leader", thus protecting his rule. At the same time, he tried to gain the citizens' personal loyalty. For the North Koreans, he might have seemed to be a shaman who, thanks to magical forces, has deep insights, a picture in accordance with traditional beliefs.

Kim was born Kim Song Ju on 15 April 1912 in Nam-ri, a place southwest of Pyongyang. He was the eldest of the three sons of Kim Hyong Jik and Kang Pan Sok. He went with his parents to Manchuria where he continued to go to school. He had reached the eighth grade of a Chinese middle school in Jilin when he was expelled because of illegal activities in a communist youth organization in 1929. After being released from jail, he organized a small group of partisans and joined Chinese communist guerrilla units which were fighting against the Japanese in southern and southeastern Manchuria. He had, meanwhile, adopted the pseudonym Kim Il Sung. He commanded a unit called a division of the "Chinese Northeast Anti-Japanese United Army", and launched a number of brave and successful attacks against the Japanese. His most celebrated success was a raid on Japanese installations at Pochonbo, a small place within Korea just across the border from Manchuria in June 1937. During the encounter, several Japanese police officers were killed. When the Japanese succeeded in crushing the activities of the partisans in Manchuria, Kim Il Sung was lucky to survive and had no other chance but to flee to the Soviet Union in March 1941.

He and many other Koreans and Chinese partisans were trained by the Soviets in a camp near Vladivostock. The purpose of the training is not quite clear. The Soviets probably intended to use the Korean and Chinese partisans against the Japanese in Manchuria if the need arose. During his stay in the Soviet Union, Kim Il Sung married a fellow partisan, Kim Chong Suk; their son, Kim Jong Il, was born on 16 February 1942.

The sudden capitulation by Japan and the generosity of the US allowed the Soviet Union to occupy the North of Korea. The 25th Division of the Soviet Army, under the command of Colonel General Chistiakov, moved into Korea in August 1945, reaching Pyongyang on 26 August; Kim Il Sung returned to

---

[2]International Herald Tribune, 7 September 1988.

Korea together with his fellow partisans in mid-September 1945, wearing the uniform of a Soviet captain. He was a young man of 33 years and only a communist leader among others. Due to his stay in the Soviet Union, he had the advantage of being closely associated with the Soviet military. He could rely on the backing of the military when they set up a communist system in North Korea. Before becoming the unchallenged boss in the North, however, he had to fight the worst of all Korean political diseases, factionalism, which had also infected the Korean communist movement. Kim Il Sung compared a factionalist with a mouse scurrying around at night when everyone was asleep.[3] He managed to catch the mice with cleverness and brutality.

Kim's Rise to Power

His own group of partisans who had fought against the Japanese in Manchuria, therefore called the Manchurian faction — or the Kapsan faction — was rather small. It comprised probably not more than 200 people, among them Kim Chaek, Choe Yong Kon, Kim Il, Choe Hyon and Im Chun Chu.[4]

An important group was the Soviet faction, made up of Korean communists who had belonged to the Korean minority in the Soviet Union. They had been educated there, and had returned to North Korea together with the Soviet troops. Their leading figures were Ho Kai, Park Chang Ok and Nam Il.

The Korean communists returning to North Korea met communist guerrillas who had stayed in Korea and had fought against the Japanese occupation power. O Ki Sop and Hyon Chun Hyok were the most prominent leaders of the domestic faction. Hyon, an idealist and rather independent, was murdered in September 1945.

Somewhat later, another group of Korean communists arrived in North Korea. This group had lived in China and fought together with the Chinese against the Japanese until the end of the war. Because of its close connection with the Chinese communists, this group was called the Yenan faction. It was lead by Kim Tu Bong, Choe Chang Ik and Mu Jong. The Yenan group was not really welcome in North Korea, because the Manchurian and the Soviet factions were afraid of getting a competitor for power.

---

[3]Suh Dae Sook p. 142.

[4]Suh Dae Sook p. 73.

Another group made itself felt in the North; the South Korean communists. On 11 September 1945, Park Hon Yong had founded the Korean Communist Party in South Korea. When it became clear in 1948 that communists were no longer tolerated in the South, many of them fled to the North.

In order to establish a communist system in North Korea, it was necessary to bring the various communist groups together. Already in October 1945, a new communist organization was founded. With respect to the Korean Communist Party existing in Seoul, it was called the North Korea Branch Bureau of the Korean Communist Party. At first, it was headed by a representative from the domestic faction, but in December 1945, Kim Il Sung took over. In June 1946, the Bureau was renamed the North Korean Communist Party, illustrating the result of the efforts of Kim Il Sung to detach it from the Korean Communist Party in Seoul.

Integrating the Yenan faction into the North Korean Communist Party was not easy because it had formed its own party, the New Democratic Party, in March 1946. Since the Soviet authorities insisted on a merger of the North Korean Communist Party and the New Democratic Party, this was done during a congress of both parties in August 1946, creating the North Korean Workers Party. The Political Committee of the new party, consisting of five members, was chaired by Kim Tu Bong, the head of the Yenan faction. The other four members of the Political Committee were Choe Chang Ik from the Yenan faction, Ho Kai from the Soviet faction, Kim Il Sung from the Manchurian faction and Chu Yong Ha from the domestic group.

The first victim of Kim's fight for power was the domestic faction. Its leading members had opposed the efforts of Kim Il Sung to organize a separate communist party in the North. Now, Kim Il Sung thus took revenge. During the Second Party Congress in March 1948, he attacked O Ki Sop and other members of the domestic group for factionalism and individual heroism. He was supported by members of the Soviet faction. O Ki Sop and others had to apologize. A new Political Bureau of now seven members was elected. All five members, including O Ki Sop were reelected, Park Il U from the Yenan faction and Kim Chaek from the Manchurian group were added. The domestic faction lost its influence even though O Ki Sop was expelled from the party only in 1958.

In June 1949, the Korean Workers' Party (KWP) was founded by uniting the North Korean and the South Korean Workers' Parties. South Korean communists who had fled to the North were integrated into the North Korean party machinery. Park Hon Yong, who had been the boss of the South Korean communists, became one of the deputy chairmen of the KWP, along with Ho Kai from the Soviet faction. Kim Il Sung continued to head the party.

The end of the Korean War provided an opportunity to conduct trials against 12 members from the South Korean faction; they were charged with espionage, destruction of democratic forces in the South and an attempted coup d'état in the North. Ten of them were sentenced to death in August 1953.[5] The same charges were leveled against Park Hon Yong at the end of 1955; he was additionally accused of having worked for the Japanese and the Americans. Park Hon Yong was also sentenced to death. After the Armistice Agreement of 27 June 1953 had removed the chance to extend the communist system to the South, the South Korean faction lost its importance. Since they were no longer needed, Kim Il Sung could get rid of his troublesome competition. When the Political Bureau was reshuffled in August 1953, only Kim Il Sung and Kim Tu Bong retained their posts. From the domestic group, only Park Chang Ok continued to belong to the upper echelon. He had maintained his stature because he had unconditionally cooperated with the returning groups.

Opposition against Kim Il Sung continued to exist and found its expression during a Central Committee meeting at the end of August 1956. His opponents criticized him and his policies. Kim Il Sung fought back brutally. He had "the resilience and resoluteness of a guerrilla fighter" as Suh Dae-Sook has put it.[6] The purges Kim Il Sung initiated in the years from 1956 to 1958 deprived the Yenan faction, as well as the Soviet group, of their influence. It was favorable for Kim's endeavors that some of the most prominent representatives of these groups had been eliminated earlier on. In December 1950, Mu Jong, a member of the Yenan group and a potential competitor of Kim Il Sung, was charged with disobeying orders and with killing retreating soldiers; he was expelled from the party. A year later, Ho Kai, for a long time the most prominent representative of the Soviet faction, was driven to suicide. Ho Kai, the party's organization expert, had favored an elite communist party and clashed with Kim Il Sung who wished to build a mass party. Since it were the Chinese and not the Soviets who had saved North Korea from being conquered, the Soviet faction had lost its main benefactor. After the "August incident" it was the

[5]For details see Suh Dae Sook p. 131.

[6]Suh Dae Sook p. 107.

turn of Kim Tu Bong and Choe Chang Ik, the remaining leaders of the Yenan faction, and of Park Chang Ok of the Soviet faction to lose their positions.

At the 4th Party Congress in September 1961, Kim Il Sung could state that factionalism was eliminated. He then controlled the party together with his Manchurian faction. The former Manchurian partisans occupied 9 of the 11 seats in the Central Committee's Standing Committee. Nam Il from the Soviet faction and Kim Chang Man from the Yenan faction, the other two members of the Committee, were not regarded as opponents of Kim Il Sung.

Party and State

In North Korea politics have been strongly determined by the Korean Workers' Party. In its charter, the KWP calls itself a Marxist-Leninist party and is organized like a communist party.[7] Its structures permeate the society. The KWP has a monopoly; private initiative outside the sphere controlled by the party is not allowed.

The highest organ of the party is the Party Congress. The congresses of the North Korean Workers' Party in August 1946 and March 1948 counted as first and second congresses, the one in June 1949, by which the Northern and the Southern wings were united, counted as the third. The following party congresses were not convened once every five years as had been provided for in the party's charter, but in larger intervals: the fourth congress was held in September 1961, the fifth in November 1970, the sixth in October 1980. The seventh congress was announced but not convened.

Party congresses seldom convened and have not come together for many years. To suffice for this, the Central Committee, which has the function to direct the work of the party between the congresses and has to hold meetings at least once every six month, has become a body of prime importance. Its approximately 150 members are elected by the Party Congress. The Central Committee elects the members of the Political Bureau, which directs the party work. Since 1980, the Political Bureau has a small Presidium. The Secretariat, also elected by the Central Committee, implements the decisions of the Political Bureau. Of great importance within the KWP apparatus is the

[7]Text in Sung Yul Yang, *The North and South Korean Political Systems. A Comparative Analysis* (Seoul 1994) pp. 905 ff.

Central Committee's Military Commission because it controls the most important pillar of the regime, the military. Kim Il Sung and his trusted followers had been guerrilla fighters and thus considered themselves to be military people. From the beginning of their rule, they had dominated the North Korean armed forces. Kim Il Sung had traced back Korea's identity to the partisan struggles; that they had fought in Manchuria under Chinese command was left out. During and after the Korean War, the North Korean military forces had expanded tremendously. Therefore, control over the military was of the essence. Kim Il Sung combined all the main functions: In May 1990, he was Secretary General of the KWP, Chairman of the Presidium and Chairman of the Military Commission.

According to its Charter (Art. 11), the KWP is organized on the principle of "democratic centralism". All leading party bodies are democratically elected. Party members are subordinate to the party organization, the minority is subordinate to the majority, a lower party body is subordinate to the higher party body, and all party organizations are absolutely subordinate to the Central Commission. Furthermore, all party bodies have to implement the party line unconditionally. In practice, this means that the leadership decides and that democracy is conspicuous by its absence.

After factionalism had been overcome, that is to say, since the beginning of the 1960s, there have been conflicts within the party. This can be gauged from the loss of leading personalities. Of the 11 members of the Political Bureau elected in 1961, only 4 retained their posts in the elections in 1970. Kim Il Sung had earlier removed a number of his own devotees, the partisan generals, because they had become overconfident, influential and independent. Those who continued in the Political Bureau were the four top officials Kim Il Sung, Choe Yong Kon, Kim Il and Choe Hyon. The principle of democratic centralism was apparently very useful to guarantee the politicians at the top to remain in power. Meanwhile, the Byzantine personality cult — mad when seen from outside, but intoxicating for those who had to live with it — had conferred on the great leader the nimbus of infallibility.[8]

The state organization was based on the constitution of 27 December 1972, which had replaced the original constitution of 1948.[9] Since its introduction,

[8]For a report of an eyewitness see Schaller pp. 17 ff.

[9]Text in Gisbert H. Flanz (editor), *Constitution of the Countries of the World, Democratic People's Republic of Korea* (New York 1997).

the DPRK had a presidential system; the president was head of state and chief executive. He was elected indirectly, namely by the Supreme People's Assembly. Government functions were distributed into two bodies, the Central People's Committee which determined government policies, and the Administration Council which implemented these policies. The Central People's Committee consisted of the President, the Vice Presidents and other elected members, approximately 15 persons. It was the backbone of the state structure. The Administrative Council consisted of the Prime Minister, his Deputies, the Ministers and the chairmen of government commissions. Within the government, the National Defense Commission was in charge of military issues. Its chairman was the Supreme Commander of the armed forces. The central government organization was a top-heavy bureaucracy.

The Supreme People's Assembly, elected for a term of five years, was the DPRK's legislature. It had a Standing Committee which was headed by the Assembly's Chairman and could pass laws when the Assembly was not in session. One observed the same tendency within the state organization which was visible in the organization of the party: the transfer of decision making to small units. The North was ruled from the center much in the same way as the South. The last article of the 1972 constitution finally made Pyongyang the DPRK's capital.

The constitution (Art. 11) defines the relationship between government and the KWP by stating that the DPRK "shall conduct all activities under the leadership of the Workers Party of Korea". In this way, the government is subjected to the party. In practice, however, a period began in which decision-making shifted from the party to the state. The Central People's Committee became a competitor of the Political Bureau and the meetings of the Central Committee of the KWP became less frequent. Kim Il Sung enjoyed being President and head of state.

Since the citizens have to respect "the collective principle" (Art. 63 and 82), "the political and ideological unity and solidarity of the people" (Art. 80) and "the socialist standards of life" (Art. 81), the constitution provides the government with a tool to exert control. Thus, the constitution is rather honest in its disregard of human rights.

Before he started transferring power to his son, Kim Jong Il, Kim Il Sung combined all important government functions: he was President, Chairman of the Central People's Committee, Supreme Commander of the Armed Forces and Chairman of the National Defense Commission. There was no need for him to fight his way to the top in the government as he had to within the party. He was the government's chief executive from the very start. He became the country's Prime Minister when the DPRK was founded on 9 September 1948. On 28 December 1972, he became North Korea's President.

Ideology and Terror

In order to motivate the North Korean population and to legitimize the communist leadership, Kim Il Sung developed an ideology, the *juche* ideology, and made great efforts to propagate it. It is not easy to discover what *juche* is about as one has to fight one's way through empty phrases, ritual repetitions, self-praise and ungrounded assumptions. The following is based on a summary which Park Sung Dok of the North Korean Academy of Social Sciences wrote on 14 May 1988.[10]

The idea of *juche* — the main constituent, in North Korea mostly translated as self-reliance — is based on the highest respect of the dignity and value of man who is the master of all things. The relationship between man and world and his role in the world is considered to be the fundamental question. *Juche* is an emancipatory idea which examines scientifically man's efforts to take his fate in his own hands. All things serve man. As master of all things, man is also master of the world and the one who plays the decisive role in developing and changing the world. It is man's social nature which attributes him a position in which he possesses independence (*chajusong*), creative force and conscience. Man is the sole master of the world. He is the master of his own fate. This is the meaning of *juche*, this is its revolutionary character.

Social progress is determined by man. The masses are the protagonists of social development and thus, the creators of history. History is a process of the creative fight of the masses for independence. The aim is an ideal society in which the masses have become the masters of all things and in which their independent and creative life is completely guaranteed.

The world has to be seen in the perspective of man's interests. These require the complete realization of man's independence which constitutes the core of

[10]North Korean Quarterly Nos. 52/53 (1988) pp. 51 ff.; see also Kim Jong Il "On the Juche Idea", text for a seminar, 31 March 1982 (www.Korea-np.co.jp/pk 062nnd-98092410.htm).

the revolution. The idea of *juche* also guarantees the independence of the state. The state's independence is the soul and the life of a country. *Juche* fights encroachments of the state's sovereignty and advocates equality, mutual respect and non-interference into the internal affairs by third countries. A state can be only independent if it follows the *juche* ideology, if it pursues a policy based on own decisions, if it is economically self-reliant relying only on its own technology and mineral resources, and if it can defend itself.

The success of the revolution and the construction depends on the mobilization of the creative capabilities of men. The mobilization depends on correct guidelines and correct policies which correspond to the demands of the masses. Material elements are of importance for the revolutionary movement, but more important is the ideological conscience of man, which has to be developed. The *juche* idea is not a theory for the sake of a theory, but it is the truth acquired by the experience during the Korean revolution. Each important event and each invaluable achievement in modern Korea are inconceivable without the idea of *juche*. So far the official concept.

Juche is said to have been developed on the basis of Marxism-Leninism by adapting it to the special situation in Korea.[11] It is, however, very doubtful whether the *juche* ideology has roots in Marxism-Leninism. The *juche* idea is based on individualism when it maintains that man is the master of all things. Marxism, on the other hand, considers man to be dependent on economic and social conditions. Marxism also does not believe in the superiority of conscience; conscience is determined by social factors. Kim Il Sung, a romantic revolutionary, believed in the priority of ideology. At best, he was a revisionist — as he was labeled by the Chinese during the Cultural Revolution.

The interrelation between the image of man as set out by the *juche* ideology and the doctrine of an independent state was rather artificial, but it was safe to guess that it was just this doctrine which was successful. One can easily understand that demands for the state's independence were well received by the North Koreans in the reconstruction period of their country. The sad experiences of being occupied by the Japanese occupation had just ended. The "admiration of China" in the preceding period of Korean history had lead to stagnation. With his *juche* idea, Kim Il Sung appealed in a clever way to Korean national pride, which had been violated for so many years. This element of the *juche* ideology amounted to nationalism, though Kim Il Sung

[11]Suh Dae Sook pp. 302 ff.

denied it, maintaining that *juche* strengthened proletarian internationalism. By appealing to the national pride of his countrymen, Kim Il Sung succeeded in mobilizing the masses and setting energies free for the reconstruction of the country.

The *juche* ideology has an origin based on the developments in North Korea's foreign relations. Kim Il Sung put forward his ideas about *juche* for the first time in 1955, when he cautiously tried to dissociate himself from the two big communist brothers. He returned to the subject in 1963 after the Soviet Union had stopped its assistance and self-reliance became imperative for North Korea. Art. 3 of the constitution (as amended on 5 September 1998) stated: "The Democratic People's Republic of Korea is guided in its activities by the *Juche* idea, a world outlook centered on people, a revolutionary ideology for achieving the independence of the masses of people".

A well organized communist party, a strictly lead government and an ideology appealing to Korean national pride were not sufficient measures to secure the rule of Kim Il Sung. The North Korean leadership developed a system of control and terror. Public North Korean sources, together with reports of diplomats who have worked and lived in North Korea, provided information about the situation in the country. Hans Maretzki, the last Ambassador of the German Democratic Republic to the DPRK from 1987 to 1990, has given a comprehensive and convincing account on which is drawn in the following summary.[12] The DPRK's internal situation is depressing.

North Korea is a work camp. Jobs are assigned to the workers by the government. The mostly long working hours as well as the low wages are fixed by the government. It is forced labor from which the North Koreans suffer. Workers are alienated, have no interest to work intensely and do not take care of their tools and other work materials, of their living quarters, public buildings and the environment. Food is rationed.

North Koreans live in material poverty. They do not own houses or apartments. Their belongings are small. An economy of shortages and an inefficient system of services add to their problems.

North Koreans live in a garrison state, life in the DPRK society is based on military methods. People are not motivated by incentives or conviction, but by instructions and, if necessary, force. Thus, military structures prevail even outside the large armed and paramilitary forces.

[12]Maretzki pp. 112–145.

North Koreans have to live with a siege mentality. The regime needs the concept of an enemy in order to maintain its radical rule. The Team Spirit Exercises of the South Korean and US armed forces provide regularly the DPRK leadership with the chance to mobilize public opinion against the perceived threat. North Korea looks like an army camp. Everywhere are military bases, posts and no-go areas, as well as artillery positions, air-raid shelters and underground tunnels to house weapons. The country is permanently preparing for war.

North Koreans lead a life in columns. They drill, march, and queue. The column is the unit, which the individual personality dissolves. On special holidays, North Koreans demonstrate how well they are drilled when they parade in huge columns along Pyongyang's avenues in front of the leadership.

The DPRK is a country of facades. The huge stadium, the sports complex, the theaters and hotels, built for the World Youth and Student Festival held in the summer of 1989, are lying idle most of the time. Also, the personality cults of Kim Il Sung and Kim Jung Il are manifestations of the paramount necessity to set up facades.

North Koreans have to live with an excessive amount of control which is exercised by the KWP, the security apparatus, the armed forces and the administration. These agencies behave autocratically and use suspicion to suppress people. Whoever travels is suspicious and needs, therefore, a permit. Those who do not cooperate are subject to sanctions.

North Koreans are kept uninformed. There is no freedom of information. All media are run by the party or by the government. It is prohibited to listen to foreign radio programs; the South Korean TV cannot be received. One hears loudspeakers blaring everywhere and they cannot be switched off. Newspapers are not sold, but distributed to functionaries who then decide what they think the masses should know. Indoctrination substitutes information.

Cultural activities are dominated by political dogmas and stagnate. Therefore, they focus on representing the revolution made possible by the *juche* ideology — on militancy, on the spirit of self-sacrifice of the workers and on the veneration of the "great leader".

The huge gap between official propaganda and the real world has left deformations. North Koreans have no chance but to live with the lies of their leadership. Speechlessness is sometimes the only possible reaction. Foreigners are potential enemies or at least, critics, and contact with them must, therefore, be avoided.

Reports of defectors contribute to enhance our knowledge of the internal situation in North Korea.[13] Thus far, the most prominent defector was Hwang Jang Yop, the architect of the *juche* ideology, former president of Kim Il Sung University, former speaker of the Supreme People's Assembly, secretary of the KWP and chairman of the Foreign Relations Committee, who went via Beijing and Manila to South Korea in the spring of 1997.[14] In an interview in September 1998, he stated that after the collapse of communism in the East Bloc at the end of the 1980s, the North Korean secret services were drastically strengthened and separate secret services existed for the military, the party and the general public.[15] He confirmed the existence of camps for prisoners and said that there are two types: labor camps for members of the elite and "isolated areas in the middle of nowhere where they are left to survive on their own". He figured that there are ten such areas with approximately 30,000 people living in each. Other estimates assume that the numbers of political prisoners is between 200,000 to 250,000.[16] It is not known, however, how well informed Hwang has been about the prison camps, but one can believe that the North Korean system is brutal and inhuman. Park Sung Dok, in his speech about *juche* on 14 May 1988, he explained that man should be free and independent, and continued by asking who on earth would want to be controlled by others; this question can only be called cynical.

The regime of Kim Il Sung was ugly. It was not the state's function to serve the citizens, but for the sake of government authorities, all citizens were controlled. The *juche* ideology as the only accepted teaching gave the pretext. Kim Il Sung and his party were the executors. The centrally planned economic system made the people completely dependent on the state. If necessary, the state proceeded with terror. The Korea of Kim Il Sung was a totalitarian state.

---

[13] Minnesota Lawyers' International Human Rights Committee and Asia Watch: *Human Rights in the DPRK* (December 1988, type-written).

[14] An extensive account is given by Oberdorfer pp. 399 ff.

[15] Far Eastern Economic Review, 15 October 1998; see also Le Monde, 14/15 March 1999.

[16] Thomas Heberer "Nordkorea zwischen Skylla und Charybdis: Beharrungsversuche und wachsender Druck von unten", in Patrick Koellner (editor), *Korea 199, Hamburg 1998* p. 302 (with additional information).

The Economy

The economy is the field where the North Korean system comes closer to communism. Factories are nationalized. Nationalization started in 1946 and did not meet much resistance, because it mostly affected enterprises which were owned by Japanese companies. Later, factories owned by Koreans were nationalized or became at least cooperative properties. Agriculture is also no longer the business of private farmers, but of collectives and government estates. Land reform was begun early; already in March 1946, more than half of all arable land was confiscated and transferred to the farmers. Collectivization started in 1954 and was completed in 1958. As in other communist countries, families of the collective farms were permitted to cultivate small plots for their own use.

The DPRK has a command economy. Planning is centralized and done by the state, which has laid down economic aims in plans since 1947. The function of the markets is suspended. Prices are fixed by the government.

When aid by the Soviet Union and China decreased after the 1960s, the DPRK focused on self-sustenance in accordance with the *juche* ideology. From now on, the North Korean government tried to build an economy with its own resources and skills. This policy was originally successful. The available information indicates that the North Korean economy was growing.[17] As economic statistics released by the North are scarce and utterly unreliable, one has to be content with estimates. An estimate by the American CIA showed that real GNP in the DPRK grew at an annual rate of 7.4% in the period from 1965 to 1976. At that time, there was fierce economic competition between the North and the South for which GNP growth rates and GNP per capita had become the measuring scale.[18] In the same period from 1965 to 1976, thanks to the energetic policy of export oriented industrialization of President Park Chung Hee, GNP in the South grew by nearly 11%. The South had overtaken the North economically.[19] During the period from the mid 1970s to the mid 1980s, growth declined in the North to less than 4% and dropped to 1% in the second half of the 80s.[20]

---

[17]See the figures in An Tai Sung (1984) p. 119 which are based on various sources.

[18]An Tai Sung (1984) pp. 139 and 140.

[19]*Korea Statistical Yearbook 1975*, published by the Economic Planning Board; *Monthly Economic Statistics 1976/1*, published by the Bank of Korea; *Major Statistics of Korean Economy 1978*, published by the Economic Planning Board.

[20]Chun Hong Taek op. cit. pp. 33 and 34; the figures are based on estimates of the CIA and the National Unification Board.

Unlike in the South, the driving force behind the economic development in the North was heavy industry. The DPRK was rich in mineral resources, including coal, iron ore, graphite, lead, zinc, tungsten, magnesite and gold. As the North also abounds in waterpower, the Japanese had established a heavy industry in the North. The new rulers strengthened mining, the machine industry and the production of fertilizers. This policy was successful. It was estimated that the share of industry of GNP increased from 23.2% to 62.3% in the period from 1945 to 1965, while at the same time, the share of agriculture decreased from 59.1% to 19.3%.[21]

Since the beginning of the 1960s, the economic plans emphasized the expansion of light industry and agriculture. Later on, the North Korean leadership had to try balancing the gap between the various sectors of the economy and improving infrastructure. The production of consumer goods, however, lagged behind. The Seven-Year Plan for the period from 1987 to 1993 focused on quick development of technology and research. Since the 1960s, the overproportional efforts to build up the military were an obstacle for a balanced economic development. According to estimates by the International Institute for Strategic Studies, North Korea, a country of 23,1 million inhabitants, maintained in 1993 armed forces of 1,128,000 and spent approximately 25% of its GDP for military purposes.[22]

In a country which wanted to be self-sufficient, agricultural production was extremely important. North Korea produced rice, corn, potatoes, millet, barley and soybeans. The yield increased in the 1980s, but observers had doubts as to whether the DPRK was self-sufficient in grain production. They noticed that the North Korean leadership often stressed the necessity to overcome nutritional problems. Kim Il Sung did so, for example, in his New Year address on 1 January 1988.[23] In mid-1995, the North Korean government had to ask for foreign food aid.

As a poor developing country, North Korea, just as South Korea, needed foreign capital and technology and received it during its first phase of economic development. Aid came from the Soviet Union, China and East European countries. The Soviet Union was by far the most important sponsor of North Korea's economic progress, providing grants of roughly 300 million rubles after

[21]An Tai Sung (1984) p. 118.

[22]*The Military Balance 1994–1995*, London 1994, pp. 178 and 179.

[23]North Korean Quarterly Nos. 52/53 (1988) p. 120.

the Korean War.[24] The Soviet Union also provided technical assistance by training North Korean students and experts and by transferring technical documents. Additional Soviet capital assistance, which had to be paid back, followed. Altogether 70 projects were built or rebuilt with Soviet aid.

Support also came from China which gave grants and loans and provided technical assistance. Fendler lists 12 projects funded by China, although the precise amount of Chinese aid is not known.[25] The East European countries also helped North Korea with grants which were used for 24 different projects.

During the 1960s, foreign assistance lapsed. The DPRK had to buy foreign modern technology, which meant Western technology. As the country had neglected the development of its export capabilities, it did not have enough foreign currency to pay for these types of imports. It had to get loans, but quickly got in arrears. The DPRK's credit rating dropped, Western deliveries were cut down, and the development of the North Korean economy slowed down.

The Democratic People's Republic of Korea was a state-trading country, however, not an important one.[26] The country exported apparel, iron, steel, cement, natural resource-based products, and arms. Iran was the major purchaser of North Korean arms during the war with Iraq.[27] North Korea imported oil, capital goods and textiles. Precise figures were not released by North Korea, but the trend of North Korea's foreign trade can be observed. Originally, the Soviet Union and East European countries were North Korea's main trading partners. In the 1970s, North Korea had to turn to the industrialized countries in order to acquire modern technology. After it could no longer repay its debts, it turned again to the Soviet Union. With the collapse of the Russian economy, China has become the DPRK's most important trading partner even before Japan and South Korea. Economic relations with Japan have been of a peculiar nature: They were dominated by remittances of pro North Korea Koreans in Japan. The amount of these remittances is completely

---

[24]See for the following Karoly Fendler, "Economic Assistance from Socialist Countries to North Korea in the Postwar Years: 1953–1963", in Han S. Park, *North Korea, Ideology, Politics, Economy* (Englewood Cliffs 1996) pp. 162 ff.

[25]Fendler op. cit. p.172.

[26]See for the following Noland (1997) pp. 50 ff.

[27]Eberstadt (1999) pp. 106–107.

unclear. Probably the remittances are not in the hundreds of millions of US dollars as often reported.[28]

Based on the information available, it seemed that North Korea's imports outweighed the exports and therefore their trade balance was negative in the period between 1970 and the mid-1997.[29] The country thus accumulated debts. In 1993, they amounted to US $7.9 billion, of which US $6.2 billion were owed to former communist countries and US $649 million were owed to western countries.

The North introduced some reforms. In 1984, they passed a law encouraging joint ventures. In 1991, they created specific free economic zones for export-oriented industries. In 1995, they allowed to establish wholly foreign-owned companies. These measures, however, did not attract much foreign investment.

The North Korean economy was in deep trouble. This was already indicated in the mid-1970s, when the country could no longer pay back its debts and lost access to long-term capital markets. As not enough goods suited for export had been developed, the country could import less and less. The withdrawal of Soviet aid and later the collapse of the Russian economy added to North Korea's difficulties. The deliberate renunciation on the advantage of the international division of labor fired back; an economy of shortages developed. A period of stagnation began in the mid-1980s. The difficulty to substitute markets by government decisions has also contributed to increasing the problems.

All in all, the policy of self-sustenance has been a failure, a failure which, however, could not be admitted to by the North Korean leaders who decided to continue along the lines of the *juche* ideology. Whether the substitution of adequate nutrition for an ideological diet will be successful in the long run is doubtful. If markets and prices will win, it will be for the benefit of North Koreans.

References

An, Tai Sung, *North Korea in Transition*, Westport 1983.

Nam, Koon Woo, *The North Korean Communist Leadership, 1945–1965*, Alabama 1974.

[28]Noland (1998) pp. 44–46.

[29]Eberstadt (1999) p. 99; see also Noland (1997) p. 51.

Lee, Chon Sik, *The Korean Workers's Party: A Short History*, Stanford 1978.

Pak, Je Kuk, *Pukhanui Kim Jong Il sungkecheje: ke munje wha joumang* (*North Korea under Kim Jong Il: Problems and Prospects*), Seoul 1985.

Lee, Dong Bok, "North Korea after the Sixth KWP Congress", in *Korea and World Affairs*, Fall 1981 pp. 415 ff.

Cho, Sung Yoon, *The Constitution of the People's Republic of Korea*, Law Library, Library of Congress (Washington 1986).

Lim, Un, *The Founding of a Dynasty. An Authentic Biography of Kim Il Sung*, translated from Japanese (1982).

Lind, Jennifer M., "Gambling with Globalism: Japanese Financial Flows to North Korea and the Sanction Policy Option", in *The Pacific Review*, Vol. 10 No. 3 1997 pp. 391–406.

Noland, Marcus, "Prospects for a North Korean External Opening", in Henriksen and Mo pp. 50 ff.

Noland, Marcus, "Prospects for the North Korean Economy", in: Suh Dae-Sook and Lee Chae-Jin (1998) pp. 33–58.

Chapter 17

North Korea Under the Son

The Great Leader's Departure

Kim Il Sung died in the early morning hours of Friday, 8 July 1994. One of South Korea's self-appointed experts on North Korea ventured on the idea that Kim Il Sung was assassinated.[1] It is most likely that he died, as his doctors have said, of "cardiac infarction". Since he was 82 years old, one could say that he died of old age.

The North Korean leadership did not announce the death of the "Great Leader" immediately, but first got prepared. When the news was made known, it came as a shock to many North Koreans. The leader was sadly missed by his people who mourned his death. A British businessman who was in Pyongyang at that time described the situation as follows: "Imagine being in a situation where everyone has lost a relative, and they all just lost the same relative, like a big extended family. People are obviously extremely upset; they are very red-eyed. Whatever a Westerner might think, he is obviously very much missed by them".[2]

People first streamed past his statue in Pyongyang, and then to the Presidential Palace where his body was put on display. A period of mourning was announced, and later extended to allow more mourners to pay their respects. The funeral was finally held on 19 July 1994. The committee for the funeral was headed by Kim Jong Il and joined by all leading North Korean officials. Two million people were said to have gathered for that occasion and watched

[1]The Washington Post, 10 July 1994.

[2]Sunday Times, 10 July 1994.

the car carrying Kim's body accompanied by other cars circle through the streets of the capital.[3]

Kim Il Sung died shortly after he had met with former US President Carter when both had found a way out of the nuclear dilemma. An American and a North Korean delegation were meeting in Geneva to discuss the nuclear issue when Kim's death was announced. President Bill Clinton extended his condolences and expressed the hope that the talks would continue.[4]

President Kim Young Sam of South Korea did not follow suit. This was surprising since a summit meeting of the leaders of the two Koreas had been scheduled for the end of July 1994. Kim Young Sam was willing to shake the hand of a living Kim Il Sung, but a dead Kim Il Sung was not worth any expression of condolence. His government even went a step further by banning visits of South Korean citizens to attend the funeral in Pyongyang. On 18 July 1994, Prime Minister Lee Yung Dook said that the government would take stern action against those who violate the National Security Act by expressing condolences over Kim's death.[5] Kim Il Sung was seen in the South only as the man who started the Korean War. The death of Kim Il Sung illustrated once again the antagonism between the two Koreas.

The Heir

When the highest leader of a communist country dies — generally the secretary general of the communist party — difficulties often arise with regards to the succession. This was not the case after the death of Kim Il Sung. The world could watch the unique spectacle that in a communist country the son was inheriting his father's position as supreme leader; a form of succession normally known from monarchic dynasties. But it was a transfer fitting for a country which had become one man's property, a country ruled by a despot. After his father's death, Kim Jong Il became North Korea's supreme leader.

The succession had been prepared for such a long time and in such a comprehensive manner that when the moment had come, the transfer happened automatically. Kim Il Sung had taken the decision to name his son his

[3]Los Angeles Times, 19 July 1994.

[4]The Washington Post, 10 July 1994.

[5]Los Angeles Times, 15 and 19 July 1994.

successor already in the early 1970s. The public received first hints of this when in 1975, Kim Jong Il was referred to as "the party center". There might have been opposition against the "great leader's" decision to make the "dear leader" his successor, but when the KWP held its 6th congress in October 1980, the signals became very convincing. Kim Jong Il assumed important positions within the structure of the party. He moved up to the number four position in the Central Committee, the Politbureau and the Presidium. He had already been elected a secretary of the Central Committee in 1973 and a member of its Political Committee in 1974. In the Military Commission of the party, he was number three after his father and General O Chin U. Later, he moved up to the number two position in all important bodies of the KWP. In December 1991, the Central Committee named him supreme commander of the armed forces, and in April 1992 he was promoted to Marshall.[6] A year later, in April 1993, he was appointed Chairman of the National Defense Commission.[7] Thus, he did not only add a government position to his many party posts but assumed control of North Korea's armed forces during his father's lifetime who took great care to swear the military in on his son. In an interview with the Washington Times in April 1992, Kim Il Sung mentioned that Kim Jong Il was running "all affairs" of the country.[8] When his father died, Kim Jong Il followed him as supreme leader not just because he was his son, but more because he was holding the key positions in the DPRK.

Not much is known about Kim Jong Il.[9] As already mentioned, he was born on 16 February 1942 in the Soviet Union. He was the oldest son of Kim Il Sung and his wife Kim Chong Suk. In 1945, he went with his parents to Korea where he lost his mother when he was seven years old. He studied political economics at the Kim Il Sung University in Pyongyang in the period from 1960 to 1964. The subject of his thesis for graduation was titled: "The Position and the Role of the Country in Socialist Construction". So, unlike his father, Kim Jong Il had a formal education which was completed with a university degree. After having graduated, he started working in the KWP. From that moment on, he has always worked within the party. He has allegedly worked

[6] Frankfurter Allgemeine Zeitung, 22 April 1992.

[7] International Herald Tribune, 10/11 April 1993.

[8] Washington, 15 April 1992.

[9] Suh Dae-Sook in Suh and Lee (1998) pp. 15–18.

together closely with artists and produced stage plays and films which glorified the "revolutionary" tradition. About the "dear leader's" character, we know even less. If one trusts the defector Hwang Jang Yop, who knew him well, Kim Jong Il could take decisions quickly, was impatient and preferred to work behind closed doors.[10] Apparently, he did not like to give public speeches. As Hwang further tells us, Kim Jong Il was clever in maneuvering. He did not try to convince people but used terror and violence. Hwang confirmed that Kim Jong Il was responsible for the massacre in Rangoon in 1983 as well as for the bombing of a South Korean passenger plane in 1987. Hwang's assertion that Kim Jong Il admired Adolf Hitler is utterly distressing.

Kim Jong Il takes Charge

When Kim Il Sung died on 8 July 1994, he was still Secretary General of the KWP. It took quite some time until his son assumed his father's position. In autumn 1997, he was elected Secretary General by provincial party organizations and not by the Central Committee. His election was announced by the Central Committee and the Military Commission on 8 October 1997.[11]

Various defections indicated that there was discontent in North Korea. The defection of Hwang Jang Yop, who had ranked number 26 within the North Korean hierarchy in the Kim Il Sung funeral committee, proved that the discontent had also reached the higher echelons of the party. Nothing indicated that the delay in the election of Kim Jong Il for Secretary General had anything to do with conflicts within the North Korean leadership. Hwang Jang Yop confirmed that Kim Jong Il was the only strong man in North Korea and did not show signs of weakness. Kim Jong Il was the first of the secretaries of the KWP; therefore, it was safe to assume that the title of Secretary General was within his grasp at any time.

After the death of his father and the old partisan leader O Chin U — who passed away on 25 February 1995 — Kim Jong Il remained the only member of the Presidium of the Political Bureau of the party's Central Committee. This underlines the fact that he was in a very strong position. The Political Bureau,

[10]See Hwang's interviews in Far Eastern Economic Review, 15 October 1998 pp. 30 ff. and Le Monde, 14/15 March 1999.

[11]Korean Central News Agency (KCNA), 8 October 1997.

the Central Committee and the Military Commission still remain active today. When Kim Yong Nam made the proposal to reelect Kim Jong Il as chairman of the National Defense Commission at the beginning of the session of the 10th Supreme People's Assembly on 5 September 1998, he mentioned that he did so upon authorization from the Political Bureau, the Central Committee and the Central Military Commission.[12] UN agencies observed that the leading party representatives played the most important role at the regional level.[13] The first session of the 10th Supreme People's Assembly at the beginning of September 1998 was a very important one because changes in the constitution and the system of rule were finalized. The elections for this Assembly were held on 26 July 1998 and had, according to the Central Election Committee, the following results: 99.85% of the registered voters took part and 100% voted for the registered candidates.[14]

Until his death, Kim Il Sung remained President of the Republic. His son never assumed that office; instead his father was made the country's "eternal president" by an amendment to the preamble — called the preface — of the constitution. It read as follows: "The DPRK and the entire Korean people will uphold the great leader Kim Il Sung as the eternal President of the Republic, defend and carry forward his ideas and exploits and complete the Juche revolution under the leadership of the Worker's Party of Korea.[15] "It seemed strange to make a dead leader the president of a country, but perhaps it was not so strange from a North Korean perspective. It gave the present North Korean leadership the chance to supply legitimacy by the man whom every North Korean has learned to adore". Kim Il Sung continues to reign in the North as B. C. Koh has rightly observed.[16]

The provisions of the constitution concerning the president were deleted by a constitutional amendment. The National Defense Commission (NDC) was given prominence. According to Article 100, the NDC had only military functions ("The National Defense Commission is the highest military organ of State power and an organ for general control over national defense"). The DPRK leadership had, however, further-reaching goals in mind, as can

---

[12]KCNA, 5 September 1998.

[13]Reese p. 21.

[14]KCNA, 27 July 1998.

[15]Unofficial translation of the Constitution as amended in September 1998 in: www.korea-np.co.jp/pk/061st_issue/98091708.htm.

[16]Koh p. 2.

be seen from the statement of Kim Yong Nam on 5 September 1998. He said: "The NDC chairmanship is the highest post of the state with which to organize and lead the work of defending the state system of the socialist country and the destinies of the people and strengthening and increasing the defense capabilities of the country and the state power as a whole through command over all the political, military and economic forces of the country. It is also a sacred, important post which symbolizes and represents the honor of our country and the dignity of the nation".[17] Although it is somewhat hidden among the many words, the intention was to make the chairman of the National Defense Commission the highest government official. Kim Jong Il was reelected to that position by the 10th Supreme People's Assembly. This was the most celebrated event of the Assembly's session.

The official who holds the highest office in a state normally also has representative functions. After all, one knows Kim Jong Il dislikes these functions. The constitution had assigned them to the President of the Supreme People's Assembly Presidium who according to Art. 111 "represents the state and receives credentials and letters of recall of diplomatic representatives accredited by a foreign state". Kim Yong Nam, a former Deputy Prime Minister and Foreign Minister, was elected President of the Assembly's Presidium and filled in for Kim Jong Il at ceremonial events.

Until his death, Kim Il Sung had been Chairman of the Central People's Committee, the policy-making body of the government. After his death, nothing was ever heard of that agency; in the fall of 1998 the new constitution abolished it.[18] The cabinet, although called an "administrative and executive body" (Art. 117), also takes part in policy-making. For example, it does so by drafting the development plans, compiling the state budget and directing the monetary and banking system (Art. 119). Hong Song Nam, who had been Deputy Prime Minister and Acting-Prime Minister, was elected Prime Minister during the meeting of the Supreme People's Assembly in September 1998.

It has often been observed that the military became more prominent since the death of Kim Il Sung.[19] A great number of reported activities of Kim

---

[17] See note 12.

[18] Koh pp. 4 and 5.

[19] See for example Vantage Point articles in Naewoe Press pp. 20, 26, 37, 56.

Jong Il were related to the military.[20] He promoted Choe Kwang and Yi Ul Sol to marshals and various other generals to vice-marshals. That the military had moved up could be taken from the ranking order of the members of the State Funeral Committee for Marshal Choe Kwang. Marshal Yi Ul Sol and Vice Marshals Cho Myong Nok and Kim Yong Chun ranked numbers 6 to 8 before three full members of the Political Bureau.[21] Also, the fact that a military parade was in the center of the celebrations of the fiftieth anniversary of the KWP's founding on 15 October 1995 emphasized the importance of the military.

It was understandable that Kim Jong Il courted the military. The position as the civilian who had to control the military was the first top responsibility he assumed. He looked back on many years of cooperation with the military, and it seemed quite natural that after being in charge of the whole country, he relied on those he knew best. At the same time, he tried to prevent, as his father had done nearly 40 years earlier, that he could be challenged by force. It is still too early to confirm the statement of Hwang Jang Yop that Kim Jong Il transformed the former dictatorship of the party into a dictatorship of the military.[22]

The elections of the members of the National Defense Commission which were held during the first session of the Supreme People's Assembly in the beginning of September 1998 confirmed the impression that the military had become extremely important. Vice-Marshal Cho Myong Rok became. Vice Chairman of the NDC, and Vice-Marshals Kim Il Chol and Yi Yong Mu Vice-Chairmen;[23] Kim Il Chol was also appointed Minister of Defense of the People's Armed Forces.[24]

The leaders whom Kim Jong Il had gathered around him had belonged to the top echelons of the DPRK, but had been considerably promoted by him. This was illustrated by the much lower ranks the new leaders had in the Kim Il Sung funeral committee in 1994: Kim Yong Nam — 8, Hong Song Nam — 17, Cho Myong Rok — 89, Kim Il Chol — 90, Yi Yong Mu — 55.[25] No doubt, Kim Jong Il has set up his own junta.

[20] See the examples given by Koh p. 3 for 1995.

[21] Suh and Lee, Appendix 2 pp. 248 ff.

[22] Far Eastern Economic Review, 15 October 1998, p. 30.

[23] KCNA, 5 September 1997.

[24] KCNA, 8 September 1997.

[25] Suh Dae Sook and Lee Chae Jin pp. 245 ff.

The regime of Kim Jong Il is as ugly as his father's. The policy to deny the North Koreans their basic rights continues.[26] They do not enjoy freedom of speech, the press, assembly and association. They are arbitrarily detained, many are held as political prisoners. There are reports about extra-judicial killings and disappearances. Contacts with foreigners are kept to a minimum. The average citizen is not allowed to leave the country. North Korea is largely isolated from outside information. Life in North Korea for all those who do not belong to the *nomenclatura* is a nightmare. The leadership has a different view. It announced on radio on 14 April 1999 that the North Korean people have "all kinds of good luck, such as blessings to eat, to learn, to get medical treatment, to work, to rest, to lead a long life, and to confront imperialism".[27] This attitude is more than cynical. It is an expression of contempt of the people.

The Food Crisis

We have heard about famine in North Korea. We have seen pictures of starving North Korean children on Western television channels. If we still were not convinced, our doubts disappeared when we learned that the country, which has made self-sufficiency a dogma, all of a sudden appealed to South Korea and Japan for food aid in 1995. But what we do not know is the extent of the food crisis. The information given by North Korea is unreliable. For third parties, it is close to impossible to assess the details of the situation in a country where foreigners cannot move freely.

As long as Korea was not divided, the South had been the country's granary. After the division, the DPRK tried to achieve self-sufficiency in grain production, even though the mountains and the climate were great obstacles to such endeavors. When the North Korean economy got into trouble, agriculture was also affected. Neither enough fertilizer nor enough fuel for farm

[26]U.S. Department of State, "Democratic People's Republic of Korea 1999, Country Report on Human Rights Practices", released by the Bureau of Democracy, Human Rights, and Labor, February 26, 1999 (www.state.gov/www/global/human_rights/1998_hr_report/northkpr.html); UNHCR, Sub-Commission on Prevention of Discrimination and Protection of Minorities, Resolution 1998/2 (www.hri.ca/forthereco...98/documentation/subscommission/1998-2.htm/).

[27]Radio Pyongyang, 14 April 1999 (monitored by Yonhap News Agency and translated by FBIS-EAS-1999-04-20).

machinery could be imported, and farm machinery could not be maintained. The public distribution system collapsed. That these were the main problems was indirectly admitted by the North Korean government since the talks with UNDP in May 1998 focused on these issues.[28] Inefficiency in the collective farming system and declining soil fertility due to monocropping may have been additional reasons for the deterioration of the food situation.[29] Lost crops will have been a problem too. The problems were aggravated by a severe flooding in the summer of 1995 and natural disasters in the following years. The government's abilities to cope with the difficulties were limited to reducing the food rations and to drawing on its grain stocks. These measures, however, were not sufficient and the situation became critical. The DPRK's government in mid-1995, for the first time, appealed to Japan and South Korea for food aid.[30]

At the end of May 1995, North Korea asked Japan for emergency rice supplies. Japan let South Korea go ahead, and the two Koreas took up negotiations in Beijing. After North Korea had given in to South Korea's demands to present its request for rice in writing, the South Korean government agreed in mid-June 1995 to deliver 150,000 tons of rice free of charge. An agreement with Japan about a delivery of 300,000 tons of rice, half free and half on a deferred payment bases, followed quickly. After the terrible flooding in August 1995, North Korea launched an international appeal for US $500 million in food aid.

South Korea and Japan were not the only countries which provided food since 1995. North Korea's main bilateral supplier was China. The international community channeled its assistance through the World Food Program (WFP) and various non-governmental organizations. International assistance was hampered by the DPRK which, although being in severe difficulties, treated the international organizations with suspicion and did not allow them to monitor the situation.

Efforts have been made to assess the grain shortfalls and the extent of the famine, but the estimates have been vague and differ considerably from each

[28] Reese p. 33.

[29] Reese p. 28, Chung Hong-Tack, "Economic Conditions in North Korea and Prospects for Reform", in Henriksen and Mo p. 34.

[30] The Gazette (Montreal), 27 May 1995; Kydo News Service, 17 June 1995; AFP, 30 June 1995; Boston Globe 7 September 1995 (via LEXIS-NEXIS).

other.[31] North Korea has not been helpful. According to a WFP estimate, North Korea overestimated, for example, the loss due to flooding in 1995 by more than double that of the actual loss.[32] Hwang Jang Yop asserted that more than 3 million people died from hunger or malnutrition between 1995 and 1998.[33] Reese felt that this figure was much too high.[34] The real figures of the grain short-fall and of the victims of the famine are unknown. The worst seems, however, to be over. It has been reassuring to hear from the head of the WFP in August 1999 that North Korea currently receives enough food to prevent starvation.[35]

The Prospects

North Korea is in dire need of reforms. The need to reform the economy is too obvious to be overlooked. In a letter addressed to the KWP activists' conference in January 1997, Kim Jong Il admitted the urgency of solving the economic problems and raising the people's living standards. He appealed to the farmers' "patriotic devotions and labor zeal". For a general economic restoration, he recommended a rapid increase in coal and steel production, hoping that this would contribute to enlarge electric generation, to smoothen railroad transportation and to normalize operation in other industries. He also emphasized the need to expand foreign trade and called for establishing joint ventures. A law passed by the 2nd session of the Supreme People's Assembly on 8 April 1999 confirms the orthodox line of running the economy by insisting that only the state manages and operates the economy.[36] The private farmer's markets, which were observed already in 1992, have meanwhile been sanctioned by the government.[37]

North Korea has already exerted all of its energies to increase agricultural and industrial production. It has been to no avail. Since 1990, the North

---

[31] Reese p. 29, Chun Hong Tack pp. 34–36.
[32] Chun Hong Taek pp. 35–37.
[33] Le Monde, 14/15 March 1999.
[34] Reese p. 30.
[35] International Herald Tribune, 16 August 1999.
[36] KCNA, 9 April 1999.
[37] Schaller pp. 68 ff.

Korean economy has had negative growth rates, i.e. it was contracting.[38] The International Monetary Fund (IMF) has estimated that between 1992 and 1996, North Korea's GNP has contracted by more than 50%.[39] It is difficult to see how efforts relying only on North Korean resources — as Kim Jong Il recommends — might help to improve the situation.

He also advocated the promotion of foreign trade. Since the DPRK's economy did not produce enough goods which found markets abroad, with the exception of arms, foreign financial and technological assistance was necessary. So far, only China has been willing to give unconditional aid as it has an interest to sustain the DPRK. North Korean migrants in search of food are already causing problems in China and the Chinese government wants to avoid receiving more of them.[40] China, furthermore, prefers having a communist neighbor south of the Yalu River. But China's resources are limited. Therefore, sources for development aid can only be from Western countries or international financial organizations which tend to be heavily influenced by Western countries. These sources, however, want to be involved in the development progress and are used to setting up conditions which, in the view of the many failures of development assistance, have a tendency to get more explicit and stringent. Donors have at least insisted on sound management and monitoring possibilities in the developing country. The main aim of the process is institutional development and policy reforms. It is difficult to see how the gap between these prerequisites and the *juche*-based efforts for radical autarky can be bridged.

If North Korea is to receive development assistance, its international contacts will expand. This will be felt also by the North Korean citizens. Foreign experts will come to the DPRK, North Koreans will go to other countries to be trained. By and by, North Koreans will be exposed to the truth, the truth of their own comparative misery and even worse to the better living conditions in South Korea. So far, North Korea's seclusion provided its leadership unrestricted opportunities for indoctrination. At the beginning of the 1990s, an observer noted that the leadership had total control of the people, that the people would do whatever they were ordered to do, and would not even shy

[38] Noland, in Suh and Lee p. 39; Pollack and Lee p. 33.

[39] Reese p. 24.

[40] Far Eastern Economic Review, 19 April 1999; Korea Times, 13 and 14 October 1999, 1 February 2000.

away from death.[41] The seclusion is an indispensable condition for upholding the despotic rule. It is difficult to see how the North Korean leadership can give up the protecting shield of dis-information.

Meanwhile, Western countries and international organizations might be willing to continue providing humanitarian assistance to alleviate the fate of the poorest. Donors want to know what has happened to their aid. If aid cannot be adequately monitored, it is likely that donors will become suspicious and reluctant to give more. They want to be sure that the aid is not being channeled to the military. If the North Korean leadership continues to prevent monitoring, it runs the risk that donors will withdraw.[42] The aid agency Medecins sans Frontières already reacted in this way and withdrew in September 1990.[43] Then, there was also the possibility that the Democratic People's Republic of Korea collapses because of insurmountable economic difficulties. The country has, however, shown remarkable resilience and survived a decade of severe economic difficulties. Furthermore, ideology still takes precedence over nutrition. On 14 April 1999, Radio Pyongyang complained about the difficult food situation, but added: "However, our people today are experiencing happiness by having special ideology and emotion".[44]

References

Koh, B. C., "Recent Political Developments in North Korea", in Henriksen and Mo pp. 1 ff.

Pohl, Manfred, "Nordkorea 1997/98: Wirtschaft und Politik", in Patrick Köllner, *Korea 1998* (Hamburg 1998) pp. 267 ff.

Pollack, Jonathan D. and Lee, Chung Min, *Preparing for Korean Unification. Scenarios and Implications* (Rand 1999).

Sakai, Takashi, "The Power Base of Kim Jong Il: Focusing on its Formation Process", in Han S. Park, *North Korea. Ideology, Politics, Economy* (Englewood Cliffs 1996) pp. 105 ff.

---

[41] Schaller p. 107.

[42] See a report prepared for Congress by the General Accounting Office in Washington, New York Times, 12 October 1999.

[43] Amnesty International, *Annual Report 1999: Korea* (www.amnesty.org/ailib/airepot/ar99/asa24.htm).

[44] See note 27.

Satterwhite, David H., "North Korea in 1996. Belligerence Subsiding, Hunger Worsens", in *Asian Survey* Vol. XXXVII, No. 1 January 1997 pp. 10–19.

Scalapino, Rohert A., *North Korea at a Crossroad* (1997).

Suh, Dae Sook, "Kim Jong Il and New Leadership in North Korea", in Suh and Lee (1998) pp. 13–31.

PART V

Foreign Relations

Chapter 18

South Korea's Great Partner

The Alliance

The Republic of Korea was America's creation. Therefore, the new state had no choice but to cooperate closely with the USA. The security of South Korea could not be ensured without US support. The country's economy could not be developed without active US assistance and participation. In addition, the Americans were willing to assist the Koreans in the process of modernization which had been started by the Japanese. Koreans learned from the Americans; a network of close contacts between South Koreans and Americans was the result.

The United States was prepared to face the enormous challenge of ensuring South Korea's security. The basis for this assurance was the Mutual Defense Treaty, concluded on 1 October 1953.[1] After the Korean War had ended, the US had reduced its forces in South Korea from approximately 300,000 in July 1953 to approximately 60,000 in December 1955.[2] The US government was willing to leave its troops stationed in South Korea. The US trained South Korean officers supplied them weapons. It made "contributions" to South Korea's defense budget, which until the mid-1960s had comprised of the largest portion of the budget. The motives for the American commitment were obvious. After the original disengagement policy had been revised because of the attack from the North, and after South Korea had become the test case for

[1] Kim Se-Jin (1976) pp. 185 ff.

[2] Lee Chae-Jin in Kihl (1994) p. 76.

the containment policy, it was necessary for the US to preserve the success of their policy. An emotional element was also added because South Koreans and Americans had fought together in Korea and in Vietnam. It was this feeling which President Ford was speaking of during his visit to South Korea on 22 November 1974. He observed that nothing united people more than having fought side by side.[3]

To Withdraw or Not to Withdraw

The structure of the relations between the two countries was asymmetrical. For South Korea, cooperation with the US was indispensable, for the US cooperation with the smaller partner was variable. The relationship was not a mere function of US policy in Asia and the Pacific Rim, but was depending on it. This policy was not only determined by regional interest of the US, but also by global interests. On the other hand, the smaller partner had become much stronger. Therefore, the share of South Korea's responsibility within the alliance had expanded. With a view to increase South Korean participation in the structure of military planning, a Combined Forces Command (CFC) was established on 7 November 1978 to which operational control of South Korean forces, so far exercised by the United Nations Command, was transferred. The South Korean forces over which the CFC had operational control were the First and Third Army stationed in frontline positions; the Second Army, which served as reserve was under South Korean operational control.[4] Operational control of the CFC also included the US forces in Korea. The Combined Forces Command is commanded by a four-star US general, the commander of US forces in Korea, and has a Korean four-star general as deputy commander. Bi-national manning is implemented throughout the command structure. The United Nations Command continues to exist with the task of maintaining the Armistice Agreement; it is headed by the same US general who commands the CFC.

When the US administration started reviewing its policy in Asia, relations to South Korea were affected. The review was caused by the developments in Vietnam where, unlike in Korea 20 years ago, the limited war could not be

[3]Korea Times, 23 November 1974.
[4]Wickham p. 21.

won. Large parts of American public opinion were convinced that the US's commitment in Vietnam was out of proportion and not justified with regards to US interests. The review of the war by the US government resulted in a new assessment of the American role in the Pacific. President Richard M. Nixon expressed new ideas in a talk with journalists at Guam on 25 July 1969. He argued that the US should continue to play a significant role in Asia, but he added "But as far as our role is concerned, we must avoid that kind of policy that will make countries in Asia so dependent upon us that we are dragged into conflicts such as the one that we have in Vietnam".[5] He further argued that in the future, the US would expect that security problems be handled by the Asian countries themselves. He underlined that the US would keep, however, its treaty commitments. His remarks, which became known as the Nixon doctrine, remained somewhat vague as he tried to envisage a reduction of the US forces in Asia while at the same time keep American commitments. The Nixon doctrine meant that the containment policy in Asia would be abandoned. The policy of global presence was modified in favor of disengagement. This policy had to be supported by a détente in relations with the two big communist powers. Here, US foreign policy was successful. Relations improved not only with the Soviet Union but also with China. President Nixon's visit to China at the beginning of 1972 went so much against traditional patterns of thinking of US allies in Asia that they were shocked by the event.

South Koreans quickly felt the effects of the new policy. In March 1970, the US government informed the South Korean government about its intentions to withdraw one of its two US divisions stationed in Korea in order to reduce the strength of American forces from 63,000 to 43,000. This announcement took the South Korean government by surprise. It tried to resist the withdrawal by arguing that a troop withdrawal was coming too early and was dangerous because it lowered the deterrence capabilities. The South Koreans were afraid that the North might once again be enticed by an American pullout to invade the South.

In August 1970, Vice-president Spiro Agnew hurried to Seoul with the mission of easing tensions between the allies. He stressed that the US would honor the commitments under the Mutual Defense Treaty. The US side, however,

---

[5] Richard P. Stebbins and Elaine P. Adam, *Documents on American Foreign Relations 1968–69* (New York 1972) p. 333.

was reluctant to go a step further and give a guarantee in writing that it would immediately assist South Korea in case of an attack. A US military aid package of $1.5 billion was offered to support a modernization program of the South Korean forces. The aid package was only partly met by a transfer of arms which the withdrawing US forces had left in Korea. In a Joint Statement on 6 February 1971, the agreement was announced.[6] In June 1971, the withdrawal of the 7th division was finished. The 2nd division, which remained in Korea, took the position that so far had been held by the 7th division. The 7th US division was disbanded. These events illustrated that South Korea, which had been the test case of the American containment policy, had become subjected to the Nixon doctrine.

The reduction of US forces in Korea remained a permanent issue within US-South Korean discussions. The Republican administration planned on withdrawing more troops, but met difficulties. As the thaw between South and North Korea in 1971 and 1972 was followed by a cold spell, larger withdrawals could not be justified. In view of the approaching debacle in Vietnam, the US government was interested in dispelling doubts of its Asian allies by showing its willingness to honor its commitments. The Joint Communiqué, published after the visit of President Ford to Seoul on 22 November 1974, mentioned Ford's assurance "that the United States has no plan to reduce the present level of United States Forces in Korea".[7]

The next energetic effort to reduce US forces in Korea was made by President Carter who had advocated a pullout already during his election campaign. Various factors had influenced Carter: The post-Vietnam mood in the US against American military involvement abroad, the poor human rights record of the Park Chung Hee government, and the tense relations with South Korea.[8] The South Korean resistance against the US withdrawal was in vain. The Joint Statement made after the 10th Annual Security Consultations on 25 and 26 July 1977 envisaged a phased withdrawal of ground combat forces over a four to five year period. This would have left air, naval, intelligence, logistics and other support available to South Korea. Measures to offset the withdrawal were also considered. The Americans stressed that the US's commitment

[6]Kim Se-Jin (1976) p. 391.

[7]Kim Se-Jin (1976) pp. 478 and 479.

[8]See Oberdorfer pp. 85 ff., Tae Hwan Kwak and Wayne Patterson, "The Security Relationship between Korea and the United States, 1960–1985", in Lee and Patterson, op.cit., p. 90.

to provide support in case of an armed attack on South Korea remained in force.

Carter's plans failed, however. For the compensatory aid, he needed the approval of Congress, but the majority of Congress was unwilling to agree to it. Many of the President's advisors who opposed the withdrawal could hide behind Congress's opposition. The doubts to whether a withdrawal of ground forces was wise increased when at the beginning of 1979, the US army's intelligence announced that the military strength of North Korea had been underestimated.[9] On 20 July 1979, the US government announced that any further withdrawals of US troops from South Korea would remain in abeyance.[10] The question was not taken up again during the Carter years.

During the Reagan years, there was no pullout debate. President Reagan assured President Chun Doo Hwan during their meeting at the beginning of 1981 "that the United States has no plans to withdraw US combat forces from the Korean peninsula".[11] The pullout debate was revived in 1989 when Congress considered budget savings. The Bush administration reacted immediately and announced in January 1990 the closure of three air force bases and the disbanding of one air force squadron in South Korea. Talks between the two allies about further reductions of US forces in South Korea followed and led to an agreement. As can be seen from the Joint Communiqué following the Security Consultative Meeting of 16 November 1990, it was agreed that the US would withdraw 5,000 ground and 2,000 air force personnel during the first stage of the pullout.[12] It was further envisaged to increase South Korea's share of financing the country's defense. Further reductions of US forces were to be taken gradually. The first stage of this withdrawal, the cut of 7,000 personnel, was completed in 1992. Further phases of troop reduction were canceled in 1992 due to tensions with North Korea caused by their nuclear efforts.[13]

The US government insisted that South Korea agree to pay an increasing part of the costs of maintaining US troops in Korea. Seoul was reluctant to accept burden sharing without power sharing. Therefore, it was logical that

---

[9]Washington Post, 31 October 1979.

[10]New York Times, 21 July 1979.

[11]Korea Annual 1981 p. 418.

[12]Korea Annual 1991 pp. 443 ff.

[13]International Herald Tribune, 13 October 1992.

peacetime operational control was transferred to South Korea; this happened on 1 December 1994.[14] Burden sharing was also implemented. In November 1995, the two allies concluded an agreement according to which South Korea was obliged to increase its direct cost-sharing contribution by 10% each year in the period from 1996 to 1998.[15] That the Republic of Korea assumed an increasingly larger share of responsibility for its own defense indicated a change in the quality of the US — South Korean partnership. The US began to retreat from a leading to a supporting role.

The changes in East Asia facilitated the transfer of more responsibilities to South Koreans. Since the end of the Korean War, the main function of the US forces in South Korea was to counteract expansionist intentions of the two big communist powers and to deter North Korea from another attack. Containment of Russia and China had become less relevant. Deterring North Korea remained, however, an important task as long as there was no viable mechanism to ease tensions on the peninsula. This task has been well performed by the US forces in Korea. The North had to take into account that in case it attacked the South, US forces would be automatically engaged. The real deterrent stems from this tripwire effect.

US forces in Korea still amount to approximately 37,000 personnel, most of them army and air force units.[16] The bulk is made up of the 2nd Infantry Division which at present has 116 tanks, 111 armored personnel and 106 armored infantry fighting vehicles as well as modern artillery. The US air force has 90 combat aircrafts. Equipment is stored for ground forces which can be brought to Korea in case of an attack. Plans on how to reinforce US troops in South Korea in case of an attack have been drawn up.

The continuing presence of US forces in Korea is questioned in the United States. In order to ensure a complete disengagement, the elimination of the tripwire forces and the cancellation of the Mutual Defense Treaty are

---

[14]Korea Annual 1994 pp. 118 and 119; 1995 pp. 118 and 119; Joint Communiqué of 27th ROK/US Security Consultative Meeting, 3 November 1995 in Institute of Foreign Affairs and National Security *Review* Vol. 4 No. 1 (February 1996) pp. 39 ff.; Defense Department Briefing on 8 October 1992, reported by Federal News Service, 8 October 1992 (available via LEXIS-NEXIS).

[15]Department of Defense, *Responsibility Sharing Report March 1998* (www.defenselink.mil/pubs/aliied_contrib/allied98_.hmtl).

[16]The International Institute for Strategic Studies, *The Military Balance 1998/99*, (London 1998) p. 28.

recommended.[17] The South Korean government on the other hand considers a redefinition of US forces in Korea only possible after the two Koreas have made meaningful progress in efforts to establish a peace structure on the peninsula.[18] There is no litmus test for the danger of war. Therefore, the precise degree of a threat from the North cannot be measured. The North continues to argue in an aggressive way; tensions on the peninsula continue to exist. There is still no mechanism to ease these tensions. As long as this state of affairs lasts, there is no better way for the US to impress upon friend and foe its willingness to enforce peace in Korea than by having forces stationed right in the area of tension. The establishment of a multilateral security framework might help bring a détente to Korea but it is not yet in place.

The US and South Korea have adapted their alliance to the changing circumstances. During their Security Consultative Meeting on 23 November 1999, they agreed "that combined defense readiness should be steadfastly maintained against a wide range of possible threats".[19] On the same occasion, the US reaffirmed its commitment to provide a nuclear umbrella for the Republic of Korea. This was welcomed by the South Korean government. The alliance continues to function.

Economic Cooperation

The American commitment to the South Korean ally has been costly. During the period from 1946 to 1976, economic assistance from the US amounted to US Dollar 5.7 billion and military assistance to 6.8 billion.[20] Not included in this sum are US war costs and expenditures on maintenance of US forces in South Korea. While the US also pursued its own interests in Korea, there is no doubt that it was willing to cope with the enormous demands of South Korea's reconstruction and development. For the most part, it was the US which enabled South Korea to develop its economy. This is a fact that should be remembered by South Koreans who, since the 1980s, delight in anti-Americanism.

---

[17] Bandow pp. 91 ff. and note 33.

[18] Presidential security advisor Lin Dong Won in Korea Times, 15 April 1999.

[19] Joint Communiqué 23 November 1999 (Yonhap News Agenc, reported and translated in BBC Summary of World Broadcast, 25 November 1999).

[20] Mason, Edward S. and others, *The Economic and Social Moderization of the Republic of Korea*, Cambridge 1980, pp. 182 and 183.

Bilateral trade with the US was essential for a country which had based its economic progress on developing an export industry. For many years, South Korea's trade balance with US was negative; the trend, however, changed in 1982 when South Korea for the first time enjoyed a surplus in bilateral trade relations with the "big brother". The surplus in 1982 was very small (US $300,000.00) but increased steeply to US $9.5 billion in 1987. In the following years the surpluses decreased, until in 1995, the South Korean trade balance with the US again became negative.[21]

Trade between South Korea and the US was affected by an important change in the trend of Korean exports during the late 1980s and the 1990s. The priority of South Korean export changed from developed to developing countries to such an extent that exports to the latter exceeded those to the former. While in 1985, the US received 35.5% of South Korea's exports, the percentage had fallen to 16.6% in 1998. The share of US exports to South Korea remained rather steady in the same period (1985: 20.8%; 1998: 21.4%).[22]

The collapse of the South Korean economy had a negative impact on the trade with the US since the lack of purchasing power in Korea slowed down imports. During the crisis, it was again the US government which, in cooperation with other bilateral donors and the international financial institutions, was instrumental in the rescue operation.

When the South Korean economy grew so tremendously, the country's importance in international trade increased steeply. In its relations to the USA, trade became a field where the asymmetry declined. In the course of this process the US — and other industrial countries — found the trade barriers, which the Republic of Korea had utilized to protect its developing economy, more and more unacceptable. In a speech before the National Assembly in Seoul on 27 February 1989, President Bush called protectionism "fool's gold".[23] When the US government began to demand a reduction or dismantling of these barriers, a number of trade conflicts developed. At first, the South Korean government tried to resist the demands for greater liberalization. Public opinion in South Korea even charged the US with harassing a small developing country. But, by and by the consideration prevailed that for a country, to have so much depending on its exports, liberalization was indispensable.

---

[21]Economic Planning Board, *Korea Statistical Yearbook 1986*, 1989; Noland (1998) p. 167.

[22]Kiheung Kim op.cit. pp. 71 ff.

[23]Korea Annual 1989 p. 374.

The first important steps taken were the reduction of import tariffs from 24.9% in 1980 to 10.6% in 1993 and the abolition of quantitative restrictions from approximately 30% in 1980 to less than 2% in 1993.[24] The decisions of the Uruguay Round resulted in further tariff cuts. Quite a number of fields of contention remained. One of them was over agricultural products. When the US tried to sell rice, fruits, vegetables, poultry and beef to Korea, they met strong and continuous resistance. The resistance was sometimes hidden behind non-tariff barriers such as standards, testing, and certification procedures which were applied arbitrarily.

From the windows of my office in Seoul, I had a view of the entrance of Namdaemun Market. One day in the fall of 1985, it attracted my attention that many traders were selling photograph albums. When I checked the situation, I found out that the albums were being sold at such low prices that I bought a box full of albums. Later, I learned the reason for the drop in prices. The photograph albums had been produced for export to the US, but could not be sold there because the US government had levied high anti-dumping tariffs. This was just one example where the US had initiated an anti-dumping case against South Korean producers arguing that they sold their goods in the US at prices below their average costs or at prices lower than those in the home market. Whether the many small companies manufacturing photograph albums had pursued a dumping policy seemed doubtful. But this and similar cases periodically spoiled South Korean–US trade relations.

Another field of contention was over intellectual property rights. The US — and other industrialized countries — had reason to complain about violations of counterfeiting, trademark infringement and by non-protection of pharmaceutical products. The South Korean government kept its market for foreign cars closed. Sometimes, it launched "buy Korean" campaigns. Another hotly debated issue, the opening of South Korea's financial markets, may have found a solution in the aftermath of the financial collapse of the country in 1997.

It has always been difficult to negotiate with Koreans because they have an inclination to knock their heads against a brick wall. Attempts to settle conflicts were additionally impaired by the Korean attitude towards law, which was aptly described in 1971 as follows: "Thus while lip service is paid by Koreans to the rule of law, the old ethical traditions still predominate which discourage resort to the courts and legislation takes on the appearance of so

[24]Noland in Tong Whan Park p. 150.

much window-dressing".[25] This assessment was confirmed by a poll done in 1972 which revealed the following: 39% of the interviewees agreed with the assertion that there were few things done as provided for by law.[26] That those who followed the law were acting unwise was accepted by 58%. Questioned on how they would react in case they had bought goods of a poor quality, only 15% agreed to take action (to report to the police), 85% preferred a passive attitude. The respect towards law was poorly developed in those years.

One might have hoped that this attitude towards law had changed over the years. A survey done in 1997, however, revealed that Koreans were still not strongly motivated to abide by the rule of law.[27] 42% replied that they would advise friends to make use of illegal services in order to get the government to do what they wanted. Surprisingly, the more the Koreans were educated, the more they were willing to neglect the law. Still, much must be done to change the Korean's attitude towards law, thus making negotiations with them more businesslike.

Friction

Although contacts between Koreans and Americans date back to the end of the last century, an extensive exchange developed only after the Second World War when the US occupied the southern part of the peninsula. Huge numbers of people took part in that encounter. US soldiers, government officials, businessmen, scholars and students, members of the Peace Corps, and private citizens came to South Korea; American missionaries continued their work, which they had begun much earlier. Conversely, Koreans came to USA in order to learn, to study and to do business. Many of them returned and made use of their knowledge acquired in the US, thus contributing to stop a brain drain from South Korea. After US immigration laws were changed in 1965, great numbers of Koreans immigrated to the US. Today, there are not

[25]Theodore B. Carter. *The Korean Attitude towards Law and the American Businessman in South Korea*, Seoul July 1971, typewritten (A copy is in the author's possession); see also Nicholas Eberstadt, "Can The Two Koreas Be One"? in *Foreign Affairs*, Winter 1992/93 pp. 163–165.

[26]Lin Hy Sop, "A Study on Legal Values in Korea: An Analysis of Attitude towards Law", in *Social Science Journal* Vol. 2, Seoul 1974 pp. 59 ff.

[27]Shin, Do C. pp. 257 and 258.

only Korean sections in Los Angeles, but a "Little Korea" exists in Manhattan south of the Empire State Building, a symbol of Korean advancement in America. Koreans and Americans in large numbers had the chance to meet and learn to understand each other. Nevertheless, friction developed and has never completely disappeared.

It was often the domestic development in the Republic of Korea which caused tension between the two countries. Originally it was sufficient, from the American point of view, that the South Korean leadership was anticommunist and pro-American. Many excuses could be found that democratic reforms and attitudes prescribed by the Americans gained a foothold only slowly. South Korea had no experience with democracy, plus they had to resist the attack from the North, had to cope with the devastation left by the war and had to fight hunger and poverty. When years went by, democratic deficits as well as the human rights violations in South Korea became more and more embarrassing for the American ally. In the US, citizen groups were organized which focused on the human rights violations in the Republic of Korea. Since the mid 1970s, critical comments from Congress began to be voiced. Succeeding US administrations made it clear to the South Korean government that it was detrimental to the South Korean image in the US that South Korea was again and again suspected of disregarding human rights. President Carter was particularly appalled by the policy of suppression in South Korea. At times, the US government intervened directly. The best known example was its intervention in January 1981 in which the life of Kim Dae Jung was saved.

A consistent American policy on how to improve the human rights situation in Korea was missing. The attitude towards Park Chung Hee and Chun Doo Hwan has been described as a gradual change "from suspicion and hostility to unenthusiastic acquiescence to strong support".[28] The reason for this attitude could be gathered from General Wickham's famous interview on 8 August 1980 with journalists from the Associated Press and Los Angeles Times. Asked whether the US would support Chun Doo Hwan as president even if his policy of political suppression and a lack of broad political participation in government continued, General Wickham answered according to the Los Angeles Time of 8 August 1980: "Yes, provided that he come to power legitimately and demonstrates, over a time, a broader base of support from the

[28]Cohen and Baker p. 171.

Korean people and does not jeopardize the security situations...here we will support him, because that, of course, is what we think the Korean people want". It is understandable that the general was angry that a background interview was attributed to him and that Chun was given an opportunity of asserting to have US support.[29] Leaving these aspects out of consideration, we can note that General Wickham only expressed the general feeling of the US government. If Chun Doo Hwan was to become South Korea's president, the US had no choice but to support him. The same was true when Park Chung Hee had seized power in 1961. It was up to the Koreans to decide which way they wanted to go. An outside power, even a mighty one like the US, had only limited influence on South Korea's internal politics. The second consideration which determined US actions was that of security. Security on the peninsula was not just of decisive importance for the South Korea, but also for the US. The United States also defended its own security in South Korea. Very often the necessity of maintaining security prevailed over all other considerations. Fortunately, the spread of *glasnost* since mid-1987 in South Korea has eased US–South Korean debates over domestic developments in South Korea.

US–South Korean relations have been asymmetrical, but one must not overdo this aspect. As the long years of cooperation have shown, the leverage of the US government over the South Korean government has been limited as far as internal developments in South Korea are concerned. None of the important domestic events of the last decades has been influenced by the US administration in a decisive way; neither the overthrow of Syngman Rhee in April 1960, nor the revolt against the democratic government in May 1961, nor the rise to power by Chun Doo Hwan, nor the start of *glasnost* by Roh Tae Woo in July 1987. South Korean leaders felt dependent on the US in many ways. They disregarded, however, American appeals when they preferred to give priority to their own interests. When Marshal Green, the US Charge d'affaires in Seoul, described his first talks with the new Park Chung Hee regime, he reported to Washington that the military leaders were often disregarding American advice, but were somewhat influenced by it.[30] This observation was true in a general way for US efforts exerting influence on Korean domestic affairs.

[29] Wickham pp. 155–158.

[30] Macdonald p. 216.

Another development, staged on the other side of the Pacific, affected the US–South Korean relationship negatively. In 1976, charges were leveled in the US that the South Korean government had tried to buy influence illegally in Washington. Suggestions were made that members of the House of Representatives had been bribed. Special committees to examine these allegations were established. Leon Jaworski, well known as the special prosecutor in the Watergate proceedings, was called in, this time as a special advisor to the House Ethics Committee. It came to light that Park Tong Sun, acting upon instructions from the KCIA, had tried to win over Representatives for South Korea's cause by bribing them. It became possible to examine Park Tong Sun, the full facts, however, were not found out. One Congressman went to jail, and others ruined their reputation. What was worse: US–South Korean relations were disturbed. The Korean government had achieved exactly the opposite of what it had been trying to achieve. Its efforts to win influential politicians over by force had backfired. Luckily for South Korea, US public opinion forgot Koreagate quickly.[31] Since American politicians had been reminded again on how difficult a partner South Korea was, they most likely did not forget the event equally as quickly as the American public had.

Public Opinion

In democracies, foreign policy is influenced by public opinion. Therefore, governments try to improve the image of their country abroad; public relations have thus become an important part of the work of embassies and consulates. In a worst-case scenario, that the Republic of Korea would have to defend itself against an attack from the North, public opinion in the US might become a crucial factor for US involvement. The tripwire effect would automatically involve US troops in South Korea into the military conflict. The US would still have to decide on whether to come to the defense of the South and by which means. A war in Korea would be a war of attrition and not a surgical war, and therefore, many casualties would have to be taken into account. This would make the decision for the US particularly difficult.

[31] Powlick p. 189.

Many surveys have been conducted to determine the level of support for the use of US troops if South Korea were to be invaded by the North.[32] As these surveys have shown, US popular support for an active military involvement in Korea has been low; support has only increased during exceptional circumstances like the nuclear crisis in the North. Even then, there was not a majority of interviewees who supported a US defense of the South. These polls indicated that it would be rather tough for the US administration to find enough public support to defend the Republic of Korea militarily against an attack from the DPRK.

It must be added that the US public's interest in Korea is on a low level.[33] What should also not be overlooked is the fact that there are persistently slightly more negative than positive impressions about South Korea in the US public. In polls taken, South Koreans got, for example, high scores for "hardworking", but also higher scores than Japan, China, Taiwan and the Philippines for being "deceitful".[34] The reasons for this negative undercurrent cannot be precisely ascertained. But one can guess that the authoritarian regimes in South Korea, the violation of human rights, the influence — peddling in the US have left their traces on US public opinion.

For many years, South Koreans have been utterly pro-American. America was identical with Western and progressive. A visitor returning to South Korea in the 1980s was surprised to observe that a militant anti–Americanism had developed and was spreading. It found its expression in demonstrations and attacks on US institutions in Korea. The charges were numerous. The Americans, so the assertions went, had intentionally divided Korea, objected to unification, supported South Korean authoritarian governments and were economically imperialistic. The South Korean government failed to stress publicly the necessity of good relations with its only ally. In the mid-1980s, it seemed that the US was no longer seen as a friend in the land of the morning freshness.

The rise of massive anti–Americanism could be traced to specific events. The catchword was Kwangju. Rumors were spreaded and people believed that the US had something to do with the quelling of the uprising and Chun's rise to power. These charges were false as has already been explained. Desperately,

---

[32]Powlick pp. 206–209.
[33]Powlick pp. 189–191.
[34]Powlick pp. 195–196.

the US authorities in Washington and Seoul tried to work towards a political solution. General Wickham and Ambassador Gleysteen, however, made the mistake of getting involved in discussions about the military actions to be taken in Kwangju even though none of the military units deployed at Kwangju was under US operational control. Chun Doo Hwan apparently got the impression that he could play around with the Americans. After the riots in Kwangju had been quelled, he told Korean publishers and editors that the US had been informed in advance of the seizure of power by the military on 12 December 1979, of his appointment as KCIA director and of the declaration of full martial law on 18 May 1980.[35] All attempts of the US side to counter these false assertions and to set the record straight were in vain; under martial law, the newspapers did not dare publish the American clarifications. Similar American efforts, at the end of the 1980s and the beginning of the 1990s, were also unsuccessful. In public opinion, the assertion of tacit American approval of the incident had meanwhile changed into a fact. It was mainly Chun Doo Hwan who was responsible for disseminating the wrong story. That he, who had contributed to damaging the image of the US in South Korea, was received with many honors in January 1981 by President Reagan is difficult to understand.

The escalation of anti-Americanism was illustrated by an incident during the Olympic Games in Seoul in 1988. After a boxing match between a South Korean and a Bulgarian where the Bulgarian was declared the winner, the following happened: South Korean officials entered the ring and physically attacked the referee from New Zealand. Also, the South Korean security guards hit the referee. The South Korean boxer staged a sit-in on the floor of the ring for one hour. The South Korean media did not blame the Koreans, who had behaved in an unfair and fanatical way, but the US's TV broadcasting company, NBC, for having given extensive coverage of the incident. While the Korean TV stations had only briefly reported the incident, NBC had given full coverage which was at the same time transmitted by AFKN, the TV network of American Forces in Korea.

The Koreans complained that the Americans did not treat them as partners. These feelings increased when the US, after South Korea's economic rise, insisted that the country's market should be opened to US competition. Koreans immediately complained about exploitation. These and similar complaints

[35] *Backgrounder* of the US Embassy in Seoul, 19 June 1989, p. 24 (see Chapter 10 note 32).

were an expression of helplessness towards the "big brother". Koreans may try as hard as they possibly can, but they will always be the "little brother". This feeling was magnified as many Koreans consider the US to be omnipotent.[36] From the American perspective, the alliance with South Korea is a "high maintenance" relationship.[37]

So there are negative undercurrents in the publics of both countries: an undercurrent of negative affect in the US and an undercurrent of resentment in South Korea. It is in the interest of both allies to counteract and hopefully reverse this process in order to avoid lasting damage for their alliance.

References

Almeida, Pedro and O'Hanlon, Michael, "Impasse in Korea: A Conventional Arms-Accord Solution"? in *Survival*, Vol. 41, No. 1 (spring 1999) pp. 58 ff.

Baek, Kwang Il, *Korea and the United States*, Seoul 1988.

Bandow, Dong, *Tripwire. Korea and United States Foreign Policy in a Changed World* (Washington 1996).

Boettcher, Robert, *Gifts of Deceit* (New York 1980).

Cohen, Jerome Alan and Baker, Edward J., "U.S. Foreign Policy and Human Rights in South Korea", in William Shaw (editor) *Human Rights in Korea. Historical and Policy Perpectives*, Cambridge 1991, pp. 171–219.

Han, Sungjoo, "The Republic of Korea and the United States. The Changing Alliance", in *Korea and World Affairs* Vol. 1 No. 2 (summer 1977) pp. 117 ff.

Kim, Young C., (editor) *Major Powers and Korea* (Silver Spring 1973).

Noland, Marcus, "US–South Korea Economic Relations", in Tong Wham Park, pp. 147–186.

Powlick, Philip J., "US Public Opinion of the Two Koreas", in Tong Wham Park, pp. 187–228.

[36]Lee Kwang Chul, Newspaper of Chonbuk University, 28 September 1987.

[37]William M. Drennan, "The U.S. Role in Korean Reunification", in *Korea and World Affairs*, Vol. 22 (summer 1989 p. 172.

Chapter 19

The Neighbor in the East

Brisk Exchanges

There are many daily flights from South Korean airports to Japan and from Japanese airports to South Korea. In 1989, the first year in which the ban on overseas travel was lifted, 600,000 Koreans visited Japan; during the same year 1.4 million Japanese came to Korea.[1] In the following years, the numbers of visitors increased. In 1995, nearly 1 million South Koreans traveled to Japan and 3.8 million Japanese came to South Korea.[2] The exchange of such large crowds of visitors indicated that their mutual dislike could not be as strong as we were often told.

As interest in Japan increased in South Korea, it became more and more popular to study the Japanese language and culture. While English is a compulsory subject at middle and high schools in South Korea, students have a choice for a second language. Japanese cultural activities in South Korea faced strong restrictions for many years due to a late reaction to Japanese colonial rule. NHK, the Japanese TV broadcasting company, managed to overcome the obstacles. Meanwhile, cultural exchanges have been possible and are promoted by both governments. The showing of Japanese films in South Korea illustrates the departure from the traditional antagonistic policy. In June 1999, a South Korean–Japanese consultation body was set up to discuss on how to promote exchanges; it consisted only of private citizens.[3] One of the first tasks of the

[1] *Business Korea Yearbook*, part VII (Seoul 1990).

[2] Korea Annual 1996 p. 235.

[3] Korea Times, 18 June 1999.

new body was to organize cultural events which would accompany the 2002 World Cup Soccer Games which are co-hosted by both countries.

A particularly close cooperation between both countries exists in the field of economy and trade. Japan has its merits with regards to South Korea's economic rise, a fact seldom mentioned in South Korea. Besides USA, Japan was the great lender of capital. There are two distinguishing phases when large amounts of capital have flown from Japan to South Korea. The first large transfers followed the 1965 Normalization Treaties in which Japan had promised grants of US $300 million and capital assistance of US $200 million. They furthermore envisaged US $300 million in the form of commercial credits. In January 1983 during the visit of Prime Minister Nakasone in Seoul, Japan promised additional loans. An agreement of the two foreign ministers, dated 12 January 1983, provided that Japan would extend US $4 billion over a period of seven years to finance Korea's major development projects.[4] US $1.65 billion were to be provided as government loans at interest rates of 4 to 4.5% and US $2.15 billion as commercial credits. In view of the country's difficult economic situation, the South Korean government had pressed for these loans for quite some time. Originally, Japan had reacted with caution as it suspected hidden requests of reparations behind the Korean wishes. Finally, the Japanese government had promised to extend huge amounts of loans, presumably hoping that much of this money would flow back to Japan.

Besides the USA, Japan has been South Korea's most important trading partner.[5] For many years, Japan was South Korea's main supplier, but its share of Korean imports began to fall from 24.3% in 1985 to 19.3% in 1997 while during the same period the US share remained rather stable around 20%. Exports to Japan declined from 15% in 1985 to 10.8% in 1997 of South Korea's total exports. Structural reasons have made it difficult to balance trade with Japan. Korean industries have insisted on manufacturing many of the goods of mass production for which Japan is famous, such as steel, ships, cars and electronics. For example, as far as ships are concerned, both countries compete for the number one spot.[6] South Korea needs to import components and

---

[4]Korea Annual 1984 p. 70.

[5]For the statistics, see: Kiheung Kim "Korea's External Economic Relations" in Joseph A. B. Winder (editor) *Korea's Economy 1999*, Korea Economic Institute of America pp. 70 ff.

[6]Korea Times, 12 October 1998.

machinery from Japan. The bilateral trade balance with Japan has remained negative for Korea (1985: US $3 billion; 1996: US $13.5 billion).

The Republic of Korea had originally discouraged foreign direct investment in order to avoid foreign, particularly Japanese, economic domination.[7] When this policy was relaxed, in the mid-1980s, Japanese businessmen used the chance to invest in South Korea. In the period from 1962 to June 1997, Japan was the second largest investor with an accumulated amount of US $5.7 billion, after the US with US $7.2 billion in the same period. When foreign capital started to flow into the country in the form of investments, Korea still continued to rely far more on loans as sources of foreign capital. How dangerous and disastrous this was, the country experienced during the 1997 collapse when the foreign loans could not be served. A law passed on 17 September 1998 facilitated investment which was basically a long-term commitment. An improved protection of intellectual property would contribute to making South Korea more attractive for foreign investment.

Apart from capital, the South Korean economy needed modern technology. It had the good luck that Japanese companies were willing to transfer technology, which they did not need any longer when they climbed up the technology ladder.[8] Japanese technology was channeled to South Korea by joint ventures, licensing, subcontracting, original equipment manufacturing and informal methods. Japan became by far the most important source of foreign technology for South Korea. For example, 57% of all license agreements concluded by South Korean companies from the period 1962 to 1984 had Japanese companies as partners.[9]

Sources of Friction

The Normalization Treaties, concluded in 1965, had focused on financial demands, fishery questions and the fate of the Koreans residing in Japan. The first of these issues had lost its importance; Japan was no longer giving development aid to South Korea and the transfer of capital from Japan to South Korea

[7]The following is based on: Peter M. Beck, "Foreign Direct Investment in Korea: From Exclusion to Inducement", in *Joint-US–Korea Academic Studies*, Vol. 9, 1999. pp. 221 ff.

[8]Castley pp. 146–166.

[9]Castley p. 162.

occurred on a commercial basis. The other two issues continued to cause conflicts between the two countries.

When the treaties of 1965 tried to solve the fisheries issue, it had been Japanese vessels which had fished in areas claimed by South Korea. The agreement had introduced a practical solution by recognizing the right of both sides to extend the fishing zone to twelve nautical miles. Meanwhile, it was the vessels of the Korean fishers which operated close to the Japanese coast. As Japan wanted to protect the marine resources before its coast, it demanded to conclude a new agreement, and as the South Korean government tried to stall negotiations, Japan announced that it would renounce the existing agreement and officially notified the Korean government of its intentions in January 1998. On 28 November 1998 a new South Korean–Japanese Fisheries Agreement was signed.[10] The accord accepted the earlier claims by both countries of an exclusive economic zone of 200 nautical miles of each country's shores as permitted by the UN Convention on the Law of the Seas of 1994. Negotiations followed to work out the details to the extent that vessels would be allowed to fish in the other country's exclusive economic zone and with what types of methods. So, the fisheries' questions did not completely die down.

The fate of the approximately 700,000 Koreans in Japan has given repeated reason for conflicts between the governments of the two countries. Most of these Koreans were born in Japan, speak mostly Japanese, want to live in Japan and have scarce contacts of Korea. They are, however, discriminated against within the Japanese society. They had been given the right to live permanently in Japan by the Normalization Treaties but their status had not been improved because they were not given parity of treatment with the Japanese.

A particular problem for Japanese authorities resulted from the fact that South and North Korea have competed for influence among the Koreans in Japan. According to official Japanese statistics, 36% of the Koreans residing in Japan are affiliated with Chosun Soren, the pro North Korean association, and 54% with Mindan, the pro South Korean organization.[11] The activities of Chosun Soren have been of concern to the Japanese government, particularly in the aftermath of the assassination attempt on President Park Chung Hee on 15 August 1974. Mun Se Kwan, the assassin, a Korean residing in Japan,

---

[10]Korea Times, 29 November 1998 and 22 January 1999.

[11]Nathaniel B. Thayer, "Korean Peninsula Trends and US–Japan–South Korea Relations", in *The Center for Strategic and International Studies* (Washington 1994) pp. 62 and 63.

allegedly operated under instructions from North Korea passed on to him by a representative from Chosen Soren in Osaka.

At the end of the 1980s, discussions centered again on the status of Koreans living in Japan. The Roh Too Woo government took up the problem energetically and worked for real improvements. These were achieved by bilateral agreements in 1990. The obligations of Korean residents to have fingerprints registered with Japanese immigration authorities and to carry an alien registration card all the time were abolished. Japan agreed to extend the validity of reentry permits from 2 to 5 years and to narrow down causes for deportation. These improvements were agreed upon in April 1990 for third-generation Koreans, and in November of the same year to first and second-generation Koreans living in Japan. These changes brought along practical improvements, but did not change the status of Koreans in any fundamental way. More and more ethnic Koreans tried, therefore, to escape their low status by using Japanese names, by marrying Japanese or by becoming naturalized. For all the others, much remains to be done. For example, the granting of voting rights in local elections was requested by President Kim Dae Jung during a visit to Tokyo in October 1998.[12] But to abolish the discrimination of Koreans in Japan is less a task for governments and more for the society. Only if the Japanese society is ready to accept the Koreans living in Japan as true fellow citizens will those problems fade away.

Another issue, the fate of the Korean comfort women, has been taken up only recently. Comfort women is a euphemism for prostitutes, young women between the age of 14 and 18, most of whom were induced by deceit, intimidation or coercion to serve in "comfort stations" for the Japanese forces during the Second World War. The precise numbers of these Korean women who had to serve as comfort women and of those who survived the war are unknown, but definitely the lives of tens of thousands of young Koreans were ruined.[13] Understandably, those who survived did not come forward with their stories. Their fate was not an issue for the Normalization Treaties of 1965.

Later, private citizens, mostly in Japan, investigated the subject, and put material together to write about it. When the civil society expanded in South Korea, groups were also formed there to take up the sad story. But only when some of the former Korean comfort women had the courage to speak up and

[12]Korea Times, 7 and 9 October 1998.

[13]Hicks p. 19 and p. 172.

even sue the Japanese government before a court in Tokyo in December 1991, asking for compensation, did the issue become prominent and a subject of a lasting and highly emotional South Korean–Japanese controversy.

At the end of the Second World War, units of the Japanese army had tried to cover up what had happened to the poor women. When the Japanese government was confronted with the issue in the beginning of the 1990s, it first tried to explain that the armed forces, i.e. the Japanese government, had not been involved. It could, however, not stick to that line, after documents were found in Japanese government archives which proved that the military had been behind the organization of the system. Prime Minister Miyazawa extended his apologies during his visit to Seoul in mid-January 1992.[14] Various Japanese administrations, however, insisted that the question of compensation had finally been dealt with by the treaties of 1965. In 1995, the Japanese government tried to settle the issue by establishing a private fund. The offer was, however, rejected by most of the women concerned who insisted on compensation by the Japanese government.

The Korean government did not take up the issue with much vigor. It saw no chance in reopening the discussion on financial issues which had arrived under so many difficulties in the Normalization Treaties. It also wanted to avoid the highly emotional issue from becoming an obstacle to the improvement of bilateral relations to which priority was given. President Kim Young Sam announced on 13 March 1993 that the Korean government would not ask the Japanese government to provide compensation but render financial assistance to the surviving victims out of its own budget.[15] His successor Kim Dae Jung followed the same line and did not take up the issue during his visit to Japan in November 1998.[16] Though the Japanese government is not urged by the South Korean government to find a solution, it might in any case be haunted by the question.

From time to time, South Koreans and Japanese get into arguments over certain islands, called "Tokdo" in Korean and "Takeshima" in Japanese. Tokdo consists of two tiny rocks without vegetation, halfway between Korea and Japan. Both countries claim territorial sovereignty over these islands. Japan

---

[14]UPI, 17 January 1992.

[15]Korea Annual 1993, p. 167, B. C. Koh, "Recent Political Developments in North Korea" in Henriksen and Mo p. 40 note 12.

[16]Korea Times, 10 November 1998.

incorporated them into the Japanese prefecture or Shimane in 1905, but South Korea had taken control of them since they proclaimed the Rhee line in 1952.[17] In the period after 1952, both sides made threatening gestures, but the basic question was not solved. What was settled, however, was the issue of fishing rights around the islands. When the new Fisheries Agreement was concluded in November 1998, a joint fishing zone was set up around the islands.[18] Thus, at least a practical solution was found.

Forever Apologies?

Koreans have felt strongly that Japan should apologize for its misdeeds in Korea. On 17 February 1965, just before the Treaty on Basic Relations between the two countries was initialed, the Japanese Foreign Minister Shiina made a remark on "an unhappy period in the long history" of the two countries.[19] This was interpreted by the South Korean government as a sort of apology. Since Shiina had only expressed regret, Korean public opinion demanded a sincere apology. Now and then, Japanese politicians reacted by making remarks about Korean participation in Korea's annexation and the benefits of Japanese rule in Korea. Each time a remark has been made, an uproar in Korea followed which forced the Japanese government to control the damage.

Both governments have been interested in improving the basics of their relationship and tried to find solutions which would allow both sides not to lose face. President Chun Doo Hwan and Prime Minister Nakasone tried particularly hard to introduce more rationality into the relationship of the two neighbors. When Nakasone paid the first official visit of a Japanese Prime Minister to Seoul, he expressed on 11 January 1983 his deep regrets about the unhappy pages in the history of Japanese–Korean relations.[20] When Chun Doo Hwan returned the visit — the first visit of a South Korean head of state to Japan — Emperor Hirohitho stated the following on 6 September 1984: "It is indeed regrettable that there was an unfortunate past between us for a period in this century".[21] When President Roh Tae Woo paid a state visit to Tokyo

[17]Kim Kwan Bong pp. 68 and 69.

[18]Korea Times, 29 November 1998.

[19]See Chapter 8.

[20]Washington Post, 12 January 1983.

[21]Korea Annual 1985 p. 15.

Emperor Akihito, Hirohito's son, went a step further by saying on 24 May 1990: "I think of the sufferings your people underwent during that unfortunate period, which was brought about by my country, and cannot but feel the deepest regret".[22] Emperor Akihito repeated that statement in March 1994 on the occasion of the official visit of President Kim Young Sam to Japan.[23] Even though these remarks were understood at that time as an explicit apology, Korean public opinion continued to request further statements by the Japanese government.

The 50th anniversary of the end of the Pacific War on 15 August 1995 made it unavoidable for the Japanese government to take a stand with regards to the past. Prime Minister Murayama made use of the opportunity by stating: "Not so long ago our country followed a national policy that was wrong and went down the path to war. This put the people of Japan in a life-or-death crisis. Through our aggression and colonial rule, we caused great damage and suffering for many countries, particularly in Asia. So that we do not go wrong in the future, I humbly acknowledge this undeniable fact of history. Once again, I express my deep remorse and heartfelt apologies."[24] A clearer language, containing the words "wrong", "aggression" and "apologies" could not be asked for. And Murayama's sincerity could not be questioned, since he had been a longtime pacifist. Nevertheless, the South Korean government found something to criticize and insisted on serious Japanese efforts to reveal the truth of history.[25] Murayama later undermined his credibility by insisting that the Treaty of Annexation of 1910 was valid under the historical circumstances. Another apology contained in a letter addressed to President Kim Young Sam followed in November 1995 in which the Japanese Prime Minister stated that the annexation treaty was signed on an unequal footing and in an imperialistic era which disregarded national prestige and dignity.[26]

Seoul's criticism of Murayama's statement of 15 August 1995 was not surprising. President Kim Young Sam not only showed inconsistency in his domestic policies, but was also unable to steer a clear course in his dealing with

[22] Korea Annual 1990 p. 89.

[23] B. C. Koh (quoted in note 15 above) pp. 36 and 37.

[24] Washington Post, 16 August 1995.

[25] Washington Post, 16 August 1995.

[26] Korea Annual 1996 p. 99 ff.

foreign countries. For the sake of long-term regional stability, reconciliation with the only like-minded partner in the area was in South Korea's national interest. Kim Young Sam, however, joined in anti-Japanese statements when the Chinese President Jiang Zemin paid a state visit to the Republic of Korea in mid-November 1995. He agreed with Jiang that Japan's new expansionism would eventually be the major factor in destabilizing the security of Northeast Asia.[27] In view of the nuclear crisis provoked by North Korea, this was a surprising statement. A different caliber in the Blue House was needed to choose a rational approach to South Korean–Japanese relations.

President Kim Dae Jung did not misuse anti-Japanese feelings for purposes of domestic policies. On the contrary, with a view to South Korea's prosperity and security, he advocated a strong, reliable and future-oriented partnership between both countries. As the Japanese government agreed with this policy, a "Joint Declaration on New ROK–Japan Partnership for 21st century" was issued by President Kim Dae Jung and Prime Minister Keizo Obuchi on 8 October 1998 in Tokyo. It stated that "Prime Minister Obuchi, looking back on the relations between Korea and Japan in this century, humbly accepted the historical fact that Japan's colonial rule inflicted incalculable damage and pain on the Korean people and expressed remorseful repentance and a heartfelt apology for Korea's ordeal".[28] The Korean President expressed his appreciation of this statement and advocated a future-oriented relationship.

It would be for the benefit of both countries if their citizens followed their leaders in reaching out to the other side. Unfortunately, one has to be afraid that voices will be heard in Korea questioning Japan's sincerity and voices in Japan questioning the reasons for humility.

Security Ties?

Seen from Japan, Korea is the nearest part of the Asian continent. Therefore, the neighboring country's strategic importance could not be overlooked by military planners in Tokyo. Korea could be seen as a buffer zone between the Japanese islands and potential attackers from the continent. Thus, there is a correlation between the security of Japan and the security of Korea.

[27] Korea Annual 1996, p. 101.

[28] Text in Korea Times, 8 October 1998.

As a reaction to Japan's military history, the country's Peace Constitution restricts military activities rigorously. The Self-Defense Forces, with approximately 240,000 men and modern equipment, are however not to be underestimated.[29] Japan has strictly followed a policy based on its economic and not on its military power. It is, therefore, understandable that it took Japan many years before officially recognizing the correlation between its own security and that of Korea. This recognition was not the result of discussions with Korea, but with the common protector, the USA. The Joint Communiqué published after the meeting between President Nixon and Prime Minister Sato on 21 November 1969 stated that the security of the Republic of Korea was "essential to Japan's own security".[30] Later, the idea that the security of both countries was interdependent was also expressed in Japanese–South Korean texts. The Joint Communiqué, published after Nakasone's visit in Seoul on 12 January 1983, mentioned "that peace and stability on the Korean peninsula are essential to those in all of East Asia including Japan...".[31]

This conviction resulted in a few practical consequences only. During the visit of the South Korean Defense Minister to Tokyo in the spring of 1994, both sides agreed to exchange visits of warships, military personnel, and military flight schedules in order to prevent accidental collisions.[32] Indeed, in December 1994 South Korean training vessels began to exchange visits.[33] In August 1999, the South Korean navy and the Japanese maritime self-defense forces had their first joint exercise: it was only a search-and-rescue mission with the scenario that a South Korean patrol vessel had caught fire.[34]

These modest steps are sometimes called confidence-building measures. This vocabulary illustrates how far apart both countries were in defense matters because confidence-building measures have been invented to overcome tensions between possible enemies.

President Kim Dae Jung and Prime Minister Obuchi did not go much further in their far-reaching plans for a South Korean–Japanese partnership

---

[29]The International Institute for Strategic Studies, *The Militar Balance 1998/99*, London 1998, pp. 18–185.

[30]Lee Chong-Shik (1985) p. 71.

[31]Korea Annual 1983 p. 379.

[32]Korea Annual 1995 p. 120.

[33]Yomiuri Shimbun, 6 August 1999.

[34]Yomiuri Shimbun, 6 August 1999.

in the 21st century. In their Joint Declaration of 8 October 1998, they agreed "to further strengthen bilateral consultations on security policy and exchanges in the field of defense on various levels".[35] They also supported establishing a multilateral security guarantee forum. At the same time, they stressed that their respective security arrangements with the US would be the basis for their defense. So far, no defense cooperation between both countries is in sight.

Both sides exercise restraint. Both sides mistrust each other. Japan faces the additional difficulty of self-imposed restrictions which also excludes the right of collective self-defense.[36] The end of the Cold War has changed perceptions in the Far East. Japan can assume that Russia no longer represents a major threat. It is the leftover from the Cold War, the tension on the neighboring peninsula, which entails dangers for Japan. The Japanese Defense Program Outline for 1996 took this situation into account.[37] The Outline mentioned the changes in the military posture in Far East Russia, but warned of large-scale military capabilities in the region. It continued "There remains uncertainty and unpredictability, such as continued tensions on the Korean Peninsula, and a stable security environment has not been fully established. Under these circumstances, the possibility of a situation in this region, which could seriously affect the security of Japan, cannot be excluded".[38] As the country's planners have reason to consider North Korea, because of its hostile attitude as a primary threat, Japan was willing to cooperate in containing a possible nuclear threat from North Korea. Japan is equally concerned about the North Korean missile development program.

It is, however, obvious that Japan has to envisage a more active role in case of a regional conflict. When an armed conflict erupts on the neighboring Korean peninsula, it might not be sufficient if Japan is only prepared to accommodate refugees.[39] In discussions with the US, the Japanese government has accepted that it has to do more. The Guidelines for US–Japan Defense Cooperation of 23 September 1997 provide for rear area and

---

[35] Korea Times, 8 October 1998.

[36] Akaneya Tasuo, "Japan", in Paul B. Stares, *The New Security Agenda. A Global Survey* (Tokyo, New York 1998) p. 179.

[37] "National Defense Program Outline in and after FY 1996 (Tentative Unofficial Translation)" in Green and Cronin pp. 359–367.

[38] Ibidem p. 361.

[39] Akaneya Tasuo p. 191.

other logistical support in case of emergency situations "in areas surrounding Japan".[40] But the question of how the two allies prepare for such a situation is left unanswered.[41]

Arrangements between Japan and the Republic of Korea on how to coordinate a response to a conflict on the peninsula are missing. Since such a conflict will effect Japan a cooperation beyond consultation and mutual visits with South Korea with a view to contain North Korea may seem advisable, more so with a view to a possible unification of Korea.[42] A united Korea may at first face economic trouble, but will be militarily strong, and will be, anyway, a good complementary partner for Japan. The idea that the US might withdraw militarily from Northeast Asia when the North Korean threat disappears and that China tries to exert leverage with Korea cannot be pleasant for the planners in Tokyo. Therefore, Japanese strategists likely noted with relief the announcement of the US administration's intention to continue US military presence in Korea and throughout the region even after the reunification of Korea.[43] Indeed, US commitment to the Far East will greatly contribute to preserve stability in the region.

Taking the difficulties of South Korean–Japanese relations during the last decades into consideration, the fighting, the emotions, the outburst of nationalism, it is not likely that both governments would opt to deepen cooperation in the field of security. Even if the governments of both countries would be willing to do so, it would not be enough. Such a policy would need public support. President Kim Dae Jung and Prime Minister Obuchi were well aware of the animosities in both countries. In order to cope with them, they envisaged in the action plan, which was attached to the Joint Declaration of 8 October 1998, a comprehensive exchange of people from all strata of the two countries.[44]

This noble effort comes late. Reconciliation is essential if both countries finally want to tackle future problems jointly and efficiently. History might be, however, stronger than reason.

---

[40]Green and Cronin pp. 333–345.

[41]Sheila A. Smith, "The Evolution of Military Cooperation in the U.S.–Japan Alliance", in Green and Cronin pp. 86–87.

[42]For a discussion of Japan's options after Korea's unification see Dujarric pp. 39 ff.

[43]The Secretary of Defense, "The United States Security Strategy for the East Asia-Pacific Region 1998", p. 62.

[44]Korea Times, 8 October 1998.

References

Akaha, Tsuneo, "Japanese Security Policy in Post-Cold War Asia", in Kwak and Olsen pp. 9 ff.

Castley, Robert, *Korea's Economic Miracle. The Crucial Role of Japan*, New York 1997.

Green, Michael J. and Patrick M. Cronin, *The U.S.–Japan Alliance. Past, Present, and Future*, New York 1999.

Han, Bae Ho, *Japan as Perceived by Korea and Asian Nations*, typewritten, Seoul 1976 (a copy is in the author's possession).

Hicks, George, *The Comfort Women. Japan's Brutal Regime of Enforced Prostitution in the Second World War* (New York 1995).

Mack, Andrew, *Island Disputes in Northeast Asia*, Working Paper 1997/2, Department of International Relations, The Australian National University.

Tagliaferri, Mariarosaria, "Ungeliebt, doch geduldet-Koreaner in Japan. Testfall fuer Tokyo's Asienpolitik", in *Asien, Deutsche Zeitschrift fuer Politik, Wirtschaft und Kultur*, No. 61, October 1996, pp. 5 ff.

Tidten, Markus, *Pax Japonica in Nordostasien. TEil I: Japans Korea-Trauma*, Stiftung Wissenschaft und Politik (Ebenhausen 1996).

Watanabe, Akio, *Japan and Korea in the Changing World*, typewritten, 1975 (A copy is in the author's possession).

Chapter 20

Northern Policy

The 1988 Olympic Games

Since the International Olympic Committee (IOC) during its session in Baden-Baden (Germany) on 30 September 1981 had awarded Seoul to host the Olympic Games in 1988, Koreans had worked hard to get prepared. It became a goal for all Koreans to demonstrate their progress and their achievements to the world. A large board opposite the city hall indicated the countdown of the last 365 days before the beginning of the Games. When the date, 17 September 1988, approached everything fell into place. Sports stadiums as well as the Olympic village were ready, parks had been built, infrastructure had been improved upon and the city was clean and nicely decorated. The political parties had agreed upon a truce for the duration of the games. The humidity of summer days had given way to a beautifully warm and dry weather with blue skies. A festive mood prevailed in South Korea's capital. Great games followed, and all those who had the good luck to be present, will not forget those days.

The Seoul Olympics were not only great games but the hitherto largest Olympics. Athletes from 160 countries participated. This was quite an achievement because the Moscow Games in 1980 had been boycotted by the West and the Los Angeles Games in 1984 had been boycotted by the Eastern bloc. In Seoul, only Cuba and North Korea were missing.

Originally, it had not been clear that so many countries would participate. From the moment the decision for Seoul had been taken, the organizers were faced with the question as to whether and in what way the other Korea, the

DPRK, would take part in the Games. The IOC wanted to avoid again having a large number of countries boycott the Games. It, therefore, offered that five competitions (archery, table tennis, women's volleyball, 100-km cycling, and qualification rounds for soccer) be held in North Korea. The DPRK's authorities considered this offer as unsatisfactory and demanded to co-host the games. With this demand, they had overbid their cards. Since the decision in Baden-Baden had awarded the Games to the city of Seoul, the South could easily reject the far-reaching demands of the North. North Korea did not co-host the Games, and its athletes did not take part in Seoul. Thus, the 1988 Olympic Games could fulfill the purpose attributed to them by the South to increase the glory and the honor of the Republic of Korea.

For quite some time, it seemed to be an open question as to whether the socialist countries would act in solidarity with North Korea and stay away from the Games. They had, after all, opposed the election of Seoul as the venue for the Games. These doubts proved unjustified. Also, the socialist countries wished to make use of the great spectacle in Seoul to demonstrate their capabilities and achievements. The months and years of preparations brought many representatives of the socialist countries to South Korea and thus into contact with South Koreans. From what they saw, heard and experienced, they got the impression that they could very well cooperate with the South Koreans. At the same time, the media of the socialist countries reported with increasing frequency on the forthcoming Games and the host country. The Games gave South Korea the chance to develop relations with the Soviet Union, China and the Eastern European countries which until then had only supported North Korea. Therefore, it is justified to note that the successful staging of the 1988 Olympic Games enabled South Korea to play a greater role in world politics.

Dynamic Changes

For many years, the lack of relations to the socialist countries was not considered unsatisfactory in Seoul. It was approved as an indispensable part of a concept which recognized only their own government as a legitimate representative of the Korean people and which excluded diplomatic relations with those states which had recognized the DPRK. When the South Korean government started to adapt its policy to the new developments which aimed at easing tensions in the Pacific area and when an improvement of the international standing could not be avoided, the South Korean government had to review its policy towards the socialist countries. It was President Park Chung Hee who left the beaten track. In a foreign policy statement on 23 June 1973, he announced that South Korea would open its doors to all nations of the world on the basis of the principles of reciprocity and equality.[1] He urged those countries whose ideologies and social institutions were different from South Korea's to open their doors to the Republic of Korea. What he had in mind was a so-called cross recognition. While the Soviet Union and China would recognize the Republic of Korea, the United States and Japan would recognize the Democratic People's Republic of Korea. Since President Park's statement, all moves of the Soviet Union, China and other socialist countries towards South Korea were watched closely in Seoul. The expectations that these contacts would develop into substantial relations have proved false, however.

It took until the end of the 1980s to break down the old structures of foreign relations, and it was the Roh Tae Woo administration which succeeded in doing so. In his inaugural speech on 25 February 1988, he stressed the aim of pursuing a northern diplomacy in order to broaden "the channel of international cooperation with the continental countries with which we have had no exchanges".[2] In a Special Declaration on 7 July 1988, he repeated that his government would continue to seek improved relations with the Soviet Union, China and other socialist countries. These steps, he said, would create "an atmosphere conducive to durable peace on the Korean peninsula".[3] So his northern policy was part of his unification policy which he approached in a new way. He demanded that the North and the South should immediately end confrontation, and he developed the concept of "a single national community" of which both the South and the North were members. He elaborated on the same subject in his address to the UN General Assembly on 18 October 1988.[4] Speaking exactly two weeks after the end of the successful Seoul Olympics, he mentioned in a convincing way that the world of confrontation and conflict was giving way to a world of détente and demanded to include the divided

[1]Korea Annual 1974 pp. 341 and 342.

[2]Inaugural Address by President Roh Tae Woo, February 25, 1988, published by KOIS, Seoul.

[3]UN Document S/19999, 8 July 1988.

[4]Korea Annual 1989 pp. 362 ff.

peninsula in that progress. He asked the socialist countries with close ties to the North to maintain these relations but also improve relations with the South. He further invited Seoul's allies to engage Pyongyang in expanding their relations.

In using the term "northern policy", an idea from the foreign policy of the Federal Republic of Germany was borrowed. The German eastern policy (*Ostpolitik*) tried to support the unification of Germany by developing relations with the Eastern European countries and thus creating an atmosphere of understanding and cooperation. Sometimes, the German word *Nordpolitik* is used for South Korea's northern policy.

The northern policy aimed at making the socialist countries interested in establishing and maintaining relations with South Korea and, therefore, in contributing to easing tensions on the peninsula. South Korea was an attractive partner because of its peaceful intentions, its strategic importance and its economic weight. The South Korean government was hoping that the socialist countries would exert a moderating influence in Pyongyang. Even if this hope proved wrong, the recognition of the Republic of Korea by the socialist countries as such would be of great importance, because the country would then enjoy worldwide recognition.

Trade and economics played an important role in South Korean considerations. The markets of the socialist countries were of interest to South Korean private business which was always searching for new markets. For the socialist countries, the Korean market was attractive as well as Korean technology and investment. In order to get organized, South Korean business organizations set up the International Private Economic Council of Korea (IPECK) which was supposed to control business with socialist countries.

Economic relations between South Korea and the socialist countries played, however, in various cases a different role. Sometimes, trade offices were established before mutual diplomatic recognition and became the forerunners of embassies. Trade offices were, for example, established in the spring of 1989 by South Korea in Moscow and by the Soviet Union in Seoul. In the beginning of 1991, trade offices were established by South Korea in Beijing and by China in Seoul. The trade offices had a semiofficial character: the South Korean side was represented by the Korea Trade Promotion Cooperation (KOTRA), the Soviet side by its Chamber of Commerce and Industry and the Chinese side by the China Council for Promotion of International Trade. But what the South Korean government always had in mind was mutual diplomatic recognition.

The northern policy could only be successful because it was introduced during a period when *glasnost* and *perestroika* spread throughout the Eastern European countries and when economic reforms were launched in China. Hungary was the first socialist country which took up diplomatic relations with the Republic of Korea. This happened on 10 February 1988, that is to say, before the collapse of the communist system in Eastern Europe. After that collapse, other Eastern European countries followed: Poland on 11 November 1989; ugoslavia on 27 December 1989; Czechoslovakia on 22 March 1990; Bulgaria on 23 March 1990; Romania on 30 March 1990; and Albania on 22 August 1991. Roh's greatest triumph was the establishment of diplomatic relations with the Soviet Union on 30 September 1990 and with China on 24 August 1992. The international environment and atmosphere had played into his hands, but it was he who had made use of the opportunity in the interest of his country. These achievements of President Roh Tae Woo deserve not to be forgotten.

Roh Tae Woo scored another important victory, the admission of the Republic of Korea to the United Nations on 17 September 1991. For many years, South Korean administrations had worked hard for the simultaneous entry of both Koreas into the UN. During the preparations for the 44th General Assembly in 1989, the South Korean government changed its policy. It insisted on South Korean membership only without opposing North Korean membership. The South argued that South Korea's admission was justified by the principle of universality and would be helpful for establishing peace on the peninsula.[5] These were convincing arguments.

For many years, the North Korean leadership had rejected the admission of both Korean states as separate entities into the UN since arguing that would perpetuate the division of the country. In its first reaction to the new South Korean policy, the North followed its old line. In a statement on 21 August 1989, a spokesman from the Foreign Ministry in Pyongyang repeated that "Korea must enter the United Nations with one nomenclature and one seat after it is reunified through confederation".[6] Nine months later, the North Korean leadership changed its mind. In a speech delivered before the Supreme People's Assembly on 24 May 1990, Kim Il Sung made a concession. If the North and the South join the UN before unification, "they must not hold two separate seats but

[5]UN Document S/20830, 5 September 1989.

[6]UN Document S/20812, 28 August 1989.

enter it jointly as one member in favor of the reunification cause".[7] This totally impractical proposal was rejected by the government of the Republic of Korea.

The admission of a state to membership in the UN requires a recommendation by the Security Council and a final decision by the General Assembly (Art. 4 UN Charter). In the past, the DPRK had been assured that the Soviet Union and China would cast a negative vote in the Security Council thus preventing the necessary recommendation for the General Assembly. But in the beginning of the 90s, the northern policy yielded its first results. North Korea could no longer rely on a negative vote by the Soviet Union against a country with which it had taken up diplomatic relations. Remained China. But North Korea's hope proved wrong. When the Chinese Prime Minister Li Peng returned from a visit to North Korea, a spokesman from the Chinese Foreign Ministry stated that the Prime Minister and his hosts had discussed the question of UN membership of both Koreas and that the Prime Minister had wished that the North and the South would find a way acceptable to both sides.[8] On the reasons why China changed its policy, one can only speculate.[9] Beijing had general misgivings of the veto of the Permanent Members of the Security Council and would have provoked the vast majority of the UN if it had to veto South Korea's UN membership. But more importantly: since China focused on economic development, stability in the neighboring countries was of the essence.

North Korea had difficulties resisting wishes of their big neighbor. The government of the DPRK had, as it stated itself,[10] "no alternative but to enter the United Nations". So on 17 September 1991, both Koreas were admitted to the UN.

Relations with the Big Bear

For many decades, South Koreans had hostile feelings towards the Soviet Union. They considered the Soviets responsible for the division of their country

[7]UN Document S/21315, 29 May 1990.

[8]Xinhua News Agency, 9 May 1991 (via LEXIS-NEXIS); see also FBIS-CHI-91-148, 1 August 1991, referring to Hong Kong sources.

[9]Lee Chae-Jin (1996) p. 121, Samuel S. King, "*The Two Koreas and World Order*", in Young Whan Kihl (1994) pp. 34–36.

[10]UN Document S/22642, 29 May 1991.

and for the Korean War. Their negative feelings had been inflamed by the downing of flight KE 007 over Sachalin. In view of these circumstances, the sudden rapprochement was surprising, but the South Korean government had good reasons, as we have seen.

It was equally surprising that the Soviet Union was taking up official relations with a country it so far had ignored, considering it to be a product of US imperialism and a springboard for the Pentagon.[11] The shift of its Korea policy fits well into the new alignment of the Soviet Union's foreign policy worldwide which substituted confrontation with cooperation. But what were the precise motives for the changes of Soviet policies under Gorbachev towards Korea? It has been asserted that the Soviet government mainly pursued the goal of profiting economically from relations with the newly industrialized country. G. F. Kunadze, a Soviet official, stated bluntly in a paper presented in Seoul in June 1991: "Our choice appeared clear: diplomatic recognition in exchange for economic benefits".[12]

This interpretation is however too one-sided. The Soviet government was very much interested in economic exchanges with the Republic of Korea and even showed a willingness to learn from the South Korea example but it also pursued strategic interests as can be seen from a statement made by Foreign Minister Eduard Shevardnadze immediately after official recognition. He argued that the Republic of Korea could no longer be overlooked in the Soviet efforts to strengthen peace in the Asian-Pacific region.[13] A rapprochement with Seoul would contribute to a relaxation of tensions on the peninsula and might help promote the normalization of relations between Pyongyang, Washington and Tokyo.

Another observation has to be added. For decades, the DPRK had been considered to be an ideological ally. With the democratization of Soviet society, an ideological gap opened up between the two countries. All of a sudden, the South seemed to be ideologically closer to the Soviet Union.[14] And many Soviet citizens who had been won over to the South Korean cause before and during the Olympic Games in Seoul now lobbied in Moscow.

---

[11] Bazhanov 1992 pp. 62 and 64.

[12] Ilpyong J. Kim, "The Soviet Union/Russia and Korea: Dynamics of New Thinking", in Kihl (1994) p. 87.

[13] Bazhanov 1992 pp. 102 and 103.

[14] Bazhanov 1992 p. 99.

The rapprochement between the two countries was promoted during a number of successive summit meetings. President Roh Tae Woo and Secretary General Gorbachev met for the first time on 4 June 1990 in San Francisco when both were guests in the United States. One has never seen a picture of a brighter smile on Roh's face than that of his first meeting with Gorbachev. Roh visited Moscow in mid-December of the same year; Gorbachev came to South Korea in April 1991. The high level contacts were continued after Russia had become the successor of the Soviet Union. President Yeltsin visited Seoul in November 1992; President Kim Young Sam visited Moscow in June 1994.

The improvement of relations also found its expression in the conclusion of a variety of bilateral treaties. Among them was a general one, called the Treaty on Basic Relations between the Republic of Korea and the Russian Federation which was signed by President Roh Tae Woo and President Yeltsin on 19 November 1992.[15] The Treaty stated that the Declaration on General Principles, which was announced on 14 December 1990 during Roh's visit to the Soviet Union, shall continue to govern relations between the two countries.[16] The more specific points of these documents are the following: both countries are committed to making Asia and the Pacific a region of peace and cooperation; for there to be peace in Asia, peace on the Korean peninsula would be important. Russia recognized the aspiration of the Korean people for unification and supported a productive inter-Korean dialogue; both sides would promote economic, scientific and technological cooperation; joint ventures and investments were encouraged; both governments would further promote broad contacts between their nationals and organizations.

These agreements were declarations of good intentions, containing a mix of political and economic issues. For the South Korean government, Russian support for an inter-Korean dialogue and a peaceful settlement of the Korean question was valuable. Even if it turned out that Russia no longer had a strong leverage with the DPRK and could not do much to moderate policies of the North, it was at least assured that Russia was not on the enemy's side. Russia, for the first time in years, made its policy towards Northeast Asia public. The prospects of getting involved in Pacific cooperation, and more so, the prospects of getting support for its ailing economy were attractive to Russia.

[15]Young Whan Kihl (1994), Appendix D, pp. 349 ff.

[16]Korea Annual 1991 pp. 429 ff.

The importance of the economic package was illustrated by the fact that the chief negotiator on the Korean side was the President's senior economic advisor, Kim Chong In. Roh Tae Woo wanted to make sure that the package was brought about quickly so that the Soviet Union would not lose interest in the process of reconciliation. The package signed on 21 January 1991 provided loans in the amount of US $1.5 billion to finance Soviet imports of Korean consumer goods and industrial raw material. It also provided export credits in the amount of US $500 million for the purchase of Korean capital goods and US $1 billion in commercial loans.[17] This was a weighty package and quite a substantial price for diplomatic recognition by the Soviet Union.

The disbursement of the loans was scheduled for a three-year period. The US $1 billion of loans were provided by ten banks, and US $470 million were also granted for the purchase of consumer goods.[18] Difficulties arose, however, because the Russian side was unable to repay the outstanding loans and interests. In May 1992, the South Korean government announced that it would suspend the remaining loans indefinitely. In May 1999, Russia's debt to Korea was allegedly US $1.7 billion.[19] Finding a way out of these difficulties had become the focus of discussions between both governments and also a source of friction. As South Korea got into severe economic difficulties at the end of 1997, it was hit hard by Russia's inability to pay back the loans. Russia repeatedly offered to repay its debts by delivering weapons to South Korea. An agreement was reached on the delivery of Russian military equipment, and at the end of 1996, the first shipments of armored fighting vehicles, tanks, and anti-aircraft missiles from Russia arrived in South Korea. How desperate the situation had become with regards to settling the Russian debts could be taken from the fact that the South Korean government considered accepting Russian submarines as part of their repayment even though South Korea had developed its own submarines based on German technology.[20] The US government was not pleased by the idea that its ally, South Korea, was receiving weapons from Russia. In a public statement on 6 April 1997, US Secretary of Defense Cohen warned the South

[17]Korea Annual 1991 pp. 95 and 96.

[18]Kim Dok Ju pp. 6 and 10.

[19]Korea Times, 12 May 1999.

[20]Korea Times, 4 June 1999.

Korean government about acquiring Russian surface-to-air missiles or SA-12 aircraft.

In November 1992, Russia and the Republic of Korea had agreed upon military exchanges for 1993 and signed a Memorandum of Understanding to this end.[21] A number of agreements on cooperation in the military field followed.[22] Meanwhile, not only officers have exchanged visits but also navy squadrons. In 1997, both countries held a joint naval exercise. Thus, the military exchanges between the Republic of Korea and the Russian Federation have surpassed those between South Korea and Japan, a development which should set planners in Tokyo thinking.

Trade between the Republic of Korea and Russia developed nicely. South Korea sold mostly finished goods and Russia sold raw materials. Exports from South Korea to Russia increased from US $520 million in 1990 to US $1.967 billion in 1996; in the same period, imports from Russia increased from US $370 million to US $1.8 billion. To put the numbers into the right proportions: export to Russia amounted to 1.5% of South Korea's US $129,72 billion exports in 1996.[23] South Korean investments in Russia did not show much progress; they amounted to just US $66 million by 1997.[24] Political and economic instability influenced bilateral economic relations negatively.

There were other developments which dampened South Korea's original enthusiasm about cooperation with Russia. Since Russia's influence in North Korea decreased, Russia could make only insignificant contributions to moderate Pyongyang's policies. The idea that "inter-linked cross relations between the Soviet Union and both Korean states" could bring both Koreas together did not work.[25] This was disappointing for the South Korean government. However, Russia also had reasons to be disappointed. On the nuclear question, it was the US which intervened actively and found a way to solve the crisis. Russia was left out. Russia was also not included in the April 1996 US–South Korea proposal of holding four party's talks (the two Koreas, the USA, China) about Korea's future.

[21] Yonhap News Agency, 21 November 1993 (reported and translated by BBC Summary of World Broadcast, 21 November 1992).

[22] Seung-Ho Joo, "Russia and Korea", in Han and Lee, pp. 97–99; Dujarric P. 105.

[23] Kiheung Kim op. cit. 70.

[24] Kim Dok Ju p. 9.

[25] Alexi D. Bogaturov, "Russian Security Policy in Northeast Asia" in Kwak and Olsen, p. 95.

The First Price

Relations between the Republic of Korea and the People's Republic of China have always been tense. Their armed forces fought each other in the Korean War. Afterwards, the Chinese government supported the policy of North Korea towards South Korea and joined the North in denouncing the policies of the South. South Koreans, however, were well aware that in the long history of Korea's relations to the great neighbor in the North, friendly periods had prevailed.

Unlike the Soviet Union, China is a completely Asian power. To take up diplomatic relations with China would be a culmination of President Roh's northern policy. He, therefore, courted China. In his address to the UN General Assembly on 18 October 1988, he said the following: "I find it significant that China, a nation which traditionally was a good neighbor of Korea, is moving to overcome the wall of separation that has lasted for nearly half a century and is expanding its mutual exchanges and cooperation with the Republic of Korea".[26] The Chinese government remained cool and rejected these attempts.

What China could not influence was the quick growing weight of a stable and prospering South Korea. This development had its bearing on relations between the two countries. Unofficial contacts developed through visits, close cooperation in emergencies and trade. Sports diplomacy was helpful in improving mutual understanding. Chinese teams took part in the 1986 Asian Games and in the 1988 Olympic Games in Seoul; a South Korean team took part in the Asian Games in Beijing in 1990. In 1991 43,200 South Koreans visited China and 44,200 Chinese visited South Korea.[27] Meetings of international organizations in China and South Korea provided the opportunity that even officials could travel to the other country. Close cooperation between Chinese and South Korean government authorities became necessary in two emergencies: in May 1983, a hijacked Chinese aircraft was forced to land in South Korea; in March 1985, a Chinese torpedo boat on which a mutiny had occurred and which was found adrift on the high seas was towed to Kunsan harbor. In both cases, Chinese and South Koreans quickly reached an agreement on how to deal with the problems. Trade was another important factor

[26] Korea Annual 1989 p. 366.

[27] Lee Chae-Jin p. 166.

in bringing both countries into close contacts. Bilateral trade expanded considerably. While the total volume had amounted to only US $280 million in 1981, it had increased to US $5.8 billion in 1991.[28] This progress was made possible by South Korea's economic uprising and China's open-door policy. This policy had been confirmed by Zhao Zijang during the fifth session of the Sixth National People's Congress in March 1987: "We shall open wider to the outside world and explore new possibilities for the effective use of foreign funds, the import of advanced technology and the earning of foreign exchange through export. In this way, our open policy will play a greater role in China's economic development and socialist modernization".[29]

Taken together, these developments suggested that, first of all, economic considerations made China agree to the establishment of diplomatic relations on 24 August 1992. A potent trade partner was living just across the Yellow Sea, and relations would be facilitated if both countries recognized each other. The expectations were not disappointing. Trade between the two countries grew. In 1994, China had a 6.6% share of South Korea's export which rose to 7.3% in 1995.[30] China's share of South Korean imports stood at 5.6% in 1994 and at 6% in 1995. China became a more and more preferred country for South Korean investments which totaled US $1.1 billion by the end of 1994.[31]

The Chinese leadership also took political aspects into consideration. As China was focusing on modernization, a peaceful neighborhood was of the essence. It could not have escaped Chinese planners that North Korea's aggressiveness was outdated and that its hopes to outdo the South had become absurd. By establishing official relations with the South and by increasing exchanges, China could contribute to ease tensions between the hostile cousins primarily because it continued to have some leverage with the North Korean regime. One does not know whether China was also trying to prepare for the possibility of Korea's unification under Southern leadership.[32] In any event, it was very useful for China to be present in the Republic of Korea.

If these considerations were the motives for China's new two-Korea policy, they paid off. China and South Korea exchanged official visitors and discussed

---

[28] Lee Chae-Jin p. 146.

[29] Lee Chae-Jin pp. 148 and 149.

[30] For the statistics, see Korea Annual 1996 pp. 151 ff.

[31] Lee Chae-Jin p. 157.

[32] Kay Moeller p. 41.

important issues. President Roh Tae Woo went to China in September 1992 and President Jiang Zemin came to Seoul in November 1995. Many other visits followed. At the end of 1999, Chinese Prime Minister Zhu Rongji was the only one of the seven members of the Political Bureau of the Chinese Communist Party who had not been to Seoul.[33] China was richly rewarded when it was finally included among the participants of the four-power conference on Korea's future proposed by the US and South Korea in April 1996. In this way, China was assured to be involved in developments on the neighboring peninsula. Relations with China were also meaningful to the South Korean government. It could now ask the only country with some leverage on North Korea to use its moderating influence in Pyongyang. And this influence has been used.

When the Republic of Korea took up diplomatic relations with the People's Republic of China in August 1992, it declared to respect "the Chinese position that there is but one China and Taiwan is part of China". Seoul then severed relations with Taipeh. This move was satisfactory for Beijing because, until that time, the Republic of Korea had been the last Asian country which maintained diplomatic relations with Taiwan. The two sides which felt betrayed by the developments — Taipeh and Pyongyang — took their revenge by entering into contact with each other in 1993 and this annoyed Beijing.[34] Neither Taipeh nor Pyongyang could risk, however, provoking the People's Republic of China.

When Roh Tae Woo delivered his last speech as President of the Republic of Korea before the UN General Assembly on 22 September 1992, he could report that his country and China had normalized relations.[35] He expressed his view that "Northeast Asia has begun to march together towards a new era of lasting peace and common prosperity". He could also inform the Assembly about the success of his Northern policy. During his term of office, which had begun in February 1988, South Korea had taken up diplomatic relations with 39 countries for a total of 165 nations. His northern policy had been a success indeed. Whether the Northern policy would achieve the long-term goal such that the new friends would exert a moderating influence in Pyongyang remains to be seen.

---

[33]Korea Times, 10 December 1999.

[34]Kay Moeller p. 41.

[35]Text in Korea Annual 1993 pp. 396–401.

The Unification Policy of the Republic of Korea

Since the Park Chung Hee era, the Republic of Korea had attempted to include northern countries into its foreign policy. The goal of this policy — whether it was called the northern policy or not — has always been the unification of the country. The unification policy of the Republic of Korea was, however, not successful.

President Park Chung Hee had focused on organizing the coexistence of the two Koreas. His successors had continued that policy. In an address to the National Assembly on 22 January 1982, President Chun Doo Hwan expounded his ideas on how a step-by-step approach could lead to unification.[36] He proposed to organize a Consultative Conference for National Reunification with participants from both sides with the task of drafting a constitution for a unified Korea. The finished draft should then be decided upon through a referendum. If the draft were to be adopted, general elections for a unified legislature and unified government would follow. The transitory period until the foundation of a united Korea will be organized by a provisional Agreement on Basic Relations.

When President Roh Tae Woo developed his concept of a single national community in his declaration on 7 July 1988, which is mentioned above, he suggested to take positive step in order to strengthen the bonds between members of the Korean nation.[37] He listed the following steps: to promote intra-Korean visits; to reunite dispersed families; to improve trade between South and North; to encourage trade between Western countries and the North; to cooperate within the international community; and to encourage cross cooperation between the US, Japan, the North on one side and Russia, China and the South on the other side. On 11 September 1989, President Roh announced a formula for a peaceful and progressively developing unification.[38] A South–North summit would work out a charter by which a Korean Commonwealth would be established as an interim stage. It would be the task of the Commonwealth to draft a constitution for a united Korea and to prepare for general elections. Roh Tae Woo appealed to Pyongyang to guarantee freedom and human rights to North Koreans. Thus, he indicated

---

[36]Korea Annual 1982 pp. 370–372.

[37]UN Document S/19999, 8 July 1988.

[38]Korea Annual 1990 pp. 389–394.

the aim he and all his predecessors had in mind: unity in freedom. This required, as Roh observed, that the North embark "on a path to openness".[39] This was exactly the path which North Korea did not dare to take because it would expose the North Korean citizens to the truth of their comparative misery. The North Korean leadership would not have failed to note that unity in freedom would mean the extension of the Southern system into the North finally.

President Kim Young Sam suggested an approach similar to the one of Roh Tae Woo.[40] He stressed that it made no sense to achieve unification hastily without having gone through a process of reconciliation. He also made it clear that final unification should be based on freedom and democracy. During his term of office (1993–1998), unity and freedom seemed suddenly possible, not as a result of unification policies but as a result of the collapse of the North which seemed to be imminent.[41] President Kim Young Sam had announced that his government would not seek "unilateral unification".[42] But he undermined his credibility by his confrontational course towards the DPRK. His administration even tried to prepare for the collapse of the North.[43]

It was quite a change when Kim Dae Jung in his inaugural address as President on 25 February 1998 declared that South Korea had no intention of undermining and absorbing North Korea.[44] He also said that his government would actively pursue reconciliation and cooperation between the South and the North and proposed to expand economic exchanges on the basis of separating economics from politics. He appealed to the North to participate in the implementation of the Basic Agreement of 1991. He insisted understandably that the South would not tolerate an armed provocation. Later, he added that he would be willing to guarantee the security of North Korea,[45] thus expressing his willingness to tolerate the DPRK's existence. If the North has

[39]Ibidem p. 393.

[40]See his speech on 15 August 1994, Korea Annual 1995 pp. 376–379.

[41]C. S. Eliot Kang, "Korean Unification: A Pandora's Box of Northeast Asia", in *Asian Perspective*, Vol. 20 Fall/Winter 1996, pp. 9–43.

[42]See his speech on 15 August 1996 (FBIS-EAS-96-159).

[43]See the speech by the Foreign Minister Yoo Chong-Ha on 8 October 1997, in: Ministry of Foreign Affairs, Seoul, IRI, Fall 1997, pp. 49–56.

[44]Mimeograph text, dated 25 February 1998 (in the author's possession).

[45]Interview with Serge Berthier in *Asian Affairs*, Summer 1999 No. 8 pp. 9–19.

ever considered striking first in order to prevent absorption by the South, the policy of the new president in Seoul might have convinced the North to give up this plan.[46]

By the end of 1999, the results of the unification policy of President Kim Dae Jung, called the sunshine policy, because it offers North Korea warm sunshine, were modest. The reactivation of the Basic Agreement could not be attained. There have been, however, some cultural and sports exchanges. In June 1999, a joint exhibition of industrial designs took place in Seoul.[47] South Korean entertainers participated in a concert in Pyongyang in December 1999.[48] North and South Korean basketball teams played matches at the end of 1999. But similar occasional exchanges had been held in the past. More significant was the presence of a number of South Koreans in the DPRK, approximately 2,000 by mid 1999. 280 of them worked for KEDO on the construction of two light-water reactors, some were aid workers and businessmen, and most of them were Hyundai employees engaged in the Mount Kumgang project.[49] This is a spectacular project. South Koreans can enter a cruise ship at Tonghae, a port at South Korea's east coast, and travel to Changjon, a port just north of the DMZ. From there, they can visit parts of Mount Kumgang, which is located close to the sea.[50] By the end of 1999, 140,000 South Koreans had made use of that chance.[51] This project was facilitated by the sunshine policy, but it was basically the achievement of Chung Ju Yung, the honorary chairman of the Hyundai group. In talks with Kim Jong Il in October 1998, Chung had gained the exclusive right to develop the Mount Kumgang area for tourism for a price totaling US $900 million.[52] This form of tourism gave South Koreans a chance to travel to the North but no chance to meet North Koreans.[53] The North Korean leadership was happy to enjoy the economic benefits of the South's conciliatory policy, but has tried to keep personal contacts between North and South Koreans as restricted as possible. Kim Dae

[46]On the broader problem, see Victor D. Cha, "Is there Still a Rational North Korean Option for War"? in *Security Dialogue*, Vol. 29 No. 4, 1988, pp. 477–490.

[47]Korea Times, 3 June 1999.

[48]Korea Times, 2 December 1999.

[49]Korea Times, 15 June 1999.

[50]New York Times, 15 February 2000.

[51]Korea Times, 17 November 1999.

[52]Frankfurter Allgemeine Zeitung, 2 November 1998; Korea Times, 25 October 1998.

[53]Korea Times, 17 November 1999.

Jung frankly admitted that he intends "to induce North Korea to change".[54] This is exactly the reason why the North Korean leaders have been reluctant to accept the sunshine policy. They are afraid that it might undermine their system.

References

Bazhanov, Eugene, "Soviet Policy towards South Korea Under Gorbachev", in Il Yung Chung (editor) *Korea and Russia, Towards the 21st Century*, Seoul 1992, pp. 61 ff.

Buszynski, Leszek, "Russia and the Asia-Pacific Region", in *Pacific Affairs*, Vol. 65 No. 4 (Winter 1992–93), pp. 486–509.

Harada, Chikahito, *Russia and North-east Asia*, Adelphi Paper 310, The International Institute for Strategic Studies, London 1997.

Kim, Dok Ju, "Cooperation between Korea and Russia: Today and Tomorrow", in *The Institute of Foreign Affairs and National Security Review* Vol. 5, No. 2 April/June 1997, pp. 1 ff.

Kwak, Tae-Hwan, *In Search of Peace and Unification on the Korean Peninsula*, Seoul 1986.

Joo, Seung Ho, "Russia's Policy Toward the Two Koreas", in Kwak and Olsen pp. 105 ff.

Lee, Chae-Jin, *China and Korea. Dynamic Relations*, Stanford, 1996.

Moeller, Kay, "China and Korea: The Godfather, Part Three", in *Journal of Northeast Asian Studies* Vol. 15 No. 4 (Winter 1996), pp. 35 ff.

Robert A. Scalapino, "The United States and the North Korea Issue: Options for the Future", in Ministry of Foreign Affairs, Seoul, *IRI Review*, Winter 1997 pp. 63–81.

Stackpole, H. C. and Jui Song, "Kim Dae Jung's Sunshine Policy and the Korean Peace Process" in *The Korean Journal of National Unification*, Vol. 7, 1988 pp. 43–58.

Whang, In Joung, "Korea's Northern Policy: A Response to a Changing World Order", in Il Yung Chung (editor), *Korea in a Turbulent World. Challenges of the New International Political Economic Order and Policy Responses*, Seoul 1992, pp. 421 ff.

[54]See interview quoted in note 45.

Chapter 21

North Korea's Foreign Partners

The Soviet Union as Patron

While South Korea was the creation of the USA, North Korea was the creation of the Soviet Union. The withdrawal of Soviet troops from North Korea by the end of 1948 indicated that Moscow considered the new state as stable and reliable. The Soviet Union was willing to support this new member of the socialist camp. When Kim Il Sung wanted to wage war against the South, Stalin's consent was decisive. During the Korean war, Stalin was helpful. The Soviet Union avoided getting directly involved militarily against the US-led UN forces, but provided arms, ammunition, military advisors and sometimes even food to the North.[1] During the war, Kim Il Sung had the great advantage that he could also rely on the other big brother, the People's Republic of China. It was the Chinese who came to his rescue. After the war, both countries continued to support his regime and his goal of unifying Korea under his command.

The pleasant situation of enjoying the support of the two big communist countries became endangered by the rift between them.[2] Already, the first phase of the Sino-Soviet conflict (1956–1961) made Kim Il Sung nervous as was illustrated by the fact that he traveled frequently to the Soviet Union and China. In particular, one of the issues under discussion bothered him, namely the Soviet emphasis on peaceful coexistence with the West because he had no

[1]See Chapter Five above.

[2]I rely on the description by Suh Dae-Sook pp. 176 ff. and Chung Chin O. pp. 27 ff.

inclination to respect the existence of the Republic of Korea. He paid lip service to the Soviet policy of peaceful coexistence, but declared it not applicable in North-South relations. He focused on avoiding siding with one or the other of the feuding giants in order to stay out of the conflict. After Kim Il Sung had returned from Moscow where he had attended the twenty-second congress of the Communist Party of the Soviet Union (CPSU), he delivered a speech before the Central Committee of the KWP on 27 November 1961. He was full of praise for the CPSU and its leadership but insisted on the independence of each communist party. He said: "All fraternal parties are completely equal and independent, and shape their policy independently, proceeding from Marxist-Leninist principles and the concrete conditions of their countries. The fraternal parties should duly learn from each other's experiences the principles of mutual respect, but the question of drawing or not drawing on each other's experiences is a question that should be decided independently by each party in accordance with its own actual conditions and needs".[3] Kim Il Sung was on his way to independence. He succeeded in remaining on friendly terms with both big brothers and even concluded treaties of friendship with both countries in the summer of 1961.

The Treaty of Friendship and Mutual Assistance with the Soviet Union was signed in Moscow on 6 July 1961 by Krushchev and Kim Il Sung. Article 1 paragraph stated: "Should either of the Contracting Parties suffer armed attack by any State and thus find itself in a state of war, the other Contracting Party shall immediately extend military and other assistance with all the means at its disposal".[4] As South Korea was a formal military ally of the United States, North Korea was now a formal military ally of the Soviet Union. The obligation of the Soviet Union towards North Korea was further reaching than that of the US towards South Korea. While the US had made a reservation to come to the South's assistance "in accordance with its constitutional process", the Soviet Union, according to the Treaty, was to become automatically involved in hostilities arising from an attack against the North.

Although this development should have brought the two allies together, disputes between them broke out in 1962 and lasted until the end of 1964. The disputes reached a first peak when, in September 1963, North Korean historians

---

[3] Alexander Dallin (editor), *Diversity in International Communism. A Documentary Record, 1961–1963* (New York and London 1963) pp. 392 and 393.

[4] Text in Byun pp. 249–258.

severely criticized mistakes they had allegedly found in a Soviet publication on Korea's history. A Pravda article ridiculed a Seminar on the Asian Economy which had been held in June 1964 in Pyongyang to which China, but not the Soviet Union, had been invited. The North Koreans hit back in strong language comparing the voice of the Pravda with the Voice of America. After Khrushchev's ouster in October 1964, the North Korean leadership tried to readjust its relations with the Soviet Union. These efforts met with success because the new Soviet leadership tried to reassert its influence on Pyongyang. A flurry of visits followed. It was helpful that Kim Il Sung himself had not come forward with anti-Soviet statements. North Korea had not changed its stance. Though arguing for the unity of the socialist camp, Kim Il Sung moved towards a more independent position by maintaining autonomy and aiming at self-reliance. He claimed that North Korea was an international revolutionary base and spoke in support of liberation movements. He fostered relations with 3rd world countries. Indeed, North Korea was not just a satellite. It criticized the withdrawal of Soviet missiles from Cuba in 1962. It did not join the Council of Economic Mutual Assistance, the organization for economic cooperation of the communist countries. And it did not support the invasion of Afghanistan by the Soviet Union at the end of 1979.

During the 1960s, when foreign assistance lapsed, the North Korean leadership had no chance but to focus on self-sustenance. Since the beginning of 1963, Kim Il Sung took up the subject of *juche* with a renewed intensity. Thus, the *juche* ideology had a function in North Korea's foreign relations; it gave a theoretical foundation for the country's own path.

From the point of view of the Soviet leaders, the ally in Northeast Asia looked somewhat strange. They disliked the personality cult of Kim Il Sung and considered the *juche* ideology a distortion of socialism and even an expression of nationalism.[5] Nevertheless, North Korea belonged to the socialist camp and was a strategic ally against the US. The Soviet Union therefore continued its relatively cool relationship with North Korea. It paid lip service to North Korea's unification policy and continued to disregard the Republic of Korea in the South. It remained the main partner of the North for aid and trade and assisted in the modernization of the Korean People's Army. Even as late as the mid 1980s, the Soviet Union delivered modern military equipment like MIG-23 aircraft, SAM-3 ground-to-air missiles, SCUD's and T-72 tanks to

---

[5]Bashanov and Bashanov p. 1126.

North Korea.[6] Military transfers from the Soviet Union to North Korea were substantial: it is estimated that they amounted to over US $5 billion between 1985 to 1990.[7] However, when Pyongyang moved too closely to Beijing, withdrawal of affection by Moscow followed. In spite of some ups and downs, the Soviet Union continued to be North Korea's main protector.

No New Thinking in Pyongyang

It was again ideological changes in Moscow which caused Kim Il Sung to review his policies. This time, the changes were far-reaching. *Perestroika*, *glasnost* and *novoe myshlenie* — restructuring, openness and new thinking — caused dramatic developments first in the Soviet Union and later in many socialist countries. Democratic ideas spread in Middle and Eastern Europe and created new societies. Communism fell into disrepute. Finally, the communist systems in Europe were overthrown. Germany was reunited and the Soviet Union disintegrated. Mikhail Gorbachev characterized the new approach to international politics as follows: "From the point of view of long-term, big-time politics, no one will be able to subordinate others. That is why only one thing — relations of equality — remains. All of us must realize this. Along with the above said realities of nuclear weapons, ecology, the scientific and technological revolution, and informatics, this also obliges us to respect one another and everybody. Such is our world — complex but not hopeless. We hold the view that everything can be resolved but everyone should rethink his role in this world and behave responsibly".[8]

Some socialist countries outside Europe introduced reforms, but this was not so in North Korea. The North Korean leadership stuck obstinately to the *juche* ideology, to the principle of self-reliance. In a speech before the Plenary of the 8th Supreme People's Congress on 29 December 1986, Kim Il Sung underlined the traditional North Korean beliefs: the pursuit of the working class interests only; the development from cooperative possession to all people's possession; the importance of the ideological, technological and

---

[6] Byun p. 219.

[7] Eberstadt (1999) pp. 35 and 36.

[8] Mikhail Gorbachev, *Perestroika. New Thinking for Our Country and the World* (New York 1987) p. 138.

cultural revolution; and the prevention of revisionist penetration into North Korea.[9]

This reaction to the revolutionary changes in the socialist camp was not surprising. The *juche* ideology had saved Kim Il Sung from getting too deeply involved in the earlier rift between the Soviet Union and China. He may have instinctively tried to use the same instrument in order to stay out of trouble again. The *juche* ideology had meanwhile developed into an elaborate system to which the leadership as well as the people in North Korea had become used to. Therefore, it was obvious that North Koreans would argue that they, thanks to the *juche* system, had already established a perfect system. Furthermore, *juche* had become a sort of belief of North Koreans, which if destroyed could be dangerous, since this could deprive the regime of one of its tools of government. The new openness Gorbachev was advocating was in conflict with the North Koreans' obsession on independence and self-sustenance. There was no real chance that the DPRK could make use of the opportunity of the reform movement in the socialist world to shed ballast.

It was not long till things got worse. On 30 September 1990, the Soviet Union took up diplomatic relations with the Republic of Korea. This was tantamount to a reversal of Soviet policies. By taking up official relations with the DPRK's archenemy, the Soviet Union indicated that it would no longer support the policy of its old friend to unite Korea on Northern terms, that is to say by destroying the existence of the Republic of Korea. It was understandable that the North Korean leadership regarded this act as a betrayal and reacted angrily.[10] Foreign Minister Shevardnadze who had come to Pyongyang in the beginning of September 1990 to explain the decision of his government and the forthcoming establishment of relations with Seoul to the North Korean leadership was treated badly. The North Korean memorandum, which was handed to the Soviet Foreign Minister, was later published by the North Korean media.[11] The North Korean view, in that memorandum expressed, that the Soviet's willingness to establish diplomatic relations with the South was a positive reaction to South Korea's northern policy and that it meant the recognition of two Koreas was correct. The assumption by North Korea that a tripartite alliance had been formed by South Korea, the US and the

[9] Byun p. 188.

[10] Kihl (1991) p. 34 ff.

[11] See Kihl (1991) p. 34.

Soviet Union in order to undermine the North Korean system went much too far. The North Korean reaction showed a sense of urgency and consternation.

The Broken Alliance

The foreign policy of the Russian Federation, the main heir of the Soviet Union, suffered from confusion. Nodong Sinmun, the KWP's newspaper, had already earlier expressed the view that its old ally was "floundering in chaos and confusion in the vortex of perestroika".[12] But only so much could be ascertained: Russia was preoccupied with trying to cope with its internal political, social and economic problems. In order to deal with this development, Russia preferred stability at its Asian borders.

President Boris Yeltsin thus tried to balance powers in the region.[13] Consequently, he agreed with President Roh Tae Woo "that unification should be realized in a peaceful manner through dialogues between the two parties concerned" (Joint Statement of 20 November 1992).[14] Russia also tried to continue cooperation with North Korea, but hopes of a moderating influence by Russia soon vanished. Moscow no longer had substantial leverage with North Korea. This became very clear during the nuclear crisis. Russia made only insignificant contributions towards a solution.

That Russia's influence in the DPRK was fading away had various reasons. As the Communist Party of the Soviet Union had fallen from power, the old party links with the KWP were no longer important. Even more so, the ideological consent which had been upheld in spite of reservations in Moscow and Pyongyang had totally disappeared. Moscow tried, therefore, to focus on state-to-state relations and sent official visitors to Pyongyang in order to maintain influence. It did so without enthusiasm because the détente with the US had weakened North Korea's strategic value. The Russian visitors to Pyongyang did not have much to offer. On the contrary, since the beginning of 1991, North Korea had to pay for imports from Russia in hard currency.[15] Since North Korea was short on hard currency, bilateral trade declined.

---

[12]Kihl (1991) p. 35.

[13]Joo pp. 110 and 111.

[14]Korea Annual 1993 p. 402.

[15]Far Eastern Economic Review, 20 November 1990, p. 30.

The North Korean memorandum published on 19 September 1990 had mentioned that the establishment of diplomatic relations between Moscow and Seoul might negatively affect the North Korean Soviet Friendship Treaty of 1961. Indeed, the clause which obliged Moscow to render automatic assistance to North Korea in case of war on the Korean peninsula no longer made much sense. During his visit to Seoul in November 1992, President Yeltsin announced that this clause would be removed.[16] In February 1993, Russian Deputy Minister Kunadze informed the DPRK government that Moscow would no longer honor that obligation.[17] On 9 February 2000, North Korea and Russia signed a new Friendship Treaty which replaced the old one from 1961.[18] The new treaty did not make the two countries military allies. The conclusion of the Treaty underlined, however, Russia's efforts to re-establish closer ties with the DPRK.

The Other Friend

North Korea's relations with China had a different quality than those with the Soviet Union. This was attributed to practical as well as ideological reasons. Many Chinese had participated together with the North Koreans in the fighting during the Korean war. There was thus a feeling of "comradeship in arms" and a unity "cemented with blood" between the two countries.[19] This common experience had its impact on politics because many Chinese veterans became influential where they reached top positions in the party and in government.[20] With regards to ideology, the North Korean leadership was mostly closer to the orthodox views of the Chinese than to the more flexible views of the Soviets; this was a fact which the North Korean leadership sometimes did not hide.

The last units of the Chinese People's Volunteers left North Korea in 1958, five years after the end of the war. On 11 July 1961, North Korea and China concluded a Treaty of Friendship, Cooperation and Mutual Assistance. Its

[16]Russian Press Digest, 20 November 1992 (Via LEXIS-NEXIS).

[17]The Wall Street Journal, 12 February 1993; Mazarr p. 96 and note 80; Lee Chae-Jin (1998) p. 214 thinks that Russia notified North Korea only in 1995 that the treaty should be abrogated or amended in 1996.

[18]New York Times, 10 February 2000, KCNA, 9 February 2000.

[19]Lee Chae Jin p. 61.

[20]For details see Lee Chae Jin pp. 74–78.

military clause (Art. 2 sentence 2) copied the North Korean–Soviet Treaty, obliging the two partners to automatically assist the other militarily in case of war.[21] A similar clause had been included in the Sino–Soviet Treaty of 1950. Thus, each of the three countries was obliged to assist the other two in case of an armed attack. For China, the DPRK was a strategic ally against the United States and against Japan. For North Korea, China's support for its unification policy was significant.

In a Joint Communiqué issued on 7 April 1970, during the visit of Zhou Enlai to Pyongyang, the following was said: "The Chinese side fully supports the correct policy of the Government of the Democratic People's Republic of Korea for the reunification of the fatherland, the policy of making the US aggressor troops withdraw from South Korea and realizing the reunification of the country by the Koreans themselves independently and free from interference by any foreign force".[22]

The publication of this communiqué, after the meeting of Zhou Enlai and Kim Il Sung, indicated that the clash between both sides was over. It had been a strange dispute.[23] No arguments were exchanged between the leaderships of the countries. Nevertheless, the conflict was so serious that both countries recalled their ambassadors for a number of years. The conflict had been caused by the Cultural Revolution and the Red Guards in China. Since the beginning of 1967, the Red Guards attacked Kim Il Sung by wall posters and articles in journals condemning his luxurious lifestyle and calling him a revisionist. An article circulated by the Red Guards in February 1968 stated that "Kim Il-song is an out-and-out counterrevolutionary revisionist of the Korean revisionist clique, as well as a millionaire, an aristocrat, and a leading bourgeois element in Korea. His house commands a full view of the Moranbong, the Taedong River, and the Pot'ong River .... The estate covers an area of several ten thousand square meters and is surrounded on all sides by high walls. All sides of the estate are dotted with sentry posts. One has to pass through five or six doors before one comes to the courtyard. This really makes one think of the great palaces of emperors in the past".[24] In Marxist history, those politicians

[21] D. C. Watt, *Documents on International Affairs 1961* (London 1965) pp. 258 and 259.

[22] Lee Chae-Jin p. 64.

[23] Suh Dae-Sook (1988) pp. 188 ff.

[24] Robert A. Scalapino and Chong Sik Lee, *Communism in Korea: The Movement* (Berkeley 1972) p. 641.

are called revisionists who try to depart from orthodox Marxism to a socialist policy. So this assertion was a great insult for Kim Il Sung.

China and Korea had border problems. One of the problems concerned the precise border demarcation in the area of the famous Paektusan, Korea's highest mountain reaching 2,744 meters. The mountain is particularly beautiful because there is a lake on top of it, the so-called Heavenly Lake (Chonji). Suh Dae Sook, referring to the fact that in 1969 photographs of Kim Il Sung standing on the top of the mountain were published, thought that the border issue played a role in the Sino-North Korean controversies in the late 1960s.[25] It is not certain whether this was really the case.[26] But it is certain that the North Korean leadership did not make great concessions regarding the boundary along Paektusan because it had made the mountain something like a sacred mountain claiming that Kim Il Sung and his partisans had fought in the area. There is no doubt the top of the mountain is accessible from the south, i.e. from the Korean side, and when climbing up, the visitor passes many revolutionary sites.[27] Since 1970, however, Sino-North Korean relations found their way back to the traditional "militant friendship".

Contacts between North Korea and China were close, and exchanges were frequent. In spite of controversies which flared up now and then, the North Korean leadership tried to make the Chinese support its policies: recognition of the DPRK as the sole legitimate government in Korea and reunification on Northern terms, accompanied by an anti-American and anti-Japanese stance. However, when China reoriented its relations with the major powers, it became obvious that North Korea was the junior partner who had to accept the developments. This became clearly visible when Beijing eased tensions with Washington, Tokyo and later with Moscow. The Nixon visit to Beijing in February 1972 and the establishment of diplomatic relations between China and Japan in September of the same year were great disappointments for North Korea because China could no longer support North Korean aggressiveness against both countries. Since China focused increasingly on economic development, a peaceful environment was essential. China therefore preferred dialogue to confrontation on the Korean peninsula. The normalization of

[25]Suh Dae-Sook (1988) pp. 197–202.

[26]Lee Chae-Jin, pp. 99 and 100, thinks that the issue was solved by secrete negotiations already in 1963.

[27]For an account of such an ascent, see Schaller pp. 132–135.

relations between China and the Soviet Union, which was started with the meeting of Deng Xiaoping and Gorbachev in Beijing in May 1989, deprived the North Korean leadership of the chance to play one "big brother" off against the other. The disappointing events reached their climax when, on 24 August 1992, the People's Republic of China and the Republic of Korea established diplomatic relations. China no longer insisted that its recognition of South Korea was dependent on the recognition of North Korea by the US and Japan. China also no longer considered North Korea the sole legitimate Korean state, but followed a two-Korea policy. This change was facilitated by the fact that the two Koreas had simultaneously been admitted to the UN and had thus become full-fledged members of the international community. The DPRK was the victim of reconciliation. It was close to a disaster to have to lose its last ally.

The Chinese, unlike the Soviets earlier on, tried everything to make their new relationship with South Korea understandable to North Korea. They informed Pyongyang in advance, arguing that the normalization with South Korea would be helpful to stabilize North Korea's position. The North Korean leadership had neither the means to obstruct the Chinese policy nor could it afford to break with its last benefactor.

After having recognized the Republic of Korea, the Chinese leaders continued to foster their ties with the North Korean leaders. The Chinese resumed their ritual exchanges of visits. They played a moderating role during the nuclear crisis. They recognized Kim Jong Il as the new leader after the death of Kim Il Sung and they delivered food to their neighbor. They tried hard to maintain friendly relations with North Korea. This could be seen by the way they handled military ties with the North. They did not formally change the military clause of the 1961 Friendship Treaty with North Korea.[28] Celebrations were even held to mark the anniversaries of the signing of the treaty. The celebrations in Pyongyang on 9 July 1998 for the occasion of the 37th anniversary of the treaty were held on a small scale and without the attendance of high-ranking officials.[29] It was clear to the North Korean leaders that their Chinese friends, focusing on their modernization program which made opening up to the outside world indispensable, had an interest in reducing

[28]See statement of Chinese Ambassador to Seoul on 30 January 1999 (BBC Summary of World Broadcast, 3 Feburary 1999, via LEXIS-NEXIS).

[29]KCNA, 10 July 1998.

military tensions on the peninsula. When a North Korean delegate, Kim Yong Nam, the number two man in Pyongyang, visited Beijing in June 1999, the Chinese President Jiang Zemin stressed that friendly relations between the two countries not only suited wishes and interests of the people, but benefited regional and world peace and stability.[30] Pyongyang also had good reasons to feel assured that policy makers in Beijing would continue to regard neighboring North Korea as a strategic shield which they would not want to lose.

Troubled Relations

The allegedly successful struggle of Kim Il Sung and his partisans against the Japanese is part of North Korean mythology. This story had been a crucial element in supplying legitimacy to the rule of the "great leader". Anti-Japanism was, therefore, considered the most natural policy in North Korea. Japan became the target of never-ending accusations and attacks in North Korea. Thus, the DPRK leadership spread an ideology of victimization. From the Japanese perspective, the DPRK was only of marginal importance. The Japanese government was concerned about the activities of the procommunist Korean residents in Japan. It was also aware of the links between these groups and North Korea as well as their remittances to North Korea. At times, Japan had to have contact with North Korea because the fate of Japanese wives, who had accompanied their Korean husbands when they were repatriated to the DPRK, had to be discussed. In 1997, it was estimated that approximately 1,800 Japanese women married to Korean husbands had left Japan for North Korea between 1959 and 1982.[31] Contact was also necessary when Japanese fishing boats and fishermen were seized by North Korea. The arrest of the captain and the engineer of a Japanese cargo vessel in November 1983 who were later given a 15-year prison sentence had particularly upset public opinion in Japan. Both countries also traded with each other. But, as with other industrialized countries, the DPRK had run up debts with Japan which caused the Japanese government to suspend the export insurance program. In 1997, North Korea exported goods to Japan amounting to 36.5 billion yen. They included textiles and some animal and vegetable products like clams and mushrooms.

[30]The People's Korea, 9 June 1999.

[31]B. C. Koh, "Japan and Korea" in Hahn and Lee (1998) p. 62.

North Korea imported goods from Japan amounting to 21.6 billion yen. Imports were mainly comprised of heavy oil and rice.[32] Japan preferred to focus on relations with the South which it had recognized in the treaty of 1965 as "the only lawful government in Korea". The Japanese government also had to take the South's sensitivities into account whenever the need arose to talk to the North. Regular and normal ties between North Korea and Japan were conspicuous by their absence.

The situation changed only when the end of the Cold War approached and South Korea, in the course of its northern policy, succeeded in improving its relations with the big brothers of North Korea. It seemed advisable that North Korea would compensate for that move by improving its relations with the big brothers of South Korea. It was thought that better relations with Japan might have even produced financial benefits, which the North needed badly. Japan felt encouraged to talk to the North by the Special Declarations made by President Roh Tae Woo on 7 July 1988 in which he offered "to cooperate with North Korea in its efforts to improve relations with countries friendly to us including the United States and Japan".[33]

Interestingly enough, the first meaningful North Korean–Japanese contacts were achieved on the political party level. A delegation of Japan's ruling Liberal Democratic Party (LDP) headed by Shin Kanemaru, and a delegation of the Japan Socialist Party (JSP) headed by Makoto Tanabe, accompanied by government officials and journalists, came to Pyongyang at the end of September 1990 to talk to the KWP about the normalization of relations. The talks were successful and resulted in a Joint Declaration on 28 September 1990.[34] The declaration of the three political parties suggested "a thorough and official apology", compensation not only for the damages suffered during the colonial period but also for losses suffered in the 45 years after the end of the Second World War, and an improvement of the status of Korean residents in Japan. The declaration also contained a clause that acknowledged "that Korea is one". This made the South Koreans suspicious of the Japanese approach. Normalization talks between the two governments followed as the declaration had suggested.[35] Altogether, eight rounds of talks were

[32]The People's Korea, 7 April 1999, based on Japanese custom clearance statistics.
[33]UN Doc. S/19999, dated 8 July 1988.
[34]Asahi Shimbun, 29 September 1990.
[35]Halloran pp. 216 and 217.

held between January 1991 and November 1992, but they failed to achieve the desired results.

The Japanese government was willing to compensate for damages done during the colonial period but only in the form of settling property claims. The North Korean tactic to raise exaggerated claims and to drag out negotiations backfired, since additional controversial issues popped up. In May 1991, evidence seemed to indicate that a Japanese woman (Yayeyo Taguchi), who had been kidnapped in 1978, was living in North Korea under the name of Li Un Hye. Her case had come to light during an investigation of Kim Hyon Hi in South Korea who had taken part in the North Korean terrorist act which destroyed Korean Air 858 in mid-air over Burma on 29 November 1987. The North Korean government rejected Tokyo's request to investigate the fate of Li Un Hye. When North Korean–Japanese negotiations were held, suspicions on Pyongyang's nuclear program arose. The North Koreans rejected the demands of the Japanese negotiators to refute these suspicions. They had underestimated how seriously the Japanese government had taken the non-proliferation issue, a policy based on a broad consent of a people which had been history's only victim of nuclear bombs.

The low level of contacts between North Korea and Japan has lasted for years. Pyongyang returned to its belligerence towards Japan hurling one abuse after the other. In Japan, there was neither consensus on how to proceed with regards to the DPRK nor much interest in making a decision. Japan supported the efforts of establishing the international consortium in charge of providing light-water reactors to North Korea (KEDO). Japan has also helped to overcome severe food shortages in North Korea by delivering grain. But whatever step it took, the Japanese government had to be aware that it would be admonished by Seoul not to proceed too quickly and not without first consulting Seoul. It was neither easy nor encouraging to have to deal with both Koreas.

Other attempts to adjust relations between Japan and North Korea were made in the spring of 1995, and again during a meeting of political parties from both sides. Representatives of the LDP, the SDP (formerly the JPS), the New Party Sakigake and the KWP promised, during a meeting in Pyongyang at the end of March 1995, "active efforts for resolution of the past and for reopening of diplomatic talks".[36] The meeting was followed by government talks; North Korea declared its readiness to allow Japanese wives of North Koreans to visit

[36]Asahi Shimbun, 31 March 1995 (NAPSNet 4 April 1995).

Japan.[37] In March 2000, both governments agreed to open up their talks in April 2000.[38]

The North tried to pressure the Japanese government to take up diplomatic relations by interpreting the two statements of the political parties as an "agreement" which also obliged the Japanese government.[39] On 31 August 1998, the DPRK fired a rocket which crossed over Japanese territory, and landed in the Pacific Ocean. Japan called the rocket a ballistic missile; the DPRK called it a rocket transporting an artificial satellite.[40] Japan felt threatened and froze its relations with North Korea. In a meeting between the Red Cross Societies of both countries in December 1999, North Korea finally agreed to Japanese demands to investigate the fate of the missing Japanese citizens.[41] The Japanese had earlier claimed that these citizens had been kidnapped by North Korea. In December 1999, another Japanese parliamentary delegation, headed by former Prime Minister Murayama, flew to Pyongyang to discuss modalities for the resumption of the normalization talks.[42]

During all these years, the DPRK continued to abuse and warn Japan. A memorandum of a North Korean committee stated, on 1 February 1999, the following: "The Japanese authorities must clearly see the present reality of the DPRK that is turning into a powerful, thriving nation through a leaping progress with vast potentials and must refrain from reckless acts that may lead to their self-destruction".[43] The reality was different: due to their intransigence, the North Korean leaders, rulers of one of the world's least developed countries, had missed many a chance to come to terms with a powerful neighbor. They had good luck that this neighbor reacted altogether with apathy towards them. If North Korea carries its policy of brinkmanship too far, things might become dangerous.

The DPRK's Unification Policy

The main goal of the DPRK has been the unification of Korea on its terms.

---

[37]AP 21 and 23 August 1977 (quoted in NAPSNet 21 and 25 August 1997).

[38]Korea Times, 22 March 2000; KCNA, 22 March 2000.

[39]People's Korea, 31 March 1999.

[40]Summary on NAPSNet 31 August and 1 September 1998.

[41]Joint Statement on DPRK-Japan Red Cross Talks, People's Korea, 22 December 1999.

[42]Korea Times, 1 December 1999.

[43]Peoples' Korea, 3 February 1999.

Strategies, on how to achieve this aim, have been put forward. In a speech on 14 August 1960, Kim Il Sung suggested establishing a Confederation of North and South Korea as a transitory institution. While the political systems in the North and the South would have been retained, a Joint Supreme National Committee would have coordinated the economic and cultural activities of both countries.[44] He varied this plan several times. In an address to the Sixth Congress of the KWP on 10 October 1980, he called the new entity the Democratic Confederate Republic Koryo. This confederation would have had a National Assembly and a Standing Committee which would have made political suggestions for both governments as they remained independent.[45] The confederation would also have had a united army and follow a policy of neutrality. Years later, Kim Il Sung talked about the three principles and the 10-point-program for unification. When he mentioned the three principles of independence, peaceful reunification and great national unity, he was referring to the agreement reached with the South on these principles in the Joint Communiqué of 4 July 1972.[46] In the ten points which Kim Il Sung developed in 1993, he did not talk much about the institutional framework for unification. He spoke of a pan-national unified state "leaving the existing two systems and two governments as they are".[47] This pattern continues to represent the DPRK's suggestions for the country's reunification in the beginning of the 21st century as revealed by the joint New Year editorial of the three important North Korean newspapers on 1 January 2000.[48]

These suggestions were not helpful at all. They were anemic and certainly unacceptable to the South because they started from the assumption of parity of both Koreas and projected, contrary to reality, the North as a democratic state. The North Korean leaders knew that their suggestions were not compatible with those of the South. They, therefore, thought of other methods to achieve unification.

---

[44]Kim Il Sung, *Works, 14, January to December 1960*, Pyongyang 1983, p. 211.

[45]Ministry of National Unification, Republic of Korea, *Peace and Cooperation. White Paper on Korean Unification 1996*, pp. 76 and 77.

[46]For example, in his speech to the 9th Supereme People's Assembly on 24 May 1990 (FBIS-EAS-90-101, 24 May 1990).

[47]KCNA on 7 April 1993 (FBIS-EAS-93-065, 7 April 1993).

[48]KCNA, 1 January 2000, see also Nodong Sinmun, 9 January 2000, quoted by KCNA on 9 January 2000.

What Kim Il Sung originally had in mind, he demonstrated in June 1950: to get control of the whole of Korea by force. As military actions against the South became increasingly futile after 1953, Kim Il Sung went looking for other possibilities to overthrow the South's system. He tried to promote a revolution in the South. This was also in perfect agreement with his revolutionary romanticism. Kim Il Sung elaborated on his ideas about a revolution in the South in a number of speeches. A particularly good insight into his thinking was given in his report on the Conference of the KWP on 5 October 1960.[49] He started saying: "Comrades, the present situation requires the rapid growth of the revolutionary forces and an acceleration of the national liberation democratic revolution by every possible means in south Korea".[50] Since the South was occupied by the US imperialists, it was the main aim of the revolution of the South to drive them out of the country. Therefore, the South Korean people had to wage a struggle to oppose the occupation by the US aggressor troops. At the same time, the landlords, comprador capitalists and reactionary bureaucrats who serve the US aggressors had to be overthrown. He called upon the South Koreans to wage a determined fight against fascist suppression and for democratic rights and freedom. He advocated the expansion of the revolutionary forces "for the decisive hour" under the guidance of a communist party.[51] He further suggested infiltrating the South Korean army. He hoped that the revolutionary movement in the South would progress quickly if the national and class–consciousness of the masses would be raised. The people of the North would do all they could to support the revolutionary struggle in the South.

Kim Il Sung did not just talk about the revolution in the South but tried to take action to promote it. He sent guerrilla units, spies and agents to the South and contacted and encouraged dissidents to take action. A Liaison Bureau was established within the KWP organization to coordinate activities in the South. Even an underground communist party, the Revolutionary Party for Reunification, was promoted by the North. Thus, the North Korean leadership provided good reasons for the South Korean government to maintain its National Security Act; a law which the North energetically demanded an

[49]Kim Il Sung, *Works, 20, November 1965 — December 1996* (Pyongyang 1984) pp. 384–398.

[50]Ibidem p. 384.

[51]Ibidem p. 387.

abolishment of. The North Korean leadership waited "for the decisive hour", but the hour never came.

The aim of fostering a revolution in the South is no longer very prominent in the North Korean propaganda, even though it is mentioned occasionally.[52] The joint New Year editorial on 1 January 2000 was speaking of a "struggle" to implement the unification policy of the DPRK.[53] Sometimes, the term of "a vigorous grand unification march" is used.[54] Is there an air of resignation?

The Hermit Nation

In view of the difficulties for the North to implement its unification policies, the question has to be raised on whether unification is still the main goal of North Korea's foreign policy at the beginning of the 21st century.

The old rhetoric is still upheld. *Nodong Sinmun* reported on 13 October 1999 that "Reunification of Korea is a matter to put an end to the outsider's domination of and interference in South Korea, establish the national sovereignty nationwide, rejoin the severed blood vein of the nation and achieve national unity as a homogeneous nation".[55] But what else could one expect? The leadership has had no choice but to continue its call for unification which is cherished by the people. Sometimes, the statements of the North Korean leadership assume a somewhat liturgical character. Take for example an article of *Nodong Sinmun* on 17 January 2000: "Kim Jong Il's outstanding and tested leadership surely guarantees accomplishment of the cause of national reunification. It is the great fruition of his wise leadership that such a nationwide organization for the reunification movement as the national alliance for the country's reunification was formed and every year pan-national rally is held, stirring up the ardent desire of the entire Korean nation for national reunification. His benevolent politics, all-embracing politics, has infinite attraction and influence which rouse all the Korean people to the movement for national reunification".[56] The article celebrated Kim Jong Il more than it stressed on unification.

---

[52]KCNA, 17 January and 9 February 2000.

[53]KCNA, 1 January 2000.

[54]KCNA, 6 January 2000.

[55]KCNA, 15 October 1999.

[56]KCNA, 18 January 2000.

In view of the political environment which had developed since the late 1980s and around the peninsula, the goal of the socialization of the South is unrealistic.[57] The DPRK is in deep economic trouble which forced its government to appeal for support to the outside world. It is not likely that a country which suffers from all sorts of shortages, food and fuel included, can uphold the battle readiness of its military forces. North Korea no longer has close friends. Both Russia and China focus on their own economic progress and are interested in peaceful developments on the neighboring Korean peninsula. South Korea, on the other hand, is economically strong, and has the world's biggest military power, the United States, as an ally, and also enjoys a close, though not trouble-free relationship with Japan. In such a situation, the idea of seizing the South is more than unrealistic. It is absurd. However, some governments even pursue absurd policies.

Also in the 1990s, the DPRK has made threatening gestures: the thinly veiled threat during the nuclear crisis; the "sea of fire" threat in March 1994; the intrusion of North Korean soldiers into the DMZ in April 1996; the firing of a rocket over Japan in August 1998; and the intrusion of north Korean naval ships into disputed waters off South Korea's northwestern coast in September 1999. These aggressive acts were unsuited to foster the aim of unification. This was also true of a threat to use nuclear weapons — if there was one. It did not make sense to expose the territory one wants to acquire to the awful power of weapons of mass destruction. It seemed more plausible that these acts were meant for domestic consumption and/or were intended to profit from the international instability they created.

In order to prepare the ground for the unification of Korea on its terms, the DPRK government had always insisted on the withdrawal of US troops from the peninsula. It knew from the experience of the Korean War that it had no chance to extend its system to the South as long as US forces were present. Since 1991, there have been a number of indications that the DPRK might accept the presence of US troops in Korea if their status be redefined. North Korea has suggested classifying them as a "peacekeeping force".[58] This suggests that the DPRK leadership may no longer have expansionist aims, and may accept the status quo. In that case, North Korea would no longer

[57]Eberstadt (1999) p. 40.

[58]Selig S. Harrison, "As North Korea Liberalizes Sanctions Should Be Eased," in *Survival*, Vol. 38, no. 4, Winter 1996/97, pp. 39 and 40; Korea Times, 7 and 15 April 1999.

be called a predator state.[59] But this is not for sure: the traditional anti-American rhetoric continues.[60] The Four Power Talks provide an excellent chance to find out the North's true intentions, particularly on whether it sees the status quo as an acceptable and even profitable alternative.

So, what is the main aim of the policy of the present DPRK leadership if it is not unification? As the country's situation has become precarious — its economy in shambles, the generous support by Russia and China gone, and the "great leader" dead — there is nothing but one central aim left, the survival of the system. The various foreign policy maneuvers can be interpreted as attempts to support this central aim.[61] Activities which are relevant to relations with the outside world are explained to the North Korean public as great successes with the intention to further the leadership's prestige. The North Korean public was informed about the missile firing which was supposed to have transported a satellite into orbit on 31 August 1998 only a couple of days after the incident and just before the beginning of the session of the 10th Supreme People's Assembly. KCNA, the North Korean press agency, informed the public that the launch had been successful and was broadcasting melodies of revolutionary hymns. The report concluded: "The successful launch of the first artificial satellite in the DPRK greatly encourages the Korean people in the effort to build the powerful socialist state under the wise leadership of General Secretary Kim Jong Il".[62]

At the beginning of 2000, there were some indications that the DPRK government was trying to improve its links with foreign countries.[63] North Korea took up diplomatic relations with Italy, resumed normalization talks with Japan, and contacted the governments of Australia, Canada, Germany, the Philippines, and the United Kingdom. One does not know whether these efforts indicate a real change of North Korea's diplomacy.[64] One has to be afraid that the leaders of the DPRK will see to it that the North Korean

---

[59]See Michael J. Mazarr, "Predator States and War: The North Korean Case", in Tong Whan Park pp. 75–95.

[60]See for example KCNA, 21 and 26 January 2000.

[61]Hyung Kook Kim pp. 71 and 72; Byeonggil Ahn po. 84.

[62]KCNA, 5 September 1998.

[63]International Herald Tribune, 18 March 2000; AFP, 5 April 2000; Asia Today (Australia), April 2000 (via LEXIS-NEXIS); Korea Times, 2 April 2000.

[64]More optimistic Rinmin Ribao, 21 March 2000, monitored by BBC Summary of World Broadcasts, 22 March 2000 (via LEXIS-NEXIS).

people will not be exposed to too much influence from outside because they wish to maintain their rule over the people's minds. It is therefore too early to bid farewell to the Hermit Kingdom in the north of the Korean peninsula.

References

Ahn, Byeounggil, "Constraints and Objectives of North Korean Foreign Policy. A Rational Actor Analysis", in Henriksen and Mo pp. 82–92.

Bashanov, Eugene and Bashanov, Natasha, "Soviet Views on North Korea. The Domestic Scene and Foreign Policy", in *Asian Survey*, Vol. XXXI, No. 12, December 1991 pp. 1123–1138.

Byun, Dae Ho, *North Korea's Foreign Policy. The Juche Ideology and the Challenge of Gorbachev's New Thinking*, Seoul 1991.

Chung, Chin O., *Pyongyang Between Peking and Moscow: North Korea's Involvement in the Sino-Soviet Dispute*, 1958–1975, Alabama 1978.

Garrett, Bauming and Glaser, Boumi, "Looking Across the Yalu: Chinese Assessments of North Korea", in: *Asian Survey* Vol. XXXV, No. 6, June 1995, pp. 528–545.

Halloran, Richard, "North Korean Relations with Japan", in Suh and Lee (1998) pp. 211–229.

Joo, Seung Ho, "Russia's Policy Toward the Two Koreas", in Kwak and Olsen pp. 110 and 111.

Lee Chae Jin, "China and North Korea: An Uncertain Relationship", in Suh and Lee (1998) pp. 193–209.

Kihl, Young Whan, "North Korea's Foreign Relations: Diplomacy of Promotive Adoption", in *Journal of Northeast Asian Studies*, Vol. 10 (Fall 1991) pp. 30–45.

Kim Hong Nack, "Japan and North Korea: Normalization Talks Between Pyongyang and Tokyo", in Kihl (1994) pp. 111–129.

Him Hyung Kook, "North Korean Foreign Policy", in *Korea and World Affairs*, Vol. 23 No. 1 Spring 1999, pp. 71–94.

Kim, Ilpyong J., "The Soviet Union/Russia and Korea: Dynamics of 'New Thinking'", in Young Whan Kihl, *Korea and the World. Beyond the Cold War*, Boulder 1994.

Satashi, Morimoto, "Confronting the North Korean Threat", in *Japanecho*, February 1999, pp. 25–29.

Yoshida, Yasuhiko, "Pyongyang Airborne Threat to Improve Diplomatic Ties", in *Japan Quarterly*, January–March 1999, pp. 10–16.

Chapter 22

Nuclear Dangers and Beyond

The Setting

Three countries maintained and continue to maintain military forces on the Korean peninsula: the Republic of Korea, the Democratic People's Republic of Korea and the USA. It is for sure that the US forces in Korea had nuclear weapons at their disposal for many years and that the US government threatened North Korea at various times to make use of them if the need arose.

In 1957, the Eisenhower administration decided (NSC Document 5702/2) to deploy nuclear weapons to South Korea. Nuclear warheads for artillery and for Honest John missiles arrived on the peninsula, later warheads for long range missiles, atomic demolition mines and gravity bombs followed. The peak of nuclear armament was reached in 1972 when 763 nuclear warheads were at the disposal of US troops in South Korea.[1] In later years, the number of nuclear warheads was reduced. The introduction of nuclear weapons on the peninsula was a severe violation of the Armistice Agreement which barred both sides from deploying new types of weapons on the peninsula. The US government considered this move necessary to be able to oppose a possible North Korean attack successfully and envisaged in its strategy an early use of nuclear weapons if necessary.

The readiness of the Americans to use all military means at their disposal in case of a North Korean attack was made clear by succeeding US administrations.[2] To give some examples: the Eisenhower administration used

[1]Oberdorfer pp. 257 and 450, quoting the research of William Arkin.

[2]Cummings p. 477.

the nuclear threat in an attempt to speed up the armistice negotiations in 1953. In 1975, Secretary of Defense James Schlesinger talked of the US nuclear weapons in South Korea and threatened to use them if necessary.[3] When President Clinton came to Panmunjom on 10 July 1993, he declared that in the event that North Koreans would use nuclear weapons "it would be the end of their country".[4] Those who were often and publicly threatened with the use of nuclear weapons on the Korean peninsula were the North Koreans. It is important to keep this fact in mind since later developments seemed to suggest that the North Koreans were the only ones playing with nuclear threats on the peninsula.

When the Soviet Union collapsed, the Bush administration announced its intention to remove all tactical nuclear weapons abroad, hoping the Soviet Union would do the same. President Bush decided to withdraw all nuclear warheads left in Korea. In prior discussions of this move, it had become evident that in view of the progress in military technology, it was no longer necessary to station nuclear warheads in Korea in order to maintain the nuclear umbrella over the ally. The Bush administration succeeded in convincing the South Korean government of the wisdom of this step and left it to President Roh Tae Woo to announce the new development which fitted well into North-South negotiations to make Korea free of nuclear weapons. On 18 December 1991, President Roh Tae Woo stated: "As I speak, there do not exist any nuclear weapons whatsoever, anywhere in the Republic of Korea".[5] In the eyes of the North Korean leadership, this was important progress but it would not have escaped their attention that even though American nuclear weapons were no longer stationed on Korean soil, the American nuclear umbrella protecting South Korea continued to exist.

It would have been surprising if the South Koreans, propelled by their "can do" spirit, had not tried to acquire nuclear weapon capability. They also had good reasons to do so at a moment when the US decisively reduced its military presence in South Korea by withdrawing the 7th US division in 1970, because the US left doubts in its ally's mind about its readiness to defend South Korea. President Park Chung Hee took the initiative that Korea should go nuclear. The considerations centered on establishing a reprocessing plant, a

---

[3]St. Louis Post-Dispatch, 21 June 1975.

[4]Oberdorfer p. 288.

[5]Korea Annual 1992 p. 395.

plant in which used fuel rods undergo a chemical process by which plutonium is extracted and then can serve as fuel for nuclear weapons. As there was no chance to cooperate with the non-proliferation conscious US government, the South Koreans turned to France. The US government, shocked by India's nuclear test in 1974, took a closer look at developments in South Korea and found enough evidence to try to discourage the South Korean government from continuing its efforts in building nuclear weapon capability.[6] The big stick, the threat that the security partnership might be endangered, had to be wielded. In 1976, Park Chung Hee finally gave in. Americans and South Koreans succeeded very well in keeping the negotiations a secret. The efforts of President Park Chung Hee to acquire nuclear weapons capability became better known to the Korean public when his daughter Park Keun Hae confirmed them publicly in 1989.[7]

It was neither the American nuclear weapons in Korea, nor the South Korean attempts to achieve nuclear weapon capability which caused great excitement, but the modest and largely undefined North Korean nuclear efforts. This happened in the beginning of the nineties. The developments gave the DPRK a prominent position in international politics, but they came also rather close — we are told — to a second Korean war.[8] The place of the drama was Yongbyon, a little town 60 miles north of Pyongyang, where North Korea had concentrated its nuclear activities.

North Korea had started these activities with a small experimental reactor provided by the Soviet Union in the sixties. In the eighties, North Korea built its own and also a larger reactor of approximately 5 MWe.[9] It tried to add two more reactors, one of 50 and another of 200 MWe capacity. The experimental reactor had been placed under the control of the International Atomic Energy Agency (IAEA) in 1977. On 12 December 1985, the DPRK joined the Non-Proliferation Treaty (NPT); the necessary safeguards agreement, however, was concluded much later on 30 January 1992 and only under international pressure. With the IAEA, there was an additional player on the field demanding to carry out not only the inspections provided for in the NPT, but also special inspections of suspicious facilities. No legal international instrument furnished

[6]Oberdorfer pp. 68 ff.; see also Los Angeles Times, 4 November 1978, and International Herald Tribune, 6 October 1995.

[7]Korea Post, December 1998 p. 50.

[8]Cummings p. 465 and 484; Oberdorfer pp. 311 ff.

[9]International Herald Tribune, 7 May 1992; Sigal pp. 20 ff.

a basis for such a demand. Nevertheless, the IAEA, which had made public secret attempts of Iraq to go nuclear in the post Gulf War period, felt justified to follow this course.[10] There seemed to be suspicious facilities in Yongbyon. The government of the DPRK denied that it tried to achieve nuclear weapon capability. Kim Il Sung stated on 20 February 1992: "As for us, as already manifested, we possess no nuclear arms, and we neither plan nor feel the need to produce them. We cannot afford a nuclear confrontation with the surrounding big powers. We can never imagine that we would develop atomic bombs that could annihilate our brethren".[11]

Growing Suspicion

There was no access to Yongbyon, so the United States had to rely on what it saw from the sky. Its satellite photographs showed a large building which experts thought could be used as a reprocessing plant, with the North Koreans calling it a "radiochemical laboratory".[12] If it was a reprocessing plant, North Korea could produce plutonium which is the fuel for nuclear weapons. As in the case of South Korea, it was the possible access to plutonium which caused alarm. The US government started to spread the news of its discovery in the first half of 1989. In November 1990, a Japanese weekly published an American satellite picture of Yongbyon.[13]

The banning of reprocessing was an issue of the South-North negotiations in 1991 which produced good results; besides the Agreement on Reconciliation, Non-Aggression and Exchanges and Co-operation between the South and the North of 13 December 1991, and a Joint Declaration on the Denuclearisation of the Korean Peninsula of 31 December 1991 banning the possession of nuclear reprocessing facilities had also been reached.

The USA had facilitated the negotiations by canceling the Team Spirit exercise for 1992 and by agreeing to bilateral talks with representatives of the North Korean government, thus meeting old Northern demands. Due to the division within the administration, the American negotiator Arnold Kanter

---

[10]International Herald Tribune, 2 and 11 February 1992.

[11]Korea Annual 1992 p. 399.

[12]International Herald Tribune, 7 May 1992.

[13]Shu kang bun shun, 29 November 1990.

received much too narrow instructions; he was not permitted to agree to a continuation of the talks or even to mention the possible normalization of relations.[14] Nevertheless, the North Korean government promised to sign the safeguards agreement with the IAEA.

The atmosphere of understanding made it possible that the Director General of the IAEA and his team were shown installations in Yongbyon, including the so-called "radiochemical laboratory" which turned out to be indeed a reprocessing plant.[15] One of the IAEA experts called it "extremely primitive" and far from ready to produce the quantity of plutonium needed for nuclear weapons.[16] In the mood of cooperation, the North Koreans even presented their guests a small quantity of plutonium which they had earlier admitted to having produced. Things seemed to be developing in the right direction.

Suspicion, however, re-emerged quickly, suspicion that North Korea had produced more plutonium than it had admitted to. Samples which the IAEA-experts had taken in Yongbyon seemed to point in that direction. The American satellite photography discovered two sites at Yongbyon which were considered to be nuclear waste facilities. In November 1992, the IAEA sought to inspect these sites, hoping that they would give a hint to whether North Korea had produced more plutonium. The agency's request was rejected by the North Korean government.

The whole atmosphere had deteriorated; South Korea and the US had contributed to this development. On 6 October 1992, the ANSP arrested 62 people charging them with being North Korean spies.[17] This made the implementation of the South-North agreements of the previous year more difficult. On 8 October 1992, the American Secretary of Defense and the Korean Defense Minister indicated that in the absence of significant improvements in the South-North dialogue, a Team Spirit exercise might be held in 1993.[18] A decision to that effect was confirmed by President Clinton on 26 January 1993. The announcement was perhaps thought to have exerted pressure on the North Korean government. What was overlooked, however, was the fact that the renunciation of the Team Spirit exercise in 1992 had meant much to North

[14]Oberdorfer pp. 266 and 267.

[15]International Herald Tribune, 2 November 1992.

[16]Oberdorfer p. 269 and notes on p. 450.

[17]Korea Annual 1993 p. 17.

[18]Federal New Service, Defense Department Briefing, 8 October 1992 (via LEXIS-NEXIS).

Korea. One has no difficulty in agreeing with the US Ambassador to South Korea, Donald Gregg, who considered this decision to hold the Team Spirit exercise in 1993 a big mistake.[19] The North Korean government became even more upset when the US presented a number of their satellite photographs of Yongbyon to an IAEA Board meeting on 22 February 1993 in Vienna in order to justify the agency's demand of special inspections.[20]

The North Koreans had been difficult, stubborn and obstinate before. They had boycotted the newly established South-North Military Commission, for example, which was supposed to meet on 12 November 1992. They did not give in to the pressure. They did not permit the inspection of the two suspected nuclear waste sites. And they demonstrated that the crisis, which was already bad enough, could be worsened. On 8 March 1993, the day before Team Spirit 1993 started, North Korea issued a war alert. On 12 March 1993, it announced its withdrawal from the NPT.

This move seemed to confirm suspicions that North Korea had something to hide, and that it had already acquired nuclear weapon capability. The real question in everybody's mind was whether the North Koreans had a nuclear bomb already and if so, how dangerous was it. The main discussions about these irritating questions were held in the United States. The US, one of the five nuclear powers, as a country committed to nuclear non-proliferation and as South Korea's godfather felt obligated to step in. The tone for the discussions was set by CIA-Director Gates when in February 1992, he told Congress that North Korea was not far away from having a bomb.[21] It was an easy exercise to find followers for a view suspecting the DPRK of having evil intentions. North Korea was a largely unknown country which had been involved in international terrorism, and had murdered many people, among them eleven high-ranking South Korean government officials at the Martyrs' Mausoleum in Rangoon in 1983 and all people aboard a Korean aircraft which was destroyed in mid-air in 1987.

In November 1993, the administration's intelligence community presented a "National Intelligence Estimate" to President Clinton. Some of the findings of the estimate were quickly leaked to the press.[22] On 26 December 1993, the New

---

[19] Quoted in Oberdorfer p. 273.

[20] Washington Post, 27 April 1993.

[21] Sigal pp. 40 and 41; International Herald Tribune, 7 May 1992.

[22] International Herald Tribune, 4/5 December 1993.

York Times revealed details of the document. Its main assertion was that there was a "better than even" chance that North Korea already had a bomb. This was the formula which was going to dominate future discussion. The document also suggested that American efforts to stop the North Korean nuclear program through negotiations or economic sanctions would barely have a chance to succeed. There was one dissenting voice, that of the State Department, which argued that North Korea could not have produced enough plutonium needed for a bomb. Some officials termed the finding of the study a "worst case" conclusion.

Negotiations

The US government had reacted considerately to the North Korean announcements of a war alert and withdrawal from the NPT in March 1993. It had engaged the DPRK government in direct talks, an action which had been taboo for a long time, but which was now of the essence if a severe conflict, possibly a military one, were to be avoided. In the first meetings between Assistant Secretary of State Robert L. Gallucci and Deputy Foreign Minister Kang Sok Ju in June 1993 in New York, a principal agreement reached was to find a peaceful solution to the conflict.[23] The second round of talks followed quickly; the delegations of both countries got together in July 1993 in Geneva. This time the North Korean negotiator, Kang Sok Ju, made an interesting proposal.[24] As it was the intention of his government to produce energy and not nuclear weapons, it would be willing to shift its nuclear program to less proliferation-prone light-water reactors (LWRs) if these could be provided by the international community. This proposal contained the key elements for a solution of the crisis; it met, however, a lukewarm reaction at that time. The US delegation promised "to support the introduction of LWRs and to explore with the DPRK ways in which the LWRs could be obtained".[25] The Americans were focusing on allowing for an IAEA inspection of the two nuclear waste sites at Yongbyon which the North Koreans continued to reject. The Clinton

[23]See the Joint Statement of the DPRK and the USA of 11 June 1993 in Sigal p. 260.

[24]Oberdorfer pp. 289 ff.

[25]Agreed Statement between the USA and the DPRK of 19 July 1993 in Sigal pp. 260 and 261.

administration had, however, succeeded in convincing the North Koreans to suspend their withdrawal from the NPT.

The US-North Korean dialogue continued into the second half of 1993 and the beginning of 1994. The talks were held on a working level only, but envisaged far-reaching changes in bilateral relations.[26] The North Koreans were supposed to agree to remain in the NPT, to accept IAEA inspections, even "special inspections", and to renew the dialogue with the South. The Americans were to end the Team Spirit exercises as well as economic sanctions and to agree to convene the third round of official talks. Even the diplomatic recognition of North Korea was mentioned as a trade-off. However, once again at the end of 1993, the atmosphere deteriorated as it had done a year ago. Again, all sides concerned contributed to the deterioration.

President Kim Young Sam made use of his visit to Washington in November 1993 to intervene as he thought the American concessions were going too far. The IAEA was allowed to send inspectors to Yongbyon in March 1994, but they were blocked from taking critical samples.[27] In the US, there was talk about possible military intervention. In a North-South meeting in Panmunjom on 19 March 1994, a North Korean official declared: "If a war breaks out, Seoul will be a sea of fire".[28] The remark was not only fanatical and reckless, but also politically dangerous as it played into the hands of the hawks in Seoul and Washington.

A Former President Steps In

During all those years, the critical question had been whether North Korea possessed enough plutonium to manufacture a nuclear device. The events can be described as a plutonium crisis. The first crisis was caused when the reprocessing plant was discovered; the second when nuclear waste sites seemed to be suited to reveal whether more plutonium had been produced than North Korea had acknowledged; the third plutonium crisis followed on 19 April 1994 when the North Korean government announced that it would unload the main reactor. The defueling would provide the opportunity to extract plutonium from the spent rods.

---

[26] New York Times, 21 November 1993.

[27] International Herald Tribune, 16 March 1994.

[28] International Herald Tribune, 3 May 1994.

The North Korean government allowed IAEA inspectors to monitor the unloading which started on 8 May 1994. They however prevented the inspectors from taking samples which could disclose whether plutonium had been discharged in the past. Without being allowed to complete their work, the inspectors left.[29] It seemed that for all sides, a sort of a self-imposed *casus belli* was approaching. The IAEA reported to the Security Council that verification was impossible. President Kim Young Sam had said on 13 May 1994 that North Korea's nuclear development should and could be stopped.[30] The US government had made it clear that it was not going to tolerate North Korea extracting plutonium from the unloaded rods and that it would therefore call for economic sanctions. North Korea made it clear that it would regard sanctions as an act of war, and Foreign Minister Kim Yong Nam threatened the South Korean leaders by declaring in Kiev on 10 June 1994: "They should remember that if they blindly follow the policies of the United States as to sanctions and finally start a war, then in the end South Korea will be devastated".[31]

In this situation, the USA and the Republic of Korea had to make special efforts. It is not surprising that they wanted at least to be prepared for a war if it broke out. The US military war plan was overhauled in February 1994 providing not just for the defense of South Korea but for a counter-offensive aimed at Pyongyang.[32] Additional US weapons were sent to South Korea, including Patriot anti-missile systems, Apache helicopters, tanks, armored carriers, and radar systems.[33] The US government, however, hesitated overdoing a military build-up fearing to provoke a pre-emptive strike by North Korea. A number of years later, Kim Young Sam claimed that he had advocated a policy of restraint. In an interview with the daily Chung Ang Ilbo, given on 3 July 1999, he stated that he had told President Clinton in a telephone call that he would not despatch even a single South Korean soldier to the frontline as long as he remained President.[34] In the US, voices advocating the preparation for war became stronger. On 15 June 1994, the Washington Post suggested destroying the reprocessing plant by military means.[35] At the beginning of June 1994,

[29]New York Times, 29 May 1994.

[30]New York Times, 13 May 1994.

[31]International Herald Tribune, 10 June 1994.

[32]International Herald Tribune, 7 February 1997; New York Times, 6 February 1994.

[33]Oberdorfer p. 313.

[34]Chung Ang Ilbo, 13 July 1999.

[35]See also W. Safire in International Herald Tribune, 10 June 1994.

the administration did not see any possibility to continue negotiations with North Korea.

It took the initiative and the courage of a former US president to find a way out of the deadlock.[36] In the beginning of June 1994, Jimmy Carter decided that he would make use of a North Korean invitation. Washington approved the trip. For quite some time, the administration had felt the need for direct high level contacts with the North Korean leadership. It happened that the visit was well-timed. On 3 June 1994, Pyongyang had publicly ventured on the idea to dismantle the "radio-chemical laboratory" in the event LWRs were provided. That subject had been raised on 9 June 1994 by an American scholar, Selig Harrison, in a talk with President Kim Il Sung who had agreed to the idea of freezing the present nuclear program in exchange for a firm US commitment on the delivery of LWRs.[37] Then, on 16 June 1999 Kim Il Sung met Jimmy Carter, the most prominent US representative who had ever gone to Pyongyang and who had the support of the US government for his mission. This time, it was the Korean host who suggested the deal of dismantling the existing reactors and returning to the NPT in exchange for the supply of LWRs. Carter asked Kim Il Sung, as had been suggested by the State Department, to freeze the North Korean nuclear program until the third round of US-North Korean negotiations and allow the IAEA inspectors to stay in Yongbyon even though North Korea had withdrawn from the IAEA. Kim Il Sung agreed. This understanding did not contain elements which were unknown, but the fact that the understanding was sanctioned by Kim Il Sung himself made the difference. Carter was correct in considering this understanding a breakthrough and a great success. In a live interview with CNN from Pyongyang, Carter informed the public of the agreement reached and urged that the third round of talks be convened quickly. By doing so, he successfully nailed down the results of his talks in Pyongyang, not to the pleasure of the US administration which felt as if it was being outdone by the former president. President Kim Young Sam and the South Korean government had been less than enthusiastic over the Carter visit to North Korea. They remembered Carter's attempts as US president to withdraw the US troops from South Korea. But their view changed

---

[36]The Carter Center, *Carter Center News*, Fall 1994 "*Cater Trip Paves the Way the U.S. — North Korean Pact*" (www.cartercenter.org/CCNEWS/CCN-F94/korea.html).

[37]Selig Harrison, "The North Korean Nuclear Crisis: From Stalemate to Breakthrough", in *Arms Control Today*, Vol. 24, November 1994, pp. 18–22.

when Carter, on his return from Pyongyang, could inform the South Korean president that Kim Il Sung was ready for a summit meeting.

The crisis was over. The preparations for war could be called off by all parties involved. Pressure had not worked, and economic sanctions would probably not have worked either, as the North Korean government was not of the type which could be scared easily. What was successful was the establishment of a channel of negotiations between the USA and the DPRK. The Clinton administration had started the negotiations with Korea but had lost its way. Carter rediscovered the track. Now, it was up to the US government to honor Carter's promises.

Back to Diplomacy

The famous third round of negotiations which had been interrupted by the death of Kim Il Sung on 8 July 1994 finally got underway on 5 August 1994 in Geneva. The negotiations proceeded well although an intervention by Kim Young Sam had to be warded off, and resulted finally in the Agreed Framework of 21 October 1994.[38] This treaty provided for the following:

- the freezing and later dismantling of the present nuclear facilities of the DPRK, monitored by the IAEA,
- the delivery of heavy oil to offset the energy forgone due to the freezing on the North Korean present nuclear facilities,
- an international consortium organized by the US to finance and supply LWRs to North Korea,
- a move toward full normalization of political and economic relations,
- cooperation for peace and security on a nuclear-free Korean peninsula, and cooperation to strengthen nuclear non-proliferation.

The next decisive step to implement the Agreement was the establishment of the consortium constituted of the USA, the Republic of Korea and Japan, called the Korean Peninsula Energy Development Organization (KEDO). Later, KEDO was joined by the European Union and various other countries

[38]Text in Sigal pp. 262 ff.; see also Foreign Press Center Briefing by Ambassador Robert Gallucci on 19 October 1994, in Publication of the Foreign Ministry of the Republic of Korea No. 42, 21 October 1994.

including Canada, Australia, and New Zealand. Additional countries such as Germany and the United Kingdom declared to participate in the financing. Further negotiations were needed to fix the details. They were held between North Korea and the US; but as South Korea was supposed to carry the largest part of the burden — US $3.22 billion of a total US $4.6 — the US had to pay regard to the interests of the ally.[39] Finally, a compromise was reached and on 15 December 1995, an agreement was concluded between KEDO and the DPRK. Article 1 § 1 of this agreement stipulated[40]: "KEDO shall provide the LWR project, consisting of two pressurized light-water reactor (LWR) units with two coolant loops and a generating capacity of approximately 1,000 MW (e) each, to the DPRK on turnkey basis. The reactor model, selected by KEDO, will be the advanced version of US-origin design and technology currently under production". The South Korean state run Korean Electric Power Corporation (KEPCO) became the main contractor for the project; a formal agreement was signed on 14 December 1999.[41] Intra-Korean difficulties and tensions, particularly the intrusion of a North Korean submarine into South Korean waters in September 1996, delayed the beginning of the construction of the LWRs. In August 1997, the construction work finally got underway in Simpo.[42]

As far as is known, North Korea has complied with the provisions of the Agreed Framework.[43] It has frozen its graphite-moderated reactors and the related facilities and allowed IAEA inspectors to monitor the freeze. The United States, however, has had difficulties to fulfill its obligations under the Agreed Framework and has fallen behind with the deliveries of heavy oil.

How High the Risk?

Already on 14 and 26 November 1991, the Chicago Tribune had called for a pre-emptive strike on Yongbyon. Similar demands followed in a US media campaign in which the North Koreans figured as natural villains. The question

[39]Dong-A Ilbo, 23 April 1999 (translated in FBIS-EAS-1999-0423).

[40]Text in my possession.

[41]Korea Times, 15 December 1999.

[42]G. Kemmerling, "Grundzüge und Tendenzen der sü dkoreanischen Außenpolitik 1997/1998", in *Korea 1997*, Institiut für Asienkunde, Hamburg 1998, pp. 169 ff.

[43]Mitchell Reiss, "Three Myths Affecting U.S. Policy Towards the DPRK and Congress' Role", PacNet 14, 7 April 2000.

remains to whether these demands had any political justification — not to mention a justification under international law. One could have only argued in favor of a military intervention if it was safe to assume that North Korea had a bomb and was going to make use of it. The claim during the crisis was that there was a better than even chance that they had the bomb. Does this assumption hold?

On 24 June 1994, the Russian daily Isvestia published a document dated 22 February 1990 allegedly originating from the KGB which said: "According to available data, the development of the first nuclear explosive device had been completed at the DPRK nuclear research center in the town of Yongbyon".[44] The document did not indicate on which data the assessment had been based upon, and its assertion ran counter to what high government officials, like Foreign Minister Kosyrev, were saying at the time when the Isvestia brought the story. Thus, no additional insight is gained.

After Hwang Jang Yop, the Secretary for International Affairs of the North Korean Workers Party, had defected to Seoul in 1997, he confirmed what he had said earlier namely that the North could annihilate the South with nuclear and chemical weapons.[45] South Korea's intelligence sources argued that Hwang Jang Yop did not have any real knowledge of the North's nuclear program but was drawing conclusions from well-known developments. So, we are back to the "better than even" formula.

This formula was an estimate, not a fact.[46] The calculation was based on the quantity of plutonium which North Korea might have extracted from the spent fuel rods. Nobody knew the exact quantity; therefore, calculations had to be made. The guess was that North Korea had extracted 12 to 13 kg of plutonium. If it was correct that 10-kg plutonium was needed for a nuclear device, then the quantity would have been sufficient for one atomic bomb. A later analysis made for the Department of Defense projected only 7 to 8 kg in North Korea's possession. With the benefit of hindsight, we have to note that it was doubtful whether in 1993, North Korea had enough plutonium available to build a bomb. The spent rods unloaded in early summer 1994, however, would have given North Korea the chance to extract enough plutonium for 5

[44]International Herald Tribune, 25/26 June 1994.

[45]Educational Foundation for Nuclear Science, Bulletin of the Atomic Sciences Vol. 53 No. 4 pp. 48 ff.

[46]For details Sigal pp. 90 ff.; Albright pp. 3–6.

to 6 bombs.[47] This was prevented by the American intervention and by the Framework Agreement.

The suspicion, however, that the DPRK had not totally sacrificed its indigenous nuclear weapon program did not die down, neither in South Korea, the United States, or in the international community. North Korea was suspected of continuing its program underground. At the end of 1998, the US discovered underground works near Kumchang-ri (25 miles northwest of Yongbyon) which seemed to be nuclear related.[48] On 17 March 1999, an agreement was reached between the DPRK and the USA which allowed the USA to inspect that underground site.[49] In May 1999, when an American delegation visited the site, it found a huge empty tunnel.[50] We can only hope that this was a symbolic revelation, but we cannot be sure. The dangers from nuclear threats emanating from North Korea were overstated in 1993 and 1994, but vigilance is called for. North Korea could contribute to a peaceful development by allowing more transparency.

Melting Enmity

At the beginning of the 1990s, the relationship between the USA and the DPRK underwent a dramatic change. For more than forty years, it had been characterized by enmity. The US had supported the claim of the South to be the sole legitimate government on Korean soil and had maintained troops in the South to deter an aggression from the North. Official ties between both countries did not exist. The US prevented trade with North Korea by imposing economic sanctions. The first sanctions, based on the Export Control Act, the Trading with the Enemy Act and the Trade Agreement Extension Act, were announced at the beginning of the Korean War. Other sanctions followed over the years.[51] The North Korean leadership considered the US to be truly responsible for Korea's division and its maintenance. The South was viewed as a US colony; the South Korean government a puppet regime established by the US imperialists. The main target of the revolution, which the North Korean

[47]Sigal p. 113.

[48]The National Journal, 5 December 1998; The Economist, 12 December 1998; Jane's Defense weekly, 27 January 1999.

[49]New York Times, 17 March 1999; Korea Times 17 March 1999.

[50]New York Times, 28 May 1999.

[51]See the overview in Eberstadt (1999) p. 87.

leaders expected to occur in the South and which they tried to foster, was "the US imperialist forces of aggression".[52] But, at the beginning of the 1990s, both countries had got in contact with each of them engaging the other.

The US had chosen an approach by small steps. In 1984, US diplomats were authorized to engage in small talk with North Korean diplomats when they met at social functions.[53] This "smile diplomacy" was advanced in October 1988 when US diplomats were allowed to hold more substantive discussions with DPRK diplomats.[54] And then a formal channel for talks was set up, the so-called Beijing channel: American and North Korean diplomats met at the International Club in Beijing and exchanged papers. This type of communication was rather strange and did not allow for any negotiations. Real negotiations were only taken up, as was already explained, when the nuclear crisis made them necessary. The US government hoped that direct talks might help to diffuse the crisis. The North Korean rulers found it attractive to enter into negotiations with the power decisive for a solution of the Korean question and they might have hoped for economic benefits. Whether they aimed at selling off their nuclear capabilities from the very beginning or whether they grasped a chance which presented itself during the talks can be left open. In any event, North Korea used the situation skillfully and gained considerable American concessions. It seemed somewhat strange that the US now had commitments to a country which it had held in disregard for so many years. Therefore, many objections were raised against this policy. Sometimes, even calling it appeasement.[55] But the US policy was successful in avoiding a war and in guiding a maverick state into the international community. The US stuck to its policy of deterrence, but supplemented it with diplomacy. There was one side effect: US–North Korea relations gained a touch of formality. Since 20 September 1995, Sweden has been protecting US consular interest in North Korea.[56]

[52]Kim Il Sung in his speech on 5 October 1966 before the conference of the KWP, in Kim Il Sung, *Works Volume 20, November 1965–December 1966* (Pyongyang 1984) p. 384. This speech is a good example of the North Korean attitude towards the US.

[53]Quinones p. 105.

[54]Department of State Bulletin, January 1989, p. 17.

[55]Fred Ikle, "U.S. Folly May Start Another Korean War", Wall Street Journal 12 October 1998.

[56]Tradeport, Democratic People's Republic of Korea (North Korea), Background Notes (www.tradeport.org/ts/countires/nkorea/bnotes).

The bilateral talks continued and soon focused on a new North Korean threat, that of missiles. For many years, North Korea has been known for manufacturing and selling short-range missiles of the Soviet SCUD type.[57] It was also known that the DPRK was developing medium-range missiles, the Nodong and the Taepodong. The firing of a missile over Japan on 31 August 1998 made it clear that the DPRK's missile technology had made progress. Although the missile failed to launch a satellite, concerns increased that the DPRK might be close to developing a missile of intercontinental range.[58] In the talks with the US, North Korea insisted that the US should lift its economic sanctions and pay compensation in return for halting missile exports.[59] At the end of May 1999, the President's coordinator for US policy towards North Korea, former Secretary of Defense William Perry, traveled to Pyongyang. He met Kim Yong Nam and had substantial discussions with Vice Foreign Minister Kang Sok Ju. He offered them a deal.[60] If North Korea suspended its nuclear weapon and missile program as well as halted the sale of their missiles, their components and their technology, then the US, Japan and South Korea would offer various economic and political benefits in return, among them a gradual lifting of economic sanctions. North Korea reacted to this policy of comprehensive engagement by its usual brinkmanship. In the beginning of July 1999, it spread the news that it was ready to fire a longer range missile,[61] indicating however on 18 August 1999 that it was prepared to negotiate.[62] The negotiations held in Berlin resulted in yet another deal.[63] On 17 September 1999, the US government announced a partial lifting of sanctions allowing North Korea to buy consumer goods in the US and to transport cargo and passengers back and

[57]For details Kay Moeller, "Das nordkoreanische Raketenprogramm: Ueberlebenspoker, Teil III" in *SWP — aktuell*, No. 23/September 1998.

[58]See the speech of Robert D. Walpole, National Intelligence Officer for Strategic and Nuclear Programs, on 8 December 1998, (http://www.cia.gov./cia/publicaffairs/speeches/walpole-speech-120898.html); for a more cautious assessment of the North Korean missile capabilities, see FAS, Nuclear Forces Guide (www.fas.org/nuke/guide/dprk/facility/nodong.htm), update 16 January 2000.

[59]Korea Times, 29 March 1999.

[60]New York Times, 27 May and 2 June 1999; Korea Times, 16 September 1999.

[61]New York Times, 4 July 1999; Frankfurter Allgemeine Zeitung 5 July 1999; International Herald Tribune, 12 and 23 July, 12 August 1999.

[62]KCNA 18 August 1999; International herald Tribune, 19 August 1999.

[63]New York Times, 14 September 1999.

forth from the US, and allowing US citizens and companies to transfer funds to invest in North Korea.[64] The DPRK government publicly stated on 24 September 1999 that it would refrain from further missile tests while talks were underway.[65]

The pattern by which the missile crisis was managed followed the one which developed during the nuclear crisis. North Korea made threatening gestures, negotiations got underway, North Korea raised the stakes, and finally a compromise was found by which the threats were reduced in return for compensation. This time, the North Korean negotiators were in a position to draw on the experience they had gathered during the nuclear crisis. They succeeded in receiving a sort of ransom for lessening bad behavior. This is exactly the aspect which drew criticism in the US Congress. The American side had, however, good reasons to be content with the result. The relaxation of the economic sanctions did not cost the US anything. The US government had taken part in delivering food-aid to hunger-stricken North Korea. How much of the sum spent on food-aid can be put into the equation is doubtful because it was humanitarian aid. This type of aid is given, above all, to alleviate the life of suffering people and often irrespective of the people's government. It is the aim of the US policy to make the DPRK join the Missile Technology Control Regime which forbids developing, deploying and exporting missiles with a range of over 300 km.[66] The agreement reached in September 1999 can be a first step in that direction.

One final observation: The engagement policy of the United States towards the DPRK is planned for the long term. This became obvious when the Agreed Framework was concluded in 1994. This policy was outlined in detail in the Perry Report, published in October 1999. In the event of compliance with the agreements and good behavior by the DPRK, the US would be willing to gradually improve ties and finally take up diplomatic relations with this country.[67] In other words, the US administration accepts the peaceful coexistence of both Korean states. Although the Perry Report tells us the contrary, its findings imply that the US accepts the *status quo* on the

[64]New York Times, 18 September 1999.

[65]KCNA, 24 September 1999; New York Times, 25 September 1999.

[66]Korea Times, 30 November 1999, quoting W. Perry.

[67]Dr. William J. Perry, "Review of United States Policy Toward North Korea: Findings and Recommendations", Unclassified Report, 12 October 1999 (www.state.gov/www/regions/eap991012_northkorea_rpt.html).

peninsula, at least for some time to come, and expects minimal changes at best. Also the other three great Pacific powers, China, Russia and Japan, will feel at ease with the situation as it is because the uncertainties which would be caused by the unification of Korea are put off. Seoul seems to be in line with this thinking. As Kim Dae Jung himself has said, it is the aim of the sunshine policy to give North Korea "a breathing space".[68] This constellation will be welcomed in Pyongyang because it gives the regime a chance to try to muddle through.

References

Albright, David, "North Korea and the "worst-case" scare-nario", in *The Bulletin of the Atomic Scientist*, Vol. 50, No. 1, January/February 1994, pp. 3–6.

Cossa, Ralph A., *The U.S. — DPRK Agreed Framework: Is it Still Viable? Is it Enough?* (http://www.csis.org/pacfor/opusdprk.pdf) April 1999.

Henriksen, Thomas H., "North Korea's Two Kims and American Foreign Policy", in Henriksen and Mo pp. 151–172.

Lee, Chae-Jin, "The United States and Korea: Dynamics of Changing Relations", in Khil (1994) pp. 69–82.

Mazarr, Michael J., *North Korea and the Bomb. A Case Study in Nonproliferation*, New York 1995.

Moeller, Kai and Zeh, Thomas, *Neue Koreapolitik der USA vor altem Dilemma*, Stiftung Wissenschaft und Politik, Ebenhausen Juni 1999.

Sigal, Leon V., *Disarming Strangers. Nuclear Diplomacy wit North Korea*, Princeton 1998.

Quinones, C. Kermeth, "North Korea: From Containment to Engagement", in Suh and Lee pp. 101–119.

[68]See the interview sited in Ch. 20 note 45.

PART VI

South–North Relations

Chapter 23

Confrontation and Dialogue

The Hostile Cousins

After the end of the Korean War, each of the two Koreas tried to find ways and means to extend their systems to the other side. Both governments understood themselves as the only legitimate representative of the Korean people. They called each other puppets and traitors and followed a course of confrontation which was only occasionally interrupted by dialogue. The hostility between the two Koreas, which lasts till today, is illustrated by their enormous efforts in the military field. Both countries maintain a huge military.[1]

In 1999, the armed forces of the Republic of Korea amounted to 672,000 men (army 560,000, navy 60,000, air force 52,000). They had modern equipment: 2,130 battle tanks, 2,500 armored personnel carriers, 4,696 field artillery tubes, 143 combatants and 14 submarines, 488 combat aircraft and missiles of various kinds.

In 1998, the armed forces of the Democratic People's Republic of Korea amounted to 1,054,000 men (army 923,000, navy 46,000, air force 85,000). They had large equipment: 3,500 battle tanks, 2,500 armored personnel carriers, 10,600 artillery tubes, 424 combatants, 26 submarines, 607 combat air craft and a variety of missiles.

It was surprising that South Korea, a developing country until the 1980s, could build up and sustain such strong forces. It was however even more surprising that North Korea, still a developing country with a population of

[1]The figures are taken from: *The Military Balance 1998/1999*, The International Institute for Strategic Studies, London 1998 pp. 185–188.

only 25 million, could create such a large force. The North Korean forces and their equipment even outnumbered the South Korean military. But the quantitative superiority did not mean too much.[2] The equipment of the North Korean forces would become, by and by, outdated and would not be replaced by modern armament as the country lacked the financial resources and access to modern technology abroad. Food and fuel shortages would also take their toll although one can assume that the armed forces received preferential treatment.[3] South Korea today has very modern equipment and can afford to keep it updated. It also has access to the arms markets, particularly to those in the US. Furthermore, it has the world's largest military power, the USA, as an ally which displayed its might in Desert Storm. Experts have concluded that the North still holds a sort of terrorist threat against the South, particularly against Seoul, but has no "plausible invasion capacity".[4]

The two hostile cousins are armed to the teeth, but have not waged war against each other again. The Demilitarized Zone (DMZ), put into place by the Armistice Agreement of 27 July 1953, has kept both sides apart. When it was established, both sides had to withdraw 2 kilometers from the Demarcation Line (DML). The DMZ was supposed to be a buffer zone. It cannot be compared to the former intra-German border: The region of the DMZ is far more militarized than the intra-German border ever was, and the division created by the DMZ is far more radical. There is no traffic across the DMZ; nearly no trade, and no communication system is in place. Mutual contacts occur only in the Joint Security Area at Panmunjom.

Incidents

Incidents, however, could not be prevented by the DMZ.[5] Gun battles in the DMZ, activities of agents and guerrilla units on the neighbor's territory, amphibious infiltration attempts, seizures of fishing boats, violations of air space, and firing at and hijacking of air crafts, clashes in the Joint Security Area were only some of the violations of the Armistice Agreement which the UN

[2] Edward A. Olsen, "The Conventional Military Strength of North Korea: Implications for Inter-Korean Security", in Suh and Lee pp. 148–152.

[3] The Seattle Times, 27 September 1997.

[4] Almeida and O'Hanlon p. 60.

[5] UN Document A/8026; Korea Herald 28 August 1976.

Commission for Unification and Reconstruction of Korea (UNCURK) registered in its annual reports until it was disbanded in 1973. These incidents cost many people their lives. In 1967 and 1968, when North Korea intensified its subversive activities, UNCURK registered 899 killed persons. South Korean activities in the northern direction also occurred, and the Southern side admitted to approximately 100 cases in which it had violated the Armistice Agreement.

The incidents reached one of their many peaks in 1968. On 21 January 1968, a group of North Korean soldiers in plain clothes came close to the Blue House before they were met by the police. 28 commandos died in shootouts with the South Korean security agents in the following days; two commandos could not be found. The only surviving North Korean soldier testified that the group was charged with the mission to kill President Park Chung Hee.

Only two days later, on 23 January 1968, North Korean patrol crafts seized the *Pueblo*, a US electronic intelligence vessel with 83 men on board, and brought it forcibly to Wonsan harbor. North Korea asserted that the *Pueblo* had intruded into the country's coastal waters. The negotiations in Panmunjom were held directly between the Americans and the North Koreans, although under the auspices of the Military Armistice Commission. This was the first time the US government dealt directly with the DPRK; an emergency made it imperative. The South Korean government viewed these contacts with suspicion. The North Korean side used the opportunity to abuse the Americans. The US side proceeded cautiously taking into account the strain of the war in Vietnam. The talks dragged out. Finally, the US side had to sign a document in which it apologized "for the grave acts of espionage committed by the US ship against the Democratic People's Republic of Korea after having intruded into the territorial waters of the Democratic People's Republic of Korea".[6] Before signing this document, the US negotiator orally repudiated its contents. One has to agree with Secretary of State Dean Rusk who called this a "strange procedure".[7] On 23 December 1978, the 82 surviving crewmembers returned via the "Bridge of No Return" in Panmunjom.

Unrest on the peninsula increased when it became known that North Korea had dug tunnels underneath and beyond the Demarcation Line.[8] One

[6]Downs p. 144.

[7]Downs p. 145.

[8]Korea Overseas Information Service, *Undermining Peace. The Fourth Infiltration Tunnel.* Seoul 1990.

hesitated to believe the news when the South Korean government claimed that the tunnels were part of an underground system intended for quick infiltration of forces and equipment behind the first line of defense of the South in case of a *blitzkrieg*. Any doubts which one might have had were dispelled when it turned out that intelligence obtained from satellite images had shown the Americans that the North Koreans were digging tunnels. In November 1974, the first tunnel northeast of Panmunjom was discovered; a second one was found in the central sector of Chorwon in March 1975; they found a third one south of Panmunjom in October 1978; and in March 1990, a fourth one was discovered in the eastern sector. A country which digs underground tunnels into another country does not have peaceful intentions.

A particularly frightening incident was caused by the North Koreans on 18 August 1976. When a work party of the United Nations Command (UNC) had started to trim a popular tree in the vicinity of the "Bridge of No Return" in the Joint Security Area, it was attacked by North Korean soldiers who killed two American security officers with axes.[9] UNC put its forces on increased readiness alert, additional US air force squadrons were deployed to Korea, and US navy vessels, among them the carrier USS *Midway*, were heading towards Korean waters. The North ordered its forces into full combat readiness. On 21 August 1976, in a message addressed to the Commander-in-Chief of the UNC, Kim Il Sung termed the incident "regretful".[10] As this statement came close to an apology, tensions were eased. Since that event, incidents in that area decreased. The meetings of the Military Armistice Commission continued to provide the opportunity to discuss violations of the Armistice Agreement, and these discussions contributed to reducing tensions.

Surprisingly, the DPRK retained its rude and belligerent behavior even after the Agreed Framework had been concluded in Geneva on 21 October 1994 which made North Korea, to a certain degree, dependent on the goodwill of the US, South Korea and Japan. When an unarmed US helicopter flew unintentionally into North Korean airspace and close to the DMZ on 17 December 1994, it was shot down and one crewmember was killed. The other crewmember was captured and released only two weeks after the US side had expressed "sincere regret".[11]

---

[9]UN War Allies Association Inc., *Axe-wielding Murder at Panmunjom*, Seoul 1976.

[10]Downs p. 155.

[11]Downs p. 262.

In the fall of 1996, a North Korean submarine landed infiltrators on the South Korean East coast near Kangnung. A number of them were hunted across South Korea. Shootouts ensued and five South Korean soldiers and four civilians were killed. Out of the approximately 25 North Korean commandos involved, one was captured alive, the others committed suicide or were killed. On 29 December 1996, the DPRK's Ministry of Foreign Affairs expressed "deep regret" for the incident.[12]

In June 1999, during a period of intense efforts of talks and reconciliation by the governments of South Korea and the US towards the North, a serious military clash occurred.[13] North Korean patrol boats had accompanied fishing vessels in crab-rich fishing grounds situated south of a line which was considered by South Korea as the demarcation line in the Yellow Sea, called the Northern Limit Line. The South Korean navy sent vessels into the area. North Korean warships continued to sail in and out of the disputed zone. First, the South Korean vessels just rammed the North Korean vessels. On 15 June 1999, ships from both sides exchanged gunfire sinking one North Korean vessel. In the days after the clash, the ships of both sides did not cross the controversial line, and tensions died down.

Expanding the Theater of Conflict

The rigor of their controversies made them extend their fighting to other countries. In the summer of 1967, 17 Koreans, among them the composer Lee Sang Yun, who lived in the Federal Republic of Germany, were kidnapped by the KCIA and forcibly brought to South Korea.[14] While six of them were soon released, eleven were indicted for espionage. They were accused of maintaining contacts with the North Korean Embassy in East Berlin, accepting propaganda pamphlets and money, giving information to the North Koreans, and traveling to North Korea. The South Korean courts passed severe sentences for the accused. The incident caused a serious German-South Korean conflict. Immediately after the kidnapping became known, the Federal Government had protested against the violation of German sovereignty, had requested to

---

[12]Downs p. 264.

[13]New York Times, 12 June 1999; Korea Times 13, 14, 15, 17 June 1999.

[14]Paul Frank, *Entschluesselte Botschaft. Ein Diplomat macht Inventur*, 2nd edition, 1982, pp. 223–247.

recall the three members of the South Korean Embassy in Bonn involved in the incident, and had demanded to return the 17 Koreans to Germany. The German government succeeded in getting all kidnapped Koreans released. For quite some time, the incident left the Federal Republic of Germany with bad feelings.

North Korea outdid South Korea because it staged terrorist attacks abroad. When the North, on 9 October 1983, tried to murder President Chun Doo Hwan in Rangoon, they instead killed eleven high-ranking South Korean officials. Four years later, North Korea proved that it was correctly classified as a terrorist country. On 29 November 1987, a South Korean passenger aircraft, KE 858, on its way from Baghdad via Bangkok to Seoul exploded in midair killing all 115 on board.[15] The explosion was caused by two time bombs which had been planted in an overhead compartment by two North Korean agents. The two agents, Kim Sung Il, an elderly man, and Kim Hyon Hee, a young woman, left the plane in Abu Dhabi and continued their journey to Bahrain posing as Japanese tourists. In Bahrain, it was detected that they traveled with forged Japanese passports and they were interrogated by the Bahrain authorities at the suggestion of South Korea. Kim Sung Il committed suicide by taking poison. Kim Hyon Hee was arrested and handed to South Korean authorities. Her confession, together with the findings of the investigation, revealed the precise course of events as well as the fact that the two terrorists were agents of the North Korean security agencies. It had been the aim of their mission, Kim Hyon Hee said, to discredit Seoul as a venue for the 1988 Olympic Games. So, the North Korean leadership had implemented what it called "a combat mission beyond the front lines".[16] In reality it was a hideous terrorist crime, illustrating how far the North Korean leadership was willing to go.

For many years, the General Assembly of the United Nations was one of the arenas used for discussing the controversies between the two Koreas. The UN had become closely involved in Korea's fate. It was one of the godfathers of

---

[15]kukhanchon kihoikpu (National Agency for Security Planning), *taehan hangkong 858 ki pokpilsakon susa kyolkwa* (*The Explosion of Korean Air 858, Results of the Investigation*), Seoul 1988; Ministry of Foreign Affairs, *Briefing on the Findings of Investigation on the Destruction of Korean Air Flight 858*, January 15, 1988.

[16]Quote from the text of the oath, Kim Hyon Hee had to make before her departure; see Agency for National Security Planning, 28 December 1987, *A Statement by Kim Hyong Hee On the Bombing of Korean Air Flight KE-858.*

the Republic of Korea who even waged war on the peninsula later. Therefore, the UN bodies were natural arenas for debates about Korea's future. The South tried to gather support for its formula that a united, independent and democratic Korea was to be established. Later, the North found increasing consent for its policy, to keep the UN's involvement in Korea on a lower level. Since both Koreas became UN members in September 1991, they enjoyed the possibilities offered to member states of the world organization.

The Joint Communiqué of 1972

The quarrels and fights between the two Koreas were occasionally interrupted by a dialogue. As contacts between the two feuding countries were so exceptional that when they occurred, they were considered sensational and were accompanied by high expectations. Two stages stand out as they resulted in agreements about joint efforts towards unification. On 4 July 1972, a Joint Communiqué was published and a Basic Agreement was signed on 13 December 1991. In both cases, the two Korean states had tried to adjust their policies to the thaw surrounding the peninsula.

The first round of talks started with a meeting of representatives from the Red Cross Societies of both countries on 20 August 1971 in Panmunjom. The aim was to alleviate the fate of the many families separated by the Korean War. It took many months to agree on an agenda for a Red Cross conference. The agenda, adopted on 16 June 1972, provided that both sides would discuss on how to trace the whereabouts of members of dispersed families, how to facilitate correspondences and visits and, finally, how to reunite them.[17]

The preliminary talks had offered a good chance to sound out the possibility of contacts on a political level. In November 1971, the North Korean side indicated its readiness for political talks. Contacts were established through secret visits of high government officials. The South was represented by no one other than Lee Hu Rak, Director of the KCIA, who traveled in May 1972 to Pyongyang where he met Kim Il Sung. The North was represented by Kim Young Joo, brother of Kim Il Sung and Director of the Organization and Guidance Department of the KWP, and by Park Sung Chul, Second Vice Prime Minister. The latter visited Seoul from 29 May to 1 June 1972 and was

[17]See the Agreed Minutes of 30 August 1972, in Kim Se-Jin (1976) p. 321.

received by President Park Chung Hee. On 4 July 1972, South and North Korea surprised the world by publishing a Joint Communiqué simultaneously in Seoul and Pyongyang which informed the public about the contacts and announced efforts to unite the country.[18] Unification, the communiqué said, should be achieved through independent efforts and by peaceful means. A great national unity should be sought transcending ideological differences. Both sides went even further. They agreed to prevent military incidents and to install a direct telephone line between the capitals. In order to promote peaceful efforts, they established a South-North Coordination Committee.

For one year, from the summer of 1992 to the summer of 1993, negotiations were held on both levels, within the Red Cross Conference and the South-North Coordination Committee. As the meetings were held alternatively in Seoul and Pyongyang, the two Korean capitals enjoyed the rare spectacle of welcoming visitors from the other side of the DMZ. Temporarily, the "Bridge of No Return" was transformed into a "Bridge of Contact". The negotiations, however, did not justify the high expectations which they had raised. During a total of seven rounds of negotiations between the Red Cross Societies, the efforts of the South to get the campaign to trace the whereabouts of members of separated families were answered by the North with the demand to stop anticommunist activities in the South. Also, the three plenary meetings of the Coordination Committee did not show any progress. The South favored a step-by-step approach, starting with economic and cultural exchanges. The North insisted on the withdrawal of US forces, a reduction of the Southern and Northern forces and the cessation of the modernization program of the South Korean forces. The North further called for a large "General National Congress" which would be entrusted to continue the discussion of the question of Korea's unification. In an address given on 28 August 1973, Kim Young Joo took up this demand and suggested that representatives from political parties, social organizations and people of all strata in the North and the South should participate in the work of the Coordination Committee.[19] It was a return to the old game. Since North Korea had not succeeded in pushing through its demands which were driven by the aim to control the whole of Korea, it ended the talks by calling the other side to be responsible for the failure and by returning to slandering and defaming the South Korean government. In his address, Kim

[18]Kim Se-Jin (1976) pp. 319 and 320.

[19]Text in Kim Se-Jin (1976) pp. 345–349.

Young Joo called Lee Hu Rak the "hangman of democracy, obstructor of peaceful reunification and inveterate betrayer who has discarded human conscience even". He demanded that Lee Hu Rak no longer be allowed to participate in the dialogue. He added some similar pleasantries by calling the Park Chung Hee government "the South Korea fascist ruling clique". Some talks followed on both channels but by and by, the dialogue was dying down. The new era of "confrontation with dialogue" which Lee Hu Rak had mentioned in a press conference on 4 July 1972 was not long lasting.[20]

When the governments of the Republic of Korea and the DPRK took up contacts at the end of 1971, they reacted to international developments. The announcement on 15 July 1971 that President Nixon would visit China made the leadership in both Koreas review their policies. The intervention of the US and China in the Korean War had been decisive in preserving the identity of both Koreas. Now, the two protectors started to normalize their relations which had been spoiled by the Korean War. It had become imperative for both Koreas to react to these developments.

For quite some time, the Republic of Korea had reasons to review its policy. The Nixon doctrine had not only resulted in a disengagement of the US but also in increased responsibilities of South Korea for its own defense. Therefore, it became urgent to try to reduce tensions on the peninsula. This could be achieved by organizing the coexistence of the two Korean states.

Kim Il Sung used the period of the dialogue with the South, which projected the picture of an independent and peace-seeking North Korea, to promote relations with Third World countries. While the DPRK had diplomatic relations with only 36 countries in 1971, the numbers had increased to 72 countries by mid-1974.[21] The DPRK had achieved another diplomatic success. The World Health Organization (WHO), one of the specialized agencies of the United Nations, accepted the DPRK as a member in May 1973. This provided North Korea with the opportunity to establish observer missions at UN headquarters in New York and Geneva. While North Korea was busy trying to overcome its isolation, it never lost sight of its main aim to unite Korea under its terms.[22]

---

[20]Koreana Quarterly, Vol. XIV, No. 3 (Autumn 1972) p. 62.

[21]Benjamin J. Min, "North Korea's Foreign Policy", in Kim, Se-jin and Cho, Chang Hyun (editors), *Government and Politics of Korea* (Silver Spring 1972), p. 241; North Korean Quarterly No. 57 (summer 1990) p. 111.

[22]Suh Dae-Sook pp. 253–260.

The Basic Agreement of 1991

For many years, silence prevailed in intra-Korean relations. Closer ties developed again in the mid-1980s. The starting point was remarkable. In the summer of 1984, the monsoon had brought great floods to South Korea. North Korea offered its support and South Korea accepted it hoping that an opportunity was being provided to take up the dialogue. And, indeed, a new channel of dialogue was established, that of economic talks.[23] The various rounds of talks in the period between November 1984 and November 1985 did not result, however, in an agreement.

More successful were the negotiations between the Red Cross Societies which were resumed in May 1985. Both sides agreed to a limited exchange of visitors. In the period from 20 to 23 September 1985, a party of 151 persons from the South and the North visited the other part of the country. As 50 members of each of the delegations were originally from the other side, they had the chance to meet their relatives. Since the South Korean TV stations reported extensively about these meetings, many South Koreans came to realize how far apart both parts of Korea had drifted. One member of the South Korean group told me, when he summed up the impressions he had gathered in the North, that he had been a guest not only in a foreign country but in another world. Parliamentary talks were envisaged, but were never started because the two sides could not agree on an agenda. In January 1986, the intermediate stage of the South-North talks came to an end as the DPRK suspended the talks in every field because of the forthcoming "Team Spirit" exercise of South Korea and US forces.

The great thaw of the year 1990, which started to melt the ice stemming from the glacier of the cold war, also reached the Korean peninsula. North Korea was about to lose the full support of its two main allies, Russia and China, which made it advisable to give talks with South Korea another try. The South, encouraged by the success of the Northern policy of President Roh Tae Woo, could afford to be lenient with the North. Since the beginning of September 1991, talks were held between the Prime Ministers of the two Koreas Yon Hyong Mok from the North and Kang Yong Hun, Ro Jai Bong and Chung Won Shik from the South — who followed each other in short intervals. These talks became known as the "South-North

---

[23]White Paper pp. 94–96.

High-level Talks".[24] They produced surprising results. On 13 December 1991, an Agreement on Reconciliation, Non-aggression and Exchanges and Cooperation between the South and the North (called the Basic Agreement) was signed, followed by a Joint Declaration of the Denuclearization of the Korean peninsula which was signed on 20 January 1992. Both agreements entered into force on 19 February 1992.[25] Never before had the two hostile cousins reached agreement in such a wide field of controversial questions.

In the preamble of the Basic Agreement, the South and the North tried to define their relationship. They insisted that it was "a special interim relationship" and not "a relationship between states".[26] This was reminiscent of the definition Chancellor Willy Brandt gave to the relationship between the two Germanies on 28 October 1969 before the Federal German Parliament. He also talked of a special relationship, but called both parts of Germany states which, however, could not be foreign countries to each other.[27] This final approach to reality was missing in the Korean-Korean agreement. On the background of the traditional disregard of the other side, the new formula however indicated progress.

The two sides had indeed reached an understanding on many basic issues. They agreed on:

- mutual recognition of and respect for each other's system,
- non-interference into the other's internal affairs,
- stopping of propaganda,
- stopping of attempts to overthrow each other,
- transforming of the armistice into a state of peace,
- cooperation in the international arena,
- nonuse of force and non-aggression,
- economic cooperation,
- cultural exchanges, and improvements of infrastructure and contacts.

The machinery was provided to implement these far-reaching goals. Liaison offices were to be established in Panmunjom. A Political Committee, a Joint

---

[24]For details, see White Paper pp. 96–102.

[25]Texts in White Paper pp. 200–209.

[26]White Paper p. 200.

[27]Auswaertiges Amt, unter Mitwirkung eines wissenschaftlichen Beirats, *Die Auswaertige Politik der Bundesrepublik Deutschland*, Koeln 1972, p. 702.

Military Commission, and Economic Exchanges and Cooperation Committee were going to be set up.

In September 1991, both Koreas had entered the UN. They then tried to live peacefully side by side on the peninsula. Both countries had come to the conclusion that it was preferable to cooperate with each other than to work against each other. For the North Koreans, this way of thinking was a great leap forward. After they had called succeeding South Korean government's puppets of the US imperialists, they then decided to enter into far-reaching agreements with them. They now respected peaceful coexistence — so it seemed.

The beginning of the 1990s were the years of the nuclear crisis. Therefore, it was of utmost importance that South and North had agreed not to "test, manufacture, produce, receive, possess, store, deploy or use nuclear weapons" and not to "possess nuclear reprocessing and uranium enrichment facilities" (Joint Declaration of 20 January 1992). Also in this case, the establishment of a mechanism, a Joint Nuclear Control Commission, was envisaged.

During 1992, quite a number of South-North meetings followed to put the institutions into place and to discuss details. However, the shadow of the nuclear crisis loomed large over the relations between South and North. The atmosphere deteriorated, and the US and South Korea had contributed to this development as has already been shown.[28] The North resented the renewal of the Team Spirit exercise for 1993 particularly and referred to that development when it called off the talks by various declarations.[29] Once again, the talks were petering out. The Basic Agreement had been called a breakthrough too early.

A number of reasons may have caused the DPRK leaders to stop the normalization process. They might have felt that the agreement on non-aggression would give them a good chance to be rewarded with a quick withdrawal of American troops. This was an error. The vague definitions of the Joint Declaration on Denuclearization had further left open the question of how to conduct the envisaged inspections. The North was only willing to allow the inspection of the facilities at Yongbyong while it demanded to be allowed to inspect all US military installations in the South. The South insisted on the

[28]See Chapter 22.

[29]Radio Pyongyang, (transcripts by BBC Summary of World News, 16 October and 19 December 1992); Nodong Sinmun, 7 December 1992, monitored by BBC Summary of World Broadcasts, 9 December 1992, Kydo News Agency, 19 December 1992 (all available via LEXIS-NEXIS).

inspections of other sites in the North. The gap could not be bridged. And then the opportunity to enter into direct talks with the United States presented itself; the DPRK leadership preferred to take this direction. It was deplorable that the momentum of the great attempt of December 1991 was lost — at least temporarily.

One of the key issues of that attempt, the transformation of the Armistice Agreement of 1953 into a peace mechanism, is now dealt with in the four party talks. These talks between the two Koreas, the US and China had been suggested in April 1996 by President Kim Young Sam and President Clinton.[30] After some hesitation, the DPRK agreed to join the talks. Until the end of 1999, six rounds of talks were held in Geneva but it did not produce any results.[31] North Korea insisted on discussing the withdrawal of US forces from South Korea and the conclusion of a bilateral peace treaty with the US. These demands were rejected by Washington. It is therefore easy to understand that North Korea is more interested in the bilateral talks with the US. As of April 2000, the bilateral talks had not reached an agreement that the DPRK would send a senior envoy to Washington for discussing the possibilities of improving relations.[32]

The South-North dialogue has been resumed. On 9 April 2000, news from Seoul and Pyongyang surprised the world. Both Korean governments had agreed to a summit meeting between President Kim Dae Jung and National Defense Committee Chairman Kim Jong Il which is to be held from 12 to 14 June 2000 in Pyongyang. Since it would be the first meeting ever between the top leaders of the two Koreas, it would indicate a dramatic turn in the nation's history.

The Importance of the Armistice

Since its conclusion in 1953, the Armistice Agreement has been the most important legal basis for the relations between South and North on the Korean peninsula. Since its primary purpose was to end active hostilities, it did not provide for a normalization of relations between South and North.

---

[30] Korea Annual 1996 p. 363.

[31] Agence France Press, 10 August 1999 (via LEXIS-NEXIS).

[32] AP, 29 January 2000 (via LEXIS-NEXIS).

Attempts to that effect have been undertaken by the governments of both Koreas, particularly by the Joint Declaration of July 1972 and the Basic Agreement of December 1991. But the intra-Korean agreements which had also envisaged institutions for conflict management were not implemented. Therefore, the only way left to ease tensions in the many South-North crises was to engage the Military Armistice Commission set up by the Armistice Agreement.

For many years, the government of the DPRK had demanded the dissolution and replacement of the Armistice Agreement. In March 1991, when a South Korean officer was appointed senior delegate of the Military Armistice Commission, North Korea called it a serious situation.[33] At the end of April 1994, the DPRK government declared that it would not deal with the United Nations Command (UNC) but would prefer dealing with the US pretending, however, to faithfully abide by the Armistice Agreement.[34] Some days later, in the beginning of May 1994, the DPRK government informed the United Nations Command of its intention to withdraw from the Military Armistice Commission.[35] At the same time, it established a separate office at Panmunjom. Thus, North Korea tried to destroy and undermine the Armistice Agreement. When it was useful for the North Koreans, they, however, returned to meetings of the Military Armistice Commission, for example after the submarine incident in the fall of 1996. In mid-1998, a new channel of military communication was established in Panmunjom: Generals of UNC and North Korea would discuss "armistice-related issues".[36] The new institution seemed to work. In the summer of 1999, the return of a South Korean dredger which was swept into the North due to heavy rains was agreed upon during general-level meetings.[37]

The Armistice Agreement is in effect, however, weakened because the two main institutions established by it, the Neutral Nations Supervisory Commission and the Military Armistice Commission, are no longer functioning properly. Whether it will be replaced in the near future by a peace mechanism is doubtful because so many years have passed and because the government

---

[33] Kyodo News Service, 29 March 1991 (via LEXIS-NEXIS).

[34] Xinhua News Agency, 28 April 1994 (via LEXIS-NEXIS).

[35] AFX News, 2 May 1994 (via LEXIS-NEXIS), New York Times, 3 September 1994.

[36] New York Times, 9 June 1998.

[37] BBC Summary of World Broadcasts, 19 August and 5 November 1999 (via LEXIS-NEXIS).

of the DPRK has so often given reason to doubt that it will observe contracts loyally. A peace accord just between the USA and DPRK should be out of the question, as the belligerents, the DPRK and China on the northern side and the United Nations on the southern side, have to participate. As all sides will have to live with the present situation for quite some time, it was not wise that the Southern side agreed to setting up a new mechanism at Panmunjom.[38] The Southern side should have insisted to abide by the provisions of the Armistice Agreement what to do the North had promised in Art. 5 of the Basic Agreement of 1991.

What can perhaps be achieved is a new architecture to preserve peace on the peninsula. To agree to such a new set-up can only be risked after the North has given proof that it is willing to respect agreements. The North has ample opportunities to supply such proof: by carrying out the provision of the Agreed Framework, by returning to the Basic Agreement and by responding positively to the policy of engagement. Measures to build confidence are of the essence on the Korean peninsula.

References

Almeida, Pedro and O'Helon, Michael Downs, Chuck Henriksen, "Impasse in Korea: A Conventional Arms-Accord Solution"? in Survival, Vol. 41, No. 1, Spring 1999, pp. 58–72. *Over the Line, North Korea's Negotiating Strategy*, Washington 1999. "North Korea's Two Kims and American Foreign Policy", in Henriksen and Mo pp. 151–172.

Thomas H. Kang, G. S. Eliot, "The Four-Party Peace Talks: Lost without a Map", in *Comparative Strategy*, 17:327–344.

Ministry of National Unification Republic of Korea, *Peace and Cooperation. White Paper on Korean Unification*, Seoul 1996 (cited as White Paper).

Smith, Gaddis, "After 25 Years — the parallel", in: *The New York Times Magazine*, 22 June 1975.

[38]Chung-In Moon, "The North Korean Problem and the Role of South Korea", in Henriksen and Mo, pp. 102–104 suggest that the South should invalidate the armistice agreement in the framework of a strategic offense.

Bibliography

An, Tai Sung, *North Korea. A Political Handbook*, Washington 1984.

Cha, Victor D., "Is There Still a Rational North Korean Option for War"? in *Security Dialogue* 1998 Vol. 29 (4), pp. 477–490.

Chung, Kyung Cho, *Korea. The Third Republic*, New York 1971.

Clifford, Mark L., *Troubled Tiger. Businessmen, Bureaucrats, and Generals in South Korea*, Revised Edition, Armonk and London 1998.

Cumings, Bruce, *The Origins of the Korean War. Vol. 2, The Roaring of the Cataract, 1947–1950*, Princeton 1981.

Cumings, Bruce, *Korea's Place in the Sun. A Modern History*, New York 1997.

Croissant, Aurel, *Politischer Systemwechsel in Suedkorea (1985–1997)*, Hamburg 1998.

Dujarric, Robert, (editor) *Korea: Security Pivot in Northeast Asia*, Hudson Institute, Indianapolis 1998.

Eberstadt, Nicholas, *The End of North Korea*, Washington 1999.

Eckardt, Andre, *Korea*, Band 29 der Reihe Kultur der Nationen, Nuernberg 1972.

Eckert, Carter J., Lee Ki Baik, Robinson, Michael, and Wagner, Edward M., *Korea. Old and New. A History*, Cambridge, Massachusetts and London, Lew Young Ick, England. 1990.

Gleysteen Jr., William H., *Massive Entanglement, Marginal Influence. Carter and Korea in Crisis*, Washington 1999.

Hahm, Pyong Choon, *The Korean Political Tradition and Law*, Seoul 1971.

Hahn, Bae Ho and Lee Chae-Jin, *The Korean Peninsula and the Major Powers*, Seoul 1998.

Han, Sungjoo, *The Failure of Democracy in South Korea*, Berkeley, Los Angeles, London 1974.

Han, Woo-Keun, *The History of Korea*, translated by Lee Kyung Shik, edited by Grafton K. Mintz, Seoul 1970.

Hapdong News Agency, *Korea Annual*, Volumes 1964–1996.

Henderson, Gregory, *Korea. The Politics of the Vortex*, Cambridge, Massachusetts, and London, England, 1968.

Henriksen, Thomas H. and Mo, Jongryn, (editors) *North Korea After Kim Il Sung, Continuity or Change*? Stanford 1997.

Henthorn, William E., *A History of Korea*, New York 1974.

Kihl, Young Whan, *Politics and Policies in Divided Korea: Regimes in Contrast*, Boulder and London 1984.

Kihl, Young Whan, (editor) *Korea and the World Order. Beyond the Cold War*, Boulder, San Francisco, Oxford 1994.

Kim, Chum Kon, *The Korean War. The First Comprehensive Account of the Historical Background And Development of the Korean War (1950–1953)*, Seoul 1973.

Kim, Kwan Bong, *The Korea-Japan Treaty Crisis and the Instability of the Korean Political System*, New York, Washington, London 1971.

Kim, Se-Jin, *The Politics of Military Revolution in Korea*, Chapel Hill 1971.

Kim, Se-Jin and Cho, Chang Hyun, *Government and Politics of Korea*, Silver Spring 1972.

Kleiner, Juergen, *Korea. Betrachtungen ueber ein fernliegendes Land*, Frankfurt 1980.

Kleiner, Juergen, *Korea — Auf Steinigem Pfad*, Berlin 1992.

Koh, Byung Chul, *The Foreign Policy of North Korea*, New York 1969.

Kwack, Tae-Hwan and Olsen, Edward A., *The Major Powers of Northeast Asia. Seeking Peace and Security*, Boulder and London 1996.

Lautensach, Hermann, *Korea. Eine Landeskunde auf Grund eigener Reisen und der Literatur*, Leipzig 1945.

Lee, Chae-Jin, *China and Korea. Dynamic Relations*, Stanford 1996.

Lee, Chong-Sik, *The Politics of Korean Nationalism*, Berkeley and Los Angeles 1963.

Lee, Chong-Sik, "Kim Il Sung of North Korea", in: *Asian Survey*, Vol. VII No. 6, June 1967, pp. 374 ff.

Lee, Chong-Sik, *Japan and Korea. The Political Dimension*, Stanford 1985.

Lee, Yur-Bok and Patterson, Wayne, *Korean-American Relations 1866–1997*, Albany 1999.

Macdonald, Donald Stone, *U.S.-Korean Relations from Liberation to Self-Reliance. The Twenty Year Record*, Boulder 1992.

Nelson, M. Frederick, *Korea and the Old Orders in Eastern Asia*, Baton Rouge 1946, Royal Asiatic Society, Korean Branch, Reprint Series, Seoul 1975.

Oh, John Kie-chiang, *Korean Politics. The Quest for Democratization and Economic Development*, Ithaca and London 1999.

Oberdorfer, Don, *The Two Koreas. A Contemporary History*, 1997.

Oliver, Robert T., *Syngman Rhee. The Man Behind the Myth*, New York 1954.

Park, Tong Whan, (editor) *The U.S. and The Two Koreas. A New Triangle*, Boulder 1998.

Rees, David, *Korea: The Limited War*, New York 1964.

Reese, David, *The Prospects for North Korea's Survival*, Adelphi Paper 323, London 1998.

Reeve, W. D., *The Republic of Korea. A Political and Economic Study*, London, New York, Toronto 1963.

Scalapino, Robert A., (editor) *North Korea Today*, New York, London 1963.

Schaller, Peter, *Nordkorea. Ein Land im Banne der Kims*, Boeblingen 1994.

Shim, Doh C., *Mass Politics and Culture in Democratizing Korea*, 1999.

Sichrowsky, Harry, *Koreareport. Vom Bruderkrieg zur Wiedervereinigung?* Wien 1973.

Seidl-Hohenveldern, Ignaz, *Voelkerrecht*, 9. Neubearbeitete Auflage, Koeln 1997.

Sohn, Pow Key, Kim Chol Choon and Hong Yi Sup, *The History of Korea*, Seoul 1970.

Suh, Dae-Sook, *Kim Il Sung. The North Korean Leader*, New York 1988.

Suh, Dae-Sook and Lee, Chae-Jin, (editors) *North Korea after Kim Il Sung*, Boulder 1998.

Teissier du Cros, Remi, *Les Coreens, Frères Séparés*, Paris 1990.

Truman, Harry S., *Memoirs, Vol. II: Years of Trial and Hope*, Garden City 1956.

Wickham, John A., *Korea on the Brink. From the "12/12 Incident" to the Kwangju Uprising, 1979–1980*, Washington 1999.

Wright, Edward Reynolds, (editor) *Korean Politics in Transition*, Seattle and London 1975.

If not marked otherwise, the following sources are quoted from the following addresses on the internet:

Foreign Broadcast Information Service - East Asia (FBIS-EAS)	www.wnc.fedworld.gov/cgi_bin/
Korean Central News Agency (KNCA)	www.kcna.co.jp/
Northeast Asia Peace and Security Network Daily Report	www.nautilus.org/napsnet/dr/
The Korean Herald (as of 1 January 1999)	www.koreaherald.co.kr
The Korea Times (as of 1 January 1999)	www.koreatimes.co.kr/times/
The People's Korea	www.korea_np.co.jp/pk/

LEXIS-NEXIS quotes were found on the internet via LEXIS-NEXIS Academic Universe, address: web.lexis-nexis.com/universe.

Name Index

Subject Index

North and South Korea
124°
126°
128°
130°
Russia
China
0 75 km
0 50 mi
Onsong
Chongsong
Tumen R.
Unggi
Musan
42°
Samjiyon
Ch'ongjin
Sodu -su R.
Orang
Sinp'a
Hyesan
Yalu R.
Changjin -gang R.
Pujon- gang R.
Puktae- ch'on R.
Kanggye
P'ungsan
Kimch'aek
Pyoktong
Pujon
Iwon
Unsan
Taedong -gang R.
Songch'o- gang R.
40°
Sinuiju
Kusong
Oro
Hamhung
Chongju
Pakch'on
Yodok
Yonghung
East Sea or Sea of Japan
Sain-ni
Nam- gang R.
Wonsan
Onch'on
P'yongyang
T'ongch'on
Namp'o
Kosong
Pukhan -gang R.
Sariwon
Imjin- gang R.
Haeju
Yonch'on
Yangyang
38°
Kaesong
Ch'unch'on
Kangnung
Inch'on
Seoul
Wonju
Suwon
Han- gang R.
Hwangji-ri
Yellow Sea
P'yongt'aek
Tanyang
Sosan
Ch'onan
Ch'ongju
Yongyang
Hongsong
Sangju
Yongdok
Taejon
Naktong -gang R.
36°
Kum- gang R.
Taegu
Chonju
Anui
Chongup
Onyang
Ulsan
Somjin- gang R.
Yangsan
Kwangju
Chinju
Pusan
Samch'onp'a
Eastern Channel
Mokp'o
Yosu
Posong
Kohung
Koje-do
Huksan- Chedo
Chindo
Tsushima
Chin-do
Wando
Korea Strait
34°
Western Channel
Iki
Cheju-do
Japan
©maps.com